BUSINESS STRATEGY AND SECURITY ANALYSIS

The Key to Long-Term Investment Profits

RAYMOND K. SUUTARI

IRWIN
Professional Publishing®
Chicago • London • Singapore

To my wife, Airlie

Times Mirror
Higher Education Group

Library of Congress Cataloging-in-Publication Data

Suutari, Raymond K.
    Business strategy and security analysis: the key to long-term
investment profits / Raymond K. Suutari.
       p. cm.
    Includes bibliographical references and index.
    ISBN 0–7863–0409–X
    1. Investments. 2. Corporations—Finance. 3. Rate of return.
I. Title
HG4521.S89 1996
658.15'2—dc20   96–3565

Printed in the United States of America
1 2 3 4 5 6 7 8 9 0 BS 3 2 1 0 9 8 7 6

PREFACE

Several years ago, I was surprised to find in my files, apparently clipped to some other papers by accident, a four-year-old list of recommended investments. Though the list had been compiled by a respected stockbroker, I knew that a number of the recommended companies had not done well.

My curiosity aroused, I obtained copies of the original reports. I found that the broker's buy recommendations had been based solely on the expectation of higher earnings for the following year due to a stronger economy. The analysis contained no reference to the state of the industries in which the companies were operating, which were deteriorating, nor to the competitive positions of the companies, which were weak. Rather than being true investment advice, this list was a recommendation to speculate on the direction of the economy—at best a risky activity. The prices of some of the stocks did, in fact, rise slightly in the next year, but they dropped sharply thereafter. I did not find any sell recommendations in this analyst's subsequent reports. The companies in question appeared to have simply dropped out of the analyst's sight (although I understand that sell advice is usually given verbally). The long-term investor who followed this broker's advice would have been stuck with a bad investment, though the short-term trader, with the instinct to take a small profit, could have been a winner. The recommendations had little or nothing to do with the virtues of the companies or their industries. They were not really about investing at all, but rather about playing the market.

These discoveries led me to do further research. I went on to sample a large number of investment analyses, and I delved into several comprehensive textbooks on investment analysis. I found that buy-and-hold recommendations were based almost entirely on expected earnings per share for the next two years, and were usually highly dependent on forecasts of the state of the economy. These forecasts are often wrong, and they keep changing. In fact, the "January effect" is a recognized phenomenon. Analysts are usually optimistic early in the year, and they tend to become pessimistic as the year progresses.

I am not denying that earnings are the main determinant of share prices, nor am I denying the validity of established investment evaluation methods. My point is that the short-term perspective which dominates current recommendations is inadequate for the longer-term investor. Sharp price drops commonly occur when actual quarterly results do not meet expectations, which is indicative of this short-term focus. This book is intended to supplement established evaluation methods by adding a long-term perspective.

Some of the analyses I reviewed did try to take a long-term view, but here too I found a problem. The long-term forecasts were frequently "linear"; that is, they were extrapolations of current activities adjusted to reflect macroeconomic expectations. Those of us who were involved in corporate management during the volatile period of the 1970s and the 1980s understand the fallacy of relying heavily on economic forecasts and on the assumption that the competitive environment will remain unchanged. This can be compared to steering a car by looking in the rearview mirror; it works only if the road remains straight. Further, in my research I frequently encountered assumptions that were incorporated into net present value calculations. The results had an appearance of sophistication and credibility which they seldom deserved.

I was not surprised to discover no textbooks on economic analysis written from a strategic perspective. Traditionally, the formulation of strategy has tended to be regarded as an art, akin to black magic and heavily dependent on intuition. Michael E. Porter of Harvard University changed this with his books *Competitive Strategy: Techniques for Analyzing Industries and Competitors*, published in 1980, followed by *Competitive Advantage: Creating and Sustaining Superior Performance*, published in 1985.[1] Dr. Porter outlined a conceptual framework for analyzing industries and identifying companies that should be able to obtain superior performance within their industries. His concepts provide the foundations of this book, and I gratefully acknowledge his contribution to strategic thinking. Porter's concepts are well known to and used by academics and corporate management, and their relative newness may explain why they have not yet found their way into broader use. The logic and relative simplicity of these concepts make them an ideal tool for individuals who want to do their own homework and/or to evaluate the quality of professional analyses.

At the time when I accidentally discovered the four-year-old stock recommendation list that got me started on all this research, I was teaching strategic management at Wilfrid Laurier University and also writing a textbook on the subject. It occurred to me that the concepts used to train students—future managers—to analyze industries and to formulate strategies with the objective of making their companies superior performers could also be used by an outsider—an investor or a trader—to analyze investment opportunities. Even the comprehensive textbooks on investment analysis which I reviewed contained virtually no discussion of the role in and contribution of strategy to company performance. I found no book using management concepts to focus on the investor's perspective. Thus the idea for this book was born.

My approach here is to shift the primary basis for investment decisions away from the financial analysis and macroeconomic forecasting disciplines that dominate current thinking and onto a business and managerial economics approach. This approach involves assessing the factors that determine the profitability of industries and the actions that define the performance of companies within their industries. The importance of financial analysis and economic expectations in arriving at an investment decision is undeniable, but these factors must be put into perspective. Financial resources are only a tool which management can use to achieve results, and their availability does not assure success. Further, the macroeconomic arena is too large to provide a basis for an investment decision for a specific company in today's environment. I will demonstrate that the economic environment is only one of many elements of change which can affect the future of a company.

This is not a book for the lazy investor. It contains no hot tips or recommendations, no prophecies of boom or doom. Making an initial evaluation of a situation obviously requires considerable effort, but the investor's work does not end there. The business environment is constantly changing, and management must respond. Consequently, investors must keep up with the news, track developments as they are happening, and try to determine how they may affect the prospects of the company. Taking a long-term perspective does not mean never selling out or buying more. As investors in General Motors (GM) and International Business Machines (IBM) have found out, "long-term" does not mean "forever." A volatile world has made the buy-and-hold investment philosophy a risky proposition.

I do not pretend to be an expert investment analyst, nor am I one of those "gurus" who have made fortunes on the market (and, what is less publicized but often happens, lost them the following year). However, this does not mean that the approach I will be describing here is untried. The same basic approach has been used by one of America's most successful investors, Warren E. Buffett, whose Berkshire Hathaway Corporation earned a 29 percent compounded average return on equity (ROE) over a period of 23 years (1970–93). Buffett rejects the practice of diversifying holdings to reduce the risk. His basic rule is, Don't put too many eggs in your basket, and pick them carefully.[2] As of 1994, Berkshire Hathaway had major holdings in only nine stocks, each of which reflected Buffett's belief that decisions should reflect "both the intensity with which an investor thinks about a business and the comfort level he must feel with its economic characteristics before buying into it."[3] The issue of comfort level is important to the long-term investor, who should not have to be concerned with the day-to-day twists and turns of the market. There is, however, no sure thing in investing. My objective will be to significantly improve the odds of outperforming the market as a whole over the long term—something that, on average, the professional money managers do not do, as their records reveal.

In this book I will describe methods by which industries and companies can be analyzed to provide a basis for long-term investment decisions, and will apply these methods to North American companies. It may be argued, quite rightfully, that this focus on North America ignores excellent offshore investment opportunities, particularly in the Far East, which is a fashionable area for investments at this time. While the analytical reasoning process described here can be applied to any industry or any company anywhere in the world, I feel that the investors who are addressed in this book need a comfort level that can be derived from sticking to familiar companies and industries. Decisions on foreign investments involve complexities arising from differences in laws, business practices, accounting standards, taxation, exchange rates, and so forth. I therefore suggest that participation in offshore investment opportunities is probably best undertaken through one of the many mutual funds which specialize in this area. Managers of such funds have the knowledge to assess the risks of foreign investments and the diversity to hedge them. (Keep in mind, though, that the performance of these funds is often uneven.) This is not to say that the methodology I will describe ignores global issues. An analysis of any industry or company must fully recognize the implications of global markets, global sourcing, and global competition.

In order to make this book relevant, I include many illustrations of how the concepts I describe can be applied. To do this, I assess the current positions and prospects of a number of industries and several well-known companies, and I express opinions about companies that might be considered as long-term investment prospects. These opinions are based on the analytical methods and reasoning I describe in the book, and are mine alone. The lead time necessary to publish a book is such that my conclusions and opinions date from early 1995. Thus, the reader at a later time will have the advantage of being able to determine to what extent my opinions were right or wrong, and to draw conclusions about the reasons for my success or failure in this regard. The differences between my opinions and the subsequent performance of the companies I discuss should in themselves be instructive.

The 1994 industry and company performance statistics used in this book illustrate the nature of the data, the way these data can be interpreted, and their role in the analytical methodology. The concepts I describe are timeless and can easily be applied to future data. Therefore, the passage of time should not make this book obsolete.

Acknowledgments

In writing this book, I recognize that I am not breaking new theoretical ground, only repackaging well-established concepts for the investment context. I gratefully acknowledge the help of many people.

Foremost among these are the thinkers of our strategic craft, particularly Michael E. Porter, whose theories are the foundation of my approach. Others, such as Henry Mintzberg of McGill University, have helped me to understand how companies make their strategic decisions.

I am indebted to the journalists and business magazines whose timely reporting of events and insights further an understanding of developments and are invaluable to the astute investor. I have acknowledged many of these sources in the Notes that follow the chapters.

Several people have read the manuscript in the various phases of preparation, provided useful comments, and corrected my errors. Particularly, I offer my thanks to Stephen Bonnyman, CFA, for his useful suggestions and encouragement. I would also like to express my appreciation to David Gillen of Wilfrid Laurier University, Waterloo, Ontario, for sharing his expertise on the airlines industry.

I also thank my many academic colleagues, who, in numerous discussions, have helped to shape my thinking, and my students, whose frequent bewilderment has forced me to learn how to explain my craft more clearly.

I would also like to express my thanks and appreciation to Georgia Kornbluth for her immense contribution in editing the original manuscript. Her grasp of the concepts enabled her to point out my inconsistencies and help refine the text to make it more readily understandable.

NOTES

1. Michael E. Porter, *Competitive Strategy: Techniques for Analyzing Industries and Competitors* (New York: Free Press, 1980); and Michael E. Porter, *Competitive Advantage: Creating and Sustaining Superior Performance* (New York: Free Press, 1985).

2. Robert Lenzner, "Warren Buffett's Idea of Heaven: 'I Don't Have to Work with People I Don't Like,'" *Forbes*, October 18, 1993, p. 40.
3. "How Buffett Views Risk," *Fortune*, April 4, 1994, p. 33.

CONTENTS

PART II

INDUSTRY STRUCTURE   47

Chapter 3

The Impact of Four Internal Constraints   48

Chapter 4

The Fifth Constraint: Internal Rivalry   66

Chapter 6

The Implications of Change   147

Chapter 8

Monitoring the Investment   216

PART V

COMPREHENSIVE INDUSTRY STUDIES   243

Chapter 9

The Automobile Industry and the Automotive Parts Industry   244

Chapter 10

The Computer Industry   276

Chapter 12

The Banking Industry 317

PART VI

OVERVIEW AND UPDATE   339

Chapter 13

Overview and Update   341

LIST OF EXHIBITS

I

STRATEGIC ANALYSIS

In order to apply strategic analysis in investment decisions, it is first necessary to understand the nature of corporate strategy and its role in determining the earnings performance of a company. Part I starts with a review of the objectives of this book and goes on to describe the basic analytical concepts and the sources of data that will be used throughout.

An examination of the historical background of corporate strategy reveals how its role in company management has led to the present-day focus on short-term perspective—a focus that dominates both management action and investment analysis. The various types of corporate strategies are described, and the relative effectiveness of each is shown.

The conventional schools of thought in investment analysis are next examined, and their respective strengths and limitations are evaluated. The ways in which strategic analysis can make the conventional approaches more effective are described. Finally, the use of strategic analysis alone as a foundation for investment decisions is introduced.

1

INTRODUCTION TO STRATEGIC ANALYSIS

My objective in this book is to show the serious long-term investor how to analyze investment opportunities. The basic premise of the method I will present is that a company's strategy is the major determinant of its long-term success. It is strategy that establishes how a company will respond to changes in the economy and in its industry. It is also strategy that enables a company to outperform its competitors.

I will show that both the situation of an industry and the strategy of a company can be analyzed and understood by an outsider. Several aspects of this objective should be explained at the outset.

First, this book is designed to *assist* investors in making investment decisions, by supplementing existing securities analysis methodologies. It does not provide magic formulas for choosing investments, nor does it eliminate the need to exercise judgment. What it does do is provide a systematic, objective way of identifying and evaluating opportunities so as to minimize risks, though not to eliminate them. It also provides a context in which the implications of change may be understood.

Second, the phrase *long term* does not indicate a precise period of time. Instead, the phrase is used to show a contrast with the *short-term* perspective that dominates contemporary investment analysis—a perspective in which decisions are based on quarterly or annual earnings forecasts and on the expected direction of the stock market as a whole. Strategic action takes time to show results. For example, Lee Iacocca, upon assuming the position of chief executive officer (CEO) at Chrysler Corporation in late 1978, formulated a strategy of refocusing the company's product lines on its K cars and minivans. Not until 1984 did the logic inherent in this strategy show up in earnings, and only then did Chrysler's stock price start to outperform the broad market by a substantial margin. However, investors should keep in mind that "long term" also does not mean forever. In a volatile, highly competitive business environment, strategies must evolve in response to changes in economic, social, and political situations, as well as technological developments. Thus, the investor must remain alert. Even industry leaders may falter, as IBM did in the early 1990s.

Third, taking a long-term perspective and relying on strategic analysis are not necessarily techniques that are useful only to conservative investors. The analytical methodology described in this book is equally applicable to newer companies and/or to emerging industries in which a degree of speculation is involved. The method described here will help investors to identify the factors creating the risk, to evaluate how a company may perform, and to track its progress.

Fourth, an investment decision based on strategic analysis does not isolate a stock from market fluctuations. History has shown that the overall market moves through cycles based upon economic variables that affect earnings expectations, interest rates, and so forth. Even the best companies are affected by the overall market perceptions, but in periodic market downturns, the soundest companies can be expected to suffer a smaller decline and recover more quickly.

Fifth, the term *investment* in the context of this book is used to refer primarily to common stocks. The investor who is considering more secure instruments such as senior bonds and debentures is better served by the bond rating agencies, though even these are not necessarily infallible. However, strategic analysis can be useful for evaluating junior debt such as "junk bonds," the prices of which may depend on earnings or even on the viability of the issuer. My objective will be to optimize capital appreciation, rather than dividends, as the primary source of investment profit. The yields on strong market performers tend to be low.

In short, my objective is to provide a method for deepening the investor's understanding of the position and prospects of a company being considered as an investment. Believers in the *efficient market* hypothesis contend that the current market price of a stock reflects all available information about the company. This implies that there exists a consensus on the interpretation of the meaning of the information. In contrast, the view I am propounding here rests on an underlying assumption that the established evaluation methodologies are limited in their ability to interpret information—a shortcoming which leads to poor judgments and missed opportunities.

THE BASIC CONCEPT: STRATEGIC ANALYSIS

Decisions on purchasing a stock are motivated by some combination of two factors: the condition of the market and the value being purchased. In a *market-driven* decision, the investor expects that a rising overall market or the prospects of a particular industry will lift all stocks, and the favorable short-term earnings expectations of a particular company will cause its stock to rise even more quickly. In this approach, which is also called the *top-down approach*, the expectation is that the market will pull a stock up. The buyer is therefore speculating that the broad range of variables that determine the direction of the market as a whole will evolve in a favorable way, and that the earnings expectations of the particular company will be fulfilled. The stock buyer is therefore a market player for whom success is usually highly dependent on the ability to respond quickly to changes in expectations.

The *value-driven* buyer, taking the *bottom-up approach*, ignores the stock market as a whole and does not attempt to forecast its direction, relying instead on the ability of a company to provide consistent earnings growth over a period of time. The investor looks for opportunities to buy a share of the earnings at a price that is considered reasonable or, even better, a bargain. In this strategy, the investor hopes to recognize potential not perceived by the market as a whole. In this approach, it is expected that the inherent value of the company will eventually assert itself, and the company will outperform the market. The value-driven investor usually has a long-term perspective, but decisions are often based on rather superficial criteria, such as the company's past earnings performance, the dividend yield, the net asset values, and the price/earnings (P/E) ratio. These factors indicate only what the company has done and where it now is—not what it may do. Value-driven investors have a strong tendency to assume that past success can be extrapolated.

This book is intended to assist the value-driven investor by providing the basis for a more profound, more systematic assessment of what provides value. The term *systematic* is important here for two reasons. First, in order to analyze a company, an investor must acquire a large amount of information about the company and its industry, and must be able to assess the relevance and implications of the data. The analytical method outlined in this book provides a systematic way of acquiring and assessing the necessary data. Second, every decision made by an investor is influenced to some degree by emotion. Psychological studies have shown that investors can be unduly influenced by the prevailing investment sentiment, which causes distortions in their evaluations of risk-reward relationships. Psychologists have identified a surprising number of idiosyncrasies that can keep people from making the soundest possible choices in many different situations. (Psychological influences on investment decisions are discussed in more detail in Chapter 7.) A systematic approach can help to minimize the emotional influences upon a decision but cannot eliminate them entirely.

Consistent long-term earnings growth is the primary determinant of share prices. A company's potential for long-term earnings growth can be assessed in terms of the following two variables:

1. *The characteristics of the industry in which the company is operating.* The overall profitability and profit potential of the companies in a given industry are determined by the industry characteristics.

2. *The competitive advantage by which a company outperforms its competitors.* Occupying a comparatively favorable position in its industry and/or possessing superior capability can help a company to outperform its competitors.

The analytical method described in the chapters to follow is based on a model of industry structure that shows the relationships between the company, the industry in which it is operating, and the overall external environment. The value of this model is that it provides a conceptual framework for a welter of facts and thus allows the analyst to develop a coherent understanding of any company's situation. Further, and equally important, it provides a systematic way of coping with the huge amounts of information that are continuously provided by disclosure requirements and by the aggressive, knowledgeable media. The significance and implications of new developments can be interpreted within the same conceptual framework that has been prepared for the company's own data.

It will be shown that competitive advantage is usually more important than industry characteristics, but a systematic evaluation of both factors and their interrelationship is necessary, not only to explain the rea-

sons for the past and present performance of a company but also to provide a basis for assessing how the company is likely to perform in the
future. An investment decision may be influenced by either or both of
these factors. Obviously, a strong performer in an industry of high overall profitability would represent the best case, but a secondary performer
in a strong industry or a superior performer in a weak industry may also
be a sound long-term investment candidate.

Industry Characteristics

Michael E. Porter's model for systematically analyzing the inherent profitability of an industry is based on the theory that an industry's characteristics are affected by five forces:

1. The threat of new entrants into the industry
2. The risk of substitution by other products
3. The bargaining power of its suppliers
4. The bargaining power of its buyers
5. The intensity of internal rivalry

(These forces and the ways in which they interact are discussed in detail
in Chapters 3 and 4.)

An *industry* may be defined, in an introductory sense, as a group of
companies and their direct competitors. (A more detailed definition will
be given in Chapter 3.) Industries vary in terms of overall profitability.
This can be seen in the 1994 the performance of various industries, as
compiled by *Forbes* magazine.[1]

- The pharmaceuticals industry, with 22 companies, had a median
  after-tax profit of 8.3 percent on sales in 1994, which provided a
  20.5 percent return on equity (ROE). All the companies in the
  industry were profitable, with profit margins ranging from 22.2
  percent of sales for the best to 0.3 percent of sales for the worst.
  This can be considered an attractive industry at present, but there
  is no assurance that it will remain so.

- In contrast, at present the airlines industry is definitely unattractive. In 1994, only 5 of the 11 companies were profitable. The
  industry median ROE was only 1.0 percent. These results were
  particularly poor because the period in question was one of economic recovery. In 1993, only 2 of the 9 companies in the industry showed a profit, and the industry median ROE was a deficit.

Between these extremes lie a range of industries of varying degrees of attractiveness. For example, the restaurant chain industry had a median ROE of 14.7 percent and a profit margin of 5.3 percent of sales in 1994, with 3 of the 13 companies incurring losses.

That industries change over time is shown by the extremes exhibited in the airlines industry. In the late 1970s, prior to deregulation, the airlines industry was highly profitable, but today, any decision to invest in an airline company would depend to a significant extent on the improvement of industry conditions and company's prospects of returning to profitability.

Competitive Advantage

In 1994 the profit margins of companies in the pharmaceuticals industry, which was mentioned above as an attractive industry, ranged from a low of 0.3 percent to a high of 22.2 percent. Obviously, some companies outperformed others. They did this by achieving *competitive advantage*—a concept that is used throughout this book and is based on Michael Porter's work. Competitive advantage may be derived from either or both of the following two factors.

1. *Superior capability, or the ability to do things better.* There are no great secrets to success in the automobile industry or the fast-food industry, but Toyota Motor Corporation and McDonald's Corporation are superior performers due to their capability.

2. *The position of a company in its industry.* A company may perform well because it operates in or has a major product line in a segment of its industry in which there is comparatively little competition. Positioning can be based on a number of factors. In the pharmaceuticals industry, the most profitable companies have effective products which are protected by patents and which they can sell for high prices.

Competitive advantage is discussed in more detail in Chapter 5.

Methodology

The obvious challenge in making a long-term investment decision is to predict both the direction of future events and a company's ability to provide superior performance. The industry model that I will present, together with an understanding of the basis of competitive advantage, will explain the basis for a company's current performance. The direction of future events will be estimated by applying a historical perspective, to show how the industry has evolved and is evolving, and by analyzing the forces for change and how they may affect the structure of the industry. The next step is to assess whether the company's competitive advantage can remain effective and can be sustained in the future, in the situation it will face in its industry.

Finally, then, the investment decision will be based on expectations for the industry environment (whether the conditions that foster profitability are expected to remain favorable or to improve), on an assessment of the competitive strength of the company (whether it will be able to maintain strong performance even in unfavorable industry circumstances), or, as is most likely, on a combination of these two factors.

The Role of Judgment

No approach to analyzing industries and companies, however systematic, can do away with the need for the investor to exercise judgment. The analytical method helps to establish the value provided by an investment prospect, but investment is not an exact science. Both judgments and assumptions are always necessary in evaluating the state and direction of both a company and its industry. Even after an evaluation has been completed, it is still necessary to judge whether the price to be paid for a stock is reasonable in relation to its potential (that is, in relation to the extent to which the stock price already discounts its prospects) and/or whether the risk involved is acceptable to the investor. For example, the stock of a leading performer in an attractive industry is likely to be relatively expensive, as the market tends to assign relatively high P/E ratios to such companies. These are often the so-called glamour stocks. The less expensive stock of a secondary company in the industry, or even a leading performer in a less attractive industry, may be judged a better buy.

Judgment is also required in assessing the nature of change and its implications for an industry. Initially, the stock market viewed the deregulation of the airlines industry as a favorable development. However, many companies did not survive, and, as indicated earlier, the industry became highly unattractive. While the implications of change can be analyzed quite systematically, a wide range of judgments about the causes and ultimate effects of change will always remain necessary.

Finally, many judgments are subjective and highly personal. In 1992, it was well known that the earnings prospects of Chrysler Corporation depended heavily on the success of the company's new LH model, a radically redesigned and relatively expensive product line. Even so, investors considering the purchase of Chrysler stock based their decisions in part on their personal judgments: how they liked the car and how they thought it would sell.

THE STRUCTURE OF THIS BOOK

This book will lead readers through a systematic process of analysis and reasoning which will significantly enhance their ability to make long-range investment decisions.

Chapter 2 examines the role of strategy in the success of a company, and shows how strategy influences critical decisions. The chapter also reviews the established investment analysis approaches and examines their strengths and weaknesses to provide the basis for an explanation of the role of strategic analysis.

It has already been shown that some industries are inherently more profitable than others. The characteristics that define the inherent profitability of an industry are created by its structure. Investors must be able to answer this question about an investment candidate: Are the conditions in the industry in which the company is operating favorable to its continued profitability? The analysis of industry structure which makes it possible to answer this question begins in Chapter 3, with an examination of four of the five constraints that define the scope of an industry's operations. Starting in Chapter 3, and continuing in Chapters 4 through 6, five sample industries and selected companies within these industries are used to illustrate the concepts.

Chapter 4 examines the fifth constraint: The factors that determine the intensity of competition in an industry. These factors include the role of the industry life cycle, which is the main determinant of long-term growth. Life cycle is an important consideration in investment decisions and the source of many misconceptions and investment mistakes. Together, Chapters 3 and 4 provide a way to evaluate the quality of an industry—and it is quality that defines the overall profit potential of the industry.

Investors must also understand how and/or why a company is or might become a superior performer. Superior performance is important to the investor, as it is the basis of the sales and earnings growth upon which stock price appreciation depends. Chapter 5 addresses the question of why some companies outperform others. An examination of the basis of competitive advantage starts with an explanation of how superior capability is achieved and the situations in which it is a key factor. Next comes a discussion of the related issue of positioning in a segment of an industry where the company can effectively use its superior capability or where competition is less severe, along with the crucial question of how superior performance can be sustained. Both superior capability and positioning can enable a company to overcome, to a significant extent, the constraints on profitability created by the structure of the industry.

Up to this point in the book, the chapters have been focused on assessing an industry and a company as they now exist, but in a volatile economic and political environment, industries are constantly changing. Chapter 6 discusses the economic, political, social, and technological forces that cause change. It outlines a way by which the effects of these changes on an industry or company can be classified as either favorable or adverse.

Chapter 7 pulls together the concepts that have previously been discussed, to provide a comprehensive picture of the basis upon which a company may be evaluated. The chapter includes a checklist to guide the evaluation process. Appendix B lists sources of the information that is needed to perform the evaluation.

Chapter 8 covers the process of monitoring the long-term investment. It discusses the ways in which the quality of an investment can be affected by developments reported by the company. The implications of strategic developments, such as acquisitions and mergers or changes in management, are examined.

Chapters 9 through 12 unify and reinforce the reader's understanding of the concepts previously outlined. Each of these chapters is a study of an industry and its main companies. The objective of these studies is to provide comprehensive examples of how industries can be analyzed. The economic characteristics of each industry are evaluated, and the changes that have taken place in the industry as a whole are investigated. Then the strategies of the major companies in the industry are evaluated, and the status of each company as a long-term investment candidate is assessed.

Chapter 9 examines the automotive industry as an example of a mature manufacturing business which has long been a favorite of investors, but too often has disappointed them. Chapter 10 analyzes the computer industry, a knowledge-based business that is experiencing the volatility characteristic of the transition from the growth to the mature phase of the industry life cycle. Chapter 11 examines the forest products industry as an example of an industry based on natural resources. Chapter 12 is devoted to the banking industry, a service industry which has been a long-time favorite of conservative investors.

Chapter 13 illustrates the monitoring process. The industry and company analyses in the earlier chapters were based on 1994 data, the latest available at the time. This chapter reviews the main developments that occurred in early 1995 and assesses their implications for earlier conclusions. Thus, Chapter 13 is an example of the exercise that long-term investors must undertake periodically to check on whether their investments are performing as expected, to detect any changes, and to recognize new opportunities.

MEASUREMENT PARAMETERS

Three elements must be compared in the process of evaluating candidates for long-term investment, as follows:

1. *Industry and company performance.* The industry under consideration should be compared to other industries, and the candidate company should be compared to its competitors within the industry.
2. *Stock price performance.* The price of a company's shares should be compared to other companies' share prices, so as to study the effect of various strategies on stock prices over a period of time.
3. *Broad market movement.* The performance of the stock market as a whole is the standard against which the candidate industry and company are compared.

Industry and Company Performance

The performance of an industry as a whole and the companies within it are best assessed in terms of their respective *returns on equity (ROEs).* The ROE consists of net profits after taxes, divided by the amount invested in the form of shares (at the original issue price), plus accumulated retained earnings. This relatively simple measure of performance is expressed as a percentage. Also called *return on book equity*, it reflects a company's effectiveness in using the shareholders' money. There is a strong correlation between return on a company's (or an industry's) equity and the market performance of the company's shares. While the measure is satisfactory for our purposes, as it reflects the shareholders' perspective, it does have a number of limitations.

In the first place, ROE is based on the value of the shares as originally issued, not on present market value. An investor whose stock shows a return on book equity of 15 percent is not likely to get a similar return on the current market price of the stock.

Second, the book equity upon which the ROE calculation is based may not reflect the effective assets of the company. Financial statements primarily include only the tangible assets of a company, and even these are stated at cost rather than at their real current value. (Goodwill while intangible usually arises from an acquisition and is recorded at its net cost.) This deficiency applies particularly to knowledge-based industries, such as the software industry. At Microsoft Corporation, for example, the company's main asset is the expertise of its employees, and there are few hard assets such as plants and equipment. For producers of branded products, book equity does not recognize the continuing value of brand recognition and acceptance. Current accounting practices do not count either knowledge or brand acceptance as an asset. Obviously, a company such as Microsoft has a higher return on book equity due to the understatement of its effective asset base in comparison to a capital-intensive manufacturing company. This situation is not as one-sided as it may appear on the surface. Knowledge must be continuously updated by training, and brand acceptance must be sustained by continued advertising. Both training and advertising entail costs that reduce operating profit. Thus they have the effect of reducing the numerator in the ROE equation, even though their value is not reflected in the denominator.

Third, return on book equity is often affected by the extent to which the company is leveraged. If the amount earned by the use of borrowed money exceeds the interest cost, the surplus accrues to the ROE. A highly leveraged company may be less efficient in operations than its competitors, but its management is doing a better job of managing the company's total capital (equity plus debt) for shareholders. However, there is higher risk, due to the debt burden.

Though these limitations must be recognized, they do not disqualify return on book equity for use as the primary measurement of the comparative performance of industries and companies.

Stock Price Movement

Changes in the price of a stock over a period of time reflect the effect of industry structures and corporate strategies. Tables of historic stock prices usually show the range for the year, that is, the high and the low for the period. Since our interest here is in the relative movement of the stock prices, I will use the *mean* (the midpoint between the high and the low) as the price for a given year. It should be recognized that the mean is not the average price for the period, as the high or low may occur early or late in the year and may hold for only a short time.

Broad Market Movement

The objective of the long-term investor is assumed to be outperforming the market as a whole, so as to achieve capital appreciation. Otherwise, the investor would be content with buying indexed funds. Broad stock market performance is measured by various indexes. The Dow Jones Industrial Average, perhaps the most commonly quoted, is narrow, consisting of only 30 stocks. Standard and Poor's 500 (the S&P 500) is a broader index, representing both a larger number and a greater variety of stocks. For the sake of consistency, I will also use the various S&P industry indexes to show the performance of selected industries. As in the case of individual stocks, the mean of the index will represent the value for any year.

In order to show the effect of industry circumstances and the strategic initiatives of a company on the price of its stock, the stock market performance of selected companies will be shown in relation to the S&P 500. Since investors are primarily interested in share price performance relative to the broad market, the stock prices of the companies will be indexed to the S&P 500. Thus the *return on investment (ROI)* will be measured solely on the basis of the appreciation (or depreciation) of the share price. This method understates the real return, in that it ignores dividends and, in certain cases, even the effect of yield on a stock price. However, I do not consider these distortions to be so serious as to invalidate the comparisons, since capital appreciation, as stated above, is the investor's primary objective.

THE DATABASE: ANNUAL REPORT ON AMERICAN INDUSTRY

Thorough analysis requires readily available data. The professional analyst has both the time and the resources to develop a database on the performance of companies and industries. Such an elaborate effort is obviously beyond the reach of the average investor. Yet, in order to screen opportunities, investors must have an up-to-date database that will provide the relevant information on industries and companies.

Such databases are published annually by several business magazines. The best database for purposes of this book is provided by *Forbes* magazine (usually in the first edition issued each year), under the title

Annual Report on American Industry. For investors in Canadian stocks, virtually the same data are provided by the *Globe and Mail* in its annual Report on Business, usually issued in July, but this report does not include industry data. (See Appendix B for more detail on sources of information.)

In the 1995 edition, the *Forbes* data covered a total of 1,370 companies, divided into 21 broad industry groups, which included a total of 74 industries. For example, the Retailing Group includes seven subgroups covering the various categories of retailing. This database is sufficiently detailed to allow comparisons of the performance of industries and the companies within them. *Forbes'* industries and subgroups and their respective performance are shown in Appendix A to this book.

The data provided by *Forbes* and their values for our purposes are described below.

Return on Equity—Five-Year Average and Latest 12 Months

As indicated above, in this book ROE will be the primary criterion for comparing industries and companies. Equity is defined by *Forbes* as the book value of the common stock after the assumed conversion of any convertible preferred stock less the liquidation value of any nonconvertible preferred stock. The five-year average ROE evens out year-to-year fluctuations and is therefore a good indicator of the basic performance of an industry and a company over a period of time. Further, the statistical method of averaging used by Forbes places greater weight on the more recent years, making the average more sensitive to recent developments. The ROE for the most recent 12 months reported provides a further check on possible change. If it is significantly different from the five-year average, the reasons should be determined. For example, earnings of a company may be lower for cyclical reasons or because of losses from discontinued operations, and this circumstance may enhance future profitability.

Return on Capital and Debt as a Percentage of Capital— Latest 12 Months

In this calculation, capital includes equity (common and preferred), long-term debt, and such items as deferred taxes, investment tax credits, and minority interest in consolidated subsidiaries. The earnings that provide the return are made up of after-tax profit adjusted as if the interest paid on long-term debt were taxed. Debt as a percentage of total capital provides an indication of the degree to which the company is leveraged, and thus the extent to which the higher earnings of a company may be due to leverage.

Growth Rates of Sales and Earnings per Share—Five-Year Average and Latest 12 Months

These self-explanatory data show growth performance. The figures for the latest 12 months consist of the reported results for the most recent four quarters, which are compared to the previous comparable period.

Sales, Net Income, and Profit Margin—Latest 12 Months

These figures allow comparisons of the sizes of the various companies with their profit margins, to get an indication of the price/cost performance of each company relative to its industry and competitors.

The tables showing the averages for companies within each industry also show the industry medians for all the performance data provided. This makes it easy to see where a company stands in its industry.
This readily available database from *Forbes* provides an excellent starting point for identifying investment candidates, as it shows the relative performance of the various industries and the companies within them. Analysis of each situation will show why one industry is more profitable than others, why some companies outperform their competitors, and whether their superior performance can be sustained over the long term. How to conduct such an analysis is of course the subject of this book.

POINTS TO REMEMBER

The key points of this chapter are as follows:

1. The objective of this book is to supplement existing investment methodologies with a method that will enable the long-term investor to pick sound common stocks which should outperform the market as a whole. The focus is on establishing the value of a particular stock rather than on evaluating the state of the market as a whole.

2. The quality of an investment is determined by a combination of the characteristics of the industry and the competitive advantage of the company.

3. This book will lead the reader through a systematic process of analyzing industries and companies, assessing the effects of change, and monitoring investments to determine whether the conditions under which the investment decisions were made have changed.

4. Analysis, however thorough and objective it may be, does not eliminate the need to exercise judgment. Investors always have to choose between alternatives, and some of their choices may be based in part on the highly subjective element of how they personally feel about the products or services of the company.

5. The data needed to screen opportunities and to identify investment candidates for intensive analysis are provided in surveys published by various business magazines. For our purposes, the Annual Report on American Industry published by *Forbes* magazine is the most useful.

NOTES

1. "Annual Report on American Industry," *Forbes*, January 2, 1995, pp. 122–270.

2

THE ROLE OF STRATEGIC ANALYSIS

Strategy is the great work of the organization. In situations of life or death, it is the Tao [way] of survival and extinction. Its study cannot be neglected.

Sun Tzu (fourth century B.C.)
R. L. Wing, translator

The concept of strategy as the basis of success or failure in an organization is not new, as demonstrated by the above words, which were written over 24 centuries ago. Traditionally, the term *strategy* has been primarily used in military contexts. The word is derived from the Greek *strategos*—the art of the army general—and the primary definition in most dictionaries is derived from this military context, emphasizing the words preparation, maneuver, and deception.

In recent times, the word has, quite logically, become popular in business contexts. After all, in business there is a basis for conflict (markets), there are enemies (competitors), and there are continuing battles (competition). In fact, the word *strategy* has come to be used in a wide variety of contexts, and has even been overused. We speak of strategies for sports games, negotiations, and so forth. In most such cases what is being described is not strategies but merely actions or tactics.

This chapter begins an exploration of the uses of strategic analysis in improving long-term investment performance. First a historical perspective shows how the development of corporate strategy has led to investors' and managers' present-day preoccupation with short-term performance. Then the various kinds of company strategies and their effects on the future of a company are described. Next the basic traditional approaches to investment analysis are defined, and their uses, strengths, and weaknesses are revealed. Finally strategic analysis itself is introduced, and its role in relation to the traditional methodologies is explained.

BACKGROUND: THE DEVELOPMENT OF CORPORATE STRATEGY

Strategy is obviously a key factor in determining both the size and consistency of a company's future earnings and the way it responds to change, two factors that are important to the investor. Understanding a company's strategy and its implications is particularly important to long-term investors. In buying the stock of a company, such investors are not just buying an interest in the earnings generated by the present business but are also trusting management to reinvest on their behalf. A bit of historical perspective may be useful on this point and will also explain the market's current preoccupation with short-term earnings.

It was in the sixteenth century that investors first began to band together to share the rewards and risks of the spice trading voyages. Initially, each such venture was organized to finance a single voyage which could last for several years, with profits distributed at the end of the voyage. The practice expanded by vertical integration into the ownership of ships and into the formation of charters to exploit certain geographic areas so as to assure cargoes. Thus were born the East India Company and the Hudson Bay Company, chartered as joint stock companies by Queen Elizabeth I. Instead of paying out all profits at the end of each voyage, dividends were paid from retained earnings. This, of course, made it necessary to introduce accrual accounting to ascertain the levels of profit.[1]

Manufacturing did not begin to need the heavy capital that requires multiple investors until the industrial revolution of the nineteenth century. The industrial corporations that arose in that period were largely single-purpose ventures which left control of the profits to its relatively few shareholders. Profits were paid out in the form of annual dividends. When a business had run its course, it was liquidated and the proceeds were distributed to the shareholders. The shareholders made individual decisions on how to reinvest their returns, thereby continually redirecting capital to its most productive use. The treasurer of the company was usually its CEO—an indication that one of the prime purposes of the company was to provide a return to shareholders in the form of dividends. Money was reinvested in the company only if it promised a return, and usually only to continue in the same type of activity.[2]

This situation changed early in the twentieth century, spurred by the beginning of taxation of dividends (which made them less attractive to shareholders) and by changes in tax legislation (which favored debt financing). The level of dividends was reduced, and the corporation assumed the role of reinvesting the withheld surplus on behalf of shareholders. The shareholders thus invested not in a specific venture but in a "perpetual" corporation, which reinvested on their behalf (see Exhibit 2–1). Rather than focusing on a specific business for the benefit of its shareholders, the corporation became a method of fulfilling various other ambitions.

As shareholdings became increasingly widespread and as shareholders became passive participants, managers became the dominant stakeholders, making companies largely self-governing and self-perpetuating. (*Stakeholders* are the parties who have an interest in the success of the business, and they include shareholders, managers, employees, customers, suppliers, and the community.)

This combination of events had a number of results. First, in the absence of significant dividend yields, the returns to shareholders came to depend heavily on appreciation in the market value of shares, which received more favorable tax treatment. This placed heavy emphasis on the growth of earnings (upon which the stock price depended) and made investors highly sensitive to share prices.

Second, the practice of providing management with stock options and bonuses based on earnings arose, and thus the priorities of management and shareholders were merged. This coalition of shareholders and management pushed aside other stakeholders. Labor asserted its interest through unions, and management and unions developed an adversarial relationship. Another important stakeholder, the community, was largely ignored until recently, when the corporations discovered "social responsibility."

Third, low dividend payouts left corporations with high levels of cash which had to be reinvested. Often this money was used for acquisi-

EXHIBIT 2–1

The Saga of Nucor: A Perpetual Company

In 1904, Ransom Eli Olds started the Reo Motor Car Company and began making heavy luxury touring cars. When the market for luxury cars faded in the depression of the 1930s, the company also started to produce trucks. This helped, but not enough, and in 1938 Reo filed for protection from its creditors under Chapter XI of the Bankruptcy Act. Reorganized as Reo Motors, Inc., the company became solely a manufacturer of trucks. This business was marginal, and the company diversified into lawn mowers. At the end of 1954, the company ceased operation and sold off its physical assets. With $16 million in the bank, it started to pay out liquidating dividends.

In an earlier period, this would have been the end of the company. The venture would have been liquidated, and the proceeds would have been distributed to shareholders. In this instance, however, a group of dissident shareholders, having noticed that the company had a $3 million tax loss on its books from the discontinuation of manufacturing operations, gained control of Reo in a proxy fight. (The shareholders were aware that the tax loss could be applied to profits on any future operations.)

The dissidents forced Reo to take over a very small company, Nuclear Corporation of America. Reo thus became Nuclear Corporation, a small company with the ambition to become the General Motors of the atom. The company manufactured radiation sensors under the trade name Nucor and acquired other fledgling companies in the industry, such as Radioactive Products and Research Chemicals. However, these businesses went nowhere.

In 1960, a new president started to turn Nuclear Corporation into a conglomerate, keeping only the profitable nuclear-related businesses. Among its acquisitions of 1962 was Vulcraft Corporation in South Carolina, a fabricator of steel roof joists. Vulcraft was successful, and in 1962 a second plant was built in Nebraska. However, there were also many failures, including unsuccessful attempts to develop a new can-making process and a photocopying machine, as well as failures of various operating companies. As a result, in 1965, Nuclear defaulted on its debt and came under the control of new shareholders. Barely staving off bankruptcy by selling or liquidating divisions, the new owners focused on Vulcraft, the company's only profitable business. In order to minimize dependence on the large U.S. integrated steel companies (these companies were barely able to compete with foreign producers which often made products of erratic quality), Nuclear built a steel minimill in Darlington, South Carolina, in 1969. Due to cap-

Source: Richard Preston, *American Steel*. (Englewood Cliffs, NJ: Prentice-Hall, Inc. 1991).

Exhibit 2–1, *Concluded*

ital costs and start-up difficulties, the company once again barely staved off bankruptcy.

This venture proved to be an outstanding success, and the company name was changed to Nucor Corporation in 1972. A second minimill was built in Nebraska in 1974, a third in Texas in 1975, and a fourth in Utah in 1980. The Vulcraft business also expanded, holding an estimated one-third share of the markets for steel joists by 1991. Not surprisingly, Nucor eventually faced a host of new minimill competitors, which made the bar steel business highly competitive. In 1990, Nucor opened a pioneering new mill at Crawfordsville, Illinois, to produce high-quality sheet steel through a thin slab continuous casting process, thereby moving up from the fiercely competitive bar steel business. A second such mill was subsequently built in Arkansas. The success of the new minimills created a shortage of high-quality scrap steel, with the result that, in 1993, Nucor was forced to invest in a plant to make a scrap substitute, iron carbide, from iron ore.

In 1994, Nucor had sales of $2.3 billion, ranking 208th in the *Fortune* magazine listing of U.S. companies by sales. It earned $1.28 per share, and at year end, the stock traded at about $50 per share, giving the company a market capitalization of $4.9 billion, more than that of USX Steel Group and Bethlehem Steel (the two major integrated steel producers) combined. In 1965, control of the company had passed for 5 cents per share. A shareholder who had stayed with the company from its beginning would have seen the business pass from cars to trucks, to nuclear products, to steel joists and primary steel, with side trips into lawn mowers and other development projects. Obviously, during the history of the corporation, there were both winners and losers among investors.

The big winners among shareholders were those who invested in 1970-71. The signals were clear. The minimill segment of the steel industry, employing new technology, was attractive in that it was competitive with foreign producers, whereas the large integrated producers were not. Further, Nucor, because of its success in starting a mill and demonstrating its low cost, would likely be in the forefront of its industry. An investment of $1,000 in Nucor in 1972 was worth over $70,000 in 1993.

The vehicle for these developments was the corporation, not the businesses that it was in. There had obviously been many twists and turns in strategy. The company had stayed in automobiles as long as it was driven by the vision of Ransom Olds, but he had sold his interest and withdrawn in the 1920s. He attempted a comeback in the 1930s, proposing that the company drop luxury cars and build cheap ones, but he lost the proxy battle. Control of the company was vested in the shareholders and management, and not in the power of ideas or a personality. Nucor had indeed become a perpetual corporation.

tions or other actions which were not necessarily the most productive use of capital. Further, these high levels of cash were a significant factor in development of major corporate extravagances, such as extreme salaries, "perks," and use of corporate jets for personal travel.

Fourth, the increasing power of management allowed managers to give priority to action to preserve their positions and independence. Such antitakeover measures as use of "poison pills" and "golden parachutes," and succumbing to "greenmail," became common, even though they provided virtually no benefit to shareholders.[3] In fact, in many cases they were highly detrimental, as they diverted money that could have been more productively used elsewhere to the preservation of management freedom and the discouragement of takeover bids that might have given shareholders an immediate higher price.

A further development which changed the nature of financial markets and had a profound effect on corporate strategy arose from the immense pool of capital that accrued in the period of prosperity following World War II. This pool, in the form of savings and pension funds, has been largely entrusted to professional money managers in various institutions and mutual funds. It is estimated that more than one-half of stocks are managed by institutions.[4] Money management is a highly competitive business in which managers' performance is measured by the increase in the value of their portfolios each quarter. The close attention that these managers pay to developments and the trading volume that they can generate make the market very sensitive to short-term developments, such as the failure of the company to meet its quarterly earnings estimates. While many institutions hold large long-term positions that are too large to be sold quickly, it is not uncommon for a portion of these to be actively traded in accordance with short-term expectations, based on the expected quarterly earnings and the direction of the market. Further, the relatively large fixed holdings of the institutions reduce the trading float to the extent that the available capitalization of the company is much smaller than the number of shares outstanding would imply.

Individual investors are well aware of the resulting volatility, and they contribute to it by participating in the guessing game. Recognizing individual investors' preoccupation with the short term, investment analysts have focused their attention on this horizon—and so, of course, have corporate managers, many of whom strive to meet short-term expectations even at the expense of the longer term.

The management objective of producing consistent, predictable, quarter-after-quarter earnings growth has many effects that are detrimental to a company in the long term. For example:

- If earnings are lagging behind expectations, discretionary expenditures such as research and development, advertising and brand development, employee training, and other activities important to long-term success are often cut. Management is reluctant to undertake action which, while having long-term benefits, imposes a short-term earnings penalty. Such actions include, for example, capital expenditures on new plants and equipment which might be initially underused and impose a depreciation and interest cost burden on current earnings.
- If earnings are running ahead of expectations, money is often wasted. With earnings, the objective is consistent orderly growth. Earnings in excess of an orderly upward trend can create expectations of greater increases in the future, thus imposing greater pressures and greater risk of failure on management. Therefore, it is necessary to keep earnings growth within a trend. Preventing the waste of excessive earnings also acts as a safety net, as it can help to sustain earnings in bad years.

Put simply, some companies are being managed to achieve a high short-term share price and for the benefit of management. Exhibit 2–2 outlines a number of typical situations.

Another consequence of preoccupation with immediate share value is a move toward realizing gains in share value through the manipulation of capital, rather than using capital more productively. Leveraged buyouts (LBOs) usually burden a company with heavy debt which can impair its future competitive potential, for no purpose other than increasing immediate share value. As Lester C. Thurlow of the Massachusetts Institute of Technology, Cambridge, put it, "Any elementary economics textbook will tell you that finance exists to serve industry; now we're busy making industry into a plaything for finance."[5]

I have, in this brief history, reviewed the events that have combined to create the short-term perspective that dominates North American management thinking and investment philosophy. This is not necessarily a universal characteristic of North American companies, many of which have more balanced management philosophies. Nor is preoccupation with the short term a global trait. It is in this area—strategic priorities—that differences between North American and offshore companies show up. In catering to impatience, American managers tend to go for the home run: the quick and dramatic gains that can be provided by acquisitions. These managers have a history of neglecting their mature businesses, which can at best provide only slow earnings growth. Often the cash that mature

E X H I B I T 2–2

Focus on Short-Term Results

Preoccupation with the short term has been a characteristic of North American management since the 1960s, as shown by the experience of Reliance Electric, ITT, RJR Nabisco, and the automotive industry.

Exxon Corporation

In 1979, Exxon Corporation made a $1.2 billion bid for Reliance Electric Co., a manufacturer of electric motors whose shares were publicly traded. Exxon was seeking a vehicle to use an energy-saving control device which it had developed. The takeover bid was successful largely because of the neutrality of Reliance CEO B. Charles Ames. Ames declared, "If I had the license to stop worrying about short-term earnings, I could grow this business right through the roof." Ames was obviously frustrated by constraints on expenditures for R&D, plant expansion, and new equipment, which, while yielding long-term results, might be initially underused and place a burden on short-term earnings. He was willing to give up his independence in order to gain more freedom for long-term action. However, the frustrations of becoming an employee of Exxon apparently proved too much, and he resigned within a year.

ITT

The preoccupation with short-term earning and their influence on stock price was carried to an extreme by Harold S. Geneen, the CEO of ITT during the 1960s and 70s. Over a 19-year period, Geneen made over 350 acquisitions, each designed to contribute to the company's earnings per share. Acquisitions were made for a combination of cash generated by operations, debt, and the exchange of ITT shares for those of the acquired company. By showing consistent earnings growth, Geneen kept the P/E multiple of ITT stock high, providing a favorable exchange ratio for stock of acquired companies, which had usually had a lower P/E ratio. ITT's image as a glamour, growth company made its shares acceptable in such exchanges.

Geneen's preoccupation with short-term earnings was extreme. He was quoted as saying, "Growth in earnings per share is the only thing that counts," and "If you make your quarters, you'll make your year." The objective of steady quarterly earnings increases was an inflexible demand

Sources: "Reliance Electric: 'Neutrality' to Help a Takeover by Exxon," *Business Week*, July 16, 1979, p. 84; Brian Burroughs and John Helyar, *Barbarians at the Gate: The Fall of RJR Nabisco* (New York: Harper & Row, 1990); pp. 370–71; and Lee Iacocca with William Novak, *Iacocca—An Autobiography* (New York: Bantam, 1984) p. 304.

Exhibit 2–2, *Continued*

that preoccupied the operating management of ITT subsidiaries to the exclusion of longer-term considerations. Many of the managers of the acquired companies could not accept the tight controls and relentless pressure. When they left, they were replaced by Geneen's men, on the assumption that a good manager can manage anything. This assumption proved not to be true and was a factor in ITT's ultimate decline.

RJR Nabisco

Brian Burrough's and John Helyar's book, *Barbarians at the Gate: The Fall of RJR Nabisco*, provided an example of increasing spending to keep earnings growth in line. The detailed analysis of RJR Nabisco by one of the parties who bid for it in the 1988 LBO resulted in an interesting admission by John Greeniaus, president of Nabisco Foods Division. His mandate was to run the business on a steady basis, producing the consistent growth in earnings that would optimize the corporation's P/E ratio and therefore the market value of the stock. Greeniaus contended that he would get into trouble if his earnings rose more than 12 percent per annum. However, he felt that the business had the capability of increasing profit margins from 11 to 15 percent, increasing profit by 40 percent (amounting to $300 million) in one year, and showing annual earnings growth of 15 to 20 percent. He constrained earnings growth by extra spending on product promotion and marketing, though he acknowledged that this money was not well spent. The business was being managed for its stock price.

The Automotive Industry

The tendency toward short-term priorities dominating management thinking also arises from factors other than concern with share prices. Consider the following quotation from the autobiography of Lee Iacocca, former president of Ford Motor Company and subsequently chairman and CEO of Chrysler Corporation.

The executives at GM, Ford and Chrysler have never been overly interested in long range planning. They have been too concerned about expediency, improving the profits for the next quarter—and earning a good bonus.

They? I should say we. After all, I was one of the boys. I was a part of the system. Gradually, little by little, we gave in to virtually every union demand. We were making so much money that we didn't think twice. We were rarely willing to take a strike, and so we never stood on principle.

I sat there in the midst of it all and I said: "Discretion is the better part of valor." Give them what they want, because if they strike, we'll lose hundreds of millions of dollars, we'll lose our bonuses, and I'll personally lose half a million dollars in cash.

Exhibit 2–2, *Concluded*

Our motivation was greed. The instinct was always to settle quickly, to go for the bottom line. In this regard, our critics were right—we were always thinking of the next quarter.

"What's another dollar per hour?" we reasoned. Let the future generation worry about it. We won't be around then.

But the future has arrived and some of us are still around. Today we're all paying the price for our complacency.

---

businesses generate is used for other purposes, and these businesses slowly starve because they are denied the reinvestment funds they need to stay competitive.

This is in sharp contrast to the situation in Japan, where capital is much more patient, partially due to *keiretsu*, a form of cross ownership with banks and other companies. The Japanese priority is to continually make improvements in existing products and processes, forgoing dramatic leaps. Japanese companies spend two-thirds of their research and development (R&D) investment on process research (making a better mousetrap), and only one-third on product research (inventing a better mousetrap). In the United States, these ratios are reversed, accounting for the fact that many products invented in the United States, such as the videocassette recorder (VCR), the camcorder, and the facsimile machine, are manufactured by Japanese companies. Further, Japanese companies have taken over or challenged the global leadership of U.S. companies in a wide range of mature products, such as Yamaha Corporation in pianos (from Baldwin Piano and Organ Co.), Honda Motors Inc. in motorcycles (from Harley-Davidson), and Yoshida Kogyo K.K. Int. (YKK) in zippers (from Figgie International Inc., Talon).

While it is important to understand the short-term bias in management thinking and investment analysis, it should be kept in mind that virtually all companies have to have long-term plans. The extent to which such a plan may be compromised by short-term thinking should be determined, insofar as possible, by an investor who is conducting a securities analysis on a particular company.

TYPES OF CORPORATE STRATEGIES

The traditional, accepted definition of *corporate strategy* was stated by William F. Glueck of Harvard University, as follows:

a unified, comprehensive and integrated plan designed to assure that the basic objectives of the enterprise are met.[6]

A *strategy* is a master plan that defines the way in which a company meets its objectives. Such a plan obviously must play a central role in determining what businesses the company will be in and how it will compete. Both of these factors are determinants of a company's long-term success. The process of formulating a strategy is deliberate and rational, and a strategy specifies explicit actions which are to be carried out by the organization in a systematic way.

Virtually all CEOs try to give the impression that they are in control of the destinies of their companies and that they have comprehensive and logical strategic plans which can be expected to produce the results expected by the investor. Surprisingly, however, in many cases there is no plan. Any actions taken by the company are being dictated by competitors' initiatives or economic developments. Often, in contemporary management practice, the strategy actually used by the company is across between these two extremes. The strategy may therefore be called *planned*, *adaptive*, or *emergent*, to use the terminology of the corporate strategist.[7]

Planned Strategy

A *planned* approach to directing the future of a company is essentially proactive, seeking to make things happen in an organized way. In the extreme it may even seek to control the day-to-day affairs of the business, as was the case at ITT Corp. under Harold Geneen.

During the 1960s and the early 1970s, Harold Geneen built ITT into one of the world's largest and most diverse conglomerates by making over 350 acquisitions. To control this company, which had 250 diverse profit centers, he devised a tight, sophisticated financial control system which involved detailed planning of every aspect of operations, under his philosophy of "management must manage." The system required each ITT subsidiary to convert its long-range earnings expectations into a detailed quarterly budget, which it then had to meet. Managers' efforts were therefore focused on making happen what they had committed to a year earlier, regardless of circumstances. Consistent failure to make the numbers resulted in the replacement of managers.

This strictly planned approach worked well during the relatively stable economic environment of the 1960s, producing consistent quarterly earnings increases which made Geneen the darling of investors. However, it fell apart in the increasing economic volatility of the early 1970s. The various businesses, tied to their rigid plans, were not able to adapt to changing circumstances that often made the assumptions under which the plans had been formulated obsolete. By the late 1970s, much of the ITT empire had to be dismantled.

The ITT experience demonstrates one of the limitations of planned strategy: its difficulty in adapting to change in volatile environments. The rigidity of the actions prescribed by the plan is what causes this difficulty, which is particularly a problem for businesses that are market-dependent, that is, businesses that have to respond to changing market needs. The planned approach is not all bad, however. It can be effective in businesses in which success depends on a key factor, such as low costs, as is common with producers of commodities—metals and forest products, for instance. Here the plan focuses attention and effort on the activities that will provide the best results and is not distracted by factors beyond its control, such as the prices received for the product.

Adaptive Strategy

With an *adaptive strategy*, the company simply reacts to economic and market developments and to competitors' initiatives. This is therefore a "follower" strategy which enables the company to "muddle through." While such a strategy can be logically expected to prevail in small, unsophisticated companies, it also exists to a surprising extent in large companies. Would you believe, General Motors (GM). Consider the following:

- GM's product line and styling have consistently lagged behind its competitors' new products, from the minivan introduced by Chrysler to the aerodynamic style introduced by Ford Motor Co. in its Taurus. In most cases, by the time GM caught up, its design was out of date and a major market opportunity had been lost.
- On the technical side, front-wheel drive and four-cylinder engines were introduced and exploited by others before GM caught up.
- In the early 1980s, to keep from getting further behind in costs, GM rationalized its production lines, but it did this at the cost of losing its product differentiation. Ford's Lincoln division capitalized on this move by a series of ads poking at GM's look-alike products.

GM's strategy has been clearly adaptive, boiling down to doing a bit of everything until the market decides where it is going. In fact, there is evidence that GM did not even understand the nature of its problems. In 1983, it entered into a joint venture with Toyota to build the Japanese-designed Chevy Nova at its Fremont, California, plant. GM's objective was to get some experience in Japanese manufacturing techniques. To its surprise, it found that the key was not the manufacturing process but the organization of the labor force and giving the worker more say. Under Toyota's management, the strike-prone Fremont plant became the most efficient and highest-quality producer in the GM system.[8]

GM has lacked both leadership and a clear strategic plan. The situation was apparently not recognized by the board of directors until 1992, when it replaced the CEO. In the absence of a clear plan based on market realities, GM was being driven by a well-entrenched internal belief that it knew what the market needed and that the customer would buy what it produced. This arrogant culture persisted until the late 1980s, when tests of customers' reactions to models of its new full-sized Chevrolet Caprice indicated that they had doubts about its heavy-looking rear end. GM's reaction was, "They will come to like it."[9] Sales of this model were well below expectations.

These examples show that GM was been mainly driven by an adaptive strategy for two decades. This adaptive strategy is largely responsible for the company's weak performance. The basic limitation of adaptive strategy is the absence of clear direction and priorities. As in the case of GM, an adaptive strategy causes a company to lag behind competitors and to waste money.

Emergent Strategy

As shown above, both planned and adaptive strategies have limitations. The systematic top-down plan tends to be rigid and often does not let the business respond to change. The bottom-up adaptive plan, in which the company has no overall direction, allows circumstances to dictate the future of the business.

In *emergent strategy*, senior management sets the direction and objectives of the company, but operating management is to accomplish the objectives in a flexible way, adapting as necessary to accommodate the often volatile business environment. This combination of broad top-down direction and lower-level adaptation causes an overall strategy to "emerge." A good example of the success of this approach is provided by the experience of General Electric Company (GE) under the management of Jack Welch.[10]

Up to 1980, GE had been a solid but lackluster performer, as a diverse conglomerate managed in a rigid, top-down mode with a large middle management bureaucracy. On taking over as CEO in 1981, Welch first decided what businesses would be attractive in the future and divested a wide range of operations, including coal mining and the manufacturing of small appliances and TV sets. For the remaining businesses he gave management a mandate to become superior performers by attaining a leading position in their respective industries, and he gave them the authority to take whatever action was necessary to accomplish this goal. The results in GE's case have been excellent. By 1993, GE stock had risen to over five times higher than its 1981 price, outperforming the Dow Jones Industrial Average, which had risen to only 3.5 times its 1981 level.

GE's emergent strategy therefore combines an appropriate degree of centralized direction with freedom for operating managers to take the action necessary to its circumstances. This delegation of responsibility for action carries necessary risks, as GE found out in 1994 when its Kidder Peabody subsidiary incurred serious losses due to management's failure to establish adequate internal controls.

The GE approach relies heavily on the two levels of analysis that are fundamental to the approach which we will be using. Senior management initially made decisions about what businesses the corporation should be in on the basis of the structure of the industries that determined their inherent profitability. The operating managers develop plans on ways to achieve competitive advantage within their respective industries and thereby to outperform their competitors.

THE INVESTOR'S PERSPECTIVE

On the surface it might appear that the way in which a company derives the strategy upon which its future depends should mainly be the concern of academics and organizational designers. However, some understanding of the way in which a company derives its strategy is important to the investor, as it provides an indication of how the company is being managed. Though it is possible to get a reasonably accurate indication of a company's strategy and the way that it is formulated, by keeping up with the business press and by reading annual reports and press releases, remember that what the public sees is often a filtered version of reality.

The existence of a dominant planned strategy indicates a need for caution. Evidence that the strategy is planned is usually provided by a dictatorial CEO who publicizes ambitious, fixed growth objectives. Such objectives, as in the case of ITT, may not be realistic in the face of changes in the market and may force managers to take short-term action to meet immediate objectives at the expense of the long term. The company may do very well in the short term, but its longer-term potential is usually questionable. However, a planned strategy may be desirable in a company in which a single factor is the key to success, or to a company in which a new CEO has been brought in to turn the company around.

On the other hand, companies pursuing totally adaptive strategies usually also carry a high risk. It is necessary to distinguish between companies with emergent strategies that have a high adaptive component due to a rapidly changing environment, and companies which are primarily adaptive. The long-term investor should look for evidence of a significant degree of top-down planning, which is necessary to the effective long-term management of the company, combined with the delegation necessary to allow operating managers to use their skills to optimize results in the face of change.

INVESTMENT EVALUATION METHODS

Historically, several schools of thought have developed on how best to evaluate investment opportunities and how best to make appropriate and profitable decisions. The established schools of thought in investment analysis are *fundamental analysis, technical or chartist analysis, contrarian analysis*, and *value investment analysis*. Each of these approaches has its proponents. There is no consensus on which is most effective in the long term. Most systems in use today rely on frequent trading, and the high transaction costs that are thus incurred can erode profits or aggravate losses under any approach.

The analytical method favored by a given analyst usually depends upon whether the investment decision is to be based on a top-down or a bottom-up orientation.

A *top-down* decision is primarily influenced by the broad overall determinants of market direction, such as interest rates and the economic cycle, and on an assessment of how these determinants affect a specific company. *Timers*, whose orientation is top-down, focus on short-term expectations, moving in and out of various stocks as opportunity arises. *Sector rotators*, who move from industry to industry in anticipation of improvements in relative value, also have a top-down orientation. Economic forecasts have a strong influence on these analytical approaches, which combine fundamentalist and technical evaluations.

Analysts who have a *bottom-up* orientation ignore the market as a whole, basing their direction and their search for value on the fundamentalist and value investment methods. A high degree of discipline is required in this approach, as the commitment is for the long term and the decision is often contrary to the prevailing market sentiment.

Since strategic analysis, the method explicated in this book, is intended to supplement rather than to replace the established analytic approaches, it is important to understand how each one works, what results it provides, and how it accommodates the long-range perspective.

Fundamental Analysis

Fundamental analysis, which is widely used, is based on the premise that the basic cause of stock price movement is anticipated changes in corporate earnings per share (EPS).[11] The analysis therefore focuses almost entirely on forecasting sales, profitability, and unencumbered cash flow. These forecasts are usually heavily dependent on expectations of the state of the economy. They rely heavily on the economic variables, such as gross national product (GNP), industrial production, the unemployment rate, the interest and inflation rate, and the level of consumer confidence. These are factored into the earnings forecast in accordance with the sensitivity of the company to any of the variables.

The fundamentalist attempts to establish an "intrinsic value" for the shares by discounting the expected future earnings to their present value at the appropriate current discount rate. Such discounting causes higher values to be placed on short-term earnings. As a result, the stock is assigned a price/earnings (P/E) ratio which incorporates both the expected growth of earnings and the rate of return on investment opportunities of equivalent perceived value. The rise of the stock market in 1992–93 can be attributed only partially to expected increases in earnings, which were at best uncertain; it must be attributed also to a decrease in the discount rate as the result of declining interest rates on alternative investments.

While there is relatively little doubt about the assumption that earnings expectations are the major determinant of stock prices, the fundamentalist approach has a number of problems.

First, as discussed earlier, circumstances have tended to focus priority on short-term forecasts, leaving the long-term investor out in the cold. Even when long-term forecasting models are used, the discounting to present value process weights early results heavily. (This is also a major problem with corporations that use the discounted cash flow (DCF) rate of return to evaluate capital expenditure alternatives, as this method favors the quick payoff to the detriment of strategic projects with a long-term benefit.)

Second, short-term EPS alone are too limited a base upon which to rely for long-term share value. There are a number of reasons for this, as follows:

1. The level of earnings is relatively easily manipulated in the short term by operating practices and vague accounting rules.[12] As mentioned previously, a wide range of measures may be used to even out earnings. Accounting practices provide a great deal of leeway about how revenue and its resultant profit are booked. Write-offs of assets such as obsolete inventory and bad investments may be timed to a period where they can be absorbed. Failure to write off obsolete inventory can be used to disguise a deteriorating situation for a considerable period. Further, current costs may not reflect liabilities currently being incurred by operations undertaken for future uses, such as environmental cleanups. A number of major companies, including W.T. Grant Company, Penn Central Transportation Company, and Prime Motor Inns, have reported impressive earnings and still gone bankrupt. As Warren E. Buffett of Berkshire Hathaway once wrote to his shareholders, "So long as investors—including supposedly sophisticated institutions—place fancy valuations on reported 'earnings' that march steadily upward, you can be sure that some managers and promoters will exploit GAAP [generally accepted accounting principles] to produce such numbers, no matter what the truth may be."[13]

2. Share buybacks can increase EPS without increasing real performance that can be sustained in the long term. This is not to criticize the use of buybacks, which can be done for sound reasons, but only to point out that a buyback is a one-time manipulation of EPS and therefore is rarely sustainable.

3. The earnings as reported may not be immediately accruing to the benefit of shareholders. In companies with heavy debt, a significant portion of the cash represented by earnings will likely have to be used to pay down debt. If the investment for which the debt was incurred was marginal or poor, as is often the case with acquisitions, a significant portion of current earnings will be used to subsidize the poor past decision. Poor investments may end up as write-offs in future years.

4. In measuring only one dimension of performance, EPS ignores the amount of capital required to achieve the earnings. A heavily capitalized but inefficient firm may therefore appear to be outperforming an efficient company with lower EPS and lower risk.

5. The costs that are deducted from revenues to arrive at earnings may include the costs of employee training, market development, R&D, and other activities providing long-term benefits. While these are, in effect, investments, accounting regulations require that they be expensed, thereby understating current earnings but possibly setting the stage for bigger increases in the future. This is a criticism of reliance on EPS only, and not of the accounting standards and practices which produce them. The accounting profession is struggling to develop better ways to account for EPS.[14]

6. In periods of inflation, earnings may have to be involuntarily invested so that the company can stay in business. This applies particularly to heavy industries, such as steel and mining, where the wear and tear on equipment and facilities is in line with the depreciation charged, even though the equipment and facilities will have to be replaced at much higher cost. Thus, the company will need additional cash from earnings to replace them. However, inflation benefits companies with large real estate holdings which appreciate in value.

Third, the basis for estimating the growth of EPS tends to be superficial, focusing as it usually does on economic influences. This is likely a factor in the poor record of accuracy in fundamentalist forecasts. One major study monitoring a total 66,400 quarterly earnings forecasts from 1973 to 1988 found that only one in four estimates was within 5 percent of actual earnings.[15] Even when the margin of error was increased to 15 percent, only a little over one-half hit the target. However valid the fundamentalist assumption that expected earnings are the main determinant of share prices may be, earnings forecasts still have a serious credibility problem.

Fourth, what compounds the uncertainties involved in forecasting earnings is the problem of how to establish the rate at which future earnings should be discounted to present value. The discount rate is incorporated in the P/E ratio, the market price of stock as a multiple of present EPS. For the market as a whole, the composite P/E ratio is based on the state of the economy and the rates of return on alternative investment opportunities. The market for a specific stock is influenced by the overall market level and also by the market's perception of the state of the industry and the expected performance of the company. Some industries, labeled "growth" industries, have a high P/E multiple to discount the expected rapid growth of earnings. The problems with the P/E multiple only start with their dependence on EPS forecasts. The other problems are as follows:

1. The P/E multiple is heavily dependent on perceptions) For example, a share earning $1 may sell at $20, carrying a 20 multiple because it is expected to earn $1.25 next year. If it earns only $1.05 the next year, its price may drop to $15, a 15 multiple. The company may be perfectly sound in the long term, and the earnings growth pause may be temporary, but perceptions will have changed. This explains why companies put so much emphasis on managing EPS, as discussed earlier. Stocks carrying high P/E multiples are particularly vulnerable to changes in perceptions, explaining why value investors tend to shun them.

2. The P/E ratio for any company tends to be influenced by the industry in which the company is operating) which may be viewed as "growth" or "cyclical," for example. Even a weak company may carry a relatively high P/E ratio because of a growth industry association.

3. Expectations tend to outrun reality) This applies most commonly to the growth stocks, which carry high multiples. As will be discussed in Chapter 4, growth in any industry or company is only a phase which must end, usually in a sudden drop of stock prices.

Under the fundamentalist approach, the price of a stock has built into it the short-term earnings outlook, which is based on the average of the analysts' estimates at a given time. The stock price can be volatile in either direction, depending on the extent to which these estimates prove optimistic or pessimistic. It has been suggested that the market player can make money by critically examining the estimates and buying stocks for which the consensus forecasts appear pessimistic.[16]

Technical Analysis

Technical analysis, also called *chartist analysis*, starts with the assumption that the present price of a stock fully reflects all fundamental data about the company and that this information therefore can be used to predict price changes. The technician's premise is that future price changes can be predicted by analyzing historical information from the stock market itself. The technician looks for patterns of price changes, trading volume, short and odd lot sales, and so forth, both for the overall market and for individual stocks. The most widely known approach is the Dow theory, originally proposed by Charles Dow in 1896, on the basis of which the Dow Jones Industrial Average was initiated. This approach makes heavy use of charts and graphs to show patterns such as "head and shoulders," "double tops," "flags," "channels," and so forth, each of which is considered indicative of the future direction of prices.

Technical analysts claim a high degree of reliability for their method, and it has a relatively wide and often ardent following, which may account in part for its success. If the charts indicate that certain price movements are imminent, enough buying or selling will often be triggered to make the price movement occur, thus creating a self-fulfilling prophecy. For this reason alone, technical analysis should be a factor in investment decisions, even if it is used only for timing purposes.

The partial success of technical analysis obscures one of its weaknesses, which arises from its assumption of the existence of the efficient market—its assumption that the current price reflects all available information. There are time lags between the availability of information and its impact on market prices, and there are major differences in various technicians' interpretations of the information. Further, the interpretation of market signals is not always as precise as claimed, as shown by the differences in predictions between technicians.

Some other structural theories also have a following. The *seasonalists*, for example, can show that stocks tend to move up or down in certain months. While seasonal patterns do exist, there are usually so many exceptions that possibilities rather than certainties are what is shown.

The *Elliott wave* theorists contend that the market moves in a five-wave sequence, resulting in rhythmic patterns of price movements. There is some evidence of validity, depending on how the data are interpreted. However, proponents of this theory often have difficulty in agreeing on what movements constitute a wave. The value of the Elliott wave theory probably lies in its ability to predict broad market direction rather than individual stocks.

The Contrarian Approach

In contrast to the technical approach, the *contrarian* view is entirely psychological. It is based on the premise that the popular wisdom is incorrect. Since contrarians assume that the public is always wrong, they buy when the public is selling, and vice versa.

Contrarians gain some credibility because they buy relatively cheap stocks, as measured by such factors as the P/E ratio. Further, if public sentiment is against a stock, investors likely to sell have already done so, minimizing the downside risk. Thus, the future price movements tend to favor the upside.

Achievement of success with the contrarian theory depends on identification of a deep and widely held public opinion that has little support from facts. The main problem with this school of thought is the difficulty of measuring the depth of overall investor consensus. A group of stocks may be down but still widely enough held to create significant downside pressure as further adverse developments occur. Therefore, there is no assurance that a further decline may not occur. Undoubtedly, there is still a contrarian somewhere who remains loaded up on buggy whip stocks.

Value Investment Analysis

Value investment analysis, the most comprehensive of the evaluation methodologies, takes a long-term perspective. The *value investor*, in fact, can be defined as a patient fundamentalist with a contrarian instinct. While sharing the fundamentalist view that earnings are the main factor in stock price changes, the value approach contains some contrarian elements in that it looks for hidden values not being recognized by the current market. The value investor ignores trying to call the market as a whole, on the premise that a value stock will outperform the market over the long term.

There are two basic approaches to value investing, the quantitative method pioneered by Benjamin Graham and the qualitative one advocated by Philip Fisher. Graham (1894–1976), a teacher of finance at Columbia University in New York City, was the pioneer of the value investing approach, co-authoring the first edition of the book *Security Analysis* in 1934 with fellow faculty member David Dodd. His approach was based on finding *bargains*, defined as stocks that could be purchased for less than their working capital value (current assets less current liabilities divided by the number of shares outstanding). The number of stocks in this category tends to be limited when the market is high, but of course it increases during market declines. Opportunities using the Graham principle tend therefore to be cyclical. (Both the S&P Outlook and the Value Line Investment Survey carry lists of stocks selling below net working capital value.) Other quantitative measures of value include the relationship of the stock price to earnings, cash flow, and book value,

with the desirable ratio in each case being relatively low. The more contemporary application of Graham's approach has led to a search for hidden values, such as real estate that has appreciated in value since being
acquired, resulting in an understatement of the value of the asset on the
balance sheet.

The weakness of the quantitative value approach is its heavy
reliance on financial ratios and the value of assets. These do not necessarily lead to the growth of earnings, nor can the value of assets be realized by the investor. For example, it may comfort the investor who holds
McDonald's shares to know that the balance sheet understates the value
of the company's real estate, but if McDonald's got into trouble, these
hidden values would be quickly dissipated in the rescue effort. It happens,
unfortunately, much too rarely that management acknowledges that a
company is worth more dead than alive, folds it up, and distributes the
proceeds to shareholders. Further, as discussed earlier, many assets do not
appear on a company's balance sheet, with the result that value opportunities that are not based on financial criteria can be overlooked. To be fair
to Graham, the intangible and intellectual assets so important to many
companies today were not as important in his time.

Despite these limitations, the value investment approach is often
highly successful. The conservative financial ratios are indicative of
basic financial strength, and, by virtue of their patience, value investors
are not likely to fall victim to the whims of the market as a whole.
Studies have shown that low P/E ratio stocks are relatively resistant to
declines. This is due to unpleasant earnings surprises, which reduce the
downside risk. Thus the risk of losers' discounting the gains of winners
in a portfolio is reduced.

Graham's unease with criteria that could not be precisely measured
was not shared by the other value investment pioneer, Philip Fisher. In
1931, at the height of the Great Depression, Fisher successfully started his
own investment counseling firm, Fisher and Company, by focusing his
evaluations on qualitative characteristics. He based his estimates of companies' earnings potential on these qualitative characteristics.[17] By inter-
viewing management, suppliers, and customers, he was able to assess the
quality of management and to identify factors that would lead to the
growth of earnings in the long term. These factors could include the quality of a company's R&D program and its sales and marketing organization, as well as the accounting and cost control systems upon which the
maintenance and improvement of profit margins were based. In effect,
therefore, Fisher was assessing the overall capability of the companies he

evaluated. Unlike Graham, who looked for cheap stocks, Fisher was looking for earnings potential—and he was willing to pay prices that were high by Graham's criteria, once he found the earnings potential he sought.

The "value" label has also been used by other methods which stray significantly from Graham's relatively simple concepts. For example, the Value Line Investment Survey ranking system, perhaps the best known, uses a formula that incorporates the relative earnings momentum (based on a comparison from each company's year-to-year change in quarterly earnings, divided by the average change for all stocks), an earnings surprise factor (based on the difference between actual reported quarterly earnings and Value Line's estimate), and a value index (based upon the company's past earnings and stock price performance relative to the market). Despite the label, this is not a traditional value method but is rather a technical approach.

The Record of Professional Managers

Given the effort devoted to securities analysis and its apparent sophistication, it might be expected to yield superior investment performance. However, on average, professional managers barely outperform the market as a whole, and a significant proportion of them underperform it. A 1992 Brookings Institution study showed that the average professional investment fund manager lagged the S&P 500 by 2.6 percent per year during a seven-year period, after trading and management costs.[18] A more recent survey of 2,700 equity managers showed that only 26 percent beat the S&P 500 during a 10-year period.[19] Even among the winners, few managers are consistent over a period of time. It has been suggested that the best way to pick a manager for a period is to pick the one with the worst recent record, on the assumption that the manager's record will likely improve back to the mean. General Mills, in managing its pension fund, already does this by giving a stock picker who is down for the year more money in the next. This has contributed to the fact that the General Mills fund has outperformed the S&P 500 by an average of 1.6 percent per annum over the past 15 years, putting its performance in the top 5 percent of all pension funds.[20]

The most likely cause of the weakness of managers' overall performance is the domination of the craft of investment analysis by the short-term, market-driven perspective, catering to impatient capital. In this climate, reputations can be made quickly. In addition, the frequent trading which it encourages provides the commission income on which the brokers depend. Besides exposing the investor to the limitations of the various analytical methods, this brings into play another risk factor, timing. Timing is heavily dependent on an intangible factor, market psychology.

As previously mentioned, transaction costs in the form of commissions on purchases and sales incurred by frequent traders can erode gains and increase losses. These erosions are not always included in the investment advisers' claims about their performance. For example, in 1994 one investment advisory letter claimed that its portfolio had gained 137 percent over the past three years, more than double the market's 60 percent.[21] However, if commissions of 3 percent (the average of discount brokers on typical-sized transactions) had been included, the portfolio gain would have been shown as only 38 percent, underperforming the market. This explains in part the relatively weak returns achieved by the frequent trader who depends on fundamentalist and technical advice.

Because of the uncertainty of the traditional evaluation methods, traders place heavy reliance on the ability to get out quickly if things don't work out. As a result, they strongly emphasize high capitalization stocks, which provide liquidity. Low capitalization stocks, even attractive ones, tend to be shunned.

STRATEGIC ANALYSIS AND THE ESTABLISHED METHODS

A purist might argue that the bid price of a stock—the price a buyer is willing to pay—is its real value. Remember, however, that the bid or market price is affected by traders' perceptions of value. These perceptions in turn reflect expectations about the direction of the economy as a whole, the state of the industry under consideration, and/or developments within a company (such as a hot new product or service).

Perceptions are generally fragile and volatile. The sharp market drop in October 1987, for instance, changed the market mood overnight from optimism to fears of a repetition of the crash of 1929. These fears failed to materialize in the 1980s, and the market subsequently recovered. These extreme shifts of opinion illustrate the point that perceptions based on the top-down approach are an important factor in determining the market price of a stock.

In strategic analysis, no attempt is made to quantify future results by forecasting earnings, cash flow, and net present values. Such forecasts have proved to be highly fallible in a volatile environment, and even many major corporations have abandoned them. As pointed out by Jack Welch, CEO of General Electric, "Trying to define what will happen three to five years out, in specific quantitative terms, is a futile exercise. The world is moving too fast for that."[22]

My contention in this book is that the real value of the shares of a company lies in its capability, which is the dominant factor in determining its future earnings. Strategic analysis limits the role of perceptions by examining capability in depth. Not only does this approach explain a company's past performance, but also it gives important indicators of whether the company's past level of performance can be sustained or improved in the future.

A basic premise of strategic analysis is that consistent, long-term earnings growth is the key factor in determining the real value of a company's stocks, and therefore in stock price appreciation. Earnings growth is assumed to be dependent on two interrelated variables: the nature of the industry in which the company is operating, and the company's competitive position within the industry. The investor who understands these factors can also go on to understand how the changing economic, social, and political environments may affect the company's future ratings.

Strategic analysis adds much depth to investors' understanding of industries and companies. It can be used to correct shortcomings of some of the established methods, and it can use technical analysis as an adjunct in timing decisions. Specific interactions between strategic analysis and the established methods are discussed below.

To Fundamental Analysis

The fundamentalist approach seeks to establish "intrinsic" value, but faces problems in this regard. The fundamentalist must revert to perceptions in a range of judgments such as determining what discount and what P/E ratio are appropriate. Given the volatility of perceptions, the challenge to the long-term investor is to find a more reliable basis for determining value.

The conventional limitations of fundamental analysis include the need to rely heavily on historical earnings performance. Related to the tendency to extrapolate past performance so as to arrive at forecasts is the tendency to assume that the company will continue to operate in its customary way. The fundamentalist approach includes relatively little recognition of change. Either changes in the industry or changes in the company's competitive position due to management action can sustain or improve performance, or even cause it to deteriorate. Though in many cases the analyst can judge the probable effectiveness of management's strategic action, such educated guesses do relatively little to help in the forecasting of short-term earnings, which usually fluctuate due to immediate conditions rather than strategic causes

Specifically, for the fundamentalist, strategic analysis can improve the depth of understanding of companies in their respective industries, and thereby the quality of the assumptions that must be made in using long-range forecasting models.

To Technical Analysis

Strategic analysis has no value to the technician; indeed, technicians reject the relevance of such information. Technical analysis can, however, be a valuable tool for the long-term investor, as it can indicate favorable timing for the purchase of a specific stock. If the technical position of a stock is weak despite strong strategic fundamentals, postponing purchase until after the stock goes through a technical correction may be wise. Further, as mentioned above, many companies that offer good value to the long-term investor are cyclical. Technical analysis is useful to the strategic analyst in identifying the phase of the cycle, so that it can be recognized in the timing of commitments.

To the Contrarian Approach

Strategic analysis adds depth to the contrarian's approach by explaining why an industry or a company has a bad or a good reputation, and by analyzing the factors that may cause this reputation to change in either direction.

To Value Investment Analysis

It was pointed out earlier that the value investment methodology was divided into two schools of thought—Graham's *quantitative* and Fisher's *qualitative* approaches. Both approaches take the patient long-term perspective, focusing on the individual company and ignoring the overall state of the stock market.

Strategic analysis supplements the qualitative approach by providing it with greater depth. While strategic analysis requires an understanding of the capability of a company, it is also concerned with how effectively this capability may be used to obtain competitive advantage through the company's positioning in its industry. Thus it provides not only a comprehensive and systematic conceptual framework for understanding how the capabilities of a company are derived but also a basis for assessing the effectiveness of these capabilities in generating future earnings under the conditions of the industry in which the company is operating, as well as in response to the changes that may occur.

The investment decision-making process based on strategic analysis, which will be described later, departs from the traditional value approach by taking timing into consideration. Timing, however, is considered only in a patient long-term context, rather than on the short-term buy-and-sell basis that speculators use in playing the market. The market is rife with cyclical stocks, and the causes of cycles can be discerned by studying industries. Even if an investor intends to hold a stock for the long term, there is nothing to be gained by buying it in the expensive part of its cycle. The patient investor should also be a patient buyer.

STRATEGIC ANALYSIS AS THE PRIMARY BASIS FOR INVESTMENT DECISIONS

Strategic analysis has been described in this section as a tool for use in supplementing established methods of investment analysis. It can also be the primary basis for investment decisions, because of its ability to identify likely candidates. The stocks of a company that has decisive and sustainable competitive advantage and that is operating in an industry with favorable fundamentals will likely outperform the market as a whole.

Reliance on strategic analysis as the primary basis of an investment decision is really a supplement to and a variation of the value approach, except that it shifts the basis of the decision from past performance and present ratios (which are almost entirely financial) to a more comprehensive evaluation of future performance based on the investment candidate's capability.

The concepts used in this book to analyze and evaluate industries and companies are in fact already being used by securities analysts. Almost all of the more consistently successful fund managers are fundamentalists who are adept at gathering and interpreting information about companies, and at projecting the implications of developments. (As the performance records cited earlier in this chapter indicate, most investment managers are not so astute.) However, these successful managers put an immense amount of time and effort into their analyses of the stock market—far more than the average individual trader has available. They also have the kind of share-buying power that gives them access to senior management. The approach to strategic analysis described in this book will allow even the dedicated amateur to reach usable conclusions without the benefit of inside contacts.

POINTS TO REMEMBER

The key points of this chapter are as follows:

1. A company's strategy is the plan by which it attempts to meet its objectives. The strategy should be concerned with the businesses that the company will be in, and should indicate how the company expects to outperform its competitors and adapt to change.

2. Company strategies can be classified as planned, adaptive, or emergent. The emergent mode, which combines strong overall direction with an ability to respond to circumstances and competitors' initiatives, is generally the most favorable to the investor.

3. Strategy is important to the investor because it indicates not only the direction of operations but also how effective management may be in reinvesting surplus funds on behalf of shareholders.

4. The priorities of institutional money managers, who control over half the stock of major companies, have influenced management to focus on providing consistent short-term earnings growth, often to the detriment of the longer term.

5. There are four basic schools of thought in investment analysis: fundamentalist analysis, technical analysis, the contrarian approach, and value investment analysis. Fundamentalists focus on earnings growth, with economic activity often the main influence. Technicians rely entirely on the trading patterns of the market as a whole and of individual stocks. Contrarians base their decisions on psychology, assuming that the public is always wrong. Value investors employ a wide range of criteria, including both fundamentalist and contrarian concepts; primarily, they look for strong present positions and a good track record.

6. Each of these four schools of thought has some validity, and all of them share many of the same weaknesses, in particular a strong dependence on past performance as an indicator of future direction and a tendency toward superficiality in recognizing the factors that affect a company's performance. In addition, frequent trading is often required, causing erosion of profits by transaction costs.

7. Strategic analysis supplements the fundamentalist, contrarian, and value investment approaches. It adds depth to the trader's understanding of the basis for company performance, and it improves the investor's ability to assess long-term performance potential. Technical analysis is used in strategic analysis as one of the guides to timing of purchases.

8. Strategic analysis can be the primary factor in a long-range investment decision, on the assumption that a company with identifiable, sustainable competitive advantage operating in an industry that can be expected to remain fundamentally sound will outperform the broad market in the long term. This approach makes it unnecessary to attempt to forecast future earnings.

NOTES

1. Dana Wechler Linden, "Lies of the Bottom Line," *Forbes*, November 12, 1990, pp. 106–12.

2. Dero A. Saunders, "Fredric Dumaine: Upstreaming the Profits," *Forbes*, July 13, 1987, pp. 258–62.

3. The term *poison pill* refers to actions undertaken to make an unwelcome takeover more difficult. These actions can include changes in corporate bylaws to stagger the terms of directors, so as to prevent the immediate gain of control by the acquirer, or the granting to existing shareholders of the right to buy additional shares relatively cheaply. The term *golden parachute* means large severance payments made to existing senior executives in the event of a successful hostile takeover. In *greenmail*, an outsider with a minority share position declares the intent to launch a takeover bid. The company buys back this minority holding at a premium price, so as to have the bid withdrawn.

4. Estimate based on percentage of institutional holdings listed in "The Business Week 1000," *Business Week*, March 28, 1994.

5. Joan Berger, "Is the Financial System Shortsighted?" *Business Week*, March 3, 1986, pp. 82–83.

6. William F. Glueck, *Business Policy and Strategic Management* (New York: McGraw-Hill, 1980).

7. Henry Mintzberg, "Strategy Making in Three Modes," *California Management Review*, Winter 1973, pp. 44–53; and Henry Mintzberg, "Crafting Strategy," *Harvard Business Review*, July–August, 1987, pp. 66–83.

8. William H. Hampton and James R. Norman, "General Motors: What Went Wrong," *Business Week*, March 16, 1987, pp. 102–10.

9. Sara Rimer, "Stubborn GM Gets a Lesson on Caprice," *Globe and Mail*, July 26, 1992, p. B3.

10. Ann M. Morrison, "Trying to Bring GE to Life," *Fortune*, January 25, 1982, pp. 50–58.

11. The definitions of the fundamental, technical, contrarian, and value methodologies have been derived from a combination of the following sources: Harvey Rachlin, *The Money Encyclopedia* (New York: Harper & Row, 1984); Sidney Cottle, Roger F. Murray, and Frank E. Block, *Graham and Dodds Security Analysis*, 5th ed. (New York: McGraw-Hill, 1988); and Jerome B. Cohen, Edward D. Zinberg, and Arthur Zeikel, *Investment Analysis and Portfolio Management*, 5th ed. (Homewood, IL: Richard D. Irwin, 1987).

12. Ford S. Worthy, "Manipulating Profits: How It's Done," *Fortune*, June 25, 1984, pp. 50–54.

13. Dana Wechsler Linden, "Lies of the Bottom Line," *Forbes*, November 12, 1990, pp. 106–112.

14. Thomas A. Stewart, "Your Company's Most Valuable Asset: Intellectual Capital," *Fortune*, October 3, 1994, pp. 68–74.

15. David Dreman, "Cloudy Crystal Balls," *Forbes*, October 10, 1994, p. 154; and David Dreman, "Where Bad News Is Good," *Forbes*, March 27, 1995, p. 151.

16. Steve Kichen and Eric S. Hardy, "How to Profit from Earnings Estimates," *Forbes*, December 20, 1993, pp. 278–81.

17. Robert G. Hagstrom, Jr., *The Warren Buffett Way* (New York: John Wiley & Sons, 1994), 1994, pp. 38–43.

18. Dyan Machan, "Monkey Business," *Forbes*, October 25, 1993, pp. 184–190.

19. As reported in Jaclyn Fierman, "The Coming Investor Revolt," *Fortune*, October 31, 1994, pp. 66–73.

20. Dyan Machan, "Monkey Business," *Forbes*, October 25, 1993, pp. 184–190.

21. Mark Hubert, "Step Right Up, Folks," *Forbes*, February 14, 1994, p. 188.

22. "Jack Welch's Lessons for Success," *Fortune*, January 25, 1993, p. 86.

II

INDUSTRY STRUCTURE

The structure of an industry determines the overall profitability of the companies competing within it. Using an analogy from sports, the structure of an industry can be compared to the condition of a playing field. A soft or muddy field makes it difficult for even the best teams to perform well and thus keeps the score low. A firm, even field, on the other hand, makes it possible for all teams to perform to the best of their ability.

In Part II, the factors that determine the nature of an industry's competitive playing field are described. The five internal constraints that determine industry structure are presented, and their implications for investors are explored. These five constraints, in various combinations, create industry conditions that determine the overall profitability of the companies in the industry. Five industries, ranging from the highly profitable pharmaceuticals industry to the money-losing airlines industry, are used to illustrate how these forces work.

3

THE IMPACT OF FOUR INTERNAL CONSTRAINTS

With few exceptions, when a manager with a reputation for brilliance tackles a business with a reputation for poor fundamental economics, it is the reputation of the business which remains intact.

Warren E. Buffett
Chairman, Berkshire Hathaway Corporation

The fundamental economics to which Warren Buffett was referring are created by the structure of an industry. As chairman of Berkshire Hathaway and one of the most successful investors in the United States, he should know.

In 1993, Berkshire Hathaway had revenues of $3.1 billion, placing it 158th in *Fortune* magazine's list of the 500 largest U.S. industrial corporations. Buffett built Berkshire Hathaway by acquiring a diverse group of companies operating in the areas of insurance; newspapers; retail home furnishings; and the manufacture and distribution of uniforms, candy, vacuum cleaners, and industrial products such as compressors and burners. Buffett chooses his investments after careful consideration of the structural soundness of the companies and their respective industries. He developed this approach after making mistakes in investing in department stores

48

and farm equipment manufacture. He had also tried, over a period of 20 years, to turn around a textile manufacturer, which was producing commodity fabrics like suit linings, before closing the operation in 1985. This experience prompted the now famous comment that opens this chapter.

After acquiring an understanding of industry fundamentals by investing in smaller businesses, Buffett took Berkshire Hathaway into major investment positions in Capital Cities/ABC Inc., Gillette Company, Federal Home Loans Mortgage Corp., The Coca-Cola Company, The Washington Post Company, and General Dynamics Corporation. His record, a 29 percent compounded average rate of return over 23 years, speaks for itself.[1]

(One of Buffett's rules is that he will not invest in a company that is operating in an industry in which the conditions do not allow it to make a consistently decent profit, no matter how brilliant the management) He views the playing field as being defined by the structure of the industry, and he chooses his playing fields carefully. He avoids the ones that, to use his terms, are sloppy, keep the score down, and prevent the team from taking full advantage of its talents.

The extent to which industries differ in profitability can be seen in the summary shown in Exhibit 3–1. Here we see the main performance measurements for five industries: pharmaceuticals (drugs), tobacco, drug and discount retailing, the manufacture of recreational products, and airlines. The list includes the industry with the best median performance over the past five years, the pharmaceuticals industry, as well as the worst, the airlines. The other three are at approximately the quartile points in between. The five-year average of median returns on equity (ROEs) for these industries ranges from 22.8 percent for the drug industry to a deficit for the airlines industry, showing the large difference in the nature of their respective playing fields.

These industries and selected companies within them will be used in this chapter, and in Chapters 4 to 6, to show how the basic concepts by which we analyze industries and competitive performance apply. I have chosen these industries as examples not only because they show wide differences in performance but also because they represent a cross section of industries, including high- and low-tech manufacture (drugs, tobacco, and recreational equipment) and two service industries (retailing and travel).

This chapter begins an examination of the structure of industries and shows how structure determines the overall profit potential of the companies operating in an industry. The chapter defines what an industry is; examines the model of industry structure developed by Michael E. Porter of Harvard University, which provides the conceptual basis for understanding industries; and describes the first four components that constrain industries. Chapter 4 discusses the factors that determine the intensity of

E X H I B I T   3–1

Performance of Selected Industries, 1994
(Industry Medians, Percentages)

Industry	No. of Companies	Profitability				Growth			
		Return on Equity		Return on Capital	Sales			Earnings per Share	
		5-Year Average	Latest 12 Months	Latest 12 Months	5-Year Average	Latest 12 Months	5-Year Average	Latest 12 Months
Pharma-ceuticals (drugs)	22	22.8	20.5	16.2	12.7	8.1	14.3	14.3
Tobacco	10	18.4	2.6	4.1	6.3	–1.3	*	–37.8
Drug and discount retailing	31	12.8	12.6	9.7	7.6	7.1	*	0.0
Recreational equipment manufacturing	9	7.7	15.2	12.8	5.3	17.7	*	13.1
Airlines	11	†	1.0	4.1	9.8	7.9	*	66.7
All industries		11.4	12.6	9.4	5.5	6.3	–18.8	11.8

* Not meaningful.
† Deficit.
Source: Annual Report on American Industry, *Forbes*, January 2, 1995, pp. 268–69.

competition in an industry, the fifth component of the Porter model. Chapter 5 examines why certain companies outperform others within each of five industries, and Chapter 6 shows how these industries and the companies within them may be changing.

WHAT IS AN INDUSTRY?

The word *industry*, as commonly used, tends to be vague in what it includes. For example, the "packaging" industry includes cans, glass containers, paper, and rigid and flexible plastic products, each of which is often referred to as an industry in its own right. The "automotive" industry makes passenger cars and trucks; the "steel" industry includes both integrated producers and minimills.

Professional strategists within companies usually use *industry* to mean "all the companies that are in direct competition with us." Thus an

industry may be defined by the material it uses, the product it manufacturers, the need it satisfies, or some other criterion. Such definitions are
useful to corporate practitioners but have no relevance for investors.

(For purposes of investment analysis, the first requirement for a
usable definition of industry is that it must group together companies with
similar characteristics so as to point up the factors that define the overall
profitability of the group. Second, it must classify them in such a way that
data on the performance of the industry as a whole and the individual
companies within it will be readily available.)

As indicated in Chapter 1, the Annual Report on American Industry,
which is compiled by *Forbes* magazine, is the primary database used in
this book. The 1994 survey covers a total of 1,370 companies, divided into
21 industry groups. These are shown in Appendix A, and the 76 industries
within the 21 industry groups provide the definition of *industry* that will
be used in this book.

The *Forbes* classification system does have a limitation in that each
company is listed under its largest business, even though it may have significant sales in other areas. For example, Nabisco Holdings Corp., listed
as being in the tobacco industry, is also a major food procesor. This limitation must be recognized in any investment analysis.

The methodology that we will be using to analyze industries applies
equally to both goods-producing and service industries, but it is necessary to
recognize some differences between the two. Service industries, unlike
goods-producing industries, cannot use inventories to even out fluctuations in
sales. An empty airline or theater seat, or an unoccupied hotel room, is a revenue opportunity lost forever. Service capacity is finite: there is a limit to sales
in peak periods until capacity can be increased. Services, unlike goods, cannot be stored; they are used more frequently by the customer. Furthermore, if
the service fails, the reputation of the company can deteriorate quickly.

Keeping in mind that our working definition of *industry* is "one of
the 76 industries in the *Forbes* classification system," let us now start to
look at what determines the overall profitability of an industry.

THE PORTER MODEL OF INDUSTRY STRUCTURE

A model developed by Michael E. Porter explains why industries differ in
overall profitability. (In this model, the characteristics of an industry are
defined by five variables: (1) the threat of new entrants, (2) the risk of
substitution by new products, (3) the industry's bargaining power with
customers, (4) its bargaining power with suppliers, and (5) the intensity
of competition within the industry.)

The Porter model is diagrammed in Exhibit 3–2. It may be explained by the following analogy. Think of an industry as operating in a box with four sides, corresponding to four of the variables that define the industry: the threat of entrants, the risk of substitution by new products, the bargaining power of suppliers, and the bargaining power of customers. These four variables determine the size of the industry's markets, the number of its competitors, the costs it incurs, and the prices it can charge. These four variables are the *industry constraints*. Inside the box, a number of companies compete. The intensity or heat of their competition—the fifth variable—is primarily dependent on the rate of market growth, the cost structure of the business, and barriers to exit.

Together, these five variables determine the overall profitability of an industry. Using this model, I will show how changes in the business environment affect an industry and how a company can achieve higher profitability than its competitors.

This chapter examines the first four variables, the nature and effects of the industry constraints. Chapter 4 covers the fifth variable, the factors that influence the intensity of competition.

Barriers to Entry

The barriers to entry determine how difficult it is to get into an industry. Obviously, if it is relatively easy to enter an industry, established companies will be continually faced with new competitors. Even in industries where fierce competition forces many businesses out, new entrants tend to replace them. If entry is difficult due to high barriers, the threat of new competition which would fragment markets is obviously lower, and the more stable environment provides a potential for higher profitability.

The main barriers to entry are listed below.

1. *Lack of sufficient capital.* Raising a large amount of money to enter an industry is obviously more difficult than raising a smaller amount. Large capital requirements are caused by some combination of the following factors:

   • Large plants with automated equipment are usually necessary to be competitive in mass production manufacturing industries.

   • Sophisticated and technologically complex products may be very costly to develop.

   • Extensive advertising and promotion may be needed, to create brand recognition and to establish brand preference among customers.

EXHIBIT 3–2

The Porter Model of Industry Structure

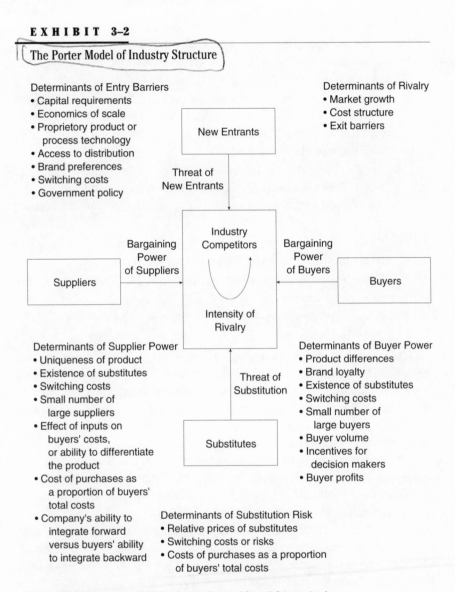

Determinants of Entry Barriers
- Capital requirements
- Economics of scale
- Proprietory product or process technology
- Access to distribution
- Brand preferences
- Switching costs
- Government policy

New Entrants

Threat of New Entrants

Determinants of Rivalry
- Market growth
- Cost structure
- Exit barriers

Industry Competitors

Bargaining Power of Suppliers

Bargaining Power of Buyers

Suppliers

Buyers

Intensity of Rivalry

Determinants of Supplier Power
- Uniqueness of product
- Existence of substitutes
- Switching costs
- Small number of large suppliers
- Effect of inputs on buyers' costs, or ability to differentiate the product
- Cost of purchases as a proportion of buyers' total costs
- Company's ability to integrate forward versus buyers' ability to integrate backward

Threat of Substitution

Substitutes

Determinants of Buyer Power
- Product differences
- Brand loyalty
- Existence of substitutes
- Switching costs
- Small number of large buyers
- Buyer volume
- Incentives for decision makers
- Buyer profits

Determinants of Substitution Risk
- Relative prices of substitutes
- Switching costs or risks
- Costs of purchases as a proportion of buyers' total costs

Source: Adapted with permission of the Free Press, a Division of Simon & Schuster, Inc. from *Competitive Advantage: Creating and Sustaining Superior Performance* by Michael E. Porter. Copyright © 1980 by Michael E. Porter.

- Operating losses will have to be covered until the business reaches the break-even point.

2. *Lack of knowledge.* Access to technology and/or specialized knowledge skills may be difficult to acquire.

3. *The need to be large in order to keep costs low.* Economies of scale are necessary with almost all mass-produced products, but acquiring a significant market share takes time.

4. *Proprietory technology in the form of patents or trade secrets about key aspects of product or process technology.* Polaroid Corporation, which initially developed instant photography, remains the only player, despite an attempt to enter by a giant like Eastman Kodak Company.

5. *Lack of access to distribution.* In food products, for example, retail shelf space is difficult to get unless a company has a well-established track record or enough capital to provide retailer incentives.

6. *Strong brand preferences and loyalties.* The market may be reluctant to try a competing product.

7. *Government regulations.* In radio and TV broadcasting, for example, licenses are required. In waste disposal, use of certain sites can engender local opposition, and strict conditions must be met.

In many industries, the barriers to entry are prohibitive, which can make these industries relatively attractive to established companies. Boeing Company, for example, is one of only three major manufacturers of commercial airliners in the world. Commercial airliner manufacture is a perfect example of an industry in which product development costs are high and must be amortized over a high volume of sales to be profitable.

Manufacture of big-ticket consumer durables, such as automobiles and appliances, is another industry with high barriers to entry. Heavy investment in production facilities and a high volume of output are required to achieve competitive costs through economies of scale. In mining, though mineral deposits can be economically mined, high exploration costs are required to find the deposits, and it takes a large amount of capital to bring them into production. This situation benefits Inco Limited, the owner of the world's largest low-cost nickel deposits.

High barriers to entry, however, are not enough to assure the profitability of an industry. Other forces affecting industry attractiveness may be unfavorable, and, indeed, barriers to entry may not be permanent. An example that has already been described (see Chapter 2) occurred in the steel industry. New technology allowed new companies to enter the steel industry via relatively low-cost minimills. A minimill costs only $250 million to build, as compared to over $2 billion for an integrated facility.

Government activity may have enormous effects on industry barriers. The U.S. government's deregulation of long distance telephone services, for instance, ended a well-established monopoly. Governments may subsidize the formation of new industries as an element of economic policy. Thus entry may become possible even when no economic justification exists on a global basis. Just such a change has occurred in shipbuilding in the Far East.

Acquisition is the most common strategy for overcoming barriers to entry. Acquisition does not seriously disturb the competitive balance in an industry. For example, in 1995, Seagram Co. sold its 24 percent stake in DuPont Co., with the goal of changing its own future direction by acquiring the entertainment conglomerate MCA Inc. MCA's movie studios, theme parks, TV production and publishing operations, and theater chain gave Seagram instant entry into the industry. Entry into this crowded industry, which had heavy capital requirements, and which also possessed control of locations, talent, and established brand names, would have otherwise presented almost insurmountable barriers. In another example, during the 1980s the tobacco company Philip Morris Companies bought food companies General Foods and Kraft, so as to diversify its operating base. Both of these food companies had well-established brands and access to retail shelf space. Otherwise, it would have taken Philip Morris years to overcome the very high barriers to entry into the industry, and the investment required would have been high and the outcome uncertain.

Threat of Substitution

The extent of the threat by substitution by a new product depends on the cost and/or performance advantages of the substitute product. At risk may be all or part of the market, as well as limitations on the price which can be charged. Copper has lost its market for data transmission wire to fiberoptics and its market in plumbing to plastics, but it retains its position in electrical wiring with no apparent threats. The use of computers, dedicated word processors, and various printers, however, has largely wiped out the market for conventional typewriters. Other common examples are the substitution of direct satellite transmission for TV cable and the substitution of facsimile transmission (fax) for conventional mail.

The threat posed by a substitute can easily be exaggerated. Superior performance does not necessarily mean that a substitute will be quickly adopted by the market. In the case of industrial products, the buyer may have to redesign its own product, risk inventory obsolescence, retrain workers, and so forth. Customers may not wish to incur the costs or risks of switching to a new and untried component unless its advantages are so clear that it is almost irresistible or even essential.

Further, consumer acceptance of a product may be slowed by established values and perceptions. This is particularly true for unique products for which no established market exists and no perception of need exists. Xerox Corporation's development of the convenient original plain-paper copier (considered initially as a substitute for carbon paper) was slowed by the difficulty of finding new investment. Even IBM declined the opportunity to participate after its study concluded that the global market was too small to justify its involvement. (If their decision had been different, imagine the size and power of a combined IBM and Xerox.)

As the above examples indicate, the main source of the risk of substitution is new technology.

Bargaining Power of Customers

Bargaining power means the extent to which one party can influence another. Customers can sometimes influence the terms of sale, limiting a company's ability to demand higher prices and to attract frequent, repeat purchases. An industry has high bargaining power with its buyers when the conditions listed below prevail.

- The product or service is unique, and no direct substitute exists.
- The buyer has a strong preference for a product with certain specifications, or for a particular brand.
- There is a large number of small customers, so that no one customer buys a significant portion of output.
- The product is consumed quickly or is perishable, and must be repurchased frequently.
- The purchase is small and does not constitute a significant cost to the purchaser.
- The purchase decision maker is not the ultimate consumer and therefore has different purchase decision motives.
- The buyer has an incentive to purchase in addition to the direct value of the product or service. Frequent flier points given by airlines are an example, in that they accrue to the individual, who in the case of the corporate business traveler is not paying the cost.

The most common way in which companies gain bargaining power over customers is by establishing brand preference. Customers will often pay a higher price for a product that they consider to be superior. (The superiority may be real or perceived, as discussed further in Chapter 5.) The extent to which buyers are willing to pay a higher price for their favorite brands was an underlying factor in many of the leveraged buyouts (LBOs) of the late 1980s. Investment bankers actively looked for situations where prices could be raised quickly without a major loss of market share, to pay the debts incurred in a buyout. As a result, the prices of such popular branded products as Ritz crackers and Oreo cookies (RJR Nabisco), Sealy mattresses (Ohio-Sealy Mattress Manufacturing Co.), and Duracell batteries (Duracell International Inc.) rose up to 30 percent upon completion of their respective LBOs.[3]

A surprisingly large number of companies make costly mistakes in their relationships with purchase decision makers. The ways in which bargaining power over buyers can be established depend on both the identity and the motives of the purchase decision maker. The key factor in bargaining may be not the characteristics of the product itself but, for instance, the service that makes the product available. An auto mechanic who buys parts to repair a customer's car makes the purchase decision but is not the end user. The mechanic therefore is likely to be less sensitive to price than is the customer who ultimately pays the bill. To the mechanic, the quick availability of the part needed to complete the job is the main determinant of the purchase decision, a fact recognized by suppliers who stress quick delivery.

Even large companies with extensive marketing experience have been known to mistake the identities of the purchase decision makers for their products. In 1988, Fisher-Price Inc., then a subsidiary of Quaker Oats and the long-time leader in the preschool toy market, was facing intense competition from Mattel Inc., Hasbro Inc., and Rubbermaid Inc., who were aggressively pushing their Disney, Playskool, and Little Tyke lines, respectively. Rather than defending its position in preschool toys aggressively, Fisher-Price introduced a sophisticated line of new products for the over-seven age group. The line flopped. In 1989 it lost $60 million, a $100 million unfavorable swing from the previous year.

Fisher-Price had forgotten that mothers make purchase decisions for preschoolers. The name and fine reputation of Fisher-Price were well known to mothers, but children over age seven, influenced by TV advertising, asked their parents to buy the toys they saw and liked on television. To this market, the name and reputation of Fisher-Price meant nothing, and apparently they didn't like what they saw.[4] Quaker Oats spun off the subsidiary to its shareholders. After Fisher-Price returned to the preschool market, it showed a good recovery.

(The industries in which bargaining power with customers is the weakest are those which supply commodities such as metals (copper, zinc, etc.), grain, and crude oil.)Here, there is no difference between the products supplied by the various producers, because the product specifications are based on industry standards. Usually, the customers are large buyers who are very price-sensitive, as the cost of commodities is a significant part of the total cost of the products into which they are processed.

Bargaining Power of Suppliers

The bargaining power of suppliers affects the availability and cost of the inputs used by an industry, including materials, labor, and various services. High bargaining power enables the industry to get these inputs on favorable terms.

The factors that establish the bargaining power of an industry over suppliers are the reverse of those that create its power over customers. After all, here the industry is the customer. Some of the factors that give an industry bargaining power over its suppliers are listed below.

- The use of standard inputs, such as commodities, having no unique characteristics.
- Substitutes for the supplier's product are available.
- There is a large number of small suppliers, none of which can dominate the market.
- The industry consists of a relatively small number of companies, each of which is a major buyer.
- The purchase can be postponed or the product stockpiled when prices are low.
- It is not feasible for the supplier to integrate forward to enter the customer's business.
- There is no shortage of the product required.
- The supplier's business does not have high barriers to entry, and the buyer has a credible possibility of being able to enter.

Besides the factors listed above, suppliers can gain high bargaining power by belonging to an association of suppliers, such as a labor union, or by participating in a commodity cartel, such as the Organization of

Petroleum Exporting Countries (OPEC). Some suppliers are able to supply technologically superior and proprietory inputs that give them high bargaining power. The earnings of Intel Corporation and Microsoft Corporation, for example, together almost equal the combined profits of the 25 major systems manufacturers that are their main customers.

The four variables discussed in this section—barriers to entry, the risk of substitution, the bargaining power of customers, and the bargaining power of suppliers—constitute the first four forces in the Porter model, which explains the profitability of industries. Before moving on to an examination of the fifth variable in Chapter 4, let's look at how the first four combine to influence the profitability of the five industries that will be used in Chapters 3 to 6 as illustrations.

CHARACTERISTICS OF FIVE SAMPLE INDUSTRIES

The four industry constraints that were described in the previous section combine in various ways to make an industry attractive or unattractive. These constraints work together to define the overall profitability of each of the five industries whose performance is shown in Exhibit 3–1.

Pharmaceuticals Industry

The five-year average return on equity (ROE) made the pharmaceuticals industry (also called the drug industry) the most attractive industry included in the *Forbes* list for 1994 (see Exhibit 3–1). The industry constraints are favorable for the following reasons:

- The barriers encountered by would-be new entrants are very high. It typically costs more than $200 million and takes an extended period of time to develop and obtain approval to market a new drug. Since already developed products are patented, they cannot be copied for a considerable period of time.
- A new entrant would have to establish an extensive marketing and sales organization to reach the doctors who make the purchase decisions.
- The risk of immediate substitution is relatively low, coming primarily from biotechnology.
- The consumer has very little influence, as it is the doctor rather than the patient who makes the purchase decision by writing a prescription. The doctor is more concerned with effectiveness than with cost.

- The market consists of a large number of relatively small buyers. There are over 60,000 retail pharmacies in the United States, none of which are big enough to exert power.[5] As a result, a General Accounting Office study showed that drug makers charged wholesalers 60 percent more in the United States than in Britain, where government is the buyer for the health care plan and can exert bargaining power.[6]
- Often there is a high degree of brand loyalty for over-the-counter drugs.
- The power of suppliers is low, because drugs are formulated out of relatively common commodity chemicals available from many sources.

As all the four industry constraints are favorable, it is not surprising that the industry as a whole has been highly profitable. *Forbes* lists 22 companies in this industry, of which only 1 company did not have a positive average ROE over the five-year period 1990–94.

While the industry remained highly attractive in 1994, its position has been deteriorating. Its market is becoming increasingly price-sensitive due to concern over the role of rising drug prices in the rapid inflation of the overall cost of health care. The government has imposed pressure on the industry to restrain price increases. A number of large cost-conscious buyers have emerged. These health maintenance organizations (HMOs) and mail-order drug distributors have started to exert the bargaining power that their size gives them. On the positive side, though the development of biotechnology continues to pose the risk of substitution, slower progress than expected has caused this threat to recede.[7]

As seen in Exhibit 3–1, price constraints were a major factor in the slowing down of the industry's sales and earnings growth, and in the decline in ROE in the latest 12 months over the five-year average.

Tobacco Industry

The tobacco industry can be regarded as relatively attractive for investors. It has the following characteristics:

- The barriers to new entrants are high. The market has strong, well-established brand preferences. Heavy investment over a considerable period of time would be required to establish a new brand well enough to make the manufacturing process efficient, to justify the marketing effort, and to acquire the necessary shelf space.

- The bargaining power of buyers is low, because the product is addictive and strong brand preferences exist.
- There are no legal substitutes (as distinct from stop-smoking aids).
- The power of suppliers is moderate. Tobacco is purchased by auction from agencies representing the growers, and manufacturers are therefore not able to exert as much influence as if they dealt individually with the large number of small suppliers.

With three of the four variables favorable, the relatively high long-term ROE of the industry is not surprising. Of the 10 companies in the industry, only one showed a negative five-year average ROE. However, as in the case of the drug industry, the industry fundamentals have been deteriorating for several years. The size of the market has been declining due to public awareness of the health risks and also because of various government-imposed curbs on smoking. Hard-core smokers appear to be becoming more price-conscious: discount cigarettes increased their market share from 11 percent in 1988 to over 30 percent in 1993.[8] This forced the major producers to discount the prices of branded products in 1993, ending a long period during which the industry had been able to increase prices regularly. The discounting did win back a significant market share, indicating that underlying brand preference remains strong but that price constraints exist.

Both the market decline and the price discounting were factors in the decline of sales and profitability in the latest 12 months in comparison to the five-year average, as shown in Exhibit 3–1.

Drug and Discount Retailing Industry

The drug and discount retailing industry is at the midpoint of the median ROE among the five sample industries we are analyzing. The industry is moderately profitable for the following reasons:

- The barriers to new entrants are high. A very high volume of sales would be required to get costs down to a level at which competitive prices could be offered. Further, it would be difficult to find suitable store locations in an already crowded industry, and a large amount of capital would be required to finance entry.
- The bargaining power of customers is very high. Most of the products sold are national brands available through other categories of retailing, and the customers are highly price-sensitive.
- Substitutes for conventional retailing are provided by mail-order and catalog houses, but these are not yet a serious risk.

• The suppliers of branded products have a moderate amount of power, which diminishes as the buyer's size and purchasing volume increase.

The dominant factor in this industry is the bargaining power of its price-sensitive customers. This industry is at best only moderately attractive, and only to the large, established companies. Of the 31 companies in this industry, 5 showed negative average annual ROEs over the five-year period 1990–94.

Recreational Products Manufacturing Industry

Companies in the recreational products manufacturing industry produce a diverse range of products, ranging from motorcycles to mobile homes and outboard motors. Thus it is different from our other sample industries, in which all the companies provide somewhat similar goods or services. However, the industry does have a common factor, in that all the companies in it compete for customers' discretionary money.

This industry has been relatively unattractive over the past five years, earning a rate of return only at the top of the lowest quartile, for the following reasons:

• The barriers to entry are only moderate, as many specialized market niches exist. In recent years, many new entrants have been successful in products such as tennis racquets and golf clubs. However, there is still strong brand preference in many products.

• Buyers' power is high, because most purchases are discretionary and can be postponed.

• There is a wide range of substitutes for virtually any recreational activity.

• Suppliers' power is low, because the materials used are relatively common commodities. In addition, many of the companies are relatively small and do not have unionized labor forces.

There are nine companies in this industry, of which eight showed positive average ROEs during the five-year period 1990–94. However, the investor should keep in mind that this period has included a significant economic recovery, and that discretionary product sales usually do improve during periods of recovery.

Airlines Industry

The airlines industry is the most unattractive of our sample industries. The industry characteristics are as follows:

- The barriers to entry are relatively low. While capital equipment requirements are heavy, airplanes can be bought used and they can also be leased. A large number of pilots and other skilled personnel are readily available, and U.S. regulations no longer significantly limit entry into the industry. Access to landing and terminal rights is limited at major airports but readily available at secondary ones.
- Cars, trains, and buses can be used as substitutes for short and medium-distance journeys.
- The industry's bargaining power with customers is low. The service has come to be regarded as a commodity, and there is little brand loyalty. Airlines offer buyer incentives to create bargaining power, and business travelers may favor a particular airline in order to accumulate frequent flier points. Price-sensitive recreational fliers have little loyalty, and high power is vested in tour operators which assemble vacation packages and buy large blocks of seats.
- The bargaining power of suppliers is high. Most employees are unionized and resistant to changes in work rules, and there are only a few aircraft manufacturers.

These characteristics make the airlines industry very unattractive. Only 3 of the 11 companies in the industry have had positive average ROEs over the past five years, and even these returns have been small.

IN CONCLUSION

This review, based on the Porter model of industry structure, of course has included only four of the five variables that define the characteristics of an industry: the threat of new entrants, the risk of substitution, the industry's bargaining power with customers, and its bargaining power with suppliers.

The implications of the fifth variable, the intensity of competition, are discussed in Chapter 4, where internal competition is shown to make a bad situation worse in the airlines industry. The intensity of internal rivalry is in part a function of the external constraints discussed in this chapter, but is also influenced by three other factors: the rate of market growth, the cost structure of an industry, and the barriers to exit. To the investor, these factors have implications beyond the intensity of competition, so that they must be looked at in more detail and separately (see Chapter 4).

It is also necessary to point out that the analysis of industry characteristics in this book is based on the present situation, or the situation at the end of 1994. In many industries, changes in circumstances are affecting industry characteristics, and some of these changes are mentioned above. The nature and implications of long-term change are discussed in more depth in Chapter 6.

POINTS TO REMEMBER

The key points of this chapter are as follows:

1. An industry can be defined as a company and all its direct competitors. For our purposes, the classifications provided by *Forbes* magazine will be used.

2. The characteristics of an industry can be analyzed with the help of a model developed by Michael E. Porter. This model shows that the profitability of an industry depends on five constraints: the threat of new entrants, the risk of substitution by other products, the bargaining power of buyers, the bargaining power of suppliers, and the intensity of internal competition.

3. The threat of new entrants depends on the size of capital requirements, the need for economies of scale, the existence of proprietory technology, brand preferences and switching costs, access to distribution, and, in some industries, government policy.

4. The risk of substitution is affected by the relative price of the substitute, the costs or risks of switching, and the importance of these advantages to the buyer.

5. Companies' bargaining power with customers and with suppliers determines the extent to which they can influence prices and the conditions of sale. The main variables that affect bargaining power are differences between products (or the uniqueness of a product), the existence of substitutes, the number of suppliers or buyers, the volumes purchased, the costs of switching, and the ability of buyers or suppliers to enter the industry.

6. Industry constraints have made the drug industry highly profitable and the airlines industry a loser.

NOTES

1. Robert Lenzner, "Warren Buffett's Idea of Heaven: 'I Don't Have to Work with People I Don't Like,'" *Forbes*, October 18, 1993, pp. 40–45.

2. The concepts of industry structure and analysis used here are drawn from Michael E. Porter, *Competitive Strategy: Techniques for Analyzing Industries and Competitors* (New York: The Free Press, 1980).

3. Stuart Flack, "Who's Really Picking Up the Tab?" *Forbes*, October 30, 1989, pp. 38–39.

4. Bill Saporito, "How Quaker Oats Got Rolled," *Fortune*, October 8, 1990, pp. 129–138.

5. Shawn Tully, "The Plot to Keep Drug Prices High," *Fortune*, December 27, 1993, pp. 120–124.

6. Gene Koretz, "Why American Drugmakers Got a Bad Rap . . .," *Business Week*, June 20, 1994, p. 30.

7. Joan O'C. Hamilton, "Biotech: An Industry Crowded with Players Faces an Ugly Reckoning," *Business Week*, September 26, 1994, pp. 84–92.

8. Subrata N. Chakravarty with Amy Feldman, "Don't Underestimate the Champ," *Forbes*, May 10, 1993, pp. 106–110.

4

THE FIFTH CONSTRAINT: INTERNAL RIVALRY

Frank: *I don't understand it. Each year we rent a truck, drive it to the mountains, pick up a load of Christmas trees at $4 each, sell them for $3.50 each and we lose our shirts. We can't go on like this!*

Ernest: *You're right! Next year we've got to get a bigger truck.*

From a cartoon by Bob Thaves

The Christmas tree retailing business will obviously remain intensely competitive and inherently unattractive as long as Frank and Ernest's reasoning prevails. Surprisingly, there are many corporate Franks and Ernests out there, as will be shown to be the case in the airlines industry.

Internal rivalry is the fifth of the constraints that determine the characteristics of an industry, according to the Porter model. In Chapter 3, internal rivalry was likened to the competitive heat in a box formed by the four external constraints (see Exhibit 3–2). Intense competition obviously makes an industry less attractive, because it squeezes profit margins. This is true even if the four external constraints, which were discussed in Chapter 3, are relatively favorable.

The factors that determine the intensity of internal rivalry are:

1. *The rate of market growth.* Fast-growing markets enable companies to meet their sales targets. They also minimize the need for offering buyer incentives, engaging in price discounting, and so forth. When market growth is slow, the battle switches to the pursuit of market share, and profit margins must often be sacrificed.

2. *The cost structure of the industry.* The extent to which total costs are fixed or variable determines the cost structure. If costs are largely fixed, profits become highly sensitive to sales volume. Flat or weak markets create intense price or other competition.

3. *The barriers to exit.* Periods of intense competition when most of the companies in an industry are losing money are prolonged if even the weakest companies find it difficult to get out of the business voluntarily, or if they are able to stay in business even though they are insolvent.

These factors are examined below.

MARKET GROWTH

The primary determinant of the long-term rate of market growth is the industry or product life cycle. Though the basic cycle progresses in an orderly and well-understood way, it is subject to variations. Cycles are affected by various causes, including shifts in demand.

Industry Life Cycles

Industries and their products and services, like people, have life cycles. For people the phases are infancy, childhood, adolescence, maturity, and aging. For products, the roughly equivalent phases are emergence, growth, transition, maturity, and decline. The progression of the life cycle can be followed by tracking the behavior of industry sales volume—its prices, costs, and profitability.[1] It is important for the long-term investor to understand the concept of life cycle, as the life cycle of an industry or a product may contain many traps for the unwary.

There are actually two product life cycles; one for nondurable or semidurable products, which are consumed relatively quickly and replaced, and another for durable goods, which last longer.

Nondurable Goods Cycle

Exhibit 4–1 shows key developments in the progression of the life cycle for nondurable goods. Below, these key events are tracked through the various phases, as shown by changes in industry sales volume, costs, prices, and profitability. The time periods represented by the horizontal scale vary from product to product, and overall cycle length can be years or centuries.

Emergence Phase A new product or industry usually emerges to fill a market need and/or because new technology develops a product that creates its own new market. Companies in the emergence phase are usually small. Prices are high, because the limited market will pay the price demanded for a unique product, because of the company's lack of expe-

E X H I B I T   4–1

Key Developments in an Industry Life Cycle

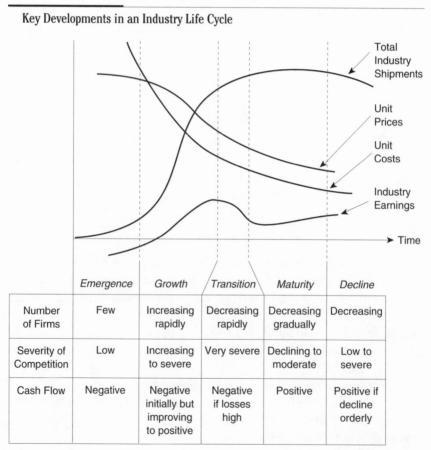

	Emergence	Growth	Transition	Maturity	Decline
Number of Firms	Few	Increasing rapidly	Decreasing rapidly	Decreasing gradually	Decreasing
Severity of Competition	Low	Increasing to severe	Very severe	Declining to moderate	Low to severe
Cash Flow	Negative	Negative initially but improving to positive	Negative if losses high	Positive	Positive if decline orderly

rience, and because limited production runs do not justify automation. A company in the emergence phase is rarely profitable. Continuous cash infusions by investors are needed, so that the company can refine the product and expand its capacity as markets grow.

Industries in the emergence phase in the early 1990s include fuel, photovoltaic cells, high-definition television (HDTV), and various areas of biotechnology.

Growth Phase   Growth starts when the product or service catches on and sales volume increases rapidly. The growth status of the new industry makes it relatively easy for new entrants to raise the necessary start-up investment, and the necessary technological and other skills are available from people leaving established firms. Prices fall rapidly because of cost reductions due to the increasing size, efficiency, and experience of the producers and the benefits of accrued R&D. Experience makes it possible to simplify the product and to refine the production process. Automated, specialized production equipment may be developed.

The combination of higher volume and declining costs means that many companies turn a profit, but there is rarely any free cash available for investors. The cash generated by operations is needed to fund the expansion of plants and to increase the level of working capital. Higher-level inventories and accounts receivables are necessary to support the higher level of sales.

Industries in the growth phase in the early 1990s include cellular telephones and compact disc (CD) players.

Transition Phase   Ultimately the market for any new product becomes saturated when most of the potential customers have tried it. Subsequent purchases are made primarily to replace product consumed, though some market growth may be available because of population increases, income growth, and so forth. Industry sales volume growth slows down, and power shifts from the producer to the distributor. Firms that did not establish a strong market position during the growth phase are forced to drop out, as they cannot attract the volume necessary to remain competitive. For such firms, a realistic assessment of long-term market growth often reveals that the prospect of reaching viable size is unlikely.

Costs and prices continue to decline, but at a slower rate, as the survivors become more efficient. The overall profitability of the industry may be adversely affected by price discounting, as marginal firms try desperately to gain the market share necessary to survive.

Maturity Phase Market growth continues to slow down, as it is derived only from factors such as population and income growth. The main characteristic of this phase is a gradual decrease in the number of firms in the industry. In order to further reduce costs and remain competitive, the larger firms gradually acquire smaller ones and concentrate production in fewer plants to increase efficiency. The industry usually becomes oligopolistic, consisting mainly of a few large firms serving mass markets. Usually there are also a number of smaller firms serving regional markets or making specialized products for smaller market segments. Prices continue to decline due to competition. Companies try to improve profits by increasing productivity and by becoming larger, often through acquisition of smaller and/or weaker competitors. This process is called the *rationalization* or *consolidation* of an industry.

The continued decline in real prices during the maturity phase, though it is often obscured by inflation, is obvious when the current dollar prices of mature products such as TV sets are compared to dollar prices of a previous time, say a decade earlier. Industries in the maturity phase are generally profitable and generate a high level of cash, as there is usually little need to invest in new plants.

Most North American industries are currently in the maturity phase. In the case of major household appliances, the number of major producers has stabilized at 5, down from more than 12 in the late 1950s.

Decline Phase The drop-off of industry shipments which occurs in a declining industry can be caused by any of a number of factors, including the following:

- Substitution of newer materials, such as plastics for metals
- Changes in social values, as in the case of tobacco products
- Governmental regulation, as in the case of DDT and PCBs

An industry may decline to extinction, as the DDT and PCB industries have done, or it may level off at a residual level of demand where the substitutes are not a threat. Though glass containers, for example, have lost a major share of market to plastic containers and metal cans, they are holding their position in wines and liquors, where glass helps to create a quality image, and in certain food products, where resistance to acids is essential.

The decline of an industry may be caused by either demand or supply factors, which vary from region to region. The decline in the demand for cigarettes in North America and certain parts of Europe due to health concerns makes the tobacco industry a declining one in these areas, but tobacco remains a mature industry in other parts of the world. Shipbuilding is a declining industry in developed nations, because it is labor-intensive, but it is a growing industry in China, which has a large supply of cheap labor.

The decline of an industry may be quite orderly if plants can be shut down gradually. This has been true in the glass container industry, which has been able to reduce production capacity gradually by closing down furnaces. In such instances, there is usually no cutthroat competition to capture the remaining markets. The companies may remain highly profitable and even increase their cash flow, as no additional or new equipment is needed. They can sometimes even withdraw cash from working capital, as inventories and accounts receivable are wound down.

On the other hand, if an industry consists of companies in a single business with highly specialized plants for which there is no other use, a sudden decline can become chaotic, involving severe price cutting and losses to all concerned. This has been the case for the integrated steel companies, which have lost market share to minimills.

Examples of industries clearly in decline in the early 1990s are the glass containers industry, which has already been described, and the long-playing (LP) record industry, which is approaching extinction due to the convenience and increasing popularity of compact disks (CDs).

Durable Goods Cycle

The durable goods cycle differs from the nondurable goods cycle primarily in the nature of its transition from growth to maturity, as shown in Exhibit 4–2. The emergence and growth phases are similar to those of the nondurable goods cycle. However, during the transition, industry volume drops off sharply. The initial market needs have been satisfied, and no replacements are required for a number of years. The decline in demand results in a shakeout of the industry, in which weaker companies are forced either to withdraw or to merge with the survivors. As inventory is liquidated, prices collapse. Eventually, replacement demand develops and the industry enters a normal maturity phase.

The severity and duration of the transition depend on the factors listed below.

- *The durability of the product, or how long it will last on average in normal use.*
- *Technological advances, which could make existing products obsolete and therefore encourage early replacement.*
- *The extent of the decline in prices.* A significant decline can attract a wider market and accelerate replacement or duplication.

Typical Life Cycle in a Durable Products Industry

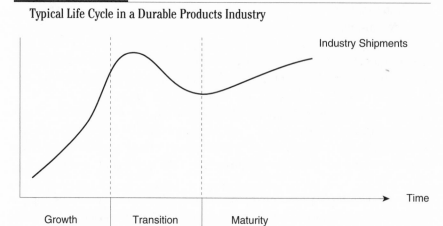

- *The cost of the purchase and customers' perceptions of whether it is a necessary or a discretionary product.* If the product is seen as expensive and discretionary, customers may decide not to replace it.

The recreational snowmobile industry provides an example of a severe transition. Introduced in the late 1950s, the snowmobile went through typical emergence and growth phases during the 1960s and the early 1970s. The growth of demand was exponential, with industry shipments peaking at 500,000 units in 1971. Once the primary market had been satisfied, however, there was no immediate replacement demand, because the snowmobile's normal product life was more than seven years. Since the product was mechanical, there was no room for either drastic price cuts or startling improvements which would have made existing products obsolete.

A weak economy depressed the demand for expensive toys like the snowmobile, and the depth and duration of this industry's transition were further accelerated by inventory liquidation. To make matters worse, in an era of rising gasoline prices and increasing environmental awareness, the snowmobile came to be seen as damaging to the ecology. The replacement rate dropped still further, limiting the chances of an industry recovery. Not surprisingly, the number of manufacturers dropped from over 30 to 5. The dropouts included some big names, such as Outboard Marine Corporation (OMC).

Another industry that has endured transitions is consumer electronic products, consisting of a wide range of products, including personal computers (PCs), videocassette recorders (VCRs), and microwave ovens. Most of the transitions in this industry have been less severe. These goods are on the whole very durable, but demand has held up for a number of reasons. The cost of manufacturing electronic equipment is very sensitive to volume; as mass markets have developed, prices have dropped sharply. VCRs, which originally cost over $1,000, can now be bought for $200. Technological developments have improved product performance in ways ranging from increased power for PCs to more convenient programming of VCRs. Further, the use of many consumer electronic products has become an integral part of North American lifestyles, making their purchase less than totally discretionary. These factors have combined to sustain demand. Transition phases tend to be less dramatic in consumer electronics than in the snowmobile industry, but have not been eliminated.

Transitions in large companies with a diversified range of products are often disguised by the facts that no one product significantly affects earnings and that new products may enter the growth phase as older products begin transition. For the investor, the danger of transition therefore lies mainly in a company's heavy reliance on a single product for a significant portion of its sales or earnings.

Variations in Industry Life Cycles

An industry does not always evolve along the relatively predictable lines described above. Variations may take the form of cyclicality, upside breakouts, or downside shifts.

Cyclicality

Cycles are fluctuations in the level of activity of an industry within the pattern of the overall life cycle. Most prominent in the maturity phase, they show up as periods of sales declines or spurts of growth, as shown in Exhibit 4–3.

Cycles can be caused by a variety of factors, including the ones listed below.

- The economic or business cycle occurs at expected though not always predictable intervals and has varying degrees of severity. The down part of a business cycle is generally an adjustment of the excesses built up in the preceding boom. Fluctuations in interest rates, which are usually associated with the economic cycle, can affect the market for major purchases such as housing.

- Replacement cycles are caused by the relatively well-defined service lives of consumer durables. Thus a strong year in auto or appliance sales will result in a replacement "echo" at some time in the future.

E X H I B I T   4–3

Industry Life-Cycle Variation: Cyclicality

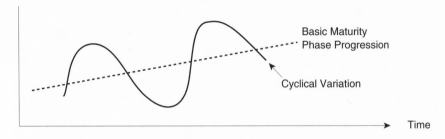

- Demographic cycles, which are tied to the pattern of births, develop slowly and predictably. For example, in the 1980s and the early 1990s there was a sharp rise in births because the large number of females born during the "baby boom" of the 1950s and the early 1960s were of childbearing age. As a result, the teenage market is starting to grow. Both the teenage market and the aging boomer generation market can now be expected to create cyclical demands for various age-related products and services.

The various causes of cycles can interact to offset or reinforce one another. For example, fulfillment of the replacement cycle can be affected by the economic cycle in the case of discretionary or postponable products. After a recession, as the economy starts to recover and consumer confidence returns, replacement sales may enhance the normal recovery, creating a boom. Infant- and child-related products as well as home improvement products weathered the early 1990s recession relatively well, as the demographically based demand offset the economic weakness.

Upside Breakouts
In the maturity phase, a change in social values or technology may suddenly popularize a product or service, or may obsolete products that are already owned by consumers. This results in an upside breakout—a sharp increase in the level of sales. After the breakout, sales return to the original cycle in the pattern shown in Exhibit 4–4.

Two breakout patterns have occurred in the roller-skating industry, the first in the early 1980s when the introduction of polyurethane wheels obsoleted wooden- or metal-wheeled skates and repopularized the sport, and the second in the early 1990s, when in-line skates were introduced. Once the stock of products in users' hands had been replaced in the early 1980s, sales

Industry Life-Cycle Variation: Upside Breakouts

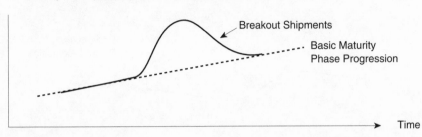

dropped to close to the former level. A similar resolution can be predicted for in-line skates. A similar pattern is occurring in the audio recording industry, as already mentioned; CDs have obsoleted vinyl records and "forced" people to replace their music libraries. Once this replacement has been completed, CD sales will likely drop off to the new-acquisitions level.

Downside Shifts

In a downside shift in the maturity phase, demand drops off quite suddenly, after which growth resumes from the lower base level, as shown in Exhibit 4–5. This pattern occurred in the automobile tire industry in the 1970s and again in the 1980s. Because of the emphasis on fuel economy, people were buying lighter-weight cars, and the popularity of power steering fell off. The industry also adopted fuel-efficient, long-lasting radial tires. This combination of factors sharply reduced the shipments of the tire industry for a time. Eventually the adjustments worked their way through the system, and growth resumed in the tire industry.

In a downside shift, the industry acts for a period like a declining industry. There is severe competition for a smaller market, and the weaker producers withdraw or are acquired by the stronger ones. In the tire industry, long-established brand names such as Firestone and Uniroyal Goodrich were absorbed by competitors.

Implications of Industry Life Cycles for the Investor

The industry or product life cycle is important to the long-term investor for two reasons. First, conditions and circumstances in each phase affect investment risks. Second, the life cycle is a major determinant of how much room for growth a company has and how such growth can be accomplished (see Chapter 5).

E X H I B I T   4–5

Industry Life-Cycle Variation: Downside Shift

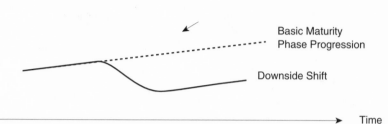

Emergence Phase The stocks of an industry in the emergence phase are inherently risky. Investment opportunities are usually in the form of initial public offerings (IPOs). These tend to be overpriced because of their glamour and their apparent potential, even though in many cases both the technology and the market potential are unproved. Their potential is therefore very difficult to assess. It is better to wait until a company enters the growth phase, when its potential becomes clearer (see Chapter 7). Many rooms have been wallpapered with stock certificates issued by emerging companies with promising technology and potential markets—technology that never fulfilled its promise and markets that never developed.

Growth Phase Though the term *growth industry* is commonly used, no such industry exists. There are, however, growth phases in every industry life cycle. The early part of the growth phase can present good investment opportunities. While there is no precise border between the emergence and the growth phases, a good indicator that an industry is passing into the growth phase is seen when the companies in the industry start to invest in plants and equipment. This development shows confidence that additional markets do exist and that they can provide higher sales. It also usually enables the companies to reduce costs and prices, thus further broadening the market. An important consideration in any investment decision is the competitive strength of the company, which may be provided by leadership in technology or by strength in a market segment (see Chapter 5).

The key to investing during the growth phase is knowing when to get out. Growth phase opportunities are not necessarily short-term trading situations; the growth phase of the computer industry lasted about 15 years. One signal that the growth phase of an industry is nearing its peak is a rapid increase in the number of new entrants and the stock market's enthusiasm for them.

It is important to distinguish between growth industries and growth companies. The rapid growth of a company in a mature or declining industry is usually based on competitive advantage. The company may be a specific market segment or using new technology which is enabling it to outperform its competitors. What growth industries and growth companies have in common is the stock market's enthusiasm for them, which often results in their being bid up to very high price/earnings (P/E) ratios. How long such growth will continue is consistently overestimated by the stock market.

As the growth phase of an industry progresses, the stocks of the companies in the industry become increasingly vulnerable to a change in the expectations of future growth. The eventual disappointment can punish investors severely. A company itself may be quite sound, but the recognition that growth will slow down can reduce the P/E ratio from, say, 50 to 25 or even lower, cutting the price of the stock by half or more. Investment in growth phase stocks is profitable only for the aggressive individual who is willing to do the extra homework involved and who has the self-discipline to get out early, even prematurely. The signal to get out can be provided by common sense and by a high level of market enthusiasm for the industry. A hot, enthusiastic market usually signals the beginning of the end for a growth stock.

Transition Phase Long-term investment in an industry in the transition phase should be avoided. The situation is usually volatile, and it is better to wait until the industry settles down and the survivors can be properly evaluated as mature companies.

Maturity Phase The maturity phase of an industry provides the large majority of investment opportunities for the long-term investor. The relative stability of this phase constitutes a comparatively sound basis for evaluation of individual companies. The key aspect in this evaluation is company performance, as provided by competitive advantage (see Chapter 5).

Decline Phase The uncertainties and frequent volatility of the decline phase tend to weigh against investment. However, there are exceptions. If the decline is orderly, and if a company remains profitable and is generating a large amount of cash, the investment decision should be based primarily on how the company is reinvesting its cash. This requires a separate evaluation of the other industries in which the company is investing. A margin of safety is provided by the continuing cash flow of the parent company. In the tobacco industry, for example, the main players began to invest heavily in acquisitions of food-processing operations when the potential decline of the tobacco industry became apparent.

Another exception occurs when the decline of an industry is being caused by high domestic costs, such as for labor. The future of a company in the industry will depend on the extent to which it can subcontract its production to lower-wage countries. The basis of the future success of the company changes from its manufacturing capability to its skill in developing and marketing products. The footwear manufacturing industry in the United States and Canada has been declining for some time due to high labor costs. Nike has done well because it has successfully transferred labor-intensive operations to low-wage countries. The company now relies on its product development and marketing skills.

Investment in a company in a declining industry must be based on the merits of the individual situation. The ability to detect the onset of decline is crucial. Cyclical changes may disguise the onset of decline or give a false signal. Some indicators of possible decline are listed below.

- *The appearance of substitutes on the market.* The use of plastic packaging for peanut butter and soft drinks were indicative of the decline of the glass container industry. New technology is almost always a threat to mature technology because of its potential for advances and refinement.

- *An industry's demands for government subsidies or for the imposition of quotas or tariffs.* Such demands indicate that the companies in the industry are not able to compete with foreign producers, usually because of labor costs.

- *A consistent, steady decline in return on equity (ROE) and/or in profit margins.*

Though these developments may occur for other reasons, they do indicate an industry in difficulty, possibly because it has entered the decline phase.

Industry and product life cycles should be considered in the timing of investment decisions. The contrarian view can be useful in this context. The stock market anticipates cyclical declines and recoveries. By the time these events actually occur, the stock market has largely discounted them. In relatively predictable cycles, such as those caused by demographic influences, an influx of new entrants pursuing the same anticipated opportunity may overcrowd the industry. This occurred in financial services, in which a strong market was expected due to the start of retirement planning by aging boomers. Thus a potentially attractive industry lost much of its appeal.

Variations in an industry's life cycle can have serious consequences for investors. Stocks of companies in upside breakout and downside shift situations should be avoided. In particular, fads or hot product situations are of short duration and very difficult to sustain or repeat. The Cabbage Patch doll drove Coleco Industries stock from a low of $3 in 1979 to a high of $65 in 1983, before it collapsed to below $10 in 1985. Companies that survive a downside shift should be considered as investment candidates, because the shakeout often leaves the industry in better condition. The industry and the companies are then in the maturity phase and should be evaluated accordingly.

Investors who are evaluating an industry's life cycle and its variations should wait until the industry has become established in a phase before making long-term investment decisions. Changes in phase and discontinuities such as upside breakouts and downside shifts create both opportunities and risks, which are best left to the speculator.

INDUSTRY COST STRUCTURES

The cost structure of an industry, the second factor that affects the intensity of competition, is actually the primary factor behind the sharp swings in the profitability of cyclical industries.

The extent to which costs in an industry are fixed—that is, the extent to which total costs tend to remain constant regardless of the level of sales revenue—is the main determinant of the industry's cost structure. A high fixed cost structure is typical of the entertainment industry, including professional sports, theater, and various recreational services. In professional sports and theater, the costs of rent, salaries, travel, and so forth are fixed for the scheduled run or season. Revenue and therefore profit or loss are dependent on paid attendance. Similarly, the cost of preparing a golf course or a ski resort for operation is the same regardless of the level of attendance.

A fixed cost structure prevails in a wide range of industries. In industries that use highly automated manufacturing and chemical processing plants, for instance, labor is a fixed cost. Workers must be present to tend machines regardless of the capacity at which the machines are being utilized. Usually, materials are the only variable costs in such industries. The only way to get rid of the fixed costs of labor is to shut down the plant, and even then, other fixed costs (such as maintenance, local taxes, and interest) continue.

Likewise, in industries where there is a high front-end cost of product development, costs are fixed. In aircraft manufacture, for instance, design, tooling, certification, and labor training costs must be amortized over the number of aircraft actually sold. If total sales fall short of expectations, the losses can be severe. On the other hand, if sales exceed expectations, profits can be enhanced significantly, as sales in excess of the break-even volume will no longer include the amortization of product development costs.

In general, the profitability of industries with high fixed cost structures is highly sensitive to total revenue, as provided by capacity utilization and the level of the average price. In the long distance telephone industry, for instance, the costs of establishing and maintaining the transmission facilities and the administrative infrastructure are almost entirely fixed, and the market is price-sensitive. Long distance carriers engage in extensive discounting of prices, special deals, and heavy advertising, with the goal of selling as much capacity as possible so as to maximize overall revenue.

A high fixed cost structure is a particular problem for industries that have no control over their prices. Producers of commodities, for example, are hit twice. First, a downturn in the economy reduces demand and capacity utilization, thereby raising unit costs. Second, prices decline due to market conditions. This accounts for the wild cyclical swings between profit and loss in the paper and mining industries. The stock market recognizes this situation by assigning a low P/E ratio to these industries.

Even in industries that have more freedom to set their own prices (rather than having prices dictated by global commodity markets), a high fixed cost structure often leads to destructive price wars during times of economic weakness. Companies try to achieve higher total revenue from the additional volume that the discounted prices attract, in the hope that this will more than the offset the effect of the lower unit price. The automobile industry has not only high product development costs, which must be amortized, but also relatively fixed labor costs, due to an automated production process and supplementary unemployment payment obligations. Companies in this industry have been practicing price cutting for years, through factory rebates.

In contemporary industrial and commercial industries, there are relatively few businesses without a significant level of fixed costs. The long-term investor must recognize the impact on earnings of fluctuations in sales and the degree to which the industry has control over these fluctuations. Beyond this, the issue becomes one of selecting the companies which, for reason of competitive advantage, are best able to take advantage of the situation. Among the sources of competitive advantage, as previously noted, are operating at the lowest costs in the industry and/or achieving bargaining power with buyers, so as to maintain sales volume and capacity utilization during periods of market weakness.

The cost structure of an industry also is a major determinant of the effect of the growth of sales on earnings. Industries with high fixed costs can often produce or service the additional volume provided by growth at relatively low incremental cost so that a high proportion of the additional sales dollar flows to the bottom line. Of course, when additional capacity has to be added, the level of fixed costs again increases. In industries where the economics of production require large plants, such as in oil refining and papermaking, these additional fixed costs may cause a temporary decline in the earnings of a company until the additional capacity can be utilized by sales growth. The sources of sales growth are discussed in Chapter 5.

BARRIERS TO EXIT

Logic would dictate that a business that had been losing money for a number of years and had little realistic prospect of returning to profitability would simply fold up. This would reduce the overcapacity in the industry and allow the survivors to improve their positions, restoring the industry to reasonable health. However, even among managers who take pride in their rational decisions, such logic does not necessarily prevail. Barriers to exit can lock companies into a losing cause, to the detriment of the industry as a whole. This is a significant problem in periods of market decline like those that occur during transitions, downside shifts, and decline phases in the durable goods industry. It is also a problem in many industries during the latter part of the maturity phase, when productivity improvement results in faster growth in production capacity than in demand. Barriers to exit perpetuate overcapacity in the industry, resulting in intense competition. There may be a number of barriers to exit in a given case, including the ones listed below.

- A company may be in a single business, the discontinuation of which would leave management unemployed. This problem is magnified if management skills are highly specialized and cannot be readily used in other industries.

- The costs of exit may be high. They may include writing off assets, making up unfunded or underfunded pension fund obligations, and covering environmental cleanup costs.

- Relatively lenient bankruptcy laws allow companies to remain in business even after they cannot meet their obligations. In 1991, 20 percent of U.S. department stores were owned by companies that were or had been in Chapter 11 bankruptcy, yet they continued to sell and to compete.

- An operation may be a relatively minor division of a larger company which will tolerate moderate losses rather than take a write-off and admit to an error in entering the business in the first place.

• If competition is global, foreign governments' influence on competitors may limit their ability to withdraw even if the business is uneconomic. Governments can threaten to expropriate the business if it closes and, in the case of mining companies, to cancel their exploration agreements. The reasons may include preservation of employment and earning foreign exchange. Costs of production such as labor are paid in local currency, but the products are sold for hard currencies. The copper mining industry in less developed countries is subject to such exit constraints.

Too often, the continuation of a marginal or losing business is justified by rosy forecasts that current management efforts will soon restore profitability. The motive for continuing is that the investment is too big to write off. Prices are cut to attract volume, with the hope of increasing capacity utilization and lowering unit costs, so as to make a profit. Competitors, who are usually in the same boat, quickly respond with their own price cuts, to avoid loss of market share. The result is a price war in which everyone loses. This situation exists in many industries, including consumer electronic retailing and a wide range of food products.[2]

In a different sort of scenario, management strategies for reducing overcapacity may self-destruct. Take the case of U.S. Steel division of USX-Marathon Group, which sold its Vineyard, Utah, mill to a group of private investors for only $40 million, on the condition that they assume the unfunded pension fund obligations. The new owners invested in new equipment, won union concessions, and returned to the market as a stronger competitor.[3]

Barriers to exit are often a function of management motives and psychology, which prevent the acknowledgment of past failures in judgment. It is not surprising that one of the first acts of a new CEO entering a company from the outside is getting rid of the losers.

The long-term investor must recognize the existence of barriers to exit as a condition which perpetuates intense competition in an industry. The tip-off is often a chronic low ROE in the industry.

IMPLICATIONS OF INTERNAL RIVALRY FOR
FIVE SAMPLE INDUSTRIES

Chapter 3 showed how the first four determinants of industry structure influenced the performance of the pharmaceuticals, tobacco, drug and discount retailing, recreational products manufacturing, and airlines industries. Now it will be useful to examine the effects of the intensity of internal rivalry on each of these industries.

Pharmaceuticals Industry

Pharmaceuticals was shown in Chapter 3 to be the highest-ROE industry among our five sample industries. Virtually every element of the external constraints was favorable, despite some recent deterioration of bargaining power with customers and despite the potential risk of substitution.

The elements of internal rivalry in this industry are also largely favorable, as follows:

- The industry is in a mature phase and continues to grow slowly. Short-term economic cycles have virtually no effect on the industry, and the long-term demographic cycle is favorable, as the aging boomer population will likely need more drugs.

- R&D costs are a high fixed cost component in the industry. Most companies hedge R&D risks by conducting a large number of research projects at any one time. The high profitability of the winners covers the losers. In the absence of cyclicality, the fixed costs are absorbed on a continuing basis without causing dramatic fluctuations in earnings.

- The products are relatively unique and patented, and are sold on the basis of effectiveness rather than price. Price wars are thus not productive. Lacking this desperation tool, companies take a realistic attitude toward their prospects in the industry. Companies that wished to leave the industry have been readily acquired by survivors, and thus there has been no continuing cutthroat competition.

Since both external constraints and the elements of internal rivalry are favorable, this is an attractive industry for investors. It is capable of providing the consistent predictable earnings which investors like without having to resort to accounting or other earnings leveling action.

Tobacco Industry

For the tobacco industry also, the external constraints are generally favorable (see Chapter 3). The barriers to entry are high, and the risk of substitution is low. While the industry's bargaining power with customers is still relatively high overall, the market has shown signs of increasing price sensitivity, forcing price reductions even in established brands. This has reduced the overall profitability of the industry. The internal rivalry situation is as follows:

- The industry is in the decline phase in most developed countries. However, the decline has been an orderly one, in which established producers are cutting output by dropping marginal brands.
- The industry has a high fixed cost component, which it has been reducing by replacing mass media advertising with cheaper and more effective database marketing. The fixed costs do not create earnings fluctuations, as there is no significant cyclicality in demand.
- The industry decline has not yet reached a stage at which consideration of exit is an important issue. The companies have ample opportunities in other countries where smoking is not yet considered a health issue. However, one major U.S. company, American Brands Inc. has sold out its tobacco operations. This is characteristic of a relatively orderly decline.

On the surface, this is an attractive industry for investors. While it can be regarded as being in the decline phase, its decline is orderly and is capable of generating a very high level of cash. However, potential changes in course may cause a significant future deterioration in the industry's attractiveness. This possibility will be taken up in Chapter 6.

Drug and Discount Retailing Industry

The favorable external constraints in the drug and discount retailing industry are the high barriers to entry and the low risk of substitution (see Chapter 3). However, the bargaining power of the price-sensitive customers is very high. The internal rivalry factors are as follows:

- The industry is in the maturity phase and continues to grow slowly. There is some cyclicality due to economic conditions. During 1993 and 1994, the industry sales growth lagged behind that of the retailing industry as a whole.
- The cost structure of the industry has a high variable component, with about 80 percent of the sales dollar required to cover the cost of products sold. Because of the low margins, high volume is necessary to cover the balance of the costs. These costs are largely fixed, creating some volatility in earnings. This industry faces competition from other categories of retailing, such as department stores, which may be able to spread their fixed costs over a broader sales base.
- Barriers to exit are low. Closing stores may involve lease termination costs, but these are rarely prohibitive. Chains and individual stores in sound locations are salable. For example, in 1993

Woolworth Corporation (Woolco) withdrew from Canada by selling out to Wal-Mart Stores Inc.

These factors of internal rivalry add an unfavorable element to an
industry structure that is already unattractive to small companies because
of the low margins; the high fixed costs; and the need for very high volume, both to cover the fixed costs and to establish bargaining power over
suppliers. The industry, however, is moderately attractive to large, established companies. Its overall attractiveness to investors is relatively low.

Recreational Products Manufacturing Industry

On the basis of external constraints, the recreational products manufacturing industry has been shown to be unattractive (see Chapter 3).
Barriers to entry are generally low, the risk of substitution is high, and
customers have high bargaining power.

The effect of the elements of internal rivalry are as follows:

- The industry is mature, but since the products are discretionary
  purchases, it is highly cyclical. This cyclicality may be attributed
  largely to economic causes.
- For the most part, the industry has high fixed costs for product
  development and manufacturing. This makes earnings volatile
  during the demand cycle.
- Barriers to exit are relatively high, because most of the companies
  in the industry are highly specialized and rely on a single product
  line. Other barriers to exit are created by management motives.

The industry as a whole is unattractive to investors because of its cyclicality. There are some favorable pockets because of the diverse range of products included in this industry, but these too tend to be cyclical. During the
1980s, we saw an upside breakout in tennis racquets as the introduction of
oversized models made with composite materials made the traditional wood-
en racquet obsolete. The 1990s have seen a similar surge in the demand for
golf clubs as the result of the development of metal *woods* and new designs
of irons. Characteristic of upside breakouts, these surges in demand will be
transient but will trap investors who get overly enthusiastic about them.

Airlines Industry

Examination of the external constraints (Chapter 3) showed the airlines
industry to be unattractive. The barriers to entry are only moderate due to

deregulation, and substitutes exist for short- and medium-distance travel. The bargaining power of customers is high. The market has become highly price-sensitive, and there is little brand loyalty. The bargaining power of the main supplier, the highly unionized labor force, remains high.

The elements of internal rivalry are as follows:

- The industry is mature, with only slow market growth. It is also highly cyclical, because vacation travel is discretionary and businesses tend to reduce their travel budgets in a weak economy. Further, it appears likely that the industry is experiencing a downside shift, since other modes of communication, such as video and teleconferencing, may be reducing the frequency of face-to-face contact in business. The proportion of business-class travel declined from 52 percent of capacity in 1982 to 40 percent in 1994.[4] If there is no recovery in the proportion of business travel, the total passenger volume will continue to grow but industry revenue will decline, because nonbusiness travelers pay a lower average price.

- The industry has a high fixed cost structure which creates high losses when capacity is underutilized. The costs of flight crew, ground crew, and fuel for a scheduled flight are virtually the same whether the flight is full or empty; the only variable cost component is meals. Attempting to minimize losses, the airlines have engaged in price wars to attract the maximum revenue per flight and have even resorted to price fixing. In 1994, 92 percent of airline travelers bought their tickets at a discount, paying on average only 35 percent of full fare.

- Barriers to exit are high. Of 36 U.S. airlines that were operational in 1980, only 11 continued to operate in 1992. Three of these were operating under Chapter 11 of the Bankruptcy Act, and were thus able to break union contracts and offer even more severe competition. Many of the companies that disappeared were absorbed by the others, so that there has not been a significant reduction of industry capacity. On international routes, many carriers, such as Air France, are government-owned and encounter strong union resistance, including violence, when they attempt to downsize. Thus industry capacity has not declined, demand has not been balanced, and capacity utilization rates have not increased to offset lower fares.

Taken together, the elements of industry structure explain the dismal ROE performance of the airlines industry and make it unattractive to investors. In this industry, only a company that is insulated from the adverse characteristics of the industry through decisive competitive advantage should be considered for investment.

This assessment of the sample industries is based on the situation as it existed in 1994. These industries may in fact be facing potential change, which must be recognized in any investment decision. (The nature and implications of potential change are discussed in Chapter 6.)

THE STOCK MARKET'S JUDGMENT

It should not be surprising that the differences in the characteristics of our five sample industries are reflected in the performance of their stocks. Exhibit 4–6 shows the market records of these industries for the period 1984–94, as measured by five S&P indexes: the Drugs Index; the Tobacco Index; the Retail: General Merchandise Chains Index; the Leisure Time Index; and the Airlines Index. These indexes are not a perfect fit with our industry classifications but are close enough to be valid.[5] The 1984–94 period has been chosen for review because it covers a complete economic cycle, with 1984 and 1994 each approximately the second year of an economic recovery.

The measurement of overall market performance is provided by the S&P 500 index, which rose at an average annual rate of 11.1 percent over the period. The tobacco, drug, and retail indexes outperformed the broad market, with average annual appreciation of 19.8, 16.1, and 14.4 percent, respectively. Leisure products and airlines underperformed the market, with average annual gains of 4.7 and 4.5 percent, respectively. These are generally in line with the relative attractiveness of the industries and their long-term average ROE performances.

There are, however, some anomalies in these industries.

S&P Tobacco Index

The second greatest five-year average ROE performer, the S&P Tobacco Index showed the largest gain over the period. It had an average gain of 30.2 percent per annum until 1992, but declined 24 percent in 1993 and 1994, leaving it with an average annual gain of 19.8 percent. However, this index overstates the performance of the industry as a whole. It is made up of only three companies and includes Philip Morris Companies, Inc., and UST Inc., both of which have been exceptional performers. Up to 1992, the five-year average ROE performance of this index was almost identical to that of the Drug Index, and the market did not appear to take seriously the threats of health-related lawsuits because of the industry's success in defending them. Philip Morris was showing growth in less vulnerable foreign markets. It diversified into food processing, a relatively high-ROE industry. The drop in 1993 and 1994 can be attributed to the discounting of prices to counter the inroads of generic products, which

EXHIBIT 4–6

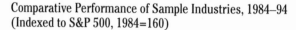

Comparative Performance of Sample Industries, 1984–94
(Indexed to S&P 500, 1984=160)

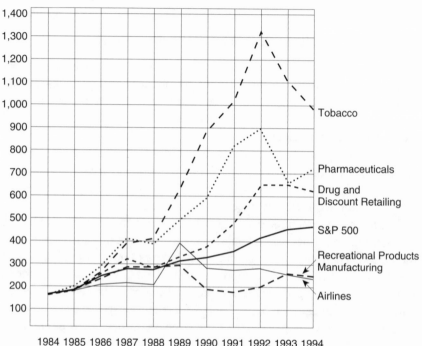

Note: The index for each year is shown at the mean between the high and the low for the period.

resulted in a 4.5 percent decline in industry earnings per share and the emerging threat of additional lawsuits. This industry has long been a favorite of investors. The industry is well understood, and the risks to it are well defined. The unfavorable implications of these risks have been cushioned by the diversification of most of the companies in the industry, so that they are no longer totally dependent on tobacco.

S&P Drug Index

The S&P Drug Index rose at an average annual rate of 24.6 percent until 1992, dropped 29 percent in 1993, but recovered somewhat in 1994 to produce an average annual increase of 16.1 percent for the period. The decline in 1993 occurred despite a 6.5 percent increase in industry earnings per share, a rate of only half the five-year average. The market's nervousness appears to have arisen over the impact of political action on health care, which threatened its traditional pricing freedom. By 1994, this threat had receded.

S&P Retail: General Merchandise Chains Index
The performance of the retail industry as a whole is probably slightly overstated by the S&P Retail: General Merchandise Chains Index, because the index includes Wal-Mart, an exceptional performer, as one of its four companies. However, the market performance reflects the industry's moderately attractive status and relatively low cyclicality.

S&P Leisure Time Index
Both relatively modest returns and cyclicality are reflected in the S&P Leisure Time Index, which turned down in 1989 in anticipation of a recession and recovered after 1991.

S&P Airlines Index
The main industry players are included in the S&P Airlines Index. The industry has held up fairly well, considering its dismal state. The market expected a recovery, which was being predicted by some analysts in mid-1994. Such a recovery would be based on an assumption that the decline in business travel is cyclical, and not a downside shift. A further assumption would be the reduction of overcapacity by the exit of some companies, a possibility not supported by the industry's historical ability to continue to operate while in a state of bankruptcy. The decline of the index in 1994 may be indicative of investors' recognition of the persistent nature of the industry's structural problems.

IN CONCLUSION

The five forces that establish the characteristics of an industry can combine in various ways to make an industry as a whole an inherently profitable one, as in the example of the pharmaceuticals industry, or a chronic loser, as in the case of the airlines industry. Stock market performance reflects the relative attractiveness of our five sample industries, as measured by their respective ROEs. Consider an astute (though imaginary) investor who, five years ago, had already recognized the accuracy of the market in this respect. This investor could have outperformed the market as a whole by investing in a basket of representative stocks in the relatively attractive tobacco, drug, and retail industries.

However, investors usually put their money into companies, not industries. In all industries, some companies outperform others and these are the best investment candidates. Our imaginary investor could have done even better by selecting for investment the specific companies in any of the five industries we are studying that, because of competitive advantage, have outperformed their competitors. Chapter 5 will show how superior performance has been achieved by companies in all five industries.

POINTS TO REMEMBER

The key points of this chapter are as follows:

1. If the rate of market growth is high, it gives companies room to grow; if low, it forces them into fierce competition for market share. The main overall determinant of market growth is the industry life cycle, with its emergence, growth, transition, maturity, and decline phases. These phases do not always progress in an orderly way, as they may be subject to variations such as cyclicality, upside breakouts, and downside shifts.

2. The long-term investor must recognize the implications of the life cycle, not only because of its effects on the intensity of rivalry but also in the context of the investment risks that it creates. To be avoided or, at a minimum, approached with caution are companies in the emergence phase that have not yet established their viability, as well as companies in the late growth phase, in which the market tends to be overly optimistic about the duration of growth. Companies in the decline phase may offer investment opportunities if the decline is orderly and if they are generating cash which is being used productively in other industries.

3. Industries with a high fixed cost structure are vulnerable to periods of intense competition during market downturns. Such companies need a minimum level of revenue and capacity utilization to cover their fixed costs. Destructive price wars may result, and may become chronic if barriers to exit are high. On the other hand, companies with high fixed costs can show dramatic improvement in earnings from growth because the additional volume can be provided at low incremental cost.

4. Barriers to exit are created by high degrees of specialization among the businesses in the industry, without alternative uses for either the assets or managers of the companies; by the ability to

continue operation even when insolvent; and by competitors that are sustained by noneconomic objectives. Barriers to exit perpetuate destructive competition.

5. Examination of the stock price performance of our five sample industries, as reflected by their industry indexes, confirms that the market recognizes the relative attractiveness of these companies. On the basis of industry characteristics alone, a long-term investment could be made in representative stocks of companies in three of these industries.

NOTES

1. The concept of an industry as evolving through a life cycle is well established. The progression and events outlined here are based on the work of Michael E. Porter, as set out in *Competitive Strategy: Techniques for Analyzing Industries and Competitors* (New York: The Free Press, 1980).

2. Bill Saporito, "Why Price Wars Never End," *Fortune*, March 23, 1992, pp. 68–78.

3. Ibid.

4. Howard Banks, "A Sixties Industry in a Nineties Economy," *Forbes*, May 9, 1994, pp. 107–112.

5. The S&P Drug Index is made up of Lilly (Eli) & Company, Merck & Co., Inc., Pfizer Incorporated, Schering-Plough Corporation, and The Upjohn Company and is representative of the industry as defined by *Forbes*. The S&P Tobacco Index includes Philip Morris, UST Inc., and American Brands Inc., but overstates industry results because of the exceptional performance of UST. The S&P Retail: General Merchandise Chains Index includes Kmart Corp., Wal-Mart Stores, Inc., Woolworth Corporation, Penney (J.C.) Co., Inc., and Sears Roebuck and Co. J.C. Penney and Sears are classified by *Forbes* as department stores, with J.C. Penney above the performance median and Sears below. The index therefore is considered to be reasonably representative of the drug and discount retailing industry for our purposes. The S&P Leisure Time Index consists of Bally Entertainment Corp., Kmart Corp., Wal-Mart Stores, Inc., Woolworth Corporation, Delta Airlines, Incorporated, Pan Am, Brunswick Corporation, Handleman Company, and Outboard Marine Corp. *Forbes* classifies Handleman under Movies and Bally under Hotels and Gaming, with Handleman a superior performer and Bally showing an ROE deficit. This index probably overstates the performance of the recreational products manufacturing industry as defined here. The S&P Airlines Index consists of Delta Air Lines, Inc., Pan Am, UAL Corp. (United Airlines), Northwest Airlines, Inc. (NWA), and USAir Group Inc. and is representative of the airlines industry as defined in this book.

PART
III
IDENTIFYING THE WINNERS

In the opening to Part II, the circumstances of the industry in which a company operates were compared to the condition of the playing field in a sports contest. No matter what condition the playing field is in, however, one team outscores the other because it has superior talent and/or a more effective game plan. Likewise, in competition between companies, some companies consistently outperform their competitors. These companies are winners because they have developed and retained competitive advantage. In Part III, the kinds of competitive advantage which are the basis of superior earnings performance are examined and the ways in which competitive advantage may be achieved and sustained are described.

To continue with the sports analogy, the playing field may not remain the same throughout the game. A day that starts out calm and sunny may become wet and windy. A team's ability to adapt to such a change usually affects the outcome of the game. Industries also change due to economic, social, political, and technological developments. When an industry changes, the companies that operate in the industry must cope with the changes. Part III also examines the causes and effects of change. Methods of assessing the implications of change for companies and their industries are described as well.

COMPETITIVE ADVANTAGE

Given the favorable conditions in the pharmaceuticals industry and the unfavorable conditions in the airlines industry, all the pharmaceuticals companies might be expected to be big winners and all the airlines companies big losers. In reality, however, some companies in any industry consistently outperform others. On the basis of comparative returns on equity (ROEs), the strongest performers in the weak airlines industry outperformed six companies in the attractive drug industry.

To illustrate this point, Exhibit 5–1 shows a leading, a median, and a weak performer in each of the five sample industries discussed in Chapters 3 and 4. (Two leading performers are shown for the tobacco industry.) The leading performer listed is not necessarily the best in the industry nor the weak performer the worst. The companies were chosen because they are similar and because they illustrate the concepts of competitive advantage to be discussed in this chapter.

Exhibit 5–1 shows that while the pharmaceuticals industry had a median five-year average ROE of 22.8 percent, the ROEs for the individual companies ranged from 49.0 percent for Merck to 16.5 percent for Pfizer. In the airlines industry, in which the aggregate five-year average

Performance of Sample Companies in Selected Industries, 1994 (Percentages)

Industry/Company	Profitability			Growth				Sales	Profit Margin
	Return on Equity %		Return on Capital %	Sales %		Earnings per Share %			
	5-Year Average	Latest 12 Months	Latest 12 Months	5-Year Average	Latest 12 Months	5-Year Average	Latest 12 Months	Latest 12 Months $ Millions	Latest 12 Months %
Pharmaceuticals									
Merck	49.0	29.2	24.0	12.5	39.6	14.7	26.6	14,099	20.6
Eli Lilly	19.6	10.0	8.9	10.7	9.9	-7.1	-63.5	6,934	6.8
Pfizer	16.5	28.2	23.8	7.3	7.2	NM	102.5	7,970	15.7
Industry medians (22 companies)	22.8	20.5	16.2	12.7	8.1	14.3	14.3	6,274	8.3
Tobacco									
UST Inc.	58.8	79.2	73.6	13.0	8.7	19.6	7.8	1,158	32.4
Philip Morris	34.4	34.3	17.9	12.7	2.5	14.5	-9.4	52,248	7.6
American Brands	19.5	15.3	11.3	3.7	2.1	5.0	-9.3	8,555	7.6
RJR Nabisco* (4 years)	0.6	D	3.5	4.7	1.5	NM	P-D	15,373	1.1
Industry medians (10 companies)	18.4	2.6	4.1	6.3	-1.3	NM	-37.8	12,049	1.9

Drug and discount retailing								
Wal-Mart	29.2	23.5	15.2	27.4	22.3	22.5	13.4	78,454	3.2
Kmart	5.0	D	D	5.6	0.9	NM	P–D	35,990	D
Woolworth	D	D	D	3.6	–14.4	NM	D–D	8,549	D
Industry medians (31 companies)	12.8	12.6	9.7	7.6	7.1	NM	0.0	1,819	1.6
Recreational equipment manufacturing									
Harley-Davidson	16.7	13.0	12.9	10.4	21.5	NM	–40.3	1,458	2.9
Fleetwood	11.3	15.4	12.8	8.0	29.2	NM	41.4	2,596	3.1
Outboard Marine	D	29.8	17.1	–4.9	4.2	NM	D–P	1,078	4.5
Industry medians (9 companies)	7.7	15.2	12.8	5.3	17.7	NM	13.1	713	3.4
Airlines									
Southwest	12.0	18.2	11.4	20.5	20.6	14.6	37.2	2,574	7.7
AMR	D	1.0	4.0	12.0	–0.4	NM	D–P	15,733	0.7
USAir	D	D	D	3.7	2.9	NM	D–D	7,118	D
Industry medians (11 companies)	D	1.0	4.1	9.8	7.9	NM	66.7	7,188	0.7

*Notes: D = deficit. NM = not meaningful. D–D = deficit to deficit. P–D = profit to deficit. D–P = deficit to profit.

Source: Annual Report on American Industry, *Forbes*, January 2, 1995.

95

ROE was at a deficit, 3 companies of the 11 listed by *Forbes* had positive returns. Southwest Airlines, the best domestic performer, showed a positive though meager 12.0 percent five-year average ROE. Overall industry performance can be explained by the characteristics of the industry, as discussed in the last two chapters. Differences in performance between companies require another level of analysis.

The achievement of superior performance by any company depends on its ability to find and sustain a basis for competitive advantage in its industry. A company with sustainable competitive advantage should be capable of producing the consistent long-term increase in earnings for which the stock market will pay a premium.

This chapter shows how competitive advantage can be developed, enhanced, and sustained. It also outlines the strategic responses that enable a company to enhance its competitive advantage. This information will help investors to determine whether management actions are likely to be productive. A company's ability to develop, enhance, and sustain competitive advantage will be the main criterion for selecting a stock for investment, as it will help to answer the key question: Which companies can be expected to consistently outperform their competitors over the long term?

SOURCES OF COMPETITIVE ADVANTAGE

To outperform its competitors, a company must be able to:

- Sell a higher volume than its competitors.
- Charge a higher unit price than its competitors.
- Operate at lower costs than its competitors.

These results of competitive advantage provide the consistent, superior earnings performance that is desirable in a candidate for long-term investment. Favorable investment status can be derived from the ability to achieve any one of these results, but exceptional performance is usually based on more than one.

Competitive advantage can be achieved by a company that has one or both of the qualities listed below.[1]

- *Superior capability*, or the ability to do better than competitors the functions that provide lower costs, and/or to provide a product or service of superior quality.
- *An advantageous position* in the market and/or between suppliers and customers. A company that has good bargaining power with

suppliers, customers, or both can consistently attract a higher sales volume, charge higher prices, or operate at lower costs.

Competitive advantage achieved through superior capability and competitive advantage derived from positioning are interrelated. Low costs provided by positioning can make it possible to sell a consistently high volume, which in turn can provide the economies of scale necessary to further reduce costs. Superior or unique capability may enable a company to provide a product or service that can command a higher price.

Superior Capability

Superior capability enables a company to provide a product or a service at lower cost and/or of higher quality than its competitors, and to distribute and market its product or service effectively. A company's capability is primarily derived from its resources, which can take many forms, including the ones listed below.

- *Financial resources* consist of cash on hand and/or borrowing power. Money has been called the universal resource. A company that has money can buy other resources—plants, equipment, and so forth. However, many resources that are necessary to success, such as knowledge and brand acceptance, must be earned rather than bought. Thus money is not the only strategic resource a company needs. In terms of developing capability and defending competitive advantage, however, money remains important.

- A *low-cost source of raw materials* is important to companies in industries such as mining and paper, where the cost and quality of raw materials are major factors in profitability.

- *Modern, state-of-the-science factories* keep costs low. *Well-located retail outlets* attract customers and offer high sales potential.

- *Superior product technology* yields a better product, whereas *superior process technology* improves the techniques of manufacturing.

- Managers and workers may have *superior skills* in manufacture, R&D, marketing, the organization and coordination of activities, and so forth.

- An *effective infrastructure*, such as an established distribution and dealer network, can provide a consistently high volume of sales.

- A *good reputation or image* and *strong brand recognition and loyalty* can cause customers to consistently favor a company or its products.

In general terms, the *resources* of a company may be defined as the materials and activities that the management organizes and coordinates to create earnings for shareholders. Not all the resources listed above appear on the balance sheet as assets. Most of the time, in fact, only financial and physical assets, such as machinery and real estate, are recognized on the balance sheet, and even these are carried at their cost, rather than at their value in producing earnings. Not shown on the balance sheet are "knowledge" resources, consisting of the various skills and information that make up the company's intellectual capital, or the value of its image and brand acceptance, which keeps customers buying the product. Some "soft" assets may be recognized on the balance sheet as "goodwill" but usually as the result of an acquisition, and here the valuation is artificial.

In this book, we will take a broader view of resources. Rather than looking only at financial resources, we will also consider knowledge, goodwill, and other so-called soft resources in the context of the capabilities that they can provide to a company.

Here are some companies at which these resources and the capabilities which they provide are important to success.

- *Inco Limited*, operating in the mining industry, is the world's largest and one of its lowest-cost producers of nickel. It has large, high-quality deposits of nickel ore in Ontario, Manitoba, and Indonesia, and it has adopted new mining methods and processing technologies.

- *Microsoft Inc.* is a leading performer in the computer software industry because of the skills of its people. This is a knowledge industry, in that the skills of employees are the primary resource.

- *Gillette Company* is a consistent leading performer in the personal products segment of the consumer nondurable goods industry. The company's aggressive development and introduction of new shaving products keep it on the leading edge of that technology.

- *Schlumberger Ltd.* is the leader in the oil field services industry because of its proprietary oil recovery technology. This company alone spends as much on R&D as all its competitors spend together.

- *Dell Computer Corporation*, started in 1984, has grown to annual sales of $4 billion on the strength of its distribution and customer service capability in the computer industry.

- *Avon Products, Incorporated* is a leading performer in the personal products segment of the consumer nondurable goods manufac-

turing industry because of its distribution and service infrastructure. Its well-established network of representatives sells cosmet-
ics and other personal products directly to the customer.

- *McDonald's Corporation* has a leading position in the resturant
  chains industry. Its large base of well-located outlets gives it an
  advantageous distribution infrastructure.

- Coca-Cola is one of the world's most recognized brand names,
  which has made *The Coca-Cola Company* the leading performer
  in the beverage industry. The company's name, logo, and image
  are established globally, representing not only a product but a
  lifestyle.

Each of these companies recognizes the importance of its superior
resources to its performance and nurtures its key resources carefully. For
example, though Gillette's Sensor razor cost over $200 million to devel-
op, the company did not hesitate to sacrifice current earnings to this
extent because it recognized the importance of continued product leadership for its future. Coca-Cola continues to spend heavily on advertising
and promotion to maintain its brand recognition.

In each of the examples listed above, superior capability derived
from the company's resources is a key factor. In several of these cases,
the company's superior capability is reinforced by its position in the
industry—the other source of competitive advantage.

Positioning

There are three ways in which a company can derive competitive advantage from its position in the industry. First, it may occupy a segment of
the market that maximizes its bargaining power with customers, enabling
it to charge high prices or to achieve high volume. Second, high bargaining power with suppliers can enable a company to get materials for low
costs. Third, a company may be able to optimize its position between customers and suppliers. Each of these possibilities is discussed below.

Bargaining Power with Customers

There are four market positions that can give a company bargaining
power with customers: (1) offering a unique product or service, (2) being
in a sheltered market, (3) occupying a value-differentiated segment, and
(4) occupying a price-differentiated position. Each of these positions can
provide various degrees of competitive advantage in different ways.

Unique Products or Services   A company can achieve competitive advantage by possessing resources that enable it to provide a product or service that cannot be directly duplicated by competitors. Barriers to entry may be provided by patents, copyrights, or trade secrecy.

- *Polaroid Corporation*, one of the leading performers in the photography and toys industry, occupies a segment that is protected from new entrants by patented, proprietary technology. While the market for "instant" photography equipment and film is not large even on a global basis, the uniqueness of the product provides bargaining power that makes it highly profitable.

- *Xerox Corporation* got its strong start in the business supplies industry by offering a unique product—office copiers—based on its technological resources.

- *IBM* had a strong starting advantage in the computer industry because its technological product, the mainframe computer with its proprietary operating systems, was unique at the time.

- The success of *The Disney (Walt) Company* in various segments of the entertainment industry is primarily based on its exclusive rights to certain popular cartoon characters. The company has global copyrights that protect its position.

Competition for unique products may be provided by substitutes. Conventional photography and electronic imaging, for example, are substitutes for instant photography. Such competition places constraints upon the price premiums that uniqueness could otherwise be expected to provide.

Sheltered Markets   A market may be sheltered by regulations or by national preference. Regulation exists in a wide range of industries, such as electrical power distribution, cable TV, pipelines, broadcasting, securities, and local telephone service. Though regulation may create barriers to entry by competitors, the ability to take advantage of the monopoly is often limited by price controls exercised by the regulating body. Regulation limits the number of competitors and prevents the fragmentation of markets. In addition to mandated regulation, voluntary regulation may be provided by exclusive dealership arrangements and franchises. Self-governing arrangements are created by professional associations, to set qualifications for entry and standards for behavior.

Shelter through national preference is provided by tariffs, quotas, and national laws. Government purchases, particularly for defense purposes and for other activities such as shipbuilding and ship operation (the Jones Act), are regulated by national laws. National preference provides protection from foreign competitors that might have a competitive advantage due to such factors as lower wages or cheaper raw materials.

Sheltered markets enhance companies' bargaining power with buyers by constraining the scope of competition. Even when such protection is provided, competition may still exist. Direct broadcast satellites and home antennas are substitutes for cable TV, and unregulated oil is a substitute for natural gas. Companies that are protected from foreign competition may still face fierce competition from other domestic firms.

Value-Differentiated Positions   Value can be real or perceived. It may be provided by a combination of the performance and quality of a product or a service, by the service that accompanies a product, or by intangible factors. The objective of value-differentiated market positions may be to charge a higher price and/or to establish consumer preference and sell a higher volume while charging the same price as competitors. If the objective is to charge a higher price, the market is usually small. The producer incurs higher costs in providing the higher value in the product but expects to more than offset these higher costs and to get a higher profit margin. If the price is the same as competitors' prices, the advantage is gained by attracting a consistently high level of sales. The high volume provides a basis for enhancing profit margins by reducing costs.

The strategic challenge for most companies is to establish recognizable differentiation for their products or services. The majority of businesses offer products or services that are virtually identical to their competitors' offerings. By catering to the mainstream tastes of the mass market, companies hope to obtain the volume of sales necessary to support the large-scale, efficient production that will achieve low costs.

The challenge to a company in such a climate is to create the perception that it is offering superior value. The battleground is advertising. It was David Ogilvy, a pioneer in advertising and the founder of the Ogilvy & Mather advertising agency, who said, "If your product is not demonstratively better than your competitor's, it pays to use emotion." Thus there are many beer commercials, for instance, that say nothing about the taste of the beer. This is because the taste of most beers is very similar. Instead of emphasizing taste, therefore, the commercials associate the company's beer with a desirable lifestyle or promote a positive self-image. The product differentiation is *perceived*. It exists only in the eyes of the beholder, and it is often fragile. The value of the product is created by the marketing skills of the company, and these skills in turn become one of the company's key resources.

When a company elects to compete in more than one value-price segment, it usually uses different brand names and even different organizations to separate the products in the eyes of the market. Thus Honda sells its luxury cars under the name Acura and through separate dealerships. The Black and Decker Corporation sells its premium line of power tools under the brand name Dewalt. The standard and premium lines are thus not directly comparable, which enhances the company's ability to provide perceived differentiation to the premium product.

In an example of highly successful value differentiation, Maytag Corporation became the leading performer in the major household appliance industry during the 1980s by pursuing a product strategy of high value for high price. It limited its product line to dishwashers and clothes washers and dryers—complex products that have a relatively short service life and are prone to breakdown. Maytag advertised its premium product on the basis of reliability rather than operating performance, using the theme of the lonely Maytag repairman. The products were priced at a 20 percent premium over competitors' prices, and the prices were maintained by the careful selection of distributors to minimize discounting, so as not to damage the premium-quality image of the product. The additional cost of producing the superior product has been estimated at $20 to $30 for each $100 of higher price. In 1985, Maytag led its industry in ROE and had a profit margin of 10.5 percent of sales. In comparison, Whirlpool Corporation, a competitor with a less differentiated product, had a 5.1 percent profit margin.

General Mills Inc. is the leading performer in the food-processing industry because of the market acceptance of a wide range of products under its Betty Crocker and other brands. Because of the popularity of its products, the company is able to command shelf space in supermarkets for both established and new products.

Differentiation by value, either real or perceived, provided to create market preference is probably the most common way of pursuing competitive advantage.

Price-Differentiated Positions   A company may choose to establish its bargaining power with customers by using the appeal of a lower price. It may choose to offer the same value as or less value than competitors' products or services.

Discount mass merchandisers offer the same value for lower price. The core of their sales is provided by nationally branded merchandise identical to that sold by competitors, so that the attraction to customers is the lower price. These companies may advertise and promote their own private brands, with the objective of establishing that they offer the same value as national brands. Success in this market position is dependent on low costs, which are usually achieved by combining high efficiency in operations with the economies of scale provided by high volume.

Less value for lower price is a position used by a wide range of businesses. Self-serve gasoline stations, discount stockbrokers, and warehouse stores all provide a lower level of service at a discount, which appeals to the price-conscious market. The same appeal is used in a range of bottom-of-the-line products, such as tires and appliances. Manufacturers produce these products to achieve volume, but devote their advertising and promotion to the higher-margin, top-of-the-line products. Again, the ability to achieve low costs is critical to profitability. The cost of the value or service omitted must more than offset the additional price discount.

A basic part of the strategy of any company involves deciding what value-price relationship it will try to establish. This relationship defines the segment of the market in which the company will compete. The decision must be based largely on the company's capability. Capability derived from resources is what enables a company to produce a differentiated product or service or to achieve the low costs necessary to assume a price-differentiated position. To be effective, a market positioning strategy must be supported by an appropriate distribution channel, which will make the product available to the buyer at the right time. The distribution channel may enhance differentiation; for example, many luxury products are sold in exclusive retail outlets. As mentioned above, Maytag chooses its distribution channels with care, so as to minimize the risk of discounting. Strong distribution channels can also help to carry a product over a difficult period. General Motors' strong dealership network has helped to sustain sales in the many periods when its products have been weak.

Bargaining Power with Suppliers

The objective of obtaining the power to bargain effectively with suppliers is to obtain a consistent supply of inputs at the lowest possible price. The uses of this bargaining power were discussed in Chapter 3. The most common way of establishing such power is to buy a very high volume of materials from a supplier and thus to become an important customer, particularly if the inputs are undifferentiated commodities. Discount merchandisers that rely on low prices to attract sales must be large enough to obtain low prices from suppliers, even if the products they sell are value-differentiated.

Positioning between Suppliers and Customers

The pursuit of competitive advantage through positioning between suppliers and customers has become common. A company may prosper even though it lacks bargaining power either with its suppliers or with its customers, so long as it can offset the lack of bargaining power with one by exploiting its bargaining power with the other. Any company, however, is doomed to chronic low profitability if it is continuously squeezed between the two. This was shown to be true in the discussion of the airlines industry in Chapter 3. To achieve and maintain competitive advantage, a company must find room for itself between its suppliers and its customers.

The basic concept involved in defining a company's position is that a company is a part of the value chain. To manufacture a product or to provide a service, a company must perform a sequence of activities (functions). The manufacture of a product, for instance, involves purchasing raw materials, processing them into semifinished materials, manufacturing components from these materials, and assembling them into the product. These activities are followed by still other activities: packaging, warehousing, distributing, selling, and servicing the product.

Traditionally, companies have had high vertical integration; that is, they have performed many of these functions themselves. Sixty years ago, Ford took in iron ore at one end of the factory and shipped cars out at the other end.

The problem with vertical integration was its inherent inefficiency. Most companies did not have the necessary expertise in each of their activities, and this lack was compounded by the difficulty of managing and coordinating a large number of coincident functions. However, this was still easier than trying to coordinate and administer the activities of a multitude of outside suppliers. This was recognized by Ronald Coase, a Nobel Laureate in economics. In his 1937 paper, "The Nature of the Firm," Coase pointed out that businesses produced goods and services internally as long as the cost of production was less than the cost of purchase on the open market.[2] One of the major costs of dealing with outsiders was transaction costs, consisting of the costs of negotiating prices, writing enforceable contracts, and tracking the transactions. These costs usually outweighed the lower prices available from even the most efficient outside supplier.

In recent years, technology—in the form of telephones, electronic mail, facsimile transmission (fax), computers, and modems, as well as rapid airline travel—has drastically improved companies' ability to communicate and coordinate. Administrative complexity and the cost and time consumed in dispersing activities to the most efficient supplier have been accordingly reduced. This has made it possible for a company to confine itself to doing what it does best: using the unique or core competence provided by its resources. This competence may, for instance, consist of developing, manufacturing, or marketing a product. Functions outside the company's core competence are contracted out to the lowest-priced or most effective supplier. The functions performed internally are those that enable the company to maximize its bargaining power between suppliers and customers.

In economic terms, this arrangement may be called *disaggregation*. It is also sometimes called *outsourcing* or *disintegration*. Outsourcing increases the efficiency of a business by focusing the company's attention on its areas of core competence, reducing distractions, and maximizing the company's bargaining power.

For example, a large domestic company may have limited bargaining power with its unionized labor force, particularly if it is a highly profitable company. If it contracts out its labor-intensive functions to a third party, it will likely gain bargaining power over this source of supply, and the problem of dealing directly with the labor force will be eliminated. The supplier's labor force will become more cooperative because its jobs will depend on satisfying a customer who has alternative sources of supply.

Disaggregation has become common in the automobile industry, where the manufacturers concentrate on designing, assembling, and marketing cars. Most of the manufacture of components is contracted out, but the assembly function is retained, giving the manufacturers direct control over quality.

Outsourcing has been the savior of many North American producers of labor-intensive products such as footwear and apparel. It is a useful practice in industries in which high domestic wage rates do not allow companies to remain competitive. Production is contracted out to low-wage countries, and the companies confine their operations to value-adding processes like product design and marketing. Large companies can take advantage of their bargaining power with suppliers, and the suppliers can obtain economies of scale by producing for a number of customers. Disaggregation has the further advantage of allowing a company to adjust to fluctuations in the market by reducing contract commitments, rather than having to resort to destructive competition so as to keep its own factories busy by trying to absorb fixed costs.

A company's position in the value chain may be based on a number of factors, including:

- Its ability to achieve low costs through some combination of inexpensive inputs (labor, materials, energy, etc.), superior process technology, the high utilization of capacity, and strong management skills.
- Its ability to charge a higher price or consistently sell a higher volume, as a consequence of success in reading the market and differentiating the product.

The key to effective disaggregation is understanding where the value is added, and therefore where the profits come from. For example, General Mills, as mentioned above, is a producer of value-differentiated food products that enjoy a large market. Its raw materials are common commodities (such as grains) that are available from a large number of suppliers. The company is thus able to exert buying power and to process low-value commodities into value-differentiated products. A significant portion of the value of its products is added through product development and through marketing efforts that develop consumer preference for its brands.

Nike Inc., a leading performer in the apparel and shoe industry, outsources by contracting out all manufacturing to lower-wage countries. The company retains only the key activities of product development and marketing, which provide the profits. Nike is an interesting example of the relative value of product development and marketing, as compared to manufacturing. In 1992, Nike paid Michael Jordan $20 million to promote its premium athletic shoe—more money than the combined total annual payrolls of the factories in Indonesia that produced them.[3]

Economies of Scale

Economies of scale can provide an important basis for competitive advantage. The term *economies of scale* describes a basic phenomenon: costs per unit produced decline as the volume produced increases, as a result of a number of advantages enjoyed by high-volume businesses. Specifically:

- Such businesses can afford specialized, highly productive automated machinery and equipment, and can employ specialized labor.
- Their high cumulative output gives them the experience necessary to improve the product and production process, and gives their workers the ability to perform repetitive tasks efficiently.

- Their high volume of purchases gives them bargaining power with suppliers.
- They can absorb fixed operating and product development costs over a large volume, reducing the cost per unit.

These advantages are not without a downside. Firms enjoying these advantages tend to be inflexible in responding to market changes. They also usually have high fixed costs, which (as pointed out in Chapter 4) create intense competition in times of market weakness.

Capability versus Positioning Situations

Competitive advantage can be derived from various combinations of capability and positioning. In general, large companies require large markets and so must rely on capability as their main basis for competitive advantage. It has already been pointed out that size itself can provide capability. Producers of commodities must also rely on the capability provided by the quality of their resources. These companies cannot influence their prices by differentiating the product and so must pursue the lowest possible costs.

Positioning strategies using unique products or value differentiation to target smaller market segments are usually necessary to smaller firms, as these strategies can provide the higher prices necessary to offset their higher costs. The histories of many highly successful companies show that they got their starts by pursuing positioning strategies but really took off after attaining the size to also improve their cost performance. The main exception to this progression occurs when a small company gets its start from superior capability provided by new technology, as the steel minimills did. (see Chapter 6).

The large company can optimize its position between suppliers and buyers through disaggregation by using its bargaining power to obtain favorable terms from suppliers. The automobile and aircraft industries have gone so far as to require subcontractors to play a role in their R&D.

Though no company can continue to exist if it has no competitive advantage, investors are interested in more than mere survival. Only companies with decisive and sustainable competitive advantage can present sound long-term investment opportunities.

Degrees of Competitive Advantage

To achieve consistent, superior earnings performance, a company must have the sort of decisive competitive advantage that will enable it to outperform its competitors by a considerable margin. This allows a company to avoid the "profitless prosperity" that often occurs in balanced competitive situations, where the advantage of any one company over its competitors is marginal. A company with decisive competitive advantage can stand above the fray. Its advantage discourages competitors' attacks. Weaker companies know they cannot win. The superior company would not only match any move they made but also retaliate by inflicting serious damage.

Decisive competitive advantage can be derived in the following two ways.

1. The stronger company can outperform its competitors by a wide margin in the key factor that determines profitability in the industry.
2. It can derive competitive advantage from two or more sources, which reinforce one another. This tactic is particularly effective when a unique capability allows the company to shift its market position away from head-to-head competition.

Let's look at some combinations that provide superior performance in various industries.

- McDonald's, among restaurant chains, has a combination of low costs (achieved through standardization of menus and advertising, as well as economies of scale) and high market share (because of the high perceived value of its products by its market). Thus it can easily weather the periodic price wars started by its competitors.
- Not only is Coca-Cola one of the world's most recognized brands, but also the company has an extensive global distribution system which enables it to exploit the popularity of its products.
- Gillette, the leader in shaving product technology, also has brand recognition and loyalty combined with a global distribution capability.

Examination of a larger sample of industry leaders would confirm what this short list shows: decisive competitive advantage is usually based on a combination of product leadership and effective distribution capability. Thus, no one customer, nor even any one group of customers, has significant bargaining power with the company. This sort of market leadership must be earned with superior products and services through a sound value-price relationship provided by some other capability, such as technological leadership.

In general, corporate strategy since the late 1980s has been to simplify the business so as to focus on a limited number of products and markets.

A large number of divestitures has resulted, for which the explanation has been, "The company is returning to its core businesses." This strategy has been based on a recognition of the complexities of managing diverse businesses in an environment of intense competition—a lesson that has long been available. For instance, three of the top five ROE companies in the food-processing industry (Wm. Wrigley Jr. Company, Kellogg Company, and Gerber Products Company) are specialized, which tends to indicate that specialization is important in establishing competitive advantage.

SUSTAINABILITY OF COMPETITIVE ADVANTAGE

Obviously, the long-term investor must be concerned about whether the competitive advantage enjoyed by an investment candidate today can be sustained over the long term. Sustainability can be assessed by asking these three questions:

1. Can the company's basis of competitive advantage be imitated by competitors?
2. Does the company indicate a willingness to continue to nurture the capabilities and/or positioning factors on which its success is based?
3. Does the company have room in its markets for further growth through which its competitive advantage can be leveraged?

The constraints upon imitation of competitive advantage are the same as the barriers to entry into an industry. The most common ones are:

- *Large size*, which provides economies of scale. In mature industries, in particular, relatively high market share is an effective barrier to imitation.
- *Strong brand preference*, which requires heavy expenditures on advertising and promotion. In consumer products, market acceptance is also necessary to get the retail shelf space necessary to distribute the product.
- *Proprietary technology*, which provides the basis for a unique or superior product or lower production costs. The technology must be protected by patents, copyrights, or maintenance of trade secrecy.

The risk of imitation depends to a significant degree on the extent to which the company's competitive advantage is based on structural or operational factors. Structural advantages include those derived from unique or superior facilities, control of favorable locations, occupation of sheltered markets, and so forth, which are relatively difficult to duplicate. Operational advantages based on how things are done within the business are more readily imitated.

Where barriers to imitation are not present, the strategic initiatives adopted by aggressive companies that show signs of success are quickly copied by competitors. The situation soon reverts to price competition. If the strategic action has added to costs, the industry is worse off than before.

Management's willingness to nurture the factors upon which the success of the company is based may include continued spending on R&D, advertising and promotion, employee training, and new equipment. Performance leaders do not rest on their laurels. Thus, one signal that should cause an investor to question a company's ability to sustain its competitive advantage is its cutting of R&D and advertising budgets in order to maintain short-term earnings.

Room for further growth is important to the investor because the growth of earnings is a major factor in determining stock values. Sustainable competitive advantage will maintain the present level of earnings, and companies can offset short-term weaknesses by measures such as share buy-backs. Ultimately, however, growth of earnings requires growth of sales revenue, through higher volume and/or through higher real prices. Opportunities for growth have the additional benefit of helping to maintain a dynamic organization and avoiding the "caretaker" mentality that afflicts many firms in the mature phase. Growth can take place in any of several directions, as follows:

- The market as a whole may grow, either because the industry is in the growth phase or because of factors such as demographics or income gains.
- A company's market share may increase, usually because the firm has decisive competitive advantage.
- Geographic expansion, or entry into other countries, may allow growth to occur.
- The company may broaden its product line by introducing new products. New products that take advantage of the company's brand acceptance and use of established channels of distribution are particularly likely to succeed.

Most situations in which companies achieve continued growth in mature industries are based on growth in a combination of the directions listed above. The most common direction in recent years has been entry into emerging nations that are enjoying rapid economic growth.

Finding room for growth is a particular challenge for companies that already dominate their industries. In this context, *dominance* can be defined as holding about 50 percent of the market, or more. Dominant companies usually find it difficult to increase their market share significantly, and furthermore, they are vulnerable to specialized competitors that may nibble at their markets. If the dominance is of long standing, the complacency and arrogance that often develop under such circumstances may present a problem. IBM, General Motors, and Xerox have all had this experience at one time or another.

COMPETITIVE ADVANTAGE IN SELECTED COMPANIES IN A BROAD SPECTRUM OF INDUSTRIES

Lets go back to some of the companies used as examples in this chapter and earlier chapters to examine the basis for and sustainability of their competitive advantage and their room for growth.

Boeing The world's leading producer of commercial aircraft, Boeing operates in an attractive industry with prohibitive barriers to entry and no substitutes. It has technological skills in product development. Its bargaining power with its large customer base is very strong, as it can supply a full line of aircraft with similar basic systems, which provides its customers with major economies in aircraft maintenance and pilot training. It has disaggregated by contracting out the development and manufacture of components, maintaining for itself the high value-added activities of product development and assembly. This combination of factors provides it with decisive competitive advantage, and it has room for growth because of the growth of aviation in general and also because of the replacement cycle.

Inco With the world's largest deposits of nickel ore under its control, Inco has invested heavily in the latest mining and processing technology, thus achieving good cost reduction results. Nickel deposits can be economically mined but have proved to be scarce. The Russian mines may be running out of readily accessible high-grade ores, and very heavy new development capital may be required in this area. Inco continues to spend heavily on exploration. The mining industry leader in metallurgical research, it sells its products in various forms which are more readily usable by its customers than are its competitors' products. Thus its products are differentiated and sell for a higher average price per pound than does raw nickel. While the metals market is highly cyclical, this company's competitive advantage is both decisive and secure, with growth potential provided by the expansion of the world economy. However, Inco must be discussed in the context of a situation, typical for commodity producers, in which global market conditions have not allowed it to translate its advantage into superior earnings. The economic recovery of 1993–94 should have provided higher nickel prices and a dramatic increase in earnings, but the collapse of the Soviet Union and the consequent drop in military demand created a continuing nickel surplus and depressed prices. Barriers to exit by foreign producers because of their importance as earners of hard currencies have kept high-cost mines in production. Such operations pay workers in soft local currencies but sell their products for hard currencies which would be otherwise difficult to obtain. In many cases, such sales are the major source of foreign currency for the country. Thus, for reasons beyond its control, Inco's competitive advantage cannot be realized until change occurs. (This situation is discussed in more depth in Chapter 6.)

Dell Computer   Dell Computer was built on the strength of its distribution and service capability and on its ability to customize its products to meet specific clients' needs, after hardware became a commodity. The company took advantage of its industry's shift of power from manufacturer to distributor—a shift which is characteristic of the transition phase of most industries. In the early 1990s, however, Dell faltered because it was slow in developing laptop and notebook lines. Its name and its reputation for customer service remain well entrenched but must be sustained by heavy advertising support. Its distribution and service performance may be readily duplicated by competitors. Further, it must reduce costs aggressively to keep up with its competitors in the computer industry. While the sustainability of its competitive advantage is therefore in doubt in the long term and its room for growth will be squeezed by aggressive competitors, it nevertheless has considerable staying power because its name and reputation have become well established.[4]

General Mills   The competitive advantage of General Mills in the food-processing industry is based on brand acceptance and on its ability to get retail shelf space for both established and new food products. This powerful combination should enable the company to maintain its competitive advantage as long as it continues to introduce new products to keep up with changes in market tastes. To find room for growth, however, it has had to enter the overcrowded restaurant chain industry (with Olive Garden and Red Lobster restaurants).

Gillette Decisive leadership in new product development and a strong consumer franchise are what gives Gillette its competitive advantage in the personal products segment of the consumer nondurable goods industry. While the company's continued new product introductions tend to obsolete existing products, there is enough residual demand for the old products to make them highly profitable as they require minimal advertising support. Wilkinson Sword Inc. beat Gillette to the market with the stainless steel blade in the 1960s, and Gillette temporarily lost market share. Since then, the company has begun to show a willingness to sacrifice current earnings so as to maintain its product development effort. Gillette's advantage is sustainable because it designs and makes its own unique manufacturing machines, thus limiting competitors' ability to imitate its products. The company's competitive advantage is therefore both decisive and sustainable. Growth is taking place in two directions: by introduction of new products, which are able to use established channels of distribution and to command premium prices, and by entry into foreign markets, particularly in emerging nations. Because Gillette applied its R&D culture to its Braun line of small appliances, it has the potential to make significant inroads into this relatively complacent industry.[5] Foreign sales account for 69 percent of Gillette's sales and provide room for market growth.

Polaroid The proprietary photographic technology that Polaroid developed creates high barriers to imitation and assures that its product remains unique. However, this technology is aging. Protective patents will expire in due course and will likely give way in part to electronic imaging, a totally different technology in which the company has relatively little background. In fact, Polaroid has indicated that the Captiva camera may be its last major conventional product development effort. Polaroid's current competitive advantage in the photography industry remains decisive, as a result of its unique product, but the long-term sustainability of this advantage is in considerable doubt.[6]

Maytag Maytag's competitive advantage in the heavy household appliance industry, based on the high perceived value of its product, is likely sustainable because the company is so well entrenched and because its products continue to be supported by an effective advertising effort. Even when it added refrigerators to its product line, the company used its customary durability theme in advertising. Other companies, however, particularly GE, are moving into the premium product market.

The market for high-value, high-priced products, which is relatively small, apparently did not provide Maytag with the room for growth that its management considered desirable. As a result, the company embarked on an acquisition program in the 1980s, broadening its product line into microwave ovens, electric ranges, freezers, and vacuum cleaners by buying Magic Chef Inc., Jenn-Air Corp., and The Hoover Co. The acquisitions were financed by heavy debt, which may have had the additional purpose of making the company a less attractive takeover target. The company's ROE performance has lapsed from its historically strong levels because the acquisitions carried lower margins than did the parent company and because there were many management problems. Even though the problems caused by the acquisitions are likely to be eventually resolved, the expanded product line does not have the competitive advantage potential of Maytag's core business. A return to the company's historical performance is not likely.

Coca-Cola   The success of The Coca-Cola Company is often attributed to the secret formula that provides the unique flavor of its main product, Coke. Even though competitors in the soft-drink industry can come close to duplicating this flavor, the task of displacing Coke's brand recognition and creating a global distribution infrastructure would pose a formidable challenge. Colas have been losing some popularity in recent years, but the company can use its distribution capability to sell competing flavors. Its competitive advantage is quite secure, and it has room in global markets for further growth, although its domestic markets are experiencing some pressure from private brands. Coca-Cola derives 78.7 percent of its operating profit from soft-drink sales in international markets, as compared to 17.7 percent from U.S. sales.[7]

Microsoft   The products of Microsoft, the world's largest developer of computer software and the Microsoft disk operating system (MS-DOS), are the standard for use in PCs. Microsoft products have been installed in over 100 million machines. MS-DOS, however, is approaching obsolescence. The race to produce the next generation of computers is on, and the winner will have a chance to dominate the computer software industry for more than a decade. The remarkable record that Microsoft has built on its proprietary technology is therefore at some risk. Further, the company's

1994 consent decree, settling an action initiated by the U.S. Department of Justice, will curtail some of the practices that have contributed to its past profitability. The door will be open to competitors in some areas of its business. Microsoft also faces the usual problem of a dominant company: finding room for growth. Despite these adverse factors, the company will not fade quickly, as it has the financial muscle to buy companies with new products and the technological skills to update and extend its own product line.

McDonald's   As mentioned earlier, McDonald's can be considered to have decisive competitive advantage because of a combination of economies of scale, the high perceived value of its products, and name recognition. Its name, like that of Coca-Cola, has become a symbol for the American lifestyle. Global markets provide the company with plenty of room for further growth.[8]

Nike Inc.   The leader in athletic footwear on the basis of its product development and marketing capability, as well as its outsourcing of manufacturing to low-wage companies, Nike has outperformed its direct competitors, Reebok International Ltd. and L.A. Gear Inc., by a substantial margin in the apparel and shoes industry. Though the company continues to spend heavily on advertising and promotion to maintain its leading position in a fickle, faddish market, consumer preferences have moved from athletic footwear to outdoor shoes and hiking boots. Nike's present market may become stagnant, and the company may lack the room to exploit its current competitive advantage by establishing its name in a different market. Both the value and the sustainability of Nike's present competitive advantage are therefore in some doubt. The company's acquisition of Canstar Sports Group Inc., the global leader in production of ice skates and in-line roller skates, indicates that management is aware of the vulnerability of its conventional products.

Most of the companies reviewed above are leading performers in their respective industries because of some basis of competitive advantage. However, it can be seen that many of them may be unable to sustain and exploit their current competitive advantage.

STRATEGIES FOR ENHANCING COMPETITIVE ADVANTAGE

One of the highest priorities of any management team is to continuously look for opportunities to improve their company's position in relation to competitors. It is obviously important for investors to be able to assess the effectiveness of candidate companies' strategic actions. In this section we will examine some of the most common strategies for enhancing competitive advantage, along with the constraints that often make action nonproductive.

Strategic action taken to improve competitive advantage can have one or both of the following objectives:

- To improve the firm's ability to increase value differentiation.
- To reposition the business to minimize the constraints imposed by the structure of its industry.

Virtually every soundly managed company maintains several basic, continuing strategies. The objectives of such strategies are to reduce costs and/or to produce a superior product or provide a superior service. The most direct actions that companies take in this regard give priority to development of the capabilities that are necessary for success in the industry, to the repositioning of products in a stronger segment of the market, and to rationalization and disaggregation.

Development of Unique Capability

Companies have been known to take many different approaches to development of unique capability, but most commonly, a company will introduce process and product technologies that its managers believe will enable the company to operate at the lowest possible costs and/or to offer a superior product or service that can be positioned in a high-value, high-priced market segment. Companies can also create and sustain unique capabilities by giving priority to R&D, employee training, or other factors. The development of capability is usually a slow process that requires dedication on the part of management. Though managers often publicize programs such as Total Quality Management, these programs are usually abandoned because they are slow to implement and because they do not cure all the company's performance problems.

Repositioning in the Market

It was pointed out in the discussion of competitive advantage that value-differentiated products and services are less price-sensitive than standard ones, because the customer is buying something more than the basic function of the product or service. Once value becomes established in the mind of customers, it is difficult to imitate. Thus, the establishment of brand loyalties, such as customers' longstanding preference for Campbell

Soup Company's line of soups, provides a major competitive advantage and is a logical strategic objective. This can be attempted by bringing out premium lines of products with recognizable differentiation, perhaps under a different name, such as Honda's Acura line and Black and Decker's Dewalt line. Upgrading value differentiation may require new or additional inputs, such as the ability to produce higher-quality goods, special marketing skills, or high advertising costs. Further, brand acceptance is difficult to transfer from one product to another, as Campbell found out through the failure of its attempt to introduce pork and beans using the Campbell name and red-and-white label.

Disaggregation

As mentioned above, disaggregation may also be called disintegration, as it involves undoing forward and backward integration. Activities are concentrated in the company's area of special competence, where it can leverage its unique capabilities. This is a positioning strategy in which competitive advantage is derived in part from the ability to optimize bargaining power between suppliers and buyers. It also has the advantage of reducing costs by minimizing the distractions caused by managing a diverse range of activities. Further, it can sharply reduce the amount of capital tied up in internal supply operations.

Disaggregation has become a major force in contemporary management thinking. The advent of computers and new communications technology has made it possible to control the multiple transactions involved in managing a disaggregated company. Disaggregation has changed the traditional adversarial bargaining relationship between suppliers and buyers into a more cooperative partnership arrangement. Companies enter into joint ventures, or strategic alliances, for various periods of time. Thus, disaggregation enhances capability by co-opting the capabilities of a broad range of suppliers for use by the company at the lowest possible costs.

Rationalization

Closing plants and concentrating production in a smaller number of plants that can be operated at a higher rate of capacity utilization is called *rationalization*. Usually, the surviving plants are specialized, that is, concentrated on a limited line of products in which they can become highly efficient. High capacity utilization is an important prerequisite for profitability in high-fixed-cost operations.

Increasing capacity utilization is one reason for the prevalence of corporate downsizing in the early 1990s. Rationalization is also the underlying strategy through which companies acquire competitors, close some of the competitors' plants, and absorb the competitors' sales volumes into their own operations. This adjustment process is a part of the transition from the growth phase to the maturity phase of an industry. As the maturity phase progresses, rationalization plays a part in the adaptation to a downside shift. It also takes place in the declining phase. Rationalization not only improves the capability of the company by providing the basis for cost reduction but also makes the industry more attractive by removing overcapacity.

The operating strategies discussed above are internal and thus difficult for the outsider to evaluate. Some clues are provided by periodic announcements of new product introductions, plant closings, contract awards, and so forth. Much more visible are other actions taken to improve the position of the company by minimizing the constraints created by the structure of the industry. The most common of these are forward integration, backward integration, horizontal integration, and entry into a substitute business.

Forward Integration

Entry into customers' line of business is often undertaken by a business that has a relatively small number of large, powerful customers with the bargaining power to seriously limit the business's earnings. This action, known as *forward integration*, may provide opportunities for differentiation that do not exist in the primary product. This situation, which is particularly common among commodity producers, has led aluminum, copper, and paper producers to enter the building products, wire, and packaging industries, respectively. Thus they gain the assured markets necessary to keep their high-fixed-cost primary operations profitable, as well as the opportunity to differentiate the quality and service of the final product. In the process, they gain a large number of relatively small customers who are unable to exert significant bargaining power.

A common problem with forward integration is that the forward businesses are rarely well managed. Managers tend to view them as existing purely to provide a benefit to the core business rather than as businesses that ought to be made highly efficient in their own right. In addition, if major competitors follow the same strategy, as they often do, the downstream portion of the industry becomes highly competitive. Recently, many companies, such as Alcan Aluminum Ltd., have become disenchanted with their forward integration into products such as building siding and have divested them.

Backward Integration

Entry into the business of a supplier that is using its bargaining power to extract high prices or to limit supply is called *backward integration*. The supplier may gain its bargaining power from its control of a scarce resource or from its ability to supply a technologically superior component. Though the backward integration may be partial, in that it may supply only a portion of the company's needs, the possibility of expanding constitutes a disciplinary threat to suppliers. In the integrated steel industry, for instance, steel companies may purchase iron mines and ships to supply a portion of their needs. One problem with backward integration is that the operations secondary to the core business are not always efficiently managed, as in forward integration.

Companies involved in the primary processing of raw materials are particularly likely to integrate backward in order to assure a consistent supply of raw materials. In 1993, Nucor, the steel minimill operator, invested in the development of a new process as well as in a plant for the production of a substitute for high-grade steel scrap. The company had been encountering higher material prices due to a shortage of such scrap, and the industry, because of the relatively low barriers to entry, had been growing. Furthermore, a supply of consistent high-quality material was vital to Nucor, which needed to maintain its capability of producing upgraded steel sheet for demanding markets. The company's managers wanted to reduce its dependence on lower-grade commodity products that were sold primarily on the basis of price. This is a good example of a company's use of backward integration not only to improve its bargaining power with suppliers but also as a move toward repositioning itself in the market.

Horizontal Integration

Broadening the business base by entry into additional product and/or geographic markets usually has the objective of finding room for growth and opportunities to use the company's unique capabilities. The effectiveness of this strategy, which is called *horizontal integration*, therefore depends on the fit of the new businesses with the established ones. Nike's acquisition of Canstar is an instance of horizontal integration which appears to be a good fit. It provides Nike with access to new markets in which its skills in marketing athletic footwear can be applied. Other examples of effective horizontal integration are Gillette's acquisition of Braun, a manufacturer of electric shavers and small appliances, and Black and Decker's purchase of GE's small household appliance operations.

Entry into Substitute Businesses

A company facing a serious threat of substitution may elect to enter the substitute business. Metal wire producers, for example, have entered the fiber optics business. This may be an effective strategy if the new business can be effectively integrated into the parent business, perhaps by using the parent company's sales force and channels of distribution for the substitute product. Otherwise, the company is entering a new, strange business in which it has no experience, and it may even be unfamiliar with the substitute technology.

Constraints on Competitive Advantage Strategies

Companies often publicize their strategic intentions, and the investor's job then is to try to predict the effectiveness of the companies' intended actions. The most common overall constraint on strategic action is the bargaining power of suppliers and buyers. In the airlines industry, for instance, as shown in earlier chapters, the continuing power of unions and the increasing power of customers has squeezed the industry and limited the scope of management action. There are three other conditions that often limit the effectiveness of a strategy: balanced competitive situations, lack of resources, and corporate cultural obstacles.

Balanced Competition

In industries with high fixed costs and without obvious differentiation of the product or service, balanced competitive situations are common. Some of the competitors pursue market share to utilize capacity by cutting prices. Others are forced to follow, and the ending is a stalemate in which nobody wins. Common examples are gasoline price wars and factory rebates in the automobile industry. Another example occurred during the 1980s, when Kraft General Foods Division of Philip Morris and The Procter and Gamble Company waged a relentless battle for market share through their Maxwell House and Folger brands of coffee. Their weapons were heavy advertising, price cutting, and coupons. The result was that coffee made no significant contribution to the profits of either company, as the competitive advantage being sought by one company could be easily and quickly imitated by the other. In contrast, Nestle's with its Hills Brothers, Nescafe, and Taster's Choice brands focused on differentiating its products and maintaining prices. While Nestle gave up market share, its businesses remained profitable.[9]

The lesson here is the folly of the belief held by many managers (though fortunately their numbers are diminishing) that size gained by high market share is in itself a basis for profitability. Only when a company can use size to derive and sustain a decisive competitive advantage—say, when it can lower costs in a manner that competitors cannot imitate—does achieving a high market share lead to profitability.

Inadequate Resources

The resources of a company play a role in virtually all strategies that involve the pursuit of competitive advantage. A company may lack the resources to pursue a strategy or even to respond effectively to competitors' initiatives. This applies particularly to industries in which intellectual capital is the key determinant of success, because such resources are the most difficult to acquire quickly. Weak financial positions also make a company vulnerable to aggressive initiatives by competitors, such as price cutting. Companies that deplete their cash or use up their borrowing power in unproductive action, such as leveraged buyouts (LBOs), can become highly vulnerable.

Cultural Constraints

The *culture* of a corporation can be defined as its "personality," or simply as "what we do around here and the way we do it." If the strategic initiatives of senior management are not compatible with the corporate culture, the organization may refuse to work actively to implement those initiatives. In the extreme, the organization may even sabotage the strategy.

In 1985 the CEO of Aluminum Company of America (Alcoa), Charles Parry, announced a new strategy which would take the company into new materials, such as composites, with the objective of deriving 50 percent of sales from these new businesses by 1995. This constituted a strategy of entering into substitute industries, and it had an inherent logic, in that new technologies could be seen as posing a long-term threat to aluminum markets. Implementation of the strategy involved closing down aluminum operations that were only marginally profitable. However, the corporation's culture was based upon a long-term effort to substitute aluminum for other metals. The managers saw the new strategy as a betrayal of the company mission and as causing the loss of their compatriots' jobs. They refused to cooperate and the strategy faltered. The defeat of the strategy was signaled when the new CEO, Paul H. O'Neill, stated in the 1988 annual report that the company was returning to its core business, aluminum.[10]

In monitoring strategy, the investor must be concerned not only with the actions of one company but also with the initiatives of its competitors. An adverse initiative by a competitor can encroach on a company's competitive advantage—for example, by invading its protected market segment. Other adverse initiatives would be competitors' moves to enhance their own capability, as signaled by new product introductions, increases in advertising, and investment in new plants. Favorable initiatives by competitors, on the other hand, can make the structure of an industry more attractive. Examples would be withdrawal from certain markets and rationalization of the industry, perhaps by acquiring another competitor and thus reducing industry overcapacity.

COMPETITIVE ADVANTAGE IN FIVE SAMPLE INDUSTRIES

In order to make informed decisions, investors need to know why, under similar situations in their respective industries, some companies outperform others. They also need to be able to identify the basis of a successful company's competitive advantage and to judge whether it is sustainable. In previous chapters, five industries—pharmaceuticals, tobacco, drug and discount retailing, recreational products manufacturing, and airlines—were used to show the effects of the various forces that determine the overall profitability of an industry. Here, both overall industry performance and the performance of a leading, a median, and a weak performer in the same five industries will be analyzed. (As before, two leading performers are analyzed for the tobacco industry.) In these analyses, references to 12-month performance are for 1994, as shown in Exhibit 5–1.

Pharmaceuticals Industry

In Chapters 3 and 4 it was established why the pharmaceuticals industry, with its 22.8 percent average of five-year average median ROEs, has been the leading performer of all industries. The barriers to entry are high, the threat of substitution is still relatively low, and bargaining power with both customers and suppliers is high. Further, while the industry is mature, advances in the science are bringing new products to a receptive market which has prospects for cyclical long-term growth due to the aging of the population.

In total, this industry remains a very attractive operating environment, despite some deterioration in recent years. Changes in the industry have resulted in a number of strategic initiatives, including the following:

- Mergers have created larger companies which are able to afford the high research expenditures necessary for success in the industry as when Roche Holding Ltd. bought Syntex Corp. in 1994. A part of this rationalization of the industry has also been motivated by companies selling off peripheral drug operations and returning to their core businesses, as when Eastman Kodak sold off its Sterling Winthrop subsidiary.
- The acquisition by drug makers of biotechnology companies has been accelerated, as drug companies attempt to establish a position in this substitute industry.
- Drug companies have also begun to integrate forward by acquiring distributors, thus rapidly increasing their bargaining power.

Within this attractive industry, the performance of individual companies varies widely. Merck, with a five-year average ROE of 49.0 percent, is among the leaders. Eli Lilly is slightly below the industry average median at 19.6 percent, and Pfizer is the weakest of the three at 16.5 percent. (Pfizer is not the weakest company listed for the industry, but the weaker performers are primarily engaged in distribution or in generic drug production, and thus do not directly compete with our sample companies in terms of activities and product lines.)

The differences in performance of these three companies can be explained in terms of their respective competitive advantages.

Merck[11]   On the strength of Merck's research effort, the company's ROE performance has been moving steadily up in its industry. Merck spends over $1.25 billion per year on its research program; its size allows it to mount this research program at a cost of about 12 percent of sales, whereas Eli Lilly would have to spend 20 percent of sales to match it. Merck's research effort has produced a broad line of highly popular, proprietary, patented prescription medications. The main market position of the company is therefore in unique and value-differentiated market segments, but it also markets other health care products. Though it is the largest company in the industry, its share of the worldwide market is only 5 percent. Merck's success in new product introductions has faltered in recent years, and the company faces severe competition from the continuous introduction of competing products by rivals. However, its research effort can reasonably be expected to provide a continuing stream of new products.

In 1993, Merck made a major strategic move, spending $6 billion to acquire Medco Containment Services, a fast-growing mail-order company with annual drug sales of more than \$2 billion. Medco contracts with big medical plan sponsors such as companies, unions, and health maintenance organizations (HMOs) to lower the cost of prescription drugs to their patients. Its customers account for 26 percent of all Americans covered by drug benefit plans. It not only has immense bargaining power with its suppliers but also monitors orders and recommends cheaper drugs to doctors.

The acquisition has four potential benefits to Merck, as follows:

1. Acquisition of Medco gives the company representation in a fast-growing field. Merck estimates that the number of Americans who are enrolled in managed health care plans will increase to 90 percent in 10 years, from 50 percent in 1994.

2. The acquisition can cut marketing and administration costs, which now account for 30 percent of sales, by providing a database on what drugs specific doctors use. With better information on the 635,000 doctors in the United States, Merck will be able to focus its sales effort. Medco also has a huge mail-order business, with access to 90 percent of U.S. pharmacies.

3. Medco's computerized patient record system will provide a database that Merck's research program can use to verify the effectiveness of its products, so as to be able to better justify the company's premium prices.

4. Medco will provide Merck with a channel of distribution for its products when the patents expire, heading off some of the competition from generic drug manufacturers. Many proprietary drug manufacturers have begun releasing copies of their patented drugs at low prices several months before the patents expire, to establish market position before competitors' copies become available. It has been shown that the generics that are released first can gain and hold up to 90 percent of market share.[12] Medco is the vehicle Merck needs to establish its own generic products in the market before copies can become available.

Like all bold strategies, this one has its risks. Merck and Medco have very different cultures, which may clash when the bias in favor of Merck products is imposed. Potentially more serious is the perception among its customers that Medco will not be totally impartial in protecting customers' interests by getting the lowest possible prices. Despite these risks, the Merck action does move toward countering an increasing threat to the profitability of the industry and may enable Merck to offset lower profit margins by the higher volume available through Medco. Not only is the gamble Merck took in acquiring Medco reasonable, but also it may be regarded as necessary.

Merck's competitors have also acquired distributors. However, Merck has acquired the best of them and is likely to maintain its competitive advantage. The attractiveness of the industry, however, may continue to deteriorate.

Eli Lilly   A smaller version of Merck, Eli Lilly has a narrower product line in pharmaceuticals. Between 1989 and 1994, products accounting for 44 percent of Eli Lilly's 1989 U.S. ethical drug sales came off patent, versus 20 percent for Merck. As a result, the company's profit margin is below Merck's. It too has been aggressive in integrating forward by acquiring McKesson's PCS Health Systems for $4 billion, and it has increased R&D spending to 15 percent of sales. It has also moved to spin off minority interests in five of its nine medical device and diagnostic products divisions. In an increasingly difficult industry environment, these actions may be enough to enable Eli Lilly to maintain its position, but they do not appear to provide basis for much improvement.

Pfizer   Though it is the same size as Eli Lilly, Pfizer has a smaller proportion of sales in high-margin prescription drugs, resulting in lower over-profit margins. Between 1989 and 1994, the patents expired on products accounting for 78 percent of the company's U.S. ethical drug sales. It had not moved toward forward integration as of mid-1994 but had increased R&D spending to a level approaching Merck's. Pfizer's remaining portfolio of patented drugs is relatively youthful and not vulnerable to early patent expiry. The company has several promising new products in the pipeline. It has announced a strategy of pursuing forward integration through contractual arrangements and strategic alliances rather than through acquisitions, and focusing on R&D and manufacturing.

Pfizer's strategy of remaining highly focused has considerable logic behind it, as it does concentrate the company's limited resources on one of the key elements of success in the industry. However, the success of the strategy will depend on the effectiveness of the R&D effort.

The Stock Market's Judgment

The stock market performance of our sample pharmaceuticals companies is shown in Exhibit 5–2. As discussed in Chapter 4, the attractive characteristics of the industry caused it to outperform the market as a whole by

Comparative Performance of Selected Companies in the
Pharmaceuticals Industry, 1984–94 (Indexed to S&P 500, 1984=160)

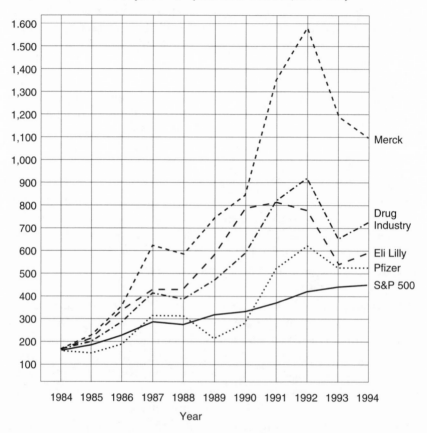

Year

Note: The index for each year is shown at the mean between the high and the low for the period.

a substantial margin in the period 1984–94, despite the dip in 1993 as a result of the market's concern over the deterioration of the industry's fundamentals. In keeping with the economic adage that a rising tide lifts all boats, all our sample companies did well. However, Merck outperformed the other samples, with an average annual appreciation of 21.3 percent versus 14.1 percent for Eli Lilly and 13.0 percent for Pfizer. However, this understates Merck's performance relative to its competitors; in 1994, it was valued at a P/E ratio of only 19 versus the industry ratio of 22 and the Eli Lilly and Pfizer ratios of 31. Thus the Merck price has less in the way of future expectations built into it than the other two.

Thus the historical stock market performance has reflected the relative ROE performance of these companies. The question whether any of them are candidates for long-term investment is taken up in Chapter 7.

Tobacco Industry

The tobacco industry has shown a relatively high five-year average median ROE of 18.4 percent. This is consistent with its relative attractiveness. Barriers to entry are high, the bargaining power of addicted customers is low, and there is little threat of substitution. The industry in North America is in the decline phase, but brand preferences remain relatively strong. In an indication of the deterioration of this industry's fundamentals, its ROE performance for the latest 12 months dropped to 2.6 percent.

Among the major companies, Phillip Morris is the leader, with an ROE of 34.4 percent, American Brands is close to the industry median at 19.5 percent, and RJR Nabisco is among the lowest at 0.6 percent. These companies are relatively similar in that they remain dependent on tobacco for a major portion of sales and earnings but have diversified into other businesses. The overall industry leader is a relatively small company, UST Inc., which has a five-year average ROE of 58.8 percent. This company provides an example of the earnings capability of a company that dominates a unique product market position.

UST Inc. Because of its unique product, UST Inc. has been in a sheltered market situation. Typically, such segments are relatively small, and this one is no exception. The company has annual sales revenues of only $1.2 billion, as compared to Philip Morris's estimated tobacco sales of $30 billion. About 86 percent of UST's sales are in smokeless (chewing) tobacco, a business which it dominates with its Copenhagen and Skoal brands. As Exhibit 5–1 shows, the company earned an exceptional 32.4 percent profit margin in the latest 12 months. Its market has been sheltered because resistance to conventional tobacco has focused on the effects of smoke and because of chewing tobacco's popularity with baseball players. Recently, however, the adverse health effects of chewing tobacco have been publicized, and major league baseball officials appear to be discouraging its use. UST's dominance in this market has discouraged entry by others.

This company's competitive strength can be regarded as decisive because of the dominance of its brands, but the company is vulnerable to the weakening of the segment of the industry upon which it is almost totally dependent.

Philip Morris[13] Tobacco provides about 70 percent of Philip Morris's operating earnings, with the Kraft General Foods Division making up the balance. The company's competitive advantage lies in the strength of its tobacco brands, particularly Marlboro, which rivals Coca-Cola in global recognition, through the image of the Marlboro man. The company holds a 42.3 percent share of the overall domestic market, but a 48.6 percent share of value-differentiated premium brands. Philip Morris, on the basis of its financial strength, undertook a bold strategy for maintaining its leadership in the premium cigarette market. It initiated the price cutting that took place in 1993 and was the main winner in the recovery of market share from discount brands. Its managers have shown a trait generally uncommon among American managers, a willingness to sacrifice short-term earnings for the sake of the long term. As a result, the company was able to increase sales and earnings in 1993, although these figures remained well below its historical rates.

The food processing industry in which the company is represented is also a relatively attractive one, with a five-year industry average median ROE of 17.0 percent. Kraft is probably a leading performer in this industry because of its economies of scale and because of the efficiency involved in marketing a broad range of products under one brand name.

The decline in domestic cigarette sales and relatively slow growth in foods will likely be offset by Philip Morris's ability to exploit its cigarette brand recognition in offshore markets, which remain strong and continue to grow at double-digit rates.

American Brands About 54 percent of American Brands' sales but only 50 percent of its operating profits have been derived from tobacco. The balance of the company's business has been a mixture of liquor, insurance, home improvement retailing, and miscellaneous operations. Its main cigarette brands, Carlton, Pall Mall, and Lucky Strike, have not been industry leaders. American Brands has held 6.8 percent of the total tobacco market but only 5.3 percent of the premium market, indicating that it has been much more dependent on low-margin discount products than Philip Morris has. American Brands is strong in the United Kingdom (UK), but this market is now facing the same health-related constraints that are affecting the U.S. market. Both the company's sales and its earnings declined in the latest 12 months shown in Exhibit 5–1. Its competitive advantage in tobacco has been at best only marginal.

American Brands has recently divested its tobacco business. This withdrawal is typical of the decline phase. In this industry, marginal performers are withdrawing in a relatively orderly way, which is consistent with the characteristics of the industry. The company's withdrawal can be considered a sound strategic move, in light of its relatively weak position in the industry.

RJR Nabisco RJR Nabisco can boast of a number of popular cigarette brands (Camel, Winston, Salem). It has a 28.8 percent share of the total tobacco market and a 27.0 share of the premium market, as well as a profitable food business. Nevertheless, this company's performance has been lagging. A part of the reason is statistical: its average ROE (Exhibit 5–1) is calculated on only a four-year period, which causes the latest down year to weigh more heavily on the average. Even taking this into account, the company underperformed the others in our sample in the latest 12 months shown in Exhibit 5–1.

Another part of the reason for the company's poor performance is its high debt load, the result of its LBO by Kohlberg Kravis Roberts (KKR) in 1989. Payment of interest consumes 9 cents of the company's sales dollar. The company has therefore had to be managed for cash flow, a major constraint on the aggressive pursuit of markets. While RJR Nabisco was forced to respond to the 1993 Philip Morris price-cutting initiative, its lack of resources meant that its response was reluctant and minimal. Philip Morris, through its aggressive action, gained 4 percent in market share; half of this gain came from other premium brands, and the financially weak RJR Nabisco was the main loser.

The company's food-processing operations contribute 43 percent of sales and include a large number of popular brands (notably Oreo and Ritz). However, the operations are fragmented into a wide range of independent products, each of which requires its own advertising support. Thus its food products do not benefit from the sort of family association that is enjoyed by Kraft products. RJR Nabisco can be regarded as having only moderate competitive strength. Its room for growth is provided primarily by the offshore tobacco market, where its brand recognition is strong.

The Stock Market's Judgment

Exhibit 5–3 shows the stock market performance of our sample tobacco companies relative to the industry index and the market as a whole. As indicated earlier, the industry index overstates the performance of the industry as a whole by a substantial margin because it covers only three companies and because it includes Philip Morris and UST Inc., both of which have been exceptional performers. The industry index therefore tracks these two companies closely.

Comparative Performance of Selected Companies in the
Tobacco Industry, 1984–94 (Indexed to S&P 500, 1984=160)

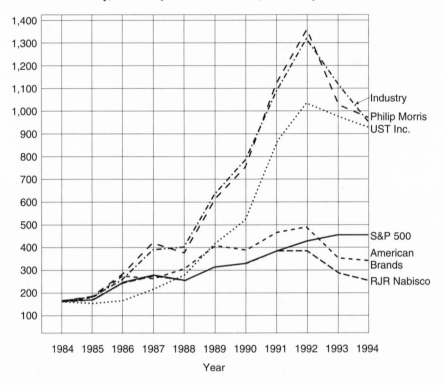

Note: The index for each year is shown at the mean between the high and the low for the period.

The 1993 Philip Morris price discounting and its implications for the value of brands took the stock market by surprise, and were the main cause of the decline in 1993. However, it should not have been a surprise, as the data on the growth of generic cigarettes were readily available. The UST stock price performance is relatively typical of the advantages of operating in a sheltered market segment. All segments of the industry appear to have been affected by the potential costs of health-related lawsuits in 1994.

Here we see the industry leaders outperforming the S&P 500 by a significant margin, but the industry median and weaker companies have been falling below it since 1993.

Drug and Discount Retailing Industry

This large industry has 31 companies of the size necessary to qualify for the *Forbes* listing. The industry has high barriers to entry but faces strong competition from alternative categories of retailing. It has relatively little bargaining power with customers, and its influence with suppliers varies from company to company, depending on size. This is a mature industry with relatively slow market growth, so that the battle for market share creates intense competition. The industry median ROE of 12.8 percent reflects these variables, which make it only moderately attractive.

Wal-Mart, the largest company in the industry, is the leading performer with a five-year average ROE of 29.2 percent. Kmart, the second largest company, is below the industry median at 5.0 percent and Woolworth is the lagging performer, with a deficit return on the five-year average ROE.

Wal-Mart[14] Started in 1954, this company has achieved exceptional growth, passing its direct competitor, Kmart, in 1990 to become the largest retailer in the United States. In 1994, its sales exceeded $78 billion, as compared to Kmart's $36 billion. Both retail a wide range of national brands and private brands. The bases of Wal-Mart's growth and superior profitability are as follows:

- The company maintains a low price policy to attract a high volume of sales. Its reputation for offering the lowest prices is such that most people probably go to Wal-Mart first, despite the surveys that have shown its prices to be only average for the industry.
- Its volume allows it to demand maximum discounts directly from manufacturers and to bypass distributors for 77 percent of its purchases.
- Sales and inventory are monitored continuously via satellite, from store to warehouse to supplier. This practice minimizes inventory levels without risking stock-outs.
- Deliveries are taken to automated warehouses which are capable of handling high volumes at low cost and can also quickly route goods to stores.
- Stores are grouped within a one-day trucking radius of the warehouses, to speed deliveries and reduce costs. Wal-Mart's distribution costs are about 3 percent of sales, about one-half what its competitors pay. The grouping of stores also allows effective use of media advertising. Thus advertising costs are kept at 0.6 percent of sales, as compared to between 2 and 3 percent for competitors.

- The company's highly motivated work force participate in a profit-sharing plan in which company proceeds are invested in Wal-Mart stock, making the employees shareholders. This is the basis for a very high level of friendly in-store service.
- Wal-Mart has found room for growth in a crowded industry by locating its stores in small outlying towns with low costs, heading off business that would otherwise go to its main competitors in higher-cost major urban locations.
- The company has been quick to broaden its base and adopt new merchandising developments, such as warehousing clubs and superstores that sell a combination of groceries and hard goods.

Wal-Mart's costs are about 6 percent below its competitors' costs, giving the company an immense and decisive competitive advantage. While some companies better Wal-Mart's net profit margin of 3.2 percent of sales, these are much smaller and more specialized operations. Wal-Mart's high level of service is a major factor in drawing customers. As mentioned above, its prices are only average for the industry. Thus, most of its lower costs flow to the bottom line. It can be argued that Wal-Mart's market position is not based on the "same-for-lower-price" image it cultivates but really on a policy of "more (service) for the same price."

Wal-Mart exploits three sources of competitive advantage: its size, which allows it to exert buying power over suppliers; its physical structure and operating practices, which keep its costs low; and its high level of service, which gives it some bargaining power with customers. As a whole, the company's competitive advantage can be considered decisive.

The sustainability of Wal-Mart's competitive advantage and growth rate rests on three questions.

1. Can Wal-Mart retain its internal cost advantage?
2. Does it have room for further growth?
3. Can it effectively control a much larger business?

The answer to each question appears to be yes. Wal-Mart's internal efficiency, which is based on both facilities and operating procedures, has had the advantage of having been built from scratch. The cost for any established competitor of imitating Wal-Mart's sources of internal efficiency would be quite high. New entrants would be foolish to challenge this company's reputation and head start. Wal-Mart's ability to grow in domestic U.S. markets will be running into limits, but it has plenty of geographic room for growth, including Canada, where it acquired the Canadian discount operations of Woolworth Corporation in 1993. Its expansions are not likely, however, to be as profitable as its domestic operations for some time, as they will initially lack the efficient infrastructure. The company's control system, based on distribution centers and groups of stores, has a balance of centralization and decentralization which can accommodate growth without becoming bureaucratic.

Kmart[15]   While Kmart can match Wal-Mart's buying power with suppliers, it has not matched its rival's internal efficiency. A much older company, Kmart is saddled with smaller, urban stores that are not grouped to minimize costs. Its strategy has been to move into specialty stores in an attempt to offset its higher costs with higher margins, but this strategy has not been pursued consistently or effectively. In the discount segment, the company has reverted to price competition. Its prices are often lower than Wal-Mart's in order to compensate for its inferior service, and the lower prices show up in the company's negative profit margins.

In 1993, Kmart embarked on a $3.5 billion "renewal" program, involving the modernization, expansion, and relocation of old stores, and the building of new discount stores from scratch. However, the implementation of the program has lagged. The most difficult aspect of the renewal is an attempt to duplicate Wal-Mart's service culture among employees, and this effort appears to be going nowhere, due to a lack of suitable leadership. Kmart's competitive advantage rests upon its bargaining power with suppliers and its many well-located stores. Taken together, these factors do not create a strong or decisive competitive advantage, which accounts for the company's relatively weak competitive performance. Its ability to challenge Wal-Mart's profitability and growth is questionable. Even if it did offer a challenge, Wal-Mart has room to sacrifice margins and cut prices.

Kmart's competitive advantage is thus only marginal, being derived primarily from its size. It will have to struggle to make gains in a competitive industry. Its ROE performance has hovered around the industry median for a decade, and little in the current plan appears to significantly improve the company's prospects. In August 1994, Kmart announced a plan to spin off majority interests in three of its specialty retailers, so as to raise funds that can be plowed back into its discount stores. It is thus indicating an intention to go head-to-head with Wal-Mart. At best, Kmart is facing a tough fight.

Woolworth   Although Woolworth is only one-sixth the size of Wal-Mart, it is the fourth largest company in the industry. Like Kmart, it operates a mix of discount and specialty stores. It also has sizable foreign operations. However, its stores are small and urban, which creates high supply costs. This structural disadvantage appears to be the main reason its average ROE performance has been consistently below the industry median for the past decade. The company has been quicker than Kmart to prune its losing and marginal operations, which accounts for its loss in the latest 12 months shown in Exhibit 5–1. Woolworth has relatively little competitive advantage in a highly competitive industry.

The Stock Market's Judgment

Exhibit 5–4 compares the stock market performance of our sample drug and discount retailing companies to the broad market and the industry index. Not surprisingly, Wal-Mart has been the strongest performer, due to its decisive competitive advantage. Woolworth stock held up well until 1993, when the depth of its problems started to become apparent. Its earlier good showing in the S&P 500 is somewhat surprising, because its ROE was been consistently below Kmart's, which consistently underperformed the S&P 500. The likely explanation is that Kmart's difficulties were widely publicized, whereas Woolworth's losses were due to restructuring costs. The market probably assumed that Woolworth would return to profitability soon. The market also appears to be skeptical about whether Kmart will be able to implement its reform program effectively.

Recreational Products Manufacturing Industry

The recreational products manufacturing industry includes the manufacturers of a wide variety of products, ranging from motorcycles to mobile homes to outboard motors. Unlike the other companies described in this book the companies in this industry are not direct competitors. They compete only for the discretionary sales dollar. These companies have been chosen because they illustrate the characteristics of various types of companies in cyclical industries.

Barriers to entry in this industry are generally high. Brand acceptance is necessary to achieve significant size, and substitutes are many. Since the products are discretionary purchases, the market is highly cyclical; thus, bargaining power with customers varies. Further, as is typical of high-volume manufacturing, the businesses have high fixed costs, causing volatility of earnings in the cyclical market.

Comparative Performance of Selected Companies in the Drug and
Discount Retailing Industry, 1984–94 (Indexed to S&P 500, 1984=160)

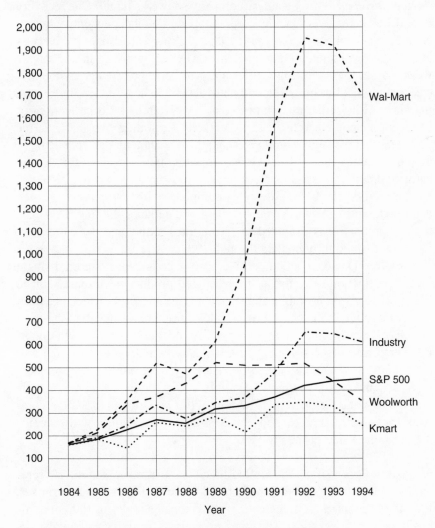

Note: The index for each year is shown at the mean between the high and the low for the period.

The industry average median ROE of 7.7 percent (shown in Exhibit
5–1) reflects the cyclicality, as it includes the recession years 1991–93.
Despite the cyclical influence, Harley-Davidson had an average ROE of
16.7 percent; Fleetwood Industries was somewhat above the industry

median at 11.3 percent and three companies, including Outboard Marine, had deficits.

Harley-Davidson This legendary company showed a remarkable recovery after it was taken over from its corporate parent by independent, entrepreneurial management in the early 1980s. Harley-Davidson's recovery is even more remarkable in that much of it was accomplished in a relatively weak market for cyclical industries and with a single product, a motorcycle of antiquated design. The company accomplished this feat by resolving many of its earlier quality problems, by obtaining tariff protection for heavy-weight motorcycles, and by cleverly exploiting two markets: the police market for large motorcycles and the nostalgia market consisting of aging, affluent males.[16] The average nostalgia buyer is 40 years old and earns $50,000 per year. For these buyers, the company has marketed not just a motorcycle but a lifestyle, complete with company-sponsored Harley-Davidson Owners Groups, rallies, and a line of clothing. This marketing approach was extended to Japan and Europe, and the company's factory remained fully booked through 1994 as a result.

Harley-Davidson's competitive advantage is dependent on a single factor, production of a highly differentiated product for a market niche based primarily on nostalgia and lifestyle. This approach, which has been highly effective in the short term, creates a trap and makes the long-term sustainability of the company's competitive advantage and growth doubtful. The product is to some extent a fad, and the market is finite and will eventually be saturated. Given the relatively long product life, replacement demand will take time to develop; and given the aging of the market, it may not develop at all. The trap in this situation is that if the company tries to stimulate sales by modernizing the design, it will sacrifice the nostalgia value of the product.

Fleetwood Enterprises The United States' largest manufacturer of recreational vehicles (RVs) and manufactured homes is Fleetwood Enterprises. RV sales accounted for 58 percent of the company's sales in 1993, but this business is highly cyclical. The company follows up all RV sales with calls to buyers, asking for suggestions and criticisms. This approach creates repeat buyers and word-of-mouth referrals in a close-knit market which meets in clubs and camps. However, brand preference in RVs is difficult to establish to any decisive degree, and the occasional use of the product gives it a long service life and a relatively low replacement rate.

Fleetwood's manufactured homes, which are built in 30 plants around the country, accounted for about 40 percent of the company's sales and gave it a 20 percent share of the U.S. manufactured home market in 1993.[17] The units are sold unbranded through independent distributors. The company's competitive advantage is based on low transportation costs, due to its many plants, plus the bargaining power that its size gives it with suppliers of materials and appliances. The product's low cost is a significant advantage in a price-sensitive, cyclical market, but is difficult to exploit fully. The purchase decision is not necessarily made by the person who will occupy the home; more often, it is made by the land developer who prepares the site. Developers often try to increase their profit opportunities by undertaking construction. In addition, small home building is a relatively common skill, and Fleetwood faces competition from a large number of small builders whose low overhead offsets much of their size disadvantage.

The company is showing an appropriate sense of priorities by pursuing competitive advantage through attempts to establish bargaining power both with its RV buyers and with its suppliers of materials for the price-sensitive manufactured home market. Its brand acceptance in RVs and its economies of scale in housing are not decisive but should be sustainable.

Outboard Marine Corp. A major producer of outboard motors, Outboard Marine Corp. (OMC) illustrates some of the worst characteristics of cyclical industries. Sales of outboard-motors, a big-ticket discretionary purchase, fluctuate greatly with consumer confidence, but since these are sophisticated products requiring expensive product development and automated manufacture, fixed costs are high. Therefore, earnings are volatile. Outboard Marine's problems have been compounded by its having let costs get out of line and by a loss of market share to Japanese entrants.

The company's competitive advantage is based primarily on its well-established brand names (Johnson and Evinrude) and on a strong dealer network, but both a sharp improvement in efficiency and a stronger market for discretionary purchases are needed before the company will be able to exploit its competitive advantage.

The Stock Market's Judgment

Exhibit 5–5 shows the stock market performance of our sample recreational products manufacturing companies. The industry index shows cyclicality, with a decline in 1990 and a recovery starting in 1992. The industry underperformed the broad market during this period.

Harley-Davidson's strong performance is not surprising, in that the company has successfully bucked the industry cycle because of its unique appeal. Harley-Davidson demonstrates a potential for operating in a

E X H I B I T   5–5

Comparative Performance of Selected Companies in the
Recreational Products Manufacturing Industry, 1984–94
(Indexed to S&P 500, 1984=160)

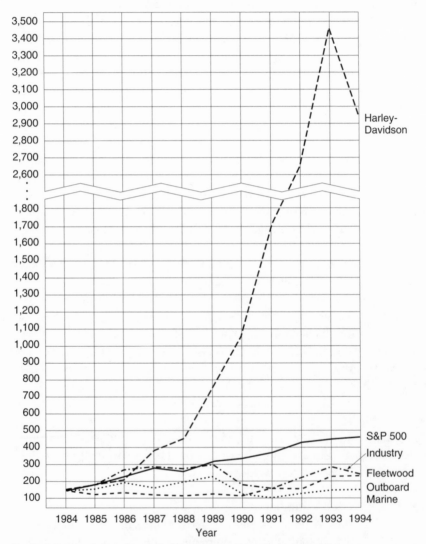

Note: The index for each year is shown at the mean between the high and the low for the period.

unique product segment, similar to UST's position in the tobacco industry. At year end 1994 Harley-Davidson carried a P/E ratio of 50, indicating continued high earnings growth expectations.

Fleetwood shows some degree of cyclicality but lacks glamour. The price of OMC reflects its potential for recovery, but the company's dismal 10-year performance is consistent with the depth of its problems.

One of the characteristics of this industry is that it is populated by relatively specialized companies. These companies can have periods of spectacular results from hot new products, such as oversized golf clubs, but such results tend to fade when the market becomes saturated and imitation develops.

Airlines Industry

The analysis of industry structure in Chapter 3 showed the airlines industry to be very unattractive, squeezed as it is between the high bargaining power of both suppliers and customers and the threat of new entrants. In addition, a high fixed cost structure makes the industry sensitive to overcapacity and cyclical declines in travel. Furthermore, the industry may be in the midst of a discontinuity in the maturity phase of its product life cycle, in the form of a downside shift in the important business market. Barriers to exit, particularly the creative use of bankruptcy laws, have perpetuated overcapacity. The strategic initiatives of various companies, such as offering frequent flier points and a range of seating classes, have been quickly imitated by others, resulting in a competitive stalemate. The plight of the industry as a whole, with its deficit five-year average ROE, is therefore not surprising.

Despite these adverse circumstances, Southwest Airlines has shown a 12.0 percent average ROE. Although this return would be regarded as marginal in most other industries, it is remarkable in the airlines industry.

Southwest Airlines[18] Southwest's relative success has been based on its recognition that airline travel has become a price-sensitive commodity, particularly for short flights (under two hours). As a result, Southwest has restructured itself into a low-cost operation capable of offering the lowest fares. The basic elements of the company's structure are:

- It flies only short-haul routes on a point-to-point basis between large population centers which provide the volume necessary to keep the planes full. Unlike the hub-and-spoke carriers, Southwest does not have to wait for connecting flights. Its idle turnaround time on the ground averages only 20 minutes, versus more than an hour for its competitors.
- The company is able to fly from secondary, less congested airports because it does not rely on connecting business. It has thus avoided a barrier to expansion of its market.

- Southwest keeps costs low by offering only no-frills service. Reservations must be made directly with Southwest (there are no hookups with travel agent reservation systems), and there are no seat assignments and no meals. Travel agents having to call in reservations encourage the customers to call themselves, saving Southwest about $30 million annually.
- Pilots and flight crew are paid on a per-flight basis rather than receiving a flat salary, which gives them an incentive for rapid turnaround. Pilots are paid about $100,000 for 70 hours of flying per month, as compared to as much as $200,000 for 50 hours for the highest-paying carriers. However, average wages are only slightly below what some other carriers pay. The main savings result from the absence of restrictive work rules which would require the expensive duplication of staff and lead to idle staff time.
- The similarity of Southwest's routes allows it to fly only one type of aircraft, providing major savings in maintenance and training.

The overall effect of these structural elements is that Southwest's costs are only 7 cents per available seat-mile, as compared to 8.8 cents for American Airlines, 9.4 cents for United Airlines, and 11.4 cents for USAir. Southwest leverages this cost advantage by concentrating on short-haul flights, on which the number of landings and the length of turnarounds create the highest costs for its competitors.

Southwest occupies a less-value-for-lower-price market position, which is made possible by its low costs. However, it offsets some of its lack of frills with the friendliness of its employees. This has given it the high capacity utilization necessary to make a profit in a business with with a high fixed cost structure. However effective this strategy may be, it does have a limitation in terms of the size of the market to which it appeals. Southwest's annual revenue of $2.6 billion is relatively small in comparison to AMR's sales of $16 billion.

The sustainability of Southwest's competitive advantage depends on the industry's ability to imitate it. The picture is mixed, for at least two reasons. First, Continental is showing that the Southwest advantage can be duplicated, and its growth will likely head off some of Southwest's opportunities for geographic expansion. In March 1994 it started to imitate Southwest's operations in the East by offering low one-class fares between major eastern points, with no advance purchase requirement. With costs of 8 cents per available seat-mile, Continental is likely to succeed in this thrust. (In so doing, of course, it will accelerate the decline of other carriers.)

Second, other airlines will likely attempt to encroach on Southwest's high-density business. This threat comes from two directions. Among the full-service airlines, United has challenged Southwest, in Southwest's own geographic market. In addition, a flood of new entrants has been attracted by Southwest's success, as both cheap airplanes and flight crews are readily available. By early 1994, there had been six new start-ups, and more than a dozen further applications had been made to the U.S. Department of Transportation.

Thus, though Southwest may to some extent be squeezed, it may still have room for some growth in longer-range traffic, for which it will start to take deliveries of suitable planes in 1997. The issue of sustainability must also take into consideration possible changes in the industry and its operating environment, which are discussed in Chapter 6.

AMR Corporation   AMR is the parent company of American Airlines, which provides 82 percent of its revenue and is the cause of all of its losses. It also operates a reservations system, Sabre, which is profitable. As the largest U.S. carrier, it offers expensive full service on a hub-and-spoke system with connections but with many low-density routes. It faces fierce union resistance to demands for concessions on wages and work rules. While the company is relatively efficient, it is trapped by the industry's weak fundamentals, particularly the power of its highly unionized labor force. As it is the largest domestic carrier, its strikes cause major inconvenience to travelers. As a result, the Clinton administration sided with the unions in the American Airlines flight attendant's strike in 1993.

Given its relatively low costs, this company will likely lead the recovery when the industry structure improves. Its extensive route system puts it in a preferred position to create strategic alliances with foreign carriers. Like all major carriers, it faces an overhang of unused frequent flier miles, which currently account for about 7 percent of the scheduled carriers' revenue.

USAir   The heaviest loser in the industry, USAir has a high-cost, relatively short-haul, hub-and-spoke system, which operates mainly in the East in a low-fare environment. Both Southwest and Continental Airlines Holdings, Inc. have invaded its markets. Further, its reputation has suffered from a series of crashes. This company must quickly win major concessions from unions if it is to stay alive. Most likely, these concessions will come piecemeal and will be followed by Chapter 11 bankruptcy, which will only delay the company's inevitable acquisition or collapse.

The only bright spot is the full-service airline situation in the international sector, which remains regulated. Here the low costs of the U.S. carriers give them an advantage, though they cannot use its advantage fully to gain volume by reducing prices, because of the regulated fares. Further, the continued subsidization of foreign carriers ($3.4 billion to Air France from the French government in 1994) will perpetuate overcapacity.

The Stock Market's Judgment

The 1984–94 stock price performance of the airlines industry and our sample companies is shown in Exhibit 5–6.

Southwest, the only domestic company outperforming the broad market, does so by a substantial margin. Its recent earnings growth has made it the darling of analysts, but the 1994 year-end P/E ratio of 12.5 indicates only moderate expectations, perhaps as a result of the market's disenchantment with the industry as a whole. AMR, perhaps the strongest of the hub-and-spoke carriers, has held up relatively well in light of the difficulties of the industry. Its airline operating losses have been in part offset by earnings from its Sabre reservation system. Though the stock of

E X H I B I T   5–6

Comparative Performance of Selected Companies in the Airlines Industry, 1984–94 (Indexed to S&P 500, 1984=160)

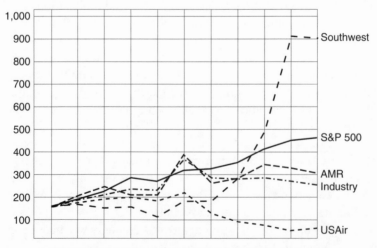

Note: The index for each year is shown at the mean between the high and the low for the period.

USAir, one of the highest-cost operators, reflects its performance, the market's expectations of company's future may still be optimistic.

IN CONCLUSION

My hypothesis to this point has been that the long-term performance of any company is based on a combination of the characteristics of the industry and the competitive strength of the company. Examination of selected companies in five sample industries confirms this hypothesis. However, we have seen that companies with strong or decisive competitive advantage have performed well despite the relative weakness of their industries, indicating that competitive strength is to a considerable extent the dominant factor in performance potential. For example, Wal-Mart, Harley-Davidson, and Southwest Airlines have performed well as to earnings and on the stock market, despite unfavorable industry circumstances. It may be that strong performance in weak industries attracts investors' interest, so that they tend to ignore the industry fundamentals that may constrain performance in the long term.

This possibility does not diminish the importance of industry characteristics. Investors must understand an industry before they can assess how change may affect it. As noted in Chapter 3, an industry's characteristics provide the playing field. To a considerable extent, they also determine the rules of the game. Thus, while Southwest has done well, its future is nevertheless affected by the nature of the airlines industry, as well as by the competitive responses which the industry condition evokes.

In this chapter, companies' performance in their respective industries has been assessed on the basis of conditions prevailing at the end of 1994. Long-term investment decisions also require judgments on how changes might affect the various industries and the performance of the companies within them. The nature and implications of change are discussed in Chapter 6.

POINTS TO REMEMBER

The key points of this chapter are as follows:

1. A company can consistently outperform its competitors by attracting a higher sales volume, being able to charge higher prices, and/or operating at lower costs. The ability to achieve one or more of these conditions is derived from competitive advantage. A company's competitive advantage in turn is based on its capability and on how

it uses that capability to position itself in its market. Advantageous positioning can be useful in enhancing the company's bargaining power with customers and with suppliers. The functions that the company performs in the value chain between its suppliers and customers may allow it to leverage its core competence.

2. Superior capability enables a company to operate at lower costs and/or to offer a better product or service than its competitors. Superior capability is derived from an effective combination of resources of various types: financial, human, physical, technological, organizational, and intangible.

3. The positions that enhance bargaining power with customers are offering a unique product or service, operating in a sheltered market, and providing a value- or price-differentiated product or service. Unique products and value-differentiated positions are based on the capabilities necessary to produce a superior product and/or the marketing skill necessary to create the perception of value. Price-differentiated positions are based on the capabilities that can provide low costs.

4. Capability and positioning advantages are combined when a company elects to use its capability to focus on a limited number of functions in which it can most effectively use its capability while at the same time optimizing its bargaining power between suppliers and buyers. Thus it occupies the part of the value chain where it can leverage its skills.

5. To achieve consistently superior performance, a company must have decisive competitive advantage. Outperforming competitors by a wide margin in the activities that are key to success in the industry is one way to attain decisive competitive advantage. Another is using two or more sources of competitive advantage in such a way that they reinforce one another. Decisive competitive advantage can help to insulate a company against cutthroat competition.

6. A company's ability to sustain competitive advantage is important to the long-term investor. Sustainability requires that competitors not be able to imitate the action of the company. Management must give continued attention to the factors responsible for the company's success, and must nurture and enhance them. Sustainability also requires room for growth, which can be provided by market growth due to the product life cycle, by continuing gains in market

share, through the creation of markets by introducing new products, and/or by entry into new geographic or global markets.

7. A company can enhance its competitive advantage by taking strategic action to increase its bargaining power with buyers and suppliers, by entering substitute industries, by rationalizing to reduce costs, or by disaggregating to focus activity on the most profitable functions. Constraints on effective strategic action include balanced competitive situations, a lack of resources, and rigidities in well-established corporate cultures.

8. The five-year average ROE performance of our sample companies is reflected in their stock market performance. Companies with a strong competitive advantage have been shown to outperform their competitors by substantial margins. While this indicates that competitive advantage is the most important factor in the longer-term performance of a company, it does not diminish the importance of industry structure as a factor in potential performance. In the pharmaceuticals industry, for instance, all three of our sample companies have outperformed the S&P 500.

NOTES

1. The explanation of the basis of competitive advantage used here is adapted from the work of Michael E. Porter, although he defined these factors as cost leadership, differentiation, and focus in Michael E. Porter, *Competitive Advantage: Creating and Sustaining Superior Performance* (New York: The Free Press, 1985), pp. 11–16.

2. Ronald H. Coase, "The Nature of the Firm," *Econometrica NS*, 1937, pp. 386–405.

3. Richard J. Barnet and John Cavanagh, *Global Dreams: Imperial Corporations and the New World Order* (New York: Simon & Schuster, 1994).

4. Toni Mack, "Michael Dell's New Religion," *Forbes*, June 6, 1994, pp. 45–46.

5. Rita Koselka, "It's My Favorite Statistic," *Forbes*, September 12, 1994, pp. 162–76.

6. Gary McWilliams, "Larry, We Hardly Knew Ye," *Business Week*, December 27, 1993, p. 40.

7. Marcia Mallory, "Behemoth on a Tear," *Business Week*, October 2, 1994, pp. 54–55; Patricia Sellers, "Pepsi Opens a Second Front," *Fortune*, August 8, 1994, pp. 70–76; John Huey, "The World's Best Brand," *Fortune*, May 31, 1993, pp. 44–54.

8. Andrew E. Serwer, "McDonald's Conquers the World," *Fortune*, October 17, 1994, pp. 103–16.

9. Bill Saporito, "Can Anyone Win the Coffee War?" *Fortune*, May 21, 1990, pp. 97–100.

10. Michael Schroader, "The Quiet Coup at Alcoa," *Business Week*, June 27, 1988, pp. 58–65.

11. Analysis and opinion on Merck and other companies in the pharmaceuticals industry are based in part on Brian O'Reilly, "Why Merck Married the Enemy," *Fortune*, September 30, 1993, pp. 60–64; Joseph Webster and Rochelle Shoretz, "Is This Rx Too Costly for Merck?" *Business Week*, August 9, 1993, p. 28.

12. Catherine Yang, "The Drugmakers vs. the Trustbusters," *Business Week*, September 5, 1994, p. 67.

13. Analysis and opinion on Philip Morris and other aspects of the tobacco industry are based in part on Subrata N. Chakravarty with Amy Feldman, "Don't Underestimate the Champ," *Forbes*, May 10, 1993, pp. 106–10.

14. Analysis and opinion on Wal-Mart and other aspects of the drug and discount retailing industry are based in part on John Huey, "Wal-Mart: Will It Take Over the World?" *Fortune*, January 30, 1989, pp. 52–64; Bill Saporito, "Is Wal-Mart Unstoppable?" *Fortune*, May 6, 1991, pp. 50–59; and Bill Saporito, "And the Winner Is Still . . . Wal-Mart," *Fortune*, May 2, 1994, pp. 62–70.

15. Analysis of Kmart is based in part on David Woodruff, Christopher Power, and Wendy Zellner, "Attention Kmart . . . Hey, Where Is Everybody?" *Business Week*, January 18, 1993, p. 38; Bill Saporito, "The High Cost of Being Second Best," Fortune, July 26, 1993, pp. 99–102; Subrata N. Chakravarty, "The Best Laid Plans . . . ," *Forbes*, January 3, 1994, pp. 44–45; James B. Treece, "Kmart: Slick Moves—or Running in Place," *Business Week*, January 17, 1994, p. 28.

16. Kevin Kelly and Karen Lowry Miller, "The Rumble Heard Round the World: Harleys," *Business Week*, May 24, 1993, pp. 58–60; Oliver Bertin, "Harley Finds Success in Cultivating Closet Brandos," *Globe and Mail*, June 2, 1994, p. B2.

17. Jerry Flint, "John Crean's Recipe for Success," *Forbes*, October 25, 1993, pp. 200–204.

18. Analysis and opinion on Southwest and other aspects of the airlines industry are based in part on Kenneth Labich, "Is Herb Kelleher America's Best CEO?" *Fortune*, May 2, 1994, pp. 44–52; Howard Banks, "A Sixties Industry in a Nineties Economy," *Forbes*, May 9, 1994, pp. 107–12; Gary Samuels, "Opportunity Beckons," *Forbes*, July 4, 1994, p. 91; Wendy Zellner, Eric Schine, and Susan Chandler, "Dogfight over California," *Business Week*, August 15, 1994, p. 32.

6

THE IMPLICATIONS OF CHANGE

Every change brings an opportunity . . .

Chinese proverb

. . . and a threat.

Murphy's addendum

The validity of the above comments on change should be apparent from the examination of industry structure and competitive advantage in Chapters 3, 4, and 5. Many instances of outstanding corporate performance have been based on a company's ability to adapt to change, and to exploit change. The long-term investor should be sensitive to change, with respect to both the opportunities it creates and the threats it poses.

Conventional analysis provides relatively little guidance on dealing with long-term change. Rather, it is primarily preoccupied with change in the context of short-term economic developments. This should not be surprising. Immediate economic developments affect markets and determine the sales and earnings upon which stock prices are based. Since stock prices are heavily influenced by expected earnings for the next year, a great deal of effort must go into estimating the direction of the economic variables upon which the performance of the company depends. The investor therefore becomes dependent on the accuracy of short-term forecasts.

As a wit has observed, "Economic forecasting exists solely to make astrology relevant." Every effective witticism contains a grain of truth, and the turbulent decades of the 1970s and the 1980s provide the foundation for this observation. During this period, economic forecasters were battered by continuing surprises, and the credibility of the craft suffered. The accuracy of short-term economic forecasts, however, has improved dramatically in recent years, to the benefit of securities analysts who regard economic developments as the primary cause of changes in stock prices.

Long-term investors, however, need to be aware that the direction of the economy is only one element of change. Analysis that covers a long period has to be concerned with a number of causes of change, including political, social, and technological forces that can change the structure of an industry and/or the competitive positions of the companies within it. This is not to say that economic changes are not important to the long-term investor. As shown in Chapter 5, many sound long-term investments are to some extent cyclical. The timing of an investment must take the economic cycle into consideration, recognizing that industries are often cyclical. So long as the fundamentals remain sound, a company can weather industry cycles and can make progress.

Change tends to be confusing because it usually comes from many directions. The challenge for the investor is to develop a systematic way of assessing the implications of change. In this chapter we will examine the forces that cause change, the ways in which change occurs, and how the effect of change on a industry and company can be analyzed. The basis for this study of the implications of change will be the Porter model of industry structure. We will trace how change can make an industry more or less attractive through its effects on barriers to entry, the risk of substitution, the bargaining power of suppliers and buyers, and the intensity of competition.

INDUSTRY STRUCTURE AND THE FORCES FOR CHANGE

Chapters 3, 4, and 5 examined the nature of industries and the ways in which companies operate within their industries. In the broader external environment, both companies and industries are affected by economic, social, political, and technological forces over which they rarely have any degree of significant control. The overall relationship between companies, industries, and the external environment is diagrammed in Exhibit 6–1.

E X H I B I T   6–1

The Relationship between Company, Industry, and External Environment

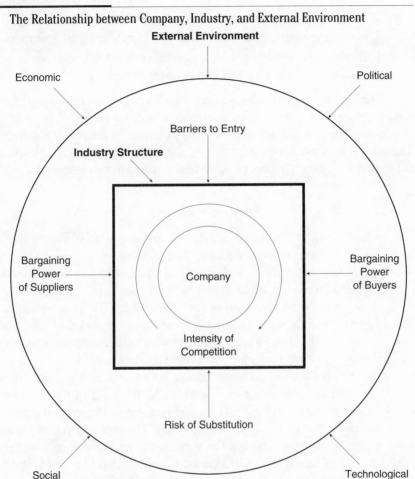

Investors need to be able to evaluate the potential effects of change on a company and on its status as a candidate for investment. Such an evaluation is based on four major factors: first, the forces for change; second, how change occurs; third, the effect of change on the industry; and fourth, the ability of a company to cope with the change.

It is convenient to place the forces for change in the four categories listed below, for purposes of study and analysis:

1. *Economic change*, which can directly affect sales and earnings
2. *Social change*, which can affect nature of markets
3. *Political change*, which can affect the competitive environment
4. *Technological change*, which can affect the structure of an industry and the position of a company within it

These categories of change and their interrelationships are examined in more detail below. For example, it will be seen that economic change can have social effects that lead to demands for political action. The effects of these four categories of change on the five variables that determine the characteristics of an industry will also be examined.

Economic Forces

The overall level of economic activity is commonly and broadly measured by the *gross national product (GNP)* and the *gross domestic product (GDP)*. The performance and prospects of most industries and companies depend on more specific economic variables, which do not necessarily move in the same direction as the GNP or the GDP. The most influential of these variables are usually *interest rates*, the *inflation rate*, and *currency exchange rates*. Exhibit 6–2 shows the main economic variables and the ways in which they can affect industry structure.

These variables can to some extent be influenced by government action through the central banks. For example, the level of interest rates can be used either to stimulate or to dampen the economy, and thus to influence the value of the domestic currency. However, in recent years, government attempts to manage the variables have become increasingly ineffective. The need to bring large deficits under control has made it difficult to exercise fiscal policy, making it necessary to rely almost entirely on monetary policy. Central banks' attempts to stabilize currencies have often been overwhelmed by massive free market currency movements. Though most of the economic variables are cyclical, they are not necessarily predictable, because they are increasingly subject to market forces.

The level of interest rates is of particular importance to the investor. Not only do interest rates affect the sizes of certain markets and influence companies' investment decisions, but also they have a direct effect on equity prices by establishing the rate at which future earnings should be discounted and determining the relative attractiveness of fixed-income investments. The influence of interest rates on corporate internal investment decisions is probably exaggerated, except when they rise above cer-

E X H I B I T   6–2

Effects of Change on Industry Structure: Economic Variables

Economic Variables	Effects on Industry Structure
GNP and GDP	Have primary effect on intensity of competition through the growth and size of markets and the extent to which fixed costs can be absorbed. Have particular effect on industries in which demand is cyclical. May change barriers to entry by affecting business confidence, which may encourage or discourage entry.
Interest rates	Affect intensity of competition through effect on market size of interest-sensitive products such as housing, cars, and capital goods. Change barriers to entry in capital-intensive industries due to the level of interest costs.
Inflation rate	Risk of substitution is affected by relative cost of substitutes. Bargaining power of suppliers and buyers is affected by their ability to pass on price increases.
Unemployment rate	Changes bargaining power with labor due to the availability and cost of labor and bargaining leverage with unions. May affect size of markets due to impact on consumer confidence.
Exchange rates	Affect intensity of competition through the size of markets due to opportunities to export and the competition from imports.

tain threshold levels. An investment in new machinery and equipment which is not considered feasible at an interest rate of, say, 8 percent is also not likely to be feasible at 5 percent, because the difference is rarely sufficient to offset other risks. Very high rates, say above 12 percent, can be a deterrent.

Social Forces

Social forces for change arise from the values of society, which are reflected in consumer preferences and consumer perceptions. *Consumer preferences*, which determine the types of goods and services that will be bought, are primarily influenced by demographic and economic factors. *Consumers' perceptions* are based on what is important to them. Changes may take place in what is considered to constitute value as well as in what is considered to pose risks. *Social values*, which are collective beliefs about what is important, can cause broad shifts in the nature of markets. Exhibit 6–3 summarizes the main components of these variables and their effects on industry structures.

EXHIBIT 6–3

Effects of Change on Industry Structure: Social Variables

Social Variables	Effects on Industry Structure
Consumer preferences	Affect intensity of competition through the growth or decline of markets, such as those based on lifestyle.
Consumer perceptions	Affect the size of markets through changes in what is considered to provide value or create risks. May create barriers to entry into areas considered to pose dangers.
Social values	Create new industries and accelerate growth or decline of established industries.

Consumer preferences about types and quantities of goods and services are a function of lifestyles, for which demographics are a major influence. The major developments of the early 1990s have been the aging of the baby boomers and the emergence of an echo of the baby boom in the form of a growing teenage market, consisting of the adolescent children of the baby boomers. Aging boomers have created relatively strong markets for home-based products, exercise equipment, and financial services. The teenage market has increased demand for footwear and apparel in the popular fashions. It should be recognized that consumer preferences based on demographics are transient. For example, when the teenage group move into the young adult phase in a few years, their priorities will change.

In recent years much has been written about *value shift*, in explanation of the growth or decline in demand for various products and services. Terms such as *cocooning* have been coined to explain growth in demand for stay-at-home products such as VCRs, but these changes may not represent significant value shifts. David Foot, a demographer at the University of Toronto, commented on recent developments by saying,

> They look like value shifts, like moving from a carefree, borrowing society to a more frugal society, but they're not two different values. On average, everyone in their teens has had similar values for the last 40 years, and everyone in their 40s and 50s has had similar values for the last 40 years. These trends are not new value systems moving through our society at all, they are a re-weighing of the traditional values."[1]

In this context, apparent changes in values become more predictable.

Social values define what is important to a given society. The main concerns of American society in recent years have been environmental protection, personal security (law and order), the cost of health care, and the quality of education. These concerns have led to the growth of industries involved in recycling, industries involved in the manufacture of burglar alarms and hand guns, health maintenance organizations, and private schools and educational aids, respectively.

Changes in consumer perceptions, as separate from basic values, can be the product of a wide range of influences, including economic circumstances and real or imagined fears. In the late 1970s and early 1980s, perceptions of value in automobiles changed; instead of status symbols, cars were seen as utilitarian transportation. The early 1990s saw a weakening of consumer preference for branded products to the extent that the price premiums of some brands had to be reduced, as noted earlier for cigarettes. Lower-priced private brands of the major merchandisers have become competitors, and it has been suggested that only the leading national brands are likely to continue to prosper.[2] A possible reason for this is that the recession of the early 1990s made consumers more price-conscious and more willing to try inexpensive products, which they often found to be of good quality. This should not be surprising, as most private brands are made in the same plants as the national brands. This suggests that competitive advantage based on brand preference may no longer be strong and that a close examination of a company's position in its market is necessary.

A more profound explanation for the apparent weakening of brands is provided in a major study by the advertising agency Young and Rubicam (Y&R). Y&R contends that the traditional measurement of brand effectiveness, name awareness based on heavy advertising, is no longer effective. In addition to name awareness, effective branding must be based on differentiation (real differences), esteem (respect for quality, etc.), and the relevance of the product to customers' needs. This suggests that brands not offering real value may be facing difficulties.

Certainly there is strong evidence that people are no longer willing to pay a high premium for branded products. During the period 1983–88, breakfast cereal producers Kellogg, General Mills, Post, and Quaker Oats raised prices by an average of 6 percent per year. Kellogg, for example, saw its market share drop from over 41 percent in 1988 to 37 percent in 1993, while the share of low-priced supermarket labels increased from 3 to 6 percent.[3] The lesson is significant, as the Kellogg brands are generally regarded as one of the strongest among cereals.

While the status of brands may be diminishing in the United States, it is flourishing in global markets, particularly in the Far East. There, the high quality of American consumer products in comparison with local products has provided strong sales even at premium prices. Certain brands, such as Coca-Cola and McDonald's, have become symbols of an affluent and leisurely lifestyle.

Another major change in perceptions has taken place in the area of what constitutes risk. Concern about the health effects of food products, for example, has resulted in the shunning of fats and a preference for high-fiber foods. Concern about the risks posed by waste disposal operations and nuclear power plants have created barriers to entry in these industries. Changes in perceptions can be transient or of long duration.

Political Forces

Governments are a major factor in virtually every aspect of social and economic life. Government influence is exercised at the federal, state or provincial, and municipal levels, and people are affected by both domestic and foreign decisions. Political action usually arises from the economic and social forces discussed above.

For purposes of this book, the influence of political forces may be categorized in the following three ways:

1. *Direct purchases of goods and services.* Government spending includes funds spent on infrastructure (roads, civil service, etc.), defense, law and order, and health care. Changing political priorities can result in the growth or decline of the industries that supply these goods and services, and can thereby change the intensity of competition. The recent decline in defense spending, for example, has forced the industry to commence rationalization.

2. *Intervention in the scope of competition.* Antitrust laws, regulation, the establishment of product and service standards, and tariffs are ways in which government intervenes in the scope of competition. The main effect of these interventions is the creation of barriers to entry through licensing requirements (in broadcasting and in cable TV) and through limits on foreign activity (the Jones Act affects the shipping industry, ownership limitations affect the airlines industry, etc.). Tariffs reduce the intensity of competition.

3. *Intervention in markets.* Governments impose quotas; grant subsidies; legislate environmental standards; set floor prices, minimum wages, and so forth; mandate the use of products (such as air bags); and intervene in markets in other ways. Quotas reduce the intensity of competition, raise barriers to entry, and reduce the bargaining power of customers (by creating sheltered markets, as

discussed in Chapter 5). The other actions listed here distort the free market by bestowing an advantage on one party.

In recent years, the U.S. government has been moving toward the deregulation of industry, but this movement has been sporadic and inconsistent at best. The structure of this government is shaped by the separation of administrative and legislative functions, the absence of consistent discipline in political parties, the power of the congressional committee chairpersons, and the short terms of members of the House of Representatives. This structure makes the U.S. government one of the most sensitive of all world governments to the lobbying of special interest groups. As a result, drastic changes of policy are relatively rare and occur only after extended consideration, which gives the investor plenty of time to react.

Global political developments can include the encouragement and toleration of cartels (as in oil and coffee), the establishment of trading blocs such as the European Economic Community (EEC) and the North American Free Trade Agreement (NAFTA), and military conflicts. Developments of this sort can affect the size and character of markets and materials, thus creating volatility even if the domestic environment is comparatively predictable.

Technological Forces

Unlike economic, social, and political forces for change, which are interrelated, technology is an independent major force for change. Every aspect of industry structure may be affected by developments in product technology (inventing the better mousetrap) and process technology (making the better mousetrap), as shown in Exhibit 6–4.

Changes in technology can combine to make an industry either more or less attractive. In the aircraft manufacturing industry, the cost of developing technologically sophisticated products has created very high barriers to entry. Technology has also enhanced the performance of the product, thus increasing bargaining power with the industry's buyers, the airlines. In contrast, a large number of industries—the integrated steel industry, for example—have been made unattractive by technology, often because of substitutes or lowered barriers to entry.

The internal combustion engine was the technological driving force of the first half of the twentieth century. To the same extent, the semiconductor has been the major technological force of the second half. The effects of the semiconductor illustrate the extent to which technology can affect industries, as shown in the following developments:

E X H I B I T   6–4

Effects of Changes on Industry Structure: Technological Variables

Element of Structure	Effect
Barriers to entry	• Raised by cost of developing increasingly technologically sophisticated products, and by automated production processes. *Example:* Aircraft.
	• Lowered by processes that diminish economies of scale. *Examples:* Computer-controlled machine tools, steel minimills versus integrated steel operations, desktop publishing.
Risk of substitution	• Raised by the introduction of cost-effective new products. *Examples:* Fiberoptics for copper, plastics and composites for metals, copiers for carbon paper.
Power of buyers	• Reduced by the ability to customize products to differentiate them for specific markets, and by technology that enhances the performance of a product.
Power of suppliers	• Increased when the supplier's component improves the performance of the product in which it is used. *Examples:* computer chips, software.
Intensity of competition:	
Market growth	• Creation of new, emerging industries. *Example:* Cellular telephones.
	• Acceleration of the progression of the product life cycle through cost reduction and the obsoleting of existing products.
Cost structure	• Move toward higher fixed costs due to technological sophistication of processes.
Barriers to exit	• Increased due to specialized products and processes that have no alternative uses.

• In the 1950s, radio broadcasting was considered a dying industry. Television was replacing it as the primary source of home entertainment. When transistors became available in the 1960s, freeing the radio from the power needs of the vacuum tube, the sale of portable units at sharply reduced prices revived the popularity of radio.

• The semiconductor was at the heart of many new products, including computers and a wide range of communications and industrial process control equipment.

• The semiconductor has enhanced the performance of a wide range of products (such as cameras and automobiles) and services (such as banking, with automated teller machines).

- The semiconductor has been the primary cause of the decline of a number of industries, including the typewriter industry and the vacuum tube industry.

As this illustration shows, technology has profound effects on the structure of industries resulting in the creation of new industries, the obsolescence of old ones, and changes in the basis of competition for almost all.

The implications of technological change must be evaluated with care. Traders have strong tendencies to exaggerate the short-term effects of change and to underestimate its longer-term effects. Technological change rarely has the immediate effects expected, for the following two reasons:

1. There is often resistance to or delay in using new technology when it threatens to obsolete existing investment or infrastructure. High-definition television (HDTV) will undoubtedly be the television of the future, but its adoption will require replacement of both broadcast facilities and home TV sets. Thus, we have a chicken-and-egg situation: stations will not invest in HDTV broadcasting capability until a market exists, and consumers will not buy HDTV sets until programs are available. On the consumer end, reluctance to buy is accentuated because limited production keeps the cost high. HDTV will therefore likely emerge gradually, consisting initially of high-end home entertainment centers dependent on videodisks. Eventually the number of such sets in use should justify broadcasting.

2. The consumer market culture may not be ready for a new product. In the early 1980s, the computer industry was predicting that the PC would soon become a common home appliance. This optimism overlooked the fact that the major portion of the home market was not computer-literate. To most consumers the computer was an expensive toy rather than a useful device. It was not until the mid-1990s that the home market started to pick up steam as a generation of computer-literate users began to emerge.

In many instances, the long-range implications of new technology are even more profound than originally anticipated. The computer, for example, is taking over a wide range of service functions. However, the investor who buys the stock of a company on the basis of the expected short-term results of a new technology is usually disappointed.

KINDS OF CHANGE

The second major factor in evaluating the potential effects of change on the status of a company as a candidate for investment is how change occurs. Change can be cyclical or it can be part of a trend. It can also be a complete surprise—a discontinuity.

Cyclical Change

Changes that occur in cycles are perhaps the most common. As discussed in Chapter 3, cycles have a wide range of causes, such as economic developments, demographic changes, and replacement requirements. Cycles may coincide and reinforce one another, with quite dramatic results. The economic recovery in the mid-1990s coincided with actual and deferred replacement requirements for automobiles, providing a very large increase in sales for the North American automobile industry.

The cycles discussed to this point have been demand-based in that they have their effect on an industry through the size of markets. There are also supply-based cycles, which investors tend to overlook because of their preoccupation with the short term. During the 1980s, investors' attention was focused on knowledge industries. "Resource" industries were disdained as archaic and were considered to be a diminishing influence on the economy.

Though raw material prices had remained depressed through much of the decade, these low prices did not justify capacity increases. In fact, they resulted in a capacity decline, due to the exit of high-cost producers and the rationalization of industries. The cumulative slow growth of demand gradually ate up the surplus capacity, and thus the economic recovery of 1993–94 resulted in shortages. Prices of metals, paper, and other raw materials increased sharply. Since lead times to bring on new capacity can be three to five years in these industries, a longer period of high prices can be expected.

Such cycles are a well-established phenomenon. They work to create the next part of the cycle, in that producers rush to increase capacity, bringing it on stream just in time to participate in the next cyclical glut.

While the underlying causes of cycles are generally well understood, a common error made by many analysts is assuming that cycles are a repetition of past events. A look at the difference between the conventional wisdom and actual events in the case of the recession of 1990–92 will be elucidating.

The conventional cyclical downturn in the economy is considered to be caused by a combination of factors. Industry capacity is thought to be overbuilt, resulting in a downturn of capital investment. This downturn, investors assume, is usually accompanied by an increase in interest rates, which is intended to dampen the inflation that usually accompanies a boom period. In typical past recessions, about two-thirds of the downturn has been caused by a decline in investment, even though investment makes up only one-third of GNP. Consumer consumption, which accounts for two-thirds of GNP, falls relatively little (about a quarter of the shortfall) because consumers, anticipating a recovery, draw on savings to maintain a relatively high level of expenditures. Further, almost all industries tend to decline together.

Consider the characteristics of the early 1990s recession in the context of this conventional wisdom.

- The drop in consumer consumption accounted for 54 percent of the shortfall of real GNP from its average growth, while the drop in investment accounted for only 38 percent of the decline. This indicates that consumers, feeling much less confident of the future, chose to cut consumption rather than dipping into savings. Consumer's lack of confidence may have been the result of concerns about such matters as job security and the trend toward increases in part-time and contract employment.

- Contrary to previous experience in which incomes started to improve with an economic recovery, 1993 saw a continued decline of median earnings, by 2.2 percent for men and by 1.2 percent for women over 1992 earnings.[4]

- While most industries dipped together in 1990–91, the "old" industries, made up of housing, automobiles, machine tools, and so forth, recovered more slowly than the "new" industries, such as semiconductors, pharmaceuticals, computers, and telecommunications equipment. Innovation and new product introduction in the new industries appear to have driven them to recover faster than the less dynamic, older industries did.

This leads to two possible conclusions. First, this apparent recovery may be hampered by a lack of consumer confidence. After deferred demand is satisfied, it may not last as long as might be expected on the basis of past experience. Second, the conventional business cycle may no longer apply equally to all industries, and cycles in different industries may not occur concurrently. Another area to reexamine the conventional wisdom on cycles is inflation. While interest rates in late 1994 had come down significantly from earlier levels, they were high by historical standards in which real interest rates have been 2½ to 3 percent. The market continues to anticipate the cyclical resurgence of a relatively high rate of inflation. Yet, this may not occur for a number of reasons:

- Industries have been restructured through disaggregation as discussed in Chapter 5, increasing their bargaining power with suppliers, particularly their internal labor forces. Disaggregation has been made possible by advances in computer and communications technology.

- The globalization of business has extended the outsourcing process involved in disaggregation to lower wage countries. Advances in both communications and transportation technology have made this possible. The combination of disaggregation and globalization have significantly broken the wage-price spiral which has been a significant factor in past surges of inflation and its persistence.

- Governments are taking a more resolute stand against inflation in their monetary and fiscal policy. At one time it could have been argued that the government benefited from inflation because it increased their revenue and made possible the payment of their debts with cheaper dollars. Further, economic policies required to bring down inflation tend to be politically unpopular. However, the size of the debt has blossomed to the level where interest costs have become the dominant consideration. The government now has a strong incentive to keep inflation, and as a result, interest rates, low. Hence, monetary and fiscal policies in which vigilance against renewed inflation is a high priority.

Thus, analysis of investment opportunities should not be blindly based on the conventional wisdom about cycles. Rather, what is required is in-depth examination of the underlying forces.

Investors also tend to make the mistake of thinking of cycles primarily in the context of their effect on markets and demand. Cycles can also affect competitive advantage, either diminishing it or enhancing it, though often temporarily. For example, Outboard Marine will likely be helped by the weak U.S. dollar in relation to the yen. This assistance, combined with a cyclical recovery of markets, could yield a significant improvement in earnings for the company. Inco was mentioned earlier as a company that was unable to realize its competitive advantage because of political developments; these too are in part cyclical.

Cycles are difficult to analyze. Research has shown that investors, including professional fund managers, tend to confuse temporary or cyclical developments with long-lasting trends. It therefore becomes particularly important that this basic tendency be overcome with sound analysis.

Trends

A *trend* can be defined as the general direction or dominant movement of events. Accordingly, trends are evolutionary in character. In analysis, trends are often described in statistical terms. In statistical analysis, trends that are of sufficient duration and consistency, and the underlying causes of which are understood, can be extrapolated for forecasting purposes. Trend analysis can be a valid indicator of change, provided the underlying reasons for and correlations of the trends analyzed are understood. Thus, many trends, such as consumption patterns based on demographics and income levels, can be used with a relatively high level of confidence to predict changes.

The adage that Trend is not destiny should always be kept in mind. In recent years we have seen many reversals of trends that had been considered major and enduring. For example, there is a well-established trend in which the government has been imposing increasingly strict regulations on U.S. industry, so as to protect the environment. These regulations are being dismantled in 1995 by the Republican-controlled Congress. The Republican proposals would require that future regulations be based on cost-benefit analysis. Companies depending on the environmental protection market will obviously be affected. Another example is provided by the fact that more than three decades of steadily rising real personal income came to a halt in the early 1990s. This halt is to a significant extent the result of the disaggregation of corporations and the globalization of competition, which were discussed earlier as factors underlying the dapening of the inflation cycle. This may last for some time and will affect industries dependent on discretionary spending.

Discontinuities

Companies have also made major errors in strategy because they regarded changes caused by discontinuities as trends. A *discontinuity* is a change that falls outside the normal range of expectations. If trends are regarded as evolutionary, discontinuities can be considered revolutionary. They may be caused by natural phenomena or by political or technological developments. Discontinuities are rarely caused by social forces, because changes in attitudes of a magnitude sufficient to cause significant socially based change rarely take place quickly. An example of discontinuity occurred when a change in the Humboldt current off Peru in 1973 resulted in the failure of the anchovy harvest. Because this harvest had traditionally supplied a major portion of global animal feed, the failure caused a sharp increase in the demand for grains, soybeans, and corn as substitutes. This increased demand ignited inflation, which was already smoldering because of errors in the Nixon administration's economic policy. The Organization of Petroleum Exporting Companies (OPEC), angered by U.S. support of Israel and the increase in the rate of inflation, became surprisingly aggressive and embargoed oil shipments, starting the oil price run-up which was the primary cause of the high inflation of the 1970s and the early 1980s.

Another example is the collapse of communism in the late 1980s. Because of the basic inefficiency of communism, its collapse was expected eventually, but the speed at which it occurred was a complete surprise. The defense industry in the United States, which had been confident of a continuation of the long and profitable Cold War, was in disarray. Many commodity producers, particularly those in base metals, have faced depressed prices because of the black market dumping of Russian inventories.

The two events described above, each of which has had major investment consequences, were complete surprises. Discontinuities are obviously unpredictable by nature. They obviously can create a degree of vulnerability for the long-term investor, but the risks from discontinuities can be minimized by avoiding investment in companies whose future depends on the stability or predictability of an important variable, such as inflation or oil prices, or even on a continuation of a major historical event such as the Cold War.

While discontinuities are disruptive and require major adjustments on the part of companies, the disruption is transient until a new equilibrium is reached. For example, higher oil prices resulted in lower consumption and eventually brought on new sources of supply, causing prices to drop dramatically from their high points. Governments were forced to take the drastic and painful action necessary to bring inflation under control. Thus the effects of the discontinuity were transient. A number of companies have made the fatal error of regarding a discontinuity as a trend. Consider the two examples described below.

Dome Petroleum was a favorite of Canadian investors through the 1970s and into the early 1980s. Under the aggressive management of its CEO, Jack Gallagher, Dome was acquiring smaller companies with oil reserves at relatively high prices. At the same time the company was spending heavily on Arctic exploration. The acquisitions program culminated with the acquisition of Hudson Bay Oil and Gas in 1981 for $4 billion, raising Dome's total debt to over $7 billion. The assumption underlying this strategy was that rising oil prices were not part of a discontinuity but an enduring trend. Gallagher's assumption was that the increase in oil prices which had started in 1973 would continue and that oil prices would exceed $50 per barrel by 1985. The oil price increase of 1979 was interpreted as confirming this trend. Had the company's expectations in this regard proved true, even the expensive reserves acquired by purchase and exploration would eventually have come to seem a bargain. Before Dome could refinance its debt with equity, however, it collapsed along with oil prices in 1983. Gallagher had, in effect, bet the company on the continuation of a trend and had compounded the risk by financing acquisitions with debt which the company had no hope of servicing if higher prices did not materialize. Evidence that high prices were curtailing demand and that alternative sources of supply were becoming available were ignored. A surprising element of the situation was that a number of normally conservative Canadian banks agreed with Gallagher's assumptions and took major write-offs on their loans.

Starting in the early 1960s, the Reichmann family of Toronto, led by Paul Reichmann, built Olympia and York Developments (O&Y) into one of the world's largest commercial real estate companies, with major holdings in Toronto, New York, and London. During the 1980s the family also made large investments in Canadian resource industries by buying controlling interests in Gulf Resources Corp. (oil and gas) and in Abitibi-Price Inc. (forestry products). This rapid growth was financed with heavy debt. O&Y's buildings were mortgaged above cost on the strength of lease revenues. The assumption underlying this strategy was that inflation would continue, thereby increasing the value of O&Y's real estate. The lenders obviously agreed that this increased value would provide ample security for their loans. The acquisition of the resource companies provided further evidence of the inflation assumption, because such companies are the major beneficiaries of inflation. When the inflation rate dropped in the early 1990s and the recession dampened the demand for rental space, O&Y collapsed, leaving its lenders with major losses. Investors were spared losses because O&Y was a private company, but the banks took heavy write-offs.

In both of these examples, the strategy was based on the misinterpretation of a discontinuity as an enduring trend—and the success of the strategy was dependent on one variable. The lesson should be obvious.

ASSESSING THE EFFECTS OF CHANGE ON A COMPANY

We have been dealing with change in the context of its effect on an industry. Its effect on an individual company can be assessed by answering these two questions:

1. Is the company more or less vulnerable to change than others because of its position in the industry?

2. Does the company have the capability to respond strategically, so as either to counter the adverse affects of change or to take advantage of the opportunities it presents?

Vulnerability to Change

A company may be more or less vulnerable to a change that affects the industry as a whole because of the position that the company occupies in the industry. It sometimes happens that a company has a mix of resources that give it a superior ability to cope with change. For example, as previously pointed out, UST has benefited from changes in the tobacco industry caused by regulation and by social attitudes toward smoking, because its product does not create the smoke that has drawn attention as a threat to health.

In an instance of change in social values resulting in political action, in 1993 the Clinton administration reacted to pressure from environmentalists by reducing the allowable cut of timber on federal lands by more than 50 percent, commencing in 1994. By exercising its bargaining power as a supplier, the government created a shortage of timber which has resulted in higher lumber prices and curtailed the operations of many companies. Four companies, Georgia-Pacific Corp., Weyerhaeuser Company, Boise Cascade Corporation, and Louisiana Pacific Corporation, own extensive timber tracts and are to some extent insulated from supply constraints and higher costs. The lack of backward integration (control over their sources of materials) had previously been an advantage for companies that got their timber from public land, because they did not have to tie up capital in land ownership. This same lack of backward integration suddenly became a disadvantage, as the affected companies no longer had a reliable source of supply. Thus, the change in government regulations hurt some companies but benefited others. The four companies that were not adversely affected had been only median or worse performers in their industries over the previous five years, but their performance is now expected to improve significantly, particularly because the investment cycle in the industry has left it short of capacity to meet demand in the intermediate term. (The forest products industry is discussed in more detail in Chapter 11.)

In general, the integrated steel industry has been a weak performer in recent years. Technological change has resulted in the emergence of minimills with lower costs for production of commodity products. Yet, some companies, such as Allegheny Ludlum Corporation, have been strong performers. These are companies that have concentrated on market segments such as specialty alloys and have developed the capability

of economically producing the relatively short production runs characteristic of this market.

These examples show that, while a change affecting an industry is
the starting point for analysis, the impact on any one company can be
quite different because of the company's position in its industry.

Strategic Responses to Change

A company's ability to make appropriate and effective strategic responses
to change depends on three factors: the company's available scope for
strategic action, the nature and quantity of its resources, and the extent of
the internal inertia inhibiting its ability to respond. These factors are closely related to the factors that determine a company's ability to enhance its
competitive advantage, which have already been discussed.

Scope for Strategic Action

The natural strategic response to a threat created by a change in industry
structure is to try to hedge the risks or neutralize the adverse effects of the
change. Thus, when plastic containers began to emerge as a substitute for
glass, most glass container manufacturers started to make plastic containers,
even though they were significantly less profitable than glass. Similarly, it is
a relatively common strategic response for a company to acquire a customer
or a supplier that has achieved significant bargaining power.

However, while the direction of a strategic response may seem obvious, the action itself may not be feasible. Lets take the case of the possible threat to a branded product manufacturer, say General Mills, being
posed by changes in consumers' values and the increasing power of the
distributors. Theoretically, a company's best strategic response to such a
development would be to acquire one of its distributors—a distributor
which, in turn, has relatively high bargaining power over a large number
of small customers. However, this would involve General Mills's buying
a supermarket chain, which would not be a realistic option. No one chain
distributes a significant part of General Mills's output. In addition, the
company would antagonize its other customers by entering into competition with them. Thus, the company's strategic action in response to
change is limited to an attempt to reinforce its brand position in line with
the new consumer perceptions.

In contrast to this scenario is the case of the drug industry, in which
forward integration was possible because bargaining power was being
exercised by a relatively small number of large buyers.

Similarly, attempts to respond to threats by moving in another direction, such as entering the substitute industry or acquiring a supplier, may have a limited effect in relation to the cost involved. When this is the case, a threatened industry or company may not be able to avoid the damage caused by an adverse development.

An interesting example of the strategic twists and turns that companies make in trying to escape the problems of change is provided by the history of Silcorp in Canada. This company started as Silverwoods Dairies in the 1920s. By the 1950s, it had grown into one of Canada's largest dairy operations and was enjoying attractive industry circumstances. Its bargaining power with a large number of small dairy farmers was high, as was its bargaining power with customers, who were served by home delivery routes. In the 1950s, however, the Canadian provincial governments established milk marketing boards. These boards set quotas and prices for farmers, creating bargaining power on their behalf. Concurrently, a postwar exodus of the market to the suburbs began. This exodus sharply increased travel distances and reduced the density of customers, destroying the economic basis of labor-intensive home delivery. The distribution of milk was thus moved into supermarkets, which had immense bargaining power. Milk became a commodity, as it was no longer differentiated by the reliability of the company, the convenience of home delivery, or even the personality of the home deliverer. Silverwood was squeezed between the suppliers and the buyers, as a result of these political and social changes.

The company's strategic response was to integrate forward, in an attempt to reestablish bargaining power with its buyers. It established neighborhood milk stores, which provided the convenience of local availability. The stores also carried a number of other grocery and confectionery items, to help absorb overhead. These milk stores were allowed to stay open on Sundays, when the laws of most Canadian provinces forced supermarkets to close. The convenience stores were so successful that by the early 1980s all of Silverwood's dairy operations had been sold. The company assumed the name Silcorp Ltd. and began to expand its convenience store business by buying several chains in the United States, financing them by heavy debt. Competition proved to be more severe in the United States than in Canada. In addition, the Canadian cash cow encountered further adverse change. The sales of cigarettes, long a mainstay, declined. Furthermore changing laws in Canada permitted supermarkets to remain open on Sundays, which sharply reduced convenience store sales. The company had to be reorganized under bankruptcy laws.

When it entered the convenience store industry, Silcorp had committed its future to an inherently unattractive industry. Barriers to entry in this industry are low, and location provides the only bargaining power over customers. While Silcorp had some bargaining power over suppliers due to its high-volume purchases, this power was usually more than offset by the inexpensive family labor available to the independent stores. Silcorp's competitive advantage was therefore limited.

At the time of the original squeeze, the company had another option. It could have pursued lower costs by acquiring other dairies and rationalizing the industry. This strategy has been pursued with moderate success by other companies. Even so, the dairy industry remains unattractive at best, as it continues to be squeezed between suppliers and buyers.

It can be argued that Silcorp was more the victim of bad luck than of poor strategy. However, the company's basic problem arose because it made a commitment to an unattractive industry and assumed a heavy debt burden. An option which did not likely occur to management (although it would have been the option of choice in an earlier time) was to pay out liquidating dividends at the time the dairy business was sold.

Availability of Resources

In general, a strong resource position provides a company with staying power and therefore with the time needed to adapt to change. A combination of cash reserves, a low level of debt, and strong continuing cash flow obviously provides a company with more time and a wider scope for action than are available to its weaker competitors. To cite an example from the tobacco industry that has already been mentioned, RJR Nabisco lost ground to Philip Morris because it responded slowly and reluctantly to its competitor's initiative (cutting prices to offset the decline in the value of brands), mainly because of its high debt.

Strategic Inertia

Though it may seem obvious to an observer that a company should respond to change in a certain way, this does not necessarily mean that the company can actually make the appropriate response. The company's ability to act may be constrained not only by a shortage of resources, as discussed above, but also by internal inertia. Like a supertanker steaming at full speed, the large corporation is difficult to turn around. Possible internal obstacles include large, specialized plants; uncooperative labor unions; and management attitudes steeped in the culture of the company. The integrated steel industry, for example, as mentioned above, has been slow to enter minimill production. This change would obsolete much of the industry's existing plant, and there is also a strong tradition in the industry that dictates, "This is not the way steel should be made." The integrated steel producers have also been severely limited in their ability to introduce cost-saving production procedures and work rules, because of the resistance of powerful unions.

The computer industry offers another example. Not only was IBM late to enter the PC market, but its effort was riddled with strategic errors. Instead of being based on a recognition of the PC as a new market, IBM's entry was to a significant degree defensive. The company's primary motivation was to protect the mainframe business on which its profitability was based. It also had a secondary motivation of trying to avoid cannibalizing its other products, such as typewriters. The company's culture had a big influence on its slowness in responding to technological change. This sort of development, though ironic for the company, is not uncommon among technological leaders. Newer, smaller companies often lead in introducing new technologies. The question for larger, established firms is now they will respond.

EFFECTS OF CHANGE ON SELECTED COMPANIES IN A BROAD SPECTRUM OF INDUSTRIES

The examples cited above illustrate the point that the existence of a need to respond to change does not mean that a company will be able to respond in time to avoid a serious setback. To further explore the implications of change, let's look at how changes may be expected to affect some of the leading corporate performers that have been discussed in past chapters.

Inco Not only is the mining industry (also called the base metals industry) highly cyclical, but also Inco is still in the process of adjusting to a discontinuity. It was a combination of the collapse of economic order in Russia, the sharp decline in Russian military demand, and the resulting dumping of metal inventories on world markets that caused this discontinuity in nickel markets. However, low-cost Russian ore reserves are known to be near exhaustion, and large new investment will be required to sustain production. The excess supply can therefore be expected to dry up, and prices to improve. Inco's lowest-cost source of supply is its mine in Indonesia. The company is expanding this mine, and thus will be exposed to the political uncertainties of that country.

Schlumberger The leadership position in oil field technology which Schlumberger now holds should enable the company to maintain strong performance at current low oil prices. The present trend toward higher world oil consumption, combined with possible limitations in the increase in supply, has led some analysts to conclude that oil prices could rise, later in the 1990s.[5] The consequent increase in exploration and development activity would be very favorable to Schlumberger.

Polaroid Heavily dependent on a single, aging technology, Polaroid is vulnerable to substitution by new technologies that are being developed in the photography and toys industry.

Coca-Cola As the dominant brand in the soft-drink industry, Coca-Cola should be able to hold its position, particularly because it is strong in foreign markets, where brand preference has not yet shown signs of erosion. The company refuses to make products for private brands, thus minimizing the risk of imitation.

Gillette Also strong in foreign markets, and for the same reason as Coca-Cola, is Gillette. This company, which has previously been cited as the leader in the personal products segment of the consumer nondurable goods industry, is likely to maintain its dominant position. Its strategy for discouraging imitation resembles Coca-Cola's strategy and is equally effective.

General Mills Because General Mills is heavily dependent on branded products, and because the distributors who control the shelf space for which companies in the food-processing industry must compete are becoming ever more powerful, the company may be vulnerable. General Mills had an ROE of 32.4 percent for the 12 months ending December 31, 1994, as compared to its previous five-year average of 37.7 percent. Its profit margin for 1994 declined to 5.4 percent, down from 6.2 percent for the previous year.

Boeing Despite the sad state of the airlines industry, its fleet is aging and will eventually have to be replaced. The necessity for replacement is being accelerated by government regulations requiring noise reduction of aircraft. Of the 9,000 commercial airliners now in service in the industry, about one-third are approaching or have exceeded their normal service life of 20 years. This is more than enough to absorb the 1,000 relatively modern aircraft which various companies in the industry have in mothballs. The global trend toward the privatization of industry may eventually reach Boeing's main competitor in the commercial aircraft industry, Airbus Industries, reducing its government support and perhaps curbing its fierce competitive instincts.

Nike Consumer preferences in the apparel and shoes industry are moving away from athletic shoes toward casual shoes and hiking boots, markets in which Nike is not well represented. The company's strength in athletic shoes should sustain it, but a major promotional effort will be required. Nike integrated horizontally by acquiring Canstar, and this move provides it with access to growing markets.

EFFECTS OF CHANGE ON FIVE SAMPLE INDUSTRIES

Up to this point, the discussions of structure and sustainable competitive advantage in five sample industries have been based on the situations that existed in these industries in late 1994. These situations included events in progress, which were making the industries more or less attractive. We will now examine how these industries may be further affected, either favorably or unfavorably, by these events and the effects that they may have.

Pharmaceuticals Industry

The pharmaceuticals industry remains a top long-term performer, despite some deterioration of the fundamentals over the past few years. As previously noted, the industry structure has been weakened by the emergence of biotechnological substitutes and by customers' increasing price sensitivity. Large buyer groups have been developed, and government pressure has constrained price increases.

While this industry is not cyclical, a number of trends—both favorable and unfavorable—are inherent in the current situation. The first favorable trend is caused by the demographic cycle and by recent political developments.

- A large segment of the population, the baby boomers, are entering a phase of life that might be described as late middle-aged. As a part of the aging process, they are tending to develop a need for more health care services and more drugs.
- The "Contract with America" which forms the agenda of the Republican-controlled U.S. Congress elected in November 1994 includes deregulation. The Federal Drug Administration (FDA) may thus be forced to approve new products more quickly, significantly reducing the cost of new product approvals for the industry. The changes in regulations would make testing requirements less stringent.

The trends that are unfavorable to the pharmaceutical industry are as follows:

- Despite the respite provided by the election of this Republican Congress, increasing government involvement in health care is still a serious threat in the long term, which will inevitably put pressures on all components of the health care industry to constrain price increases and even to reduce prices. The U.S. government may encourage the use of cheaper generic drugs for the Medicaid program, as the Canadian government has done for some time. The cost and accessibility of health care will continue to be a significant political issue in the United States in the long term.

- The health insurance industry, which increasingly controls the practice of medicine in the United States, will continue to exert strong cost constraints on all aspects of the health care industry. The emergence of health maintenance organizations (HMOs) will concentrate buyer bargaining power into larger, more powerful units.

- Biotechnology, which is still in its infancy, will eventually provide increasingly powerful substitutes for drugs. In the extreme, it has the potential to virtually replace the chemical-based drug industry.[6]

The unfavorable developments of the past few years, of which some of the trends listed above are an extension, have already resulted in some rationalization of the industry through acquisitions, mergers and joint ventures, and forward integration. As health care providers move toward increasing assumption of power, it has been suggested that they may begin to require drug makers to guarantee the long-term cost effectiveness of their products, rather than only their immediate therapeutic effects. Under such an arrangement, the drug companies would bear the cost of the ultimate treatment, such as surgery, if the drugs were not effective. This would move the drug companies into the care provider and health insurance business, a drastic change in the industry.[7] This would be a very long-term development, if indeed it came to pass.

Despite some deterioration of the fundamentals, the industry remains relatively attractive. The expected changes are evolutionary, and no discontinuities can be foreseen. A decision to invest in the industry should therefore be based on the ability of the particular company to sustain its competitive advantage and to cope with and adapt to expected changes.

In this respect, Merck should fare well. As discussed earlier, this company has the size and resources to maintain a research program of the scope necessary for survival in the industry. Its strategic initiative in integrating forward carries some risks, though not the risk of outright failure. What is in question is the degree to which forward integration will contribute to earnings. The current political stalemate over the role of government in health care will allow market forces to govern the industry, likely for some time. This suits Merck particularly well, as the company has moved to restore its bargaining power. Further, its managers have demonstrated an awareness of the implications of change and a willingness to take action. Though industry developments will likely slow the rate of sales growth from the company's historical double-digit levels, Merck should remain consistently strong relative to other industries. The stock market may well have discounted the unfavorable developments that took place in 1992 and 1993.

Tobacco Industry

It has already been shown that the tobacco industry is declining in North America and Europe but has remained relatively strong elsewhere. The present and future of the industry are being affected by three developments. First, well-established brand loyalties have weakened. Inroads by discount brands to the extent of a 30 percent market share have forced both Philip Morris and RJR Nabisco to reduce prices on their premium brands. It has been argued that the 30 percent of the population who continue to smoke represent a hard core of smokers to whom obtaining nicotine at low cost may be more important than taste.

Second, a large increase in tobacco taxes was considered by the Clinton administration to finance a national plan for medical care. Canadian experience has shown that each 10 percent increase in cigarette prices results in a 4 percent decline in smoking. The Clinton proposal will likely be shelved as a result of the midterm election results of 1994, but the underlying forces for such action are strong. It would be foolish to consider the current situation permanent.

Third, in 1994 the state of Mississippi launched a lawsuit against tobacco companies, claiming compensation for health care costs due to smoking. Mississippi's suit was followed by other state suits. The chance of success for these suits cannot be estimated on the basis of the precedent of the individual suits to date (which have not resulted in significant damages), as the basis for the claims is different.[8] The filing of class action suits is also being permitted. Class actions have more resources than individual actions, thus may have a greater chance of success. As noted in Chapter 4, the stock market has tended to ignore the risks arising from the health issue. The downward movement of industry stocks in 1993 was primarily caused by the threat to profitability posed by the discounting of premium brands. The market's indifference to the health issue is surprising, in view of a parallel with the earlier asbestos industry situation. If the tobacco suits that are now in process and upcoming succeed, they will obviously be followed by other suits. This could drive tobacco companies to seek bankruptcy protection, as Manville Corporation did in response to the asbestos suits.

These three developments together constitute a very strong, even strengthening, trend against cigarette sales, along with an increasing risk of large product liability damages. The bright spots for the industry include strong foreign sales and the popularity of major U.S. brands. A remotely possible but significant discontinuity would be the early discovery of ways to cure or prevent cancer and heart disease, which would reduce the main pressures on the industry.

Risks to the companies in the tobacco industry range from serious to catastrophic. Many of these companies have significant nontobacco businesses which would also be at risk if the tobacco lawsuits were successful. This suggests that if an investor is keen on obtaining a stake in the tobacco industry, an investment in a British company would provide better representation in the foreign markets and protection from the harsh U.S. product liability laws. Foreign investment, however, creates other risks, such as those arising from variations in exchange rates.

Of the U.S. tobacco companies, UST is the strongest. It would not be immediately affected by unfavorable legal decisions based on the effects of tobacco smoke, but in the long term it will become vulnerable, as evidence of the damaging effects of its smokeless tobacco products is emerging. Philip Morris is the strongest of the conventional tobacco companies. It is establishing itself as the leader in a declining industry, and it will be the one which eventually turns off the light—but it may do so with its pockets full of cash. If, as expected, cigarette taxes are eventually increased, the makers of premium brands with their higher margins will have room to absorb some of the tax increase and to narrow the price difference between their brands and the generic products. If an investor felt that the product liability risks were not too threatening, Philip Morris would be the preferred investment, because of the competitive strength provided by its resources.

Drug and Discount Retailing Industry

The drug and discount retailing industry has already been assessed as only moderately attractive, due primarily to intense competition. Superior earnings performance such as that achieved by Wal-Mart requires low costs. Low prices and/or a high level of customer service, which can create customer preference, can only be achieved if costs are low. The high volume achieved through customer preference provides bargaining power with suppliers.

No foreseeable changes, either favorable or unfavorable, are likely to alter the industry fundamentals. While much has been written about the threat of substitution created by new technology that would allow home shopping via interactive TV, it would be years before this infrastructure would become so extensive that it would affect conventional retailing. Further, such a development would primarily pose a threat to specialty retailers rather than to discounters who sell price-sensitive, frequently purchased products.

In the absence of any risk of change in industry fundamentals, investment in this industry can be based on current or expected competitive advantage. Wal-Mart is the preferred long-term investment, due to the sustainability of its competitive advantage.

Recreational Products Manufacturing Industry

Developments in the recreational products manufacturing industry arise from a combination of cycles and trends. The cyclical influence is due to the discretionary nature of the products. Purchases are influenced by such economic variables as consumer confidence, disposable income, and even interest rates. Sensitivity to these cycles will remain a fundamental characteristic of the industry but may be modified to some extent by trends. Since the companies being used as examples in this industry serve somewhat different markets, each company must be considered separately.

Harley-Davidson The analysis of Harley-Davidson in Chapter 5 raised questions about its room for growth in its market niche (high-income males with an average age of 40). The company's market appeal is based on image and nostalgia. The baby boomers who constitute this market niche are aging, and the upcoming affluent group were brought up on Hondas. The demographic cycle is therefore going against the company. As it runs out of market room, it is likely to become vulnerable to the cyclical declines that are characteristic of this industry as a whole. The company was able to avoid these declines in the early 1990s by meeting a backlog of demand in its specialized market segment.

Fleetwood Enterprises An underlying demographic trend which is favorable to Fleetwood is the increasing size of the retiree market, which should increase sales of mobile homes and small factory-built houses.

This trend should help to cushion the low points of the cycles that are inherent in the business. A prolonged period of high inflation which would raise prices above the levels affordable by fixed-income customers would create a discontinuity of potential concern to businesses dependent on the retiree market.

Outboard Marine   The major portion of the market for outboard motors and boats is recreational. For this reason, and because these products are big-ticket purchases, Outboard Marine is highly sensitive to economic forces. Replacement cycles are also a factor in demand. The high fixed cost structure of the business will continue to result in dramatic swings in earnings. An economic recovery, combined with the high value of the Japanese yen, is likely to produce a recovery through the mid-1990s because Japanese competitors will be at an exchange rate disadvantage. Recent concerns about two-cycle outboard motors polluting water with oil and gasoline residues have given rise to U.S. government regulations which will force manufacturers to convert to four-cycle power, at considerable R&D and retooling costs. OMC has obtained the marine rights to a German fuel injection technology which will reduce emissions and lower product costs. Introduction of this system in 1995 may give the company some competitive advantage, but it is not known whether this technology will meet the more stringent government standards which will take effect in 1998.

To sum up, an interesting situation prevails in the recreational products manufacturing industry, in that the historically strongest performer, Harley-Davidson, is at the greatest risk, whereas one of the weakest, Outboard Marine, has good though cyclical recovery potential.

Airlines Industry

There are no long-term investment candidates in the airlines industry at this time, due to its weak fundamentals. The short-term speculator, however, may be able to find some opportunities. Any change in investment potential would depend on favorable developments in industry structure which would improve the industry environment. Such developments may or may not occur, but there are some possibilities.

The government may re-regulate the industry, thereby creating barriers to entry, protecting markets, and limiting price wars. It is hard to see this as a realistic prospect. Further, many of the potential benefits of re-regulation would likely be dissipated by restoration of the power of the unions.

Continuing losses may exhaust the financial resources of many companies, overcoming the barriers to exit and accelerating the rationalization of the industry. Rationalization would have to take place on a global basis, incorporating the unregulated domestic and semiregulated international routes, so as to provide cross feeding of traffic and subsidization of highly competitive situations. The carriers that survived the shakeout could then obtain the volume and prices necessary to make a profit. As a side effect, airline travel would likely lose its elite status and take on many of the characteristics of bus travel.

In short, the airlines industry as a whole is not attractive to the long-term investor and will not be so for some years, until the shakeout is complete and the capabilities of the survivors can be assessed. The improvement in industry profitability in 1994 will likely delay the shakeout by providing interim hope to the beleaguered carriers, though this hope cannot be justified in the longer term. However, the nimble short-term investor may find some opportunities in companies in which remedial strategies are working at least temporarily.

THE INVESTOR'S PERSPECTIVE

While every investor must be sensitive to change, the priorities of the long-term investor are different from those of the speculator, or market player. The market player must be concerned about the effects of immediate change on earnings per share (EPS). As pointed out earlier, investors tend to overestimate the immediate impact of change and to underestimate its longer-term effects. The market reacts almost immediately to expected developments in the direction of the economy, contracts won or lost, the level of interest rates, and so forth. Thus the market player must keep track of day-to-day developments and be willing to get into or out of the market quickly.

The long-term investor, recognizing that short-term fluctuations are a part of the normal course of many businesses, should be concerned only about changes that affect the fundamental economics of the industry and/or the competitive position of a company in it. All investors, whether they take a short view or hold a long-term perspective, are willing to accept different degrees of risk in relation to the potential rewards. The conservative investor likely prefers to take positions in well-managed companies in stable industries, or in industries in which change is gradual and reasonably foreseeable. Aggressive investors may wish to take advantage of the returns that can be provided by an expected favorable change in industry fundamentals or in the position of a company.

Levels of Risk

Possession of decisive or strong competitive advantage is a necessity for any company that an investor is considering as a long-term investment. Even a company that has this requisite, however, is subject to the influence of change that affects its industry as a whole. In this context, change entails three levels of risk.

The lowest level of risk is presented by companies operating in relatively stable industries in which little change is expected. The relative performance of companies in a stable competitive environment usually tends to change slowly. Among our sample companies, this category includes Avon, Gillette, Coca-Cola, MacDonald's, and Wal-Mart. A decision to invest in a company of this sort may be based on the investor's assessment of the company's sustainable competitive advantage.

A somewhat higher level of risk is presented by companies operating in industries in which change is occurring in a relatively orderly and predictable way. A company with an effective strategy can widen the performance differences between itself and other companies. This category includes Merck, Nike, and Boeing, among our sample companies. In order to make an investment decision, the trader must assess not only the company's degree of competitive advantage but also the effectiveness of the strategic initiatives it is undertaking in an effort to cope with the change.

The highest risks are presented by companies operating in industries in which a major change in a favorable direction is expected or possible. Here, an improvement in earnings is expected to be derived from the company's anticipated ability to leverage its competitive advantage in a more attractive industry environment. The improvement in earnings can be quite dramatic. Inco and Schlumberger are in this category. It should be recognized that both of these companies are basically sound industry leaders. They are capable of weathering adverse developments and thus are not totally dependent on higher commodity prices. If the nature of the expected development is fully understood, the investor's uncertainty is usually likely to lie more in the issue of timing than in the direction of events.

At each of these three levels of risk, an investor should be able to confidently assume that the company is capable of both coping with and taking advantage of any change, either expected or unexpected. The basis for such an assumption is provided by well-managed corporations' demonstrated ability to adapt to managing change. In the relatively orderly business environment of the 1960s and the early 1970s, most corporations had corporate planning departments which carried out the detailed economic forecasting and planning upon which the corporation's decisions were based. (The planned strategy was discussed in Chapter 2.) When the economic environment became more volatile, starting in the mid-1970s, prediction became virtually impossible. Rather than continuing the futile exercise of making detailed long-range plans, corporations began to make only broad assumptions about the shape of future developments, such as economic growth. Managers reshaped their organizations to make them flexible enough to adapt to and take advantage of evolving situations. With the return of a somewhat more orderly environment in the 1980s, companies began to plan strategy while retaining both the ability to adapt to short-term changes in the industry and the ability to react to competitors' actions. That is, they adopted an emergent strategy. A company's ability to cope with change is usually confirmed by consistently superior long-term performance, as indicated by a high average ROE.

Assessing Change

Investors, like companies, must find ways to cope with change. Again like companies, they may initially find the prospect of change quite intimidating, or even crippling. Awareness of the kinds of change that affect companies and industries can help. So can careful assessment of the probable effects of change upon a company that is a candidate for investment, and of the industry in which it operates. After performing such an assessment, many investors realize that coping with change is not so formidable as it first appeared.

The investor must recognize that cycles are a normal occurrence in most businesses. An upturn in an industry cycle will at least temporarily improve the earnings prospects of companies in the industry. While cycles are inherently short-term developments, their occurrence does not disqualify an industry for long-term investment. Due consideration must be given to the selection of companies for investment and to the timing of purchases and sales.

To be a viable candidate for long-term investment, a company should have strong, preferably decisive, competitive advantage in its industry. Such an advantage will probably enable the company to weather the ensuing cyclical downturn better than its competitors do, and to perform more consistently than its competitors do over the long term. An in-depth academic study of 64 companies has confirmed that the successful ones in a hostile external environment were those which achieved competetive advantage either by having the lowest cost or most differentiated positions in their respective industries.[9]

In considering the timing of purchases and sales, investors must remember that stock prices anticipate cycles and run ahead of them. A reasoned contrarian view is helpful in timing these decisions. Comparing a company's current P/E ratio to its historical pattern indicates the extent to which the current price discounts an expected improvement in earnings.

The intensity, duration, and predictability of cyclical change are quite different between industries. Hence, generalizations are risky. For example, both the forest products and the automotive industries are known to be highly cyclical, yet automotive stocks swing wildly in price (as discussed in Chapter 9), while forest products stocks remain comparatively stable (see Chapter 11). Thus, the timing of investment decisions in cyclical situations should take into consideration the characteristics of the industry involved.

Favorable trends, if soundly based, can serve to reinforce the position and the potential of either an industry or a company, if it is fundamentally sound, as suggested in the discussion of Fleetwood Industries. In a cyclical industry, a favorable trend will reduce the depth of the next downturn. There is a risk, however, in basing a stock primarily on the expectation that a trend will improve the industry fundamentals. A trend may be recognized by many companies, which then rush into the industry (if barriers to entry are low), to take advantage of the expected situation. The industry becomes overcrowded, and much of the potential is diluted. For example, the increasing affluence of aging baby boomers was long expected to provide a strong market for financial services. The industry became overcrowded by the early 1990s, and competition was particularly intense. On the other hand, if a company is already sound and if the industry has barriers to entry, a favorable trend can reinforce the company's position.

Discontinuities usually have a transient effect unless the future of a company is based almost totally on a single assumption, as was the case with Dome Petroleum and with Olympia &York, which were discussed earlier in this chapter. Even these companies would likely have survived had they not been so heavily leveraged. In such cases, stock buyers should be aware that they are not investing but speculating. A discontinuity may cause a setback to even a sound, well-managed company, but such a company will usually recover. As previously mentioned, the aerospace and defense industry has been hit with a major discontinuity in the form of the unexpected end of the Cold War. Not surprisingly, its five-year average ROE declined from 18.5 percent in the early 1980s to 12.7 percent in the five-year period 1990–94, from the upper quartile to the all-industry median. Yet, many companies such as Rockwell International Corporation have maintained their ROE through various combinations of acquisitions to rationalize the industry and conversions of technology to civil applications—that is, by showing their ability to cope with change.

In conclusion, coping with change in the context of making investment decisions is not necessarily as formidable as it initially appears.

POINTS TO REMEMBER

The key points of this chapter are as follows:

1. Change can be caused by economic, social, political, or technological forces. These forces are often interrelated. Two or more
   of them may act together to affect the structure of an industry
   and/or the competitive position of a company.

2. Change can occur either as part of a recognizable cycle or trend
   or as a complete surprise—a discontinuity in the expected course
   of events. Cycles are the most common causes of change.
   Investors should be aware that, while cycles do recur, their
   underlying causes may be different.

3. The effects of a change can be assessed by first determining how
   it will affect the five variables that define the industry's structure
   and thus how it will alter the fundamental characteristics of the
   industry. Next the trader should evaluate the company's vulnerability to the change in comparison to its competitors' vulnerability, so as to determine whether the competitive balance in the
   industry will be changed. Companies may or may not be able to
   take strategic action either to offset the adverse effects of change
   or to take advantage of them.

4. Change is not necessarily an issue in all investment decisions. If
   an industry is expected to be relatively stable over a long period
   of time, investment decisions are based primarily on a company's
   degree of competitive advantage. If an industry is changing in
   gradual and relatively predictable ways, a company's strategy for
   coping with change must also be assessed. In a fast-changing
   industry, however, investment decisions must be based almost
   entirely on a company's ability to use its competitive advantage
   to cope with the changes in the industry.

5. The effects of cycles must be recognized in planning the timing
   of an investment. The stock market anticipates cycles, and prices
   move ahead of actual developments.

6. A trend can reinforce or weaken a company's present and/or
   potential performance, but investing solely on the basis of a trend

is risky. If the trend has been broadly recognized, the industry may be overcrowded by the time it takes effect.

7. The effects of discontinuities may be serious but are usually transient. A well-managed company can weather a transient or minor discontinuity. However, when a business is totally dependent on an assumed course of events, and is structured in such a way as to leave little room for error, even a transient discontinuity can cause major risk. Discontinuities of the proportions of the Cold War and the change in the Humboldt current, which were described in this chapter, can have extensive and long-lasting effects on an industry.

NOTES

1. Quoted from Don Marston, "The Great Boom and Bust Ahead," *Cashing in . . . Tapped Out*, published by The Courtyard Group of Companies and Transitions Support Management, Inc., Winter 1995, pp. 5–6.

2. Patricia Sellers, "Brands: It's Thrive or Die," *Fortune*, August 23, 1993, pp. 52–56.

3. Andrew E. Serwer, "Kellogg: What Price Brand Loyalty," *Fortune*, January 10, 1994, pp. 108–109.

4. Christopher Georges, "When Hard Work Doesn't Pay," *Globe and Mail*, November 9, 1994, p. A15.

5. Robert Lenzner and James M. Clash, "Wrong Again," *Forbes*, June 6, 1994, pp. 44–45.

6. John Carey and Jeoffrey Smith, "The Next Wonder Drug May Not Be a Drug," *Business Week*, May 9, 1994, pp. 84–86.

7. Brian O'Reilly, "Why Merck Married the Enemy," *Fortune*, September 20, 1994, pp. 60-64.

8. Maria Mallory with David Greising, Richard S. Dunham, and Mary Beth Regan, "Is the Smoking Lamp Going Out for Good?" *Business Week*, April 11, 1994, pp. 30–31; and Maria Mallory with John Carey, "These Days, Where There's Smoke, There's a Lawsuit," *Business Week*, June 6, 1994, p. 36.

9. William K. Hall, "Survival Strategies in a Hostile Environment," *Harvard Business Review*, September–October 1980, pp. 75–85.

IV

THE INVESTMENT

Though the insights into the potential earnings performance of a company provided by understanding the characteristics of its industry and the extent of its competitive advantage, as described in Parts II and III, provide no investment profits in themselves, they can be used to make an investment decision. To quoted Warren Buffett's Noah principle: "Predicting rain doesn't count; building arks does."

Part IV deals with two aspects of investment decisions: first, the initial purchase decision, which is made by applying the understanding of the industry and company that was gained in Parts II and III, and second, the continuing decisions that are made as a result of the monitoring of the investment. Monitoring is done on a continuing basis to assure that the circumstances and assumptions upon which the decision to purchase was based remain valid and that the investor can continue to hold the stock. Effective monitoring must cover not only assessment of the earnings and financial situation of the company but also an evaluation of any strategic actions being taken by the company, as well as interpretation of the implications of such developments as changes in management.

7

THE INVESTMENT DECISION

The analytical methodology and reasoning of strategic analysis provide a foundation for a long-term investment decision. Why some industries are more profitable than others and why some companies consistently outperform their competitors has already been shown. Even armed with all this high-quality information, the investor may find the actual investment decision difficult. Many variables are involved, each of which requires the exercise of judgment—and the necessary judgments may be subjective in nature. As if this weren't enough, the relative importance of these subjectively evaluated variables must then be weighed.

This chapter leads the investor through the complex and difficult process of actually making an investment decision. It provides:

- A list of questions to ask in determining the characteristics of an industry
- A list of questions to ask in assessing a company
- Guidelines for evaluating management
- A method for ranking investment options
- A method for establishing the risk-reward relationships for investment candidates

- An examination of the kinds of judgments involved in making an investment decision
- Two sets of actual company evaluations

THE DECISION-MAKING PROCESS

There are several steps in the process of choosing a company for long-term investment. First the industries and companies under consideration must be evaluated, and the companies' management must be assessed. Next the various investment alternatives must be ranked so that they can be compared on the basis of a combination of the characteristics of the industries and the performance potential of the companies—for it is this combination that will determine the future earnings of the companies. The prices of the stocks and their present price/earnings (P/E) ratios are also important factors in the eventual decision, which is based on the risk-reward relationship.

Analyzing an Industry's Characteristics

For the long-term investor, long-term return on equity (ROE) performance, changes in recent ROE performance as compared to the long-term average, and the extent and direction of future changes in profitability are the essential characteristics of industry structure. These characteristics can be defined for any industry by answering the questions listed below.

1. What is the five-year average of industry median ROEs? What is the ROE for the most recent year? How do these figures compare to the all-industry ROEs? What is the trend in the direction of the industry ROE?

2. What overall characteristics of the industry explain this ROE performance? Specifically:

   - What is the nature of the barriers to entry? What is the risk of new entrants?
   - What is the threat of substitutes? What is the industry's vulnerability to these substitutes?
   - What is the industry's bargaining power with its customers? What factors create this bargaining power?
   - What is the industry's bargaining power with suppliers? What factors create this bargaining power?

- How intense is the competition within the industry? What are the causes of this competition, including the life-cycle phase of the industry, the industry cost structure, and barriers to exit?

3. What changes already taking place within the industry explain the ROE trend? What further changes are inherent in the current structure of the industry? Include such factors as change of industry phase and emerging substitutes.

4. What changes are possible in the industry's economic, social, political, and technological environments? What elements of industry structure might be affected by these changes? How might these changes affect the structure and profitability of the industry? Are any of these changes cyclical, or based on trends? Is the future of the industry based on a key variable which is at risk of a possible discontinuity?

Analyzing a Company's Performance within Its Industry

After the investor has determined the characteristics of the industry in which a candidate company is operating, the next step is to answer the questions listed below, which pertain to the company and its competitors. However, the investor is not likely to be able to answer all these questions completely. It will probably be necessary to make estimates or draw conclusions from circumstantial evidence. Even so, the reasons for differences in long-term ROE performance between the candidate and other companies in its industry should be established in adequate detail, and any changes that have taken place in recent years should be explained. Even so, these answers should help to provide an acceptable basis for an investment decision.

The questions that need to be asked about an investment candidate and its competitors are as follows:

1. How does the company rank in its industry, in terms of ROE, return on capital, and profit margins? In comparison to competitors, in what direction and to what extent has the company's performance been changing?

2. What combination of capability and positioning gives the company the competitive advantage that provides this performance? On what resources does the capability depend? Does the company appear to be nurturing these resources?

3. What is the magnitude of the company's competitive advantage relative to that of competitors—marginal, strong, or decisive? To

what extent is the company's competitive advantage sustainable? Does the company have room for continued growth?

4. What is the company's apparent strategy for enhancing its competitive strength and responding to potential change? Can this strategy be expected to be effective?

5. What are the competitors doing strategically? Are their actions making the industry structure more favorable or less favorable?

6. Is the company's basis of competitive advantage threatened or strengthened by possible future changes in industry structure? Does the company have the resources to weather unexpected changes or discontinuities?

Evaluating a Company's Management

The quality of a company's management is obviously an important factor in its long-term success. After all, it is the managers who diagnose the company's industry and competitive circumstances, and it is also the managers who decide on and carry out the strategy that provides the earnings. The long-term investor should attempt to answer this question: Does the company have a consistent and effective strategy for providing and sustaining competitive advantage and coping with change?

In some cases, the answer can be found in management statements. Such statements are printed in annual reports to shareholders, filed with securities regulators, included in presentations to investment analysts, and given out in interviews with the press. Remember, however, that these statements tend to be self-serving. The managers are telling you what they want you to believe and trying to create an image. This image usually exaggerates reality, but there are exceptions. When Jack Welch assumed the CEO position at General Electric in 1981, he publicly outlined his vision for the company and the basic strategy that he would be following. It has been possible to follow the fortunes of GE on the basis of Welch's strategy, which has been both consistent and effective, though not without some disappointments.

In most cases, investors must rely on circumstantial evidence when they are evaluating a company's strategy. Circumstantial evidence may be used to substantiate or to repudiate managerial statements, and also to assess managers' effectiveness. The kinds of circumstantial evidence commonly used are as follows:

- The company's performance record in improving its ROE ranking in its industry

- The action being taken by the company's managers to adapt to changes in the industry

For example, in the past five years Merck has steadily improved its five-year average ROE ranking in the pharmaceuticals industry, moving up from fifth in 1988, at 1.4 times the industry median, to first in 1994, at 2.1 times the industry median. Further, as pointed out in Chapter 6, the company has been adapting to changes in the industry structure. It attempted to restore its bargaining power with customers by making an acquisition in 1994 which expanded its influence on the market. While the industry will continue to change, Merck's performance provides reasonable assurance of its management's competence and ability to cope.

Professional investment analysts and money managers often have opportunities to question management in the course of presentations or one-on-one meetings. Thus, if these analysts have done their homework on the industry and the company, they can get answers to a number of important questions. Specifically:

1. Is the view from inside the company on both the industry and the company's position consistent with the analyst's outside view?
2. What is the company's strategy? Does the company address its strategic problems and take advantage of its opportunities?
3. Is the company's strategy realistic? Does it take into account the company's current position and resources?
4. What is the nature of the company's strategic leadership? Is the strategy planned, emergent, or adaptive? (Refer back to Chapter 2 if you need to refresh your memory on the types of strategies.)

Management's statements, however, should be taken with a grain of salt. It is surprising how often there are major differences between corporate pronouncements and reality. Use of the terms *strategic vision* and *mission* by management, with no reference to specific actions, should always be regarded as evasive.

General Motors, for example, has a long history of talking about change, with highly apparent good intentions, while achieving few results. The company's progress has been slow because of resistance to change on the part of both management and labor, and also because of the company's internal structural rigidities. General Motors announced a plan to streamline the way its cars are conceived, engineered, and built in 1984. However, 10 years later the company was continuing to have major problems caused by extended development times and shortages of new models at the critical time of their introduction.

An investor's evaluation of management must also include an assessment of its depth—an aspect that is of particular concern when the company appears to be highly dependent on one very visible person. A *management with depth* may be defined as one that has a sufficient number of capable and experienced people at senior levels to replace any departures, including the CEO. Consider the situation of Microsoft, for example. The company is highly dependent on the dynamic and visionary leadership of its founder and CEO, Bill Gates. While there is considerable depth in its talented management team, Gates is so closely identified with the company that his departure would almost certainly cause a significant decline in its stock prices. While the company would continue to do well for a while, its long-term potential without Gates's vision and drive would be questionable. The Microsoft investor is therefore only a heartbeat away from the risk of a significant loss.[1]

Another example of the effects of a company's strong dependency on the dominance and leadership of one person can be seen in a coup that took place in Saatchi & Saatchi Co., the world's fifth-largest advertising company. In late 1994, dissidents on the board of directors forced the resignation of Maurice Saatchi, the chairman of the board, who together with his brother Charles had founded the business in 1970. Unhappy with the performance of share prices, these dissidents, who represented various pension funds and mutual funds, gave excessive spending along with autocratic and belligerent management style as the reasons for their coup.

The dissidents had underestimated both the strength of Maurice Saatchi's influence and his standing in the industry. Within days, several major clients withdrew their accounts. Others put their accounts up for review. Seven key executives resigned and, together with Saatchi, set up a rival agency. Saatchi & Saatchi stock dropped by one-third, and the company's survival is in question.[2] The dissidents would have been better off selling their shares, since they were not satisfied with the company's performance. Unfortunately, it was not only the dissidents who suffered from their own shortsightedness, but also many other shareholders.

Though sound basic management is important to the long-term investor, the examples of Microsoft and Saatchi & Saatchi provide clear evidence that sound management alone is not an adequate basis for an investment decision. A statement by Warren Buffett, chairman of Berkshire Hathaway, which was cited at the beginning of Chapter 3, is worth repeating in this context: "With few exceptions, when a manager with a reputation for brilliance tackles a business with a reputation for poor fundamental economics, it is the reputation of the business which remains intact."

Ranking the Options

One basic difficulty in assessing a company as an investment candidate is the large number of variables involved, each of which carries an initially unknown degree of importance and uncertainty. Through strategic analysis, the investor is able to weigh the relative importance of two major factors—the characteristics of the industry and the company's competitive position within the industry—and to make a decision based on one or both of them. Most often, the decision is based on a balance of the two.

The process involves ranking the two major factors on the industry attractiveness-competitive strength matrix shown in Exhibit 7–1.[3] For purposes of ranking, both industries and companies are divided into four classifications, which are defined below. The important issue of change is treated in the matrix as a part of each of the two major factors. On the industry attractiveness axis, change is recognized primarily by its effect on the size of its markets through the impact of cycles and trends. On the competitive strength axis, the company's ability to respond to change is assessed on the basis of its resources and/or the strategic responses available to it (see Chapter 6).

The four classifications provided in Exhibit 7–1 are probably adequate for most purposes. If needed, however, the number of classifications can easily be expanded to five or six for either industry or company, or for both, and the classifications can be defined in more detail. The four classifications of industry attractiveness shown in Exhibit 7–1 are defined as follows:

Classifications of Industry Attractiveness	Industry Characteristics
High	Key industry fundamentals are almost all favorable, with no apparent threat from change. The industry median five-year average ROE is likely to be in the upper quartile of the *Forbes* ranking of all industries, with the latest period showing no significant deterioration that can be attributed to longer-term developments.
Favorable	The industry is competitive, but competition is constrained to some extent by fundamentals. The industry median five-year average ROE is likely to be in the third quartile of all-industry performance.
Moderate	The industry has a balanced competitive situation, with slow market growth. Battles for market share are common. The industry median ROE is likely to be in the lower half of the all-industry list.
Low	The industry is intensely competitive, with little prospect for change. The industry median ROE is in the lowest quartile of the all-industry list.

Industry Attractiveness–Competitive Strength Matrix

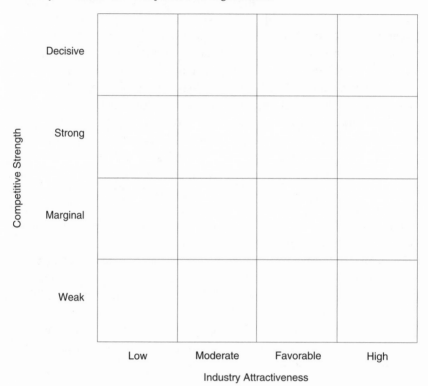

The four classifications of competitive strength shown in Exhibit 7–1 are defined as follows:

Classification of Competitive Strength	Company Characteristics
Decisive	The company derives competitive advantage from two or more sources, which reinforce each other. The risk of imitation is low, and the company has the resources to effectively counter competitive threats and/or industry changes. There is room for growth from available markets and through utilization of competitive advantage. Superior operating capability is indicated by superior profit margins with strong financial position. The company is one of the leading, performers in the industry, in terms of five-year average ROE as well as most recent period ROE.
Strong	The company's competitive advantage is derived from more than one source. There is some risk of imitation, and the advantage is

	difficult to improve significantly, but it is basically sustainable. Growth is dependent to some extent on an increase in market share. The company has the resources required to respond to change. The company's ROE performance is likely to be in the upper quartile of its industry.
. Marginal	Competitive advantage is present to the extent that the company's position can be held, but there is limited potential for significant improvement. Sales growth is heavily dependent on increase in market share, and the company's ROE performance is in the upper half of the industry.
Weak	The company's competitive advantage is weak, or the company's product or service is vulnerable to imitation. The company's ROE is in the lower half of the industry.

Establishing the Risk-Reward Relationship

Every investment involves some degree of risk. While the overall objective of all long-term investors is to achieve capital appreciation of their stock portfolios while minimizing risk, the degree of risk that is acceptable must be determined by the individual, and thus is a matter of judgment.

Criteria for Long-Term Investment

The basic principles upon which long-term investment decisions should be based have been discussed in earlier chapters. They are repeated below, as a reminder.

1. The market performance of a stock is determined by a combination of the industry's attractiveness and the company's competitive advantage. However, the dominant factor in performance potential is competitive advantage (as discussed in Chapter 5).

2. Where both of these factors are present, the industry's attractiveness must not be threatened by change and the company's competitive advantage must be sustainable. The company must also have room for growth.

3. In a less than attractive industry, the potential for improvement should be present, and industry constraints must be offset by strong or decisive competitive advantage on the part of the company.

4. If the industry is sufficiently attractive, a company that has moderate competitive strength with a strong prospect for improvement may be considered.

5. In all cases, the extent of potential earnings improvement which may already be reflected in the stock price must be taken into consideration.

Investment Zones

A company's position on the industry attractiveness-competitive strength matrix that was introduced in Exhibit 7–1 can also indicate the risk-reward relationship involved in investment in that company. The risk-reward zones are shown in Exhibit 7–2 and described below.

Primary Zone Long-term investment in a company in the primary zone can be expected to yield consistent long-term earnings growth with relatively low downside risk. The primary zone is defined as a segment in which one of two conditions occurs: either (1) decisive competitive strength is found in a company that is operating in an industry that has moderate, favorable, or high attractiveness, or (2) strong to decisive competitive strength is found in a company whose industry is highly attractive. In this zone, the degree of competitive strength is the main criterion, but the potential of a company with relatively strong competitive advantage in an attractive industry environment is also recognized.

EXHIBIT 7–2

Industry Attractiveness–Competitive Strength Matrix: Risk-Reward Zones

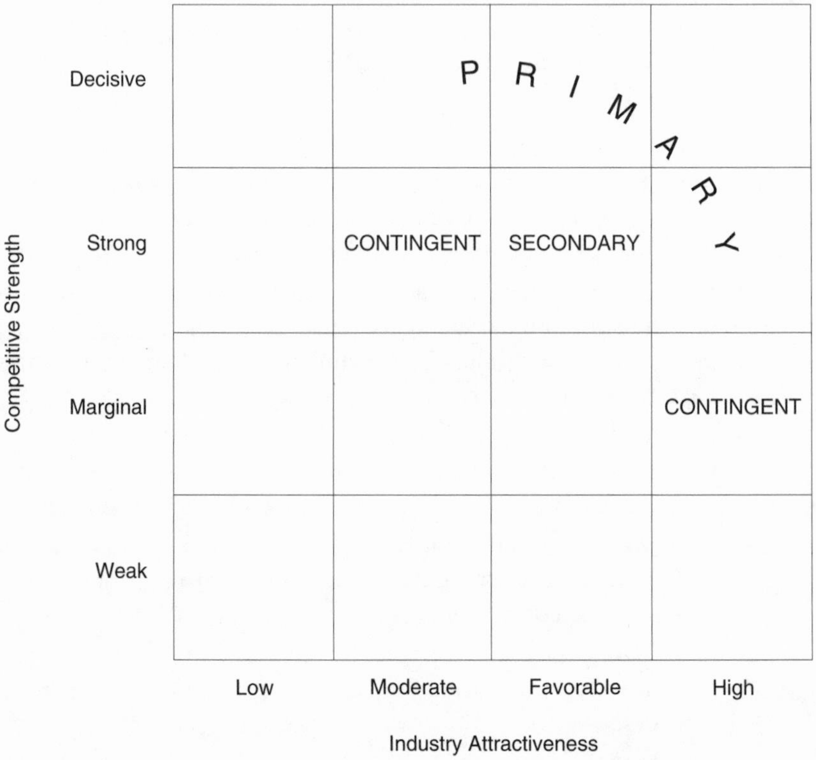

Industry Attractiveness

Secondary Zone   Companies in the secondary zone may be considered on the basis of their combination of favorable industry attractiveness and strong competitive advantage, if no adverse change in either can be foreseen. Stocks in this area have the potential for relatively high appreciation if either the attractiveness of the industry or the company's competitive advantage becomes more favorable.

Contingent Zone   A company in the contingent zone may be considered for long-term investment if there is a sound prospect of an improvement in either the industry's attractiveness or the company's competitive strength. An increase in industry attractiveness often results from cyclical changes, whereas any of the strategies discussed in Chapter 5 can enhance a company's competitive strength. Either of these types of improvement can move a company into the secondary zone or even the primary zone. Investment in companies that are currently in the contingent zone is for the relatively aggressive investor. Though such investments are speculative in nature, they are capable of providing very high returns.

Long-range investment opportunities may exist beyond these zones, but their adverse factors must be recognized and reconciled with expectations. For example, a company that has decisive competitive strength in a weak industry may present an investment opportunity. The danger here is that the weakness of the industry may cause competitors to react in such a way as to seriously threaten the sustainability of the company's competitive advantage. Since such a situation exists in the airlines industry, even the strongest performers may be disqualified as long-term investment candidates.

Stock Prices

The stock price obviously must be taken into consideration in any investment decision. The first basis of reference is the performance of the broad market, which for our purposes is the price/earnings (P/E) ratio for the S&P 500. A P/E ratio higher than that of the broad market is the premium the investor pays for either favorable industry fundamentals or decisive competitive strength.

Comparison of the P/E ratio of the company under consideration to the P/E ratios of its competitors provides another useful indicator of relative value.

What price is acceptable to the individual investor is of course a matter of judgment. Inevitably, it reflects the person's degree of confidence in the conclusions reached through strategic analysis. Investors should, however, be wary about making an across-the-board assumption that the market's judgment is necessarily right. Market prices are based in part on emotional factors and thus do not inevitably represent a rational decision. The role of emotion in determining market prices is discussed in more depth below.

Risks of Dominance

There is one caveat with respect to reliance on decisive competitive advantage as an investment criterion. This applies to companies that have been long dominant in their industries through decisive competitive advantage. *Dominance*, defined here as holding about a 50 percent or higher share of its markets, creates certain risks, which are described below.

Limited Room for Growth   Having a high market share limits a company's room for growth. A company with a 20 percent market share that gains 5 percent in share has sales growth of 25 percent; a 50 percent share company that gains the same amount has only 10 percent sales growth, and such gains are difficult for a company with high market share to achieve.

Management Problems   Dominant companies often tend to develop management problems. Top managers in these companies may tend to rest on their laurels. They may continue too long doing whatever made the companies successful in the first place. They may either ignore changes in their industries or complacently assume that their companies' dominant positions will enable them to overcome any ill effects that might arise from the changes. The experiences of General Motors and IBM in the 1980s are examples of this syndrome. GM's share of the overall U.S. market declined from 46 percent in 1980 to 37 percent in 1987 due to various failures which will be discussed in Chapter 9. IBM fell behind in the PC market when its initial product failed and has not been able to regain a leading position.

In addition, a strong position of leadership can generate an arrogant attitude in management. Intel's initial reaction to the 1994 revelation of faults in the company's pentium chips demonstrates this phenomenon. Intel initially claimed that the defect would affect only a very small proportion of users, but was forced into an overall product recall by customer protest. While the cost of this was manageable to Intel and its technological leadership enabled it to hold its leading position, its reputation was badly damaged.

In short, investors who hold stocks in dominant companies must be on the alert for signs of a variety of management problems. Even the best managers must remain dynamic and flexible in order to retain their powers, their reputations, and their ability to do a good job for investors.

Erosion by Competitors   The profitability enjoyed by dominant companies means that their markets are constantly under attack by envious competitors, who look upon them as natural targets. Usually, competitors will
try to nibble away at dominant markets by establishing specialized niches for themselves, in which they have some prospect of success.

Consequences of Failure   The consequences of product or service failure are
unusually severe for a company that dominates its industry. If, for example,
a large number of the company's products are in the hands of consumers,
recalls or adjustments may be quite expensive. In addition, the damage to the
company's reputation can be serious, due to the scale of the failure.

   Because of these risks, investors should exercise caution when they
are considering dominant companies as long-term investment candidates.

EXERCISING JUDGMENT

While the analytical and decision-making procedures described in this book
are methodical, they nevertheless rely heavily on investors' judgments.
These judgments are of two types: (1) evaluation of the relevance and reliability of the available information and (2) interpretation of the information.
   Both types of judgments contain pitfalls for the investor, which will
be discussed below. The evaluative function must be performed in a systematic and meticulous way. The interpretation of information can be a
particularly hazardous area for the investor, as it is subject to varying
kinds and degrees of influence by emotional factors. Assessing the extent
and depth of emotional influence can be difficult, as it involves a variety
of subtle factors which may be difficult to identify and understand.
Nevertheless, it is important to investigate this area, so that subjective
influences on the decision can be minimized.

Evaluating Facts

The information needed to analyze industry and company situations for
investment purposes falls into the following three categories[4]:

1. *Known information, or facts.* Investors can have reasonable confidence in this sort of information, which includes financial and
   other data published by companies; calculations based on these
   data; and industry statistics compiled by reliable authorities, such
   as governmental bodies and trade associations.

2. *Presumed information, or presumptions.* These are generally accepted interpretations of an industry's situation, such as the market shares, relative operating costs, and reputations of the companies operating in the industry. Presumptions are less reliable than facts.

3. *Assumed information, or assumptions.* The least reliable of the three categories, assumptions may involve reasoned estimates on various aspects of the stock market. They are particularly common in attempts to guess the directions of future events and developments that may affect an industry or a company.

All three of these categories of information are necessary parts of a comprehensive analysis of an industry and company. The most common error is the tendency to upgrade the quality of information—say, by treating an assumption as a presumption. This happens particularly with regard to future developments. Traders also tend to not question the "conventional wisdom" that distorts their views of the market. Further, they often give too much weight to certain information, such as the quality of management. Too frequently, a CEO with a strong performance record is given cult status and considered unable to do wrong.

One way of assessing the reliability of any bit of information is to examine how it fits into the overall picture of the company or industry. Any information that is assumed but does not logically fit the known facts should be either verified by other means or disregarded.

A further important basis for judgment is provided by trying or inspecting the company's product or service to determine whether you like it or are favorably impressed. If this is not possible, talking to some of the company's customers can be a reasonable substitute.

As investors gain experience, this experience begins to play a significant role in their exercise of judgment. It provides a historical analogy according to which the present facts can be interpreted. While experience has the obvious value of adding long-term perspective, it also creates danger. Investors may not realize the extent to which experience conditions their decisions, causing them to neglect to ask the right questions—the questions that are right for the present situation, though they may not have applied in the past. There is an old military adage that is also relevant to the stock market: "Generals are always prepared to fight the last war."

Experience must be tempered with caution. The investor must evaluate the ways in which the current situation is similar to or different from a prior event that is being used as a basis for reference. At issue here are the both thoroughness of the investor's analysis and a healthy degree of skepticism about the conventional wisdom.

Minimizing Emotional Influences

"Sometimes reason becomes the slave of passion," observed David Hume, the eighteenth-century Scottish philosopher. Human nature is much the same at the end of the twentieth century as it was in Hume's time. Even seemingly reasonable processes, such as the evaluation of facts about the stock market, are subject to distortion by perception and personal experience.

Types of Emotional Biases

Psychological studies of the decision-making process have uncovered significant biases that affects investors when they are choosing between risks and rewards.[5] These biases are of four basic types: aversion to losses, exaggeration of remote possibilities, confusion about cycles, and faulty comparisons. Some basic findings that are relevant to the process of making investment decisions are described below.

Aversion to Losses A surprisingly strong emotion—so strong, in fact, that it can prevent even knowledgeable investors from accepting good bets—is aversion to losses. Indeed, this trait may account for the large number of undervalued stocks in the marketplace. If you buy a depressed stock and it declines further, it's human nature to berate yourself for being so dumb in the first place. However, if you buy a highly rated, popular stock and it falls, this is an act of God and you are blameless. Aversion to losses is an underlying cause of the herd instinct, which magnifies both undervaluations and overvaluations.

Exaggeration of Remote Possibilities We are all poor judges of remote possibilities, and most people tend to exaggerate them, leaping to either overly optimistic or overly pessimistic conclusions about the ultimate conclusions of events that may be as yet only indistinct possibilities. Thus we overestimate the immediate impact of new technology, for instance, but underestimate its long-term implications (see Chapter 6).

On the upside, this tendency to exaggerate can result in an astronomical P/E ratio for a company with a hot new product, even when the odds are against an increase in earnings of the magnitude necessary to justify the price of the stock.

A couple of real-world examples will illustrate the downside effects of exaggeration. The 1986 nuclear accident at Chernobyl in the Ukraine, which necessitated the abandonment of the town, also caused a strong reaction on the other side of the world: a fall in the stock prices of U.S. utilities that had built nuclear plants. In 1984 the stock of Union Carbide dropped 30 percent in only a few weeks, after an accident in Bhopal, India. An accidental release of a toxic gas killed an estimated 2,000 people and injured 30,000 to 40,000. Union Carbide was eventually ordered to pay $470 million in damages, with $200 million covered by insurance. By the time of the settlement in 1989, Union Carbide stock was at twice its pre-Bhopal level. The stock market was overreacting to the remote possibility that the company would be hit with a devastating penalty. It is doubtful that moral concerns over Union Carbide's action played any role in this.

The nuclear power generation industry in North America has continued to operate without incident. However, public concern about safety, combined with a weakening of the economics of nuclear power generation in comparison with alternative sources of electricity, has resulted in no new nuclear plants being built.

Confusion about Cycles   Both investors and managers tend to take a short view of temporary or cyclical developments, confusing them with long-term trends and concluding that things will stay as they are now. Even in industries in which cycles are a long-established phenomenon, managers tend to make decisions on the basis of current conditions. Rather than adding capacity during periods of weak prices, so that it will be available when the demand cycle turns upward, they add capacity at the peak of the recovery. This contributes to the glut in the eventual downturn, thereby driving prices even lower.

This tendency may be overcome by the use of the contrarian approach. Investors are reluctant to finance expansion, either by debt or equity, in periods of low prices for products and the consequent low earnings. The attitude is that things will not improve no matter what the historical record.

Faulty Comparisons   If two things have some similar characteristics, most people tend to conclude that the two are the same. This is true even if the similarities are superficial. Compounding the risk of making faulty comparisons is a tendency to make too much of examples that can be easily recalled. For example, investors may choose a mutual fund on the basis of recent successes rather than taking the trouble to study its historical record, or they may assume that a company that has consistent earnings growth for a few years will continue this sterling performance, rather than realizing that the growth could be due to luck rather than to more trustworthy qualities such as management perspicacity or competitive advantage.

Biases, distortions, and defects in judgment make the stock market much less rational than investors would like it to be, and than many people actually believe it to be. The individual investor who has not done his or her homework is particularly vulnerable to emotional influences—that is, particularly likely to make mistakes in judgment, due to emotional factors. Even securities analysts who have been trained to be objective are often reluctant to recommend poorly regarded stocks, preferring to be identified with winners which can make their reputations much more quickly.

Investors should therefore be alert to the possibility of bias in every context—not excepting this book. Earlier in this chapter, for example, in the analysis of long-term investment candidates, the astute reader could find many instances of possible bias. One such instance is my evaluation of the possibility of a catastrophic legal judgment against the tobacco industry. An analyst who feels that my reaction to this possibility is exaggerated may wish to add Philip Morris to the list of long-term investment candidates.

The overall exercise of judgment in selecting long-term investments can be assisted by applying the following five rules, based on suggestions that were originally made by Warren Buffett.[6]

1. Think of yourself as buying part of a business, not just a stock. This approach should make a significant difference in your perspective, because a part owner of a business has a long-term view, whereas a stock owner tends to become a market player in times of doubt.

2. Make an investment only if you understand the situation in the company and its industry, and only if you feel comfortable about the economic characteristics and performance capability of the company.

3. Don't try to figure out what the market is doing. "In fact, the true investor welcomes volatility . . . because a wildly fluctuating market means that irrationally low prices will periodically be attached to solid businesses. It is impossible to see how the availability of such prices can be thought of as increasing the hazards for an investor who is totally free to either ignore the market or exploit its folly."[7]

4. Concentrate rather than diversify your holdings. "Diversification is protection against ignorance, but if you don't feel ignorant, the need for it goes down drastically."

5. After you analyze a company situation and decide you feel comfortable with it, have the courage to act on your convictions and
stay with the company as long as it remains sound.

Buffett has described his overall approach as being based on his
belief that "When proper temperament joins with proper intellectual
framework, then you get rational behavior."

This book provides an intellectual framework for rational investment behavior, and the assumption is that strong companies will outperform the market in the long term. The investor must contribute the temperament—the considerable degree of self-knowledge and self-discipline
that are needed to overcome the biases inherent in emotion-based judgments and to make rational investment decisions.

Evaluating Growth Situations

As part of the overall analysis of an industry and a company, the question
of "growth" must often be given particular attention. The term *growth*
may be applied to either an industry or a company. Rapid growth of earnings provides the basis for a high P/E ratio and a rapid rise in the stock
price. With careful analysis and the exercise of judgment in growth situations, the investor can avoid participating in the equally rapid decline in
the stock price which often follows.

Sources of Growth
Growth situations can be readily analyzed using the procedures that have
already been described. Special attention should be given to the reasons
for the rapid growth, which usually arises from some combination of the
following three circumstances:

1. The industry in which the company is operating is in the growth
   phase of its life cycle (see Chapter 3).
2. The company is offering a new product or service with particular market appeal, or is exploiting an underserviced market segment. Either of
   these situations creates strong bargaining power with buyers.
3. The company is using new technology or new concepts to
   restructure its industry, usually by lowering barriers to entry
   and/or reducing operating costs.

Life-Cycle Phase The growth phase of an industry is just that, a phase—
and it usually ends sooner than enthusiastic investors expect. Even when

industry shipments continue to grow, late in the phase, when the industry is overbuilt, earnings will tend to drop as competition becomes intense. The astute investor may recognize opportunities during the shift of power from producer to distributor. As mentioned earlier, such a shift took place as the growth phase of the PC industry entered its late stage in the second half of the 1980s, providing the basis for the emergence of Dell Computer.

Another growth situation related to industry phase arises during upside breakouts in basically mature industries. The emergence of cellular phones in the mature telecommunications industry is an example. Since mature industries are usually dominated by giants, opportunities for new companies are typically limited to market niches and often based on unique technology.

New Product or Service Growth because of a new product or service is a continuing phenomenon which has been particularly prevalent in the computer software industry. This industry has offered a wide range of opportunities for servicing specialized market segments. The problem for the investor is that while market segments offer opportunities for rapid growth, they are ultimately limited in size and therefore in possibilities for growth. If a market segment continues to grow, it will attract other players and competition will increase. The human skills which are the key resource in the computer software industry are readily available, and barriers to entry are low.

Industry Restructuring Growth due to industry restructuring is relatively rare, but, of the three sources of growth, it probably offers the most dramatic and enduring long-term investment opportunities. Restructuring is usually based on new technology which changes the basic economics of the industry. A dramatic example is provided by the emergence of steel minimills and the performance of Nucor, as discussed in Exhibit 2–1. The best investment opportunities are provided by the leaders in the new industry. These are the companies that get a fast start, have room for rapid growth, and can stay up to date in the developing technology.

An indication of the distribution of opportunities between these three categories of growth situations is provided by a 1994 survey in "Hot Growth Companies," published by *Business Week* magazine.[8] This survey ranked 100 companies based on a composite index made up of three-year results in sales growth, earnings growth, and return on invested capital. The survey, which included companies that had sales of more than $10 million but less than $150 million, showed the following sources of growth:

- *Unique product or service.* Of the growth situations surveyed, 96 were based on a unique product or service, broken down as follows: 39 in technological areas (mainly software), 9 in food service, 9 in specialty retailing, 10 in distribution, and 29 in miscellaneous areas.
- *Industry breakout.* Three growth situations were based on a breakout in the telecommunications industry.
- *Industry growth phase.* One growth situation occurred in the waste disposal industry, which was in the late growth phase of its life cycle.

Business Week's review of its 1992 listing, which accompanied the 1994 survey, indicated that the high-tech and retail categories had taken the worst beating. Several food service companies were among the best performers.

Investing in Growth Companies

In considering long-term investment in growth companies, individual investors should be particularly cautious, for three reasons. In the first place, the stocks of such companies are usually priced quite high by the time they are available to individual investors (though underwriting institutions can do well with these stocks). A *Business Week* study of initial public offerings (IPOs) indicates that individual investors have access to only a small proportion of hot deals at initial offering prices, and thus usually wind up paying a much higher price in the market.[9]

Second, two university-based studies reported by *Business Week*[10] indicate that 90 percent of returns on common stock offerings are earned by the initial buyers of the shares, who purchased them on the first day they were offered. In addition, the average annual return on IPOs held for five years is only 5 percent—which is very low in relation to the risk. The underwriters are influential in setting the initial offering price at a level at which they can quickly sell out through their brokers, thereby assuring their commission and fees on the deal.

Third, the high prices of these stocks can be justified only if their expected strong earnings performance is actually realized. Though the earnings performance may be attainable in the short term, several factors may cause difficulty in sustaining them in the long term. These factors are as follows:

- The company's basis for competitive advantage is usually narrow, usually dependent on one factor, and rarely decisive. Many opportunities are dependent on fashion, which tends to be transient. (Here, the term *fashion* is used to mean a popular style or format and can be used in relation to products or services of a wide range of businesses, from apparel to restaurants.)

- Many such opportunities are in fragmented industries, in which a large amount of capital and management depth are necessary, to increase the number of outlets upon which the growth depends.
- Fragmented industries are usually relatively easy to imitate. The barriers to entry tend to be low, and any apparent success will quickly attract imitators. In order for such a growth situation to be sustainable, an essential element is some protection against imitation. The existence of proprietary technology would be an example.

While the above cautions should be taken into account, there have been many long-term success stories that have come out of relatively small growth situations. Some companies have been able to get a fast start and establish competitive advantage through superior capability and dominance of major markets so quickly that competitors were effectively discouraged. Toys 'R' Us Inc. and Office Depot Inc. offer examples of this strategy. Both companies are retailers and are termed "category busters," offering broad product lines in their respective areas of specialization at low prices through warehouse-type outlets. Toys 'R' Us has grown to more than 581 stores with sales of more than $8 billion since its start-up in 1978. Office Depot, a more recent example, was started in 1986. By 1994 it had grown to 362 stores with sales of $3.8 billion.

In considering a particular "growth" company as a candidate for long-term investment, the investor must evaluate it in terms of the performance-limiting factors listed above, to make sure that they are not dominant issues with the company and its industry. Usually it is better to wait until the company's performance capability has been established. By this time, too, the market's valuation of the company's stocks will no longer be affected by the emotional factors that influenced the price of the initial offering.

TWO SETS OF COMPANY EVALUATIONS

In this section we follow the procedure described above to evaluate two sets of companies as candidates for long-term investment. The first set of companies is taken from the sample industries that were discussed in Chapters 3 through 6, the second from a broad spectrum of industries, as described in Chapters 5 and 6.

In each of these evaluations, several companies are positioned on an industry attractiveness-competitive strength matrix. The position of each company is determined by the characteristics of its industry and by the company's competitive capabilities. The time periods on which the evaluations are based are specified, because industry attractiveness can vacillate from favorable to moderate due to cyclical influences.

A change in position on the matrix can be driven by an expected change in industry attractiveness, a change in the company's competitive performance, or a combination of these two factors. If changes are considered to be leading the company in a different direction, the company's position on the matrix is accompanied by an arrow showing the expected direction. A straight arrow indicates that the change is a trend, and a wavy arrow indicates a cyclical change.

EVALUATING COMPANIES IN FIVE SAMPLE INDUSTRIES

Fifteen companies from the five sample industries that were discussed in Chapters 3 through 5 are evaluated as long-term investment candidates in this section. These five industries are the pharmaceuticals, tobacco, drug and discount retailing, recreational products manufacturing, and airlines industries.

Exhibit 7–3 gives brief explanations of the positions of these 15 companies on the matrix shown in Exhibit 7–4. For each company, Exhibit 7–3 indicates both the range of prices for the 52 weeks ending March 31, 1995, and the extent to which the stock price and the P/E ratio of the same date may recognize potential future developments in the industry and the company.

The broad market reference against which these prices are judged is the trailing ratio, or P/E ratio, of the S&P 500, which was 16.5 as of March 31, 1995. The *trailing ratio* is defined as the P/E ratio based on reported earnings for the latest 12 months. Some analysts feel that estimated earnings for a given year provide a more realistic basis for evaluating the present price than does the trailing ratio. However, because of the unreliability of current earnings estimates (as discussed in Chapter 2), it is best to stick to a hard factual basis.

The conclusion I derive from Exhibits 7–3 and 7–4 is that there are two long-term investment prospects on the list, as follows:

Merck   With its competitive advantage, Merck should be able to offset any weakening in the pharmaceuticals industry, particularly because the company's P/E ratio indicates relatively low expectations.

Evaluations of Selected Companies in Five Sample Industries as Long-Term Investment Candidates
(As of March 31, 1995)

Industry/ Company	Stock Price Range 52 Weeks Ending 03/31/95	Price	03/31/94 P/E Ratio	5-Year ROE % Co./Ind.	Evaluation
Pharmaceuticals industry					
Merck	45 1/8–28 18	42 5/8	17.9	49.0/22.8	Decisive competitive advantage due to size, consistent development of new products, and forward integration. Weakening of industry is partially offset by improving demographics. P/E ratio does not discount potential.
Eli Lilly	76 7/8–47	73	16.4	19.6/22.8	Marginal competitive strength is highly dependent on one popular product. Company is capable of surviving but will have to struggle to improve its ranking in industry. Potential takeover candidate in further rationalization of industry.
Pfizer	90–53 1/4	85 3/4	20.5	16.5/22.8	Competitive strength improving toward strong, but future heavily dependent on forthcoming new products and strategy of staying focused and significantly increasing R&D expenditures. P/E ratio does not unduly discount improvement potential.
Tobacco industry					
UST Inc.	32 3/8–23 5/8	31 3/4	17.0	58.8/18.4	Decisive competitive strength due to domination of sheltered market segment. Company is vulnerable to health-related litigation, particularly if legal action against rest of industry succeeds.

Exhibit 7–3, *Concluded*

Industry/ Company	Stock Price Range 52 Weeks Ending 03/31/95		03/31/94 P/E Ratio	5-Year ROE % Co./Ind.	Evaluation
		Price			
Philip Morris	68–47 1/2	65 3/8	12.0	34.4/18.4	High competitive strength due to global recognition of brands, with likely one of best food-processing operations in industry. Industry, however, is highly vulnerable.
RJR Nabisco	7–5	5 7/8	def	0.6/18.4	Competitive strength marginal on basis of some strong tobacco brands, popular food products, and global diversification. However, company is heavily leveraged in vulnerable industry.
Drug and discount retailing industry					
Wal-Mart	27 7/8–20 1/2	25 5/8	21.9	29.2/12.8	Decisive competitive strength from structurally derived low operating costs and reputation for high level of in-store service. Potential for growth not unduly discounted by P/E ratio.
Kmart	18 5/8–11 7/8	13 3/4	21.8	5.0/12.8	Only marginal competitive strength due to structural problems, which will require heavy spending to correct. Remedial action not well implemented to date. Quality of management open to question. Vulnerable to further disappointing results.
Woolworth	18 5/8–12 7/8	18 1/2	51.4	10.6/12.8	Has consistently underperformed industry in long term due to structural limitations, as geographic fragmentation works against distribution efficiency. Remedial action is unlikely to significantly change this, although foreign currency earnings converted to weak dollars may temporarily disguise problems.
Recreational products manufacturing industry					
Harley-Davidson	29 7/8–21	24	17.5	16.7/7.7	Strong competitive strength due to successful exploitation of market niche. However, company is likely to run out of room for growth, and to begin demonstrating the cyclicality inherent in industry.

Fleetwood	27 1/4–7 3/4	23 5/8	11.9	11.3/7.7	Strong competitive strength in industry with potential for improvement from both immediate economic and longer-term demographic factors. Potential not discounted in recent P/E ratio.
Outboard Marine	25 1/4–17 3/8	21	7.7	Def./7.7	A chronic underperformer in a highly cyclical industry. Cyclical strength of industry and currency exchange advantages are likely to improve performance in short term, but long-term potential depends on effectiveness of management's cost reduction and ability to cope with new environmental regulations affecting products. Company warrants watching, as it has potential for significant improvement in competitive strength to exploit its brand recognition and distribution infrastructure.
Airlines industry					
Southwest	34 3/8–15 1/2	17 7/8	14.7	12.0/Def.	Decisive competitive strength in dismal industry, for a combination of structural and operating reasons. Competitive advantage will erode as competitors adopt its practices. Room for growth likely to be limited by imitators. Remarkable record of performance has made company a favorite of analysts, so recent P/E ratio may still be optimistic.
AMR	65 7/8–48 1/8	64 3/4	28.7	Def./Def.	Strong competitive position due to size, extensive routes, and relatively low costs, despite hub-and-spoke structure. This has allowed company to return to profitability in current economic upturn. Will likely do well when industry problems are resolved, but present high cost of shares does not justify waiting.
USAir	8 3/8–3 7/8	6 1/8	Def.	Def./Def.	Weak competitive position due to high operating costs and hub-and-spoke structure. Will require extensive concessions from unions for even slim hope of survival.

Note: Def. = deficit.

EXHIBIT 7–4

Industry Attractiveness–Competitive Strength Matrix:
Sample Industries and Companies

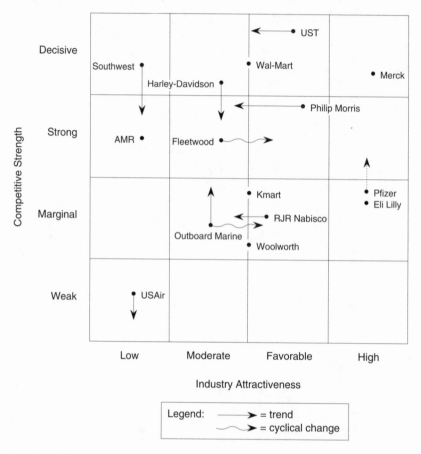

Wal-Mart This company has decisive and sustainable competitive advantage. Thus it should be able to continue to outperform the drug and discount retailing industry, which is not threatened with adverse change.

Two other companies may be considered possible future investment candidates, and therefore should be tracked closely.

Pfizer This company, operating in the pharmaceuticals industry, has a highly focused strategy of concentrating on product development and manufacture and is backing it up with a major commitment to R&D.

Fleetwood With its strong competitive position in the recreational products manufacturing industry, Fleetwood should improve its overall longterm profitability as demographics turn favorable.

This may seem like a short list, considering that 15 companies were analyzed from our five sample industries. However, remember that this sample included both median and weak industries and performers, which are less appealing investment candidates. In addition, I have ruled out two strong performers, UST and Philip Morris, because of serious threats to the tobacco industry posed by litigation. (You may disagree with my conclusions. This sort of disagreement is what makes horse races and stock markets.)

EVALUATING SELECTED COMPANIES IN A BROAD SPECTRUM OF INDUSTRIES

The explanations of analytical concepts and methodology in earlier chapters included descriptions of the situations of a number of companies in a broad spectrum of industries. To assess 12 of these companies as possible long-term investment candidates, Exhibit 7–5 gives brief explanations of their positions on the matrix shown in Exhibit 7–6. The format, dates, and broad market reference for this assessment are the same as those used in Exhibits 7–3 and 7–4.

My suggestions for long-term investment candidates among this group of companies are as follows:

Boeing The high competitive strength which Boeing has demonstrated, an improving airlines industry environment because of both cyclical and trend causes, and a P/E ratio that does not discount the future potential give the investor sufficient reason to consider investing in this company.

McDonald's This company has high competitive strength and more room to grow in the fast-food industry than its P/E ratio appears to recognize.

Schlumberger Decisive competitive advantage and a reasonable stock price, considering the potential for improvement in the oil field services industry, make Schlumberger a likely candidate.

The following companies are also worth consideration:

Coca-Cola The soft-drink industry is basically sound, and Coca-Cola is an exceptional company. Its stock price may seem high at present, but it

Evaluations of Selected Companies as Long-Term Investment Candidates
(As of March 31, 1995)

Company	Stock Price Range 52 Weeks Ending 03/31/95	Price	03/31/95 P/E Ratio	5-Year ROE % Co./Ind.	Evaluation
Avon	65 5/8–54	60 1/2	17.7	60.2/16.9	Strong competitive advantage due to established brand name and distribution structure in sound industry not threatened by change. Company is being imitated in domestic markets. Primarily dependent on foreign markets for growth. P/E ratio probably reflects potential.
Boeing	54–42 1/2	43 7/8	21.4	18.5/12.7	Strong to decisive competitive position due to product development capability, broad product line, and large customer base. Basic demand trend is favorable. Replacement cycle, which is not unduly discounted by P/E ratio, is forthcoming.
Coca-Cola	59 3/8–36 5/8	56 3/8	28.5	48.4/17.1	Competitive advantage decisive because of global recognition of brand name and distribution capability. Erosion of domestic market position to private brands can be offset by room for growth in global markets, but growth potential is at least partially discounted by P/E ratio.
Dell	47 3/4–21 1/4	43 3/4	21.3	17.5/5.6	Current competitive advantage based on reputation and distribution capability is being imitated. Performance hard to maintain. Upside potential is limited, as industry is intensely competitive and of low attractiveness.

Company					
General Mills	64 5/8–49 3/8	59 5/8	15.5	37.7/17.1	Strong competitive advantage due to product positions and leading brand names. Should be capable of withstanding erosion of brand loyalty. Profit margins likely to be eroded. Industry likely to remain favorable but slow-growing. Company has had to enter food service industry to find room for growth. Sustaining ROE performance may be difficult.
Gillette	85 3/8–62	81 5/8	26.0	36.2/16.9	Competitive advantage decisive due to leadership in product and process technology, brand acceptance, and global distribution capability, which provides room for growth with no apparent threats to the industry. Company's exceptional potential is partially discounted by its high P/E ratio.
Inco	31 1/4–21 3/8	27 7/8	185.8	11.4/4.3	Strong competitive advantage due to extensive ore reserves and low-cost production capability in a commodity with low substitution risk. Prospects for cyclical improvement are dampened by supply disruption due to political discontinuity. High recent stock price may be premature, but company will probably be a good investment prospect when its markets settle down. Purchase price of stock should recognize its strong cyclicality.
McDonald's	39 1/4–25 1/2	35 1/4	21.0	19.4/13.8	Strong to decisive competitive advantage due to low costs, high perceived value of product, and name recognition. Domestic market is mature, but company has plenty of room for growth in global markets. Room for growth is not being unduly discounted by the P/E ratio.
Microsoft	74–41	71	29.9	39.7/16.2	Leadership in product development has allowed company to dominate its industry, but its products are aging and its future depends on equally successful replacements. Company has turned to acquisitions at high prices for interim growth. An exceptional company, but the risks arising from prolonged dominance of computer industry and heavy dependence on CEO raise question of whether P/E ratio is not unduly optimistic.

Exhibit 7–5, *Concluded*

Company	Stock Price Range 52 Weeks Ending 03/31/95	Price	03/31/95 P/E Ratio	5-Year ROE % Co./Ind.	Evaluation
Nike	78–52 1/4	75	15.6	27.2/17.8	Competitive advantage has been based on product development, marketing capability, and ability to contract manufacture to low-cost suppliers. Shift in market preference to other products dilutes brand appeal. Highly dependent on the vagaries of fashion, which are unpredictable and should be of concern to the long-term investor. Acquisition of Canstar broadens product line and hedges some risks in company's primary products.
Polaroid	36 3/4–29	34 1/2	43.1	25.9/14.8	Competitive advantage is currently decisive, based on leadership in an aging technology which will remain a good cash cow for many years. Competitive advantage is not likely to be sustainable, as long-term growth depends on entry into new technologies—an effort in which company's efforts show signs of floundering.
Schlumberger	63–50	59 5/8	27.0	17.8/6.0	Decisive competitive advantage in weak, cyclical industry, based on leadership in technology for which company is able to charge premium price. Even if oil exploration activity does not increase, company has room for growth through gas development and recovery-enhancement technology. If oil prices recover, its earnings growth could be dramatic, as it will be selling technology that is already paid for. This stock offers a very low-risk way to take advantage of potential oil price increases.

E X H I B I T   7–6

Industry Attractiveness–Competitive Strength Matrix: Selected Companies

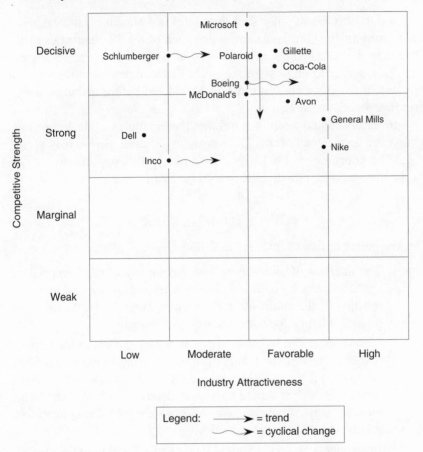

Legend: ———➤ = trend
        ⌒⌒➤ = cyclical change

should be considered for long-term investment whenever a price weakness occurs.

Gillette   Also an exceptional company, operating in the sound personal products segment of the consumer nondurable goods industry, Gillette too should be considered for investment if a price weakness makes the purchase of the stock temporarily more appealing.

Inco   After some intermediate-term supply problems in the mining industry, which have been created by a political discontinuity (as discussed in Chapter 6), have worked themselves out, Inco could be considered by investors who feel that they should have a "resource" stock, a producer of primary raw materials, in their portfolios.

Again, this list of suggested long-term investment candidates may seem surprisingly short, considering that each of the 12 companies evaluated here was selected because it had some basis of competitive advantage. This serves to emphasize the point that competitive advantage is only one of the elements that must be considered before making a long-term investment decision.

Investors should keep in mind that the examples evaluated in this section add up to a total of only 27 companies, whereas *Forbes* lists a total of 1,370 companies for 1994. Obviously, many other opportunities exist for the investor who is willing to search for them.

POINTS TO REMEMBER

The key points of this chapter are as follows:

1. The analysis of an industry and a company can be undertaken systematically by defining the characteristics of the industry, the position of the company in the industry, and the implications of possible change for both industry and company.

2. Management can be evaluated in part on the basis of the performance record of the company. The investor should be wary of companies that are highly dependent on one person for management. The analyst should attempt to determine whether the long-term strategy of the company is consistent with the competitive realities of the industry situation.

3. Investment candidates should be ranked according to the characteristics of their industries and according to their relative competitive strengths. Of these two variables, competitive strength is the more important, but it can be exercised effectively only if the industry provides appropriate scope. Investment candidates can be compared on an industry attractiveness-competitive strength matrix, and the directions in which expected developments may lead the companies can also be indicated on the matrix.

4. The risk-reward relationship must be considered in the context of balancing safety with potential for capital appreciation. The industry attractiveness-competitive strength matrix also helps to define this relationship. Long-term appreciation in the value of a

stock can be driven by improvements in industry fundamentals, by the strengthening of competitive advantage, or, in the best cases, by both of these factors.

5. A decision about long-term investment involves judgments about the relevance, importance, and reliability of information on the stock. Mistakes in judgment can be minimized by careful consideration of the source of each piece of information and the extent to which it is consistent with the overall picture. The influence of emotional factors, which may create biases in judgment, should be minimized.

6. Growth situations should be analyzed with special emphasis on the basis of the industry developments and/or the competitive advantage which is driving the growth.

NOTES

1. For a comprehensive examination of Gates's role and the company's management depth, see Brent Schlender, "What Bill Gates Really Wants," *Fortune*, January 16, 1995, pp. 34–63.

2. Paula Dwyer and Richard A. Melcher, "Uglier and Uglier at Saatch & Saatchi," *Business Week*, January 23, 1995, pp. 46–47.

3. The matrix has been adapted from a concept developed by Bernard C. Reimann. See his article, "Stock Price and Business Success: What Is the Relationship?" *Journal of Business Strategy*, Summer 1987, pp. 38–49.

4. The discussion of the hierarchy of information and the role of experience is based on Richard E. Neustadt and Ernest R. May, *Thinking in Time: The Uses of History for Decision Makers* (New York: The Free Press, 1986).

5. The studies are primarily the work of Daniel Kahneman and Amos Tversky, as reported in John J. Curran, "Why Investors Make the Wrong Choices," *Fortune*, 1987 Annual Investor's Guide, pp. 63–68.

6. Robert Lenzner, "Warren Buffett's Idea of Heaven: 'I Don't Have to Work with People I Don't Like'," *Forbes*, October 18, 1993, pp. 40–45.

7. From the Berkshire Hathaway Annual Report, 1993, as quoted in "How Buffett Views Risk," *Fortune*, April 4, 1994, p. 33.

8. Amey Stone, "Hot Growth Companies: A Roster of the Nimble and Innovative," *Business Week*, May 23, 1994, pp. 92–104.

9. Phillip L. Zweig, Leah Nathans Spiro, and Michael Schroeder, "Beware the IPO Market: Individual Investors Are at a Big Disadvantage," *Business Week*, 1994, pp. 84–89.

10. Ibid.

8

MONITORING THE INVESTMENT

Once investors have analyzed the long-term performance potential of companies and the industries in which they operate, they are able to make investment decisions with a degree of confidence. The resulting comfort level, however, should not be allowed to deteriorate into complacency.

No stock is immune to the vagaries of the stock market as a whole. Every investment must be monitored. To monitor their portfolios appropriately, investors must follow the progress of each company and industry in which they hold a position. The underlying assumptions upon which an investment decision was originally based will not remain valid forever. Eventually, the fundamentals of every industry and the competitive capability of every company will change. When this happens, the investor must consider the advisability of continuing to hold the stock.

If the time for a change has indeed arrived, the investor who has already been studying alternative candidates for long-term investment can usually avoid making hasty or ill-considered moves. For this reason, keeping track of changes that affect other companies and other industries should be a regular part of the monitoring process.

The sources of information described in Appendix B are as useful in monitoring investments as in the analytical procedures for choosing investment candidates (with which we have been concerned in Chapters 3 through 7). Even though I have specifically selected these sources for use in strategic analysis, I recognize that the investor who attempted to read all of them in detail would be deluged on a continuing basis with an overwhelming and unusable quantity of information.

Thus, monitoring must be a systematic and selective process. Rather than obsessing over every published detail about companies and industries in which they hold stocks, investors should look for specific signals which indicate developments that must be evaluated in more detail. This chapter will discuss the nature and implications of these signals and the underlying developments to which they call attention.

MONITORING AN INDUSTRY

Four external forces—economic, political, social, and technological—cause changes that affect industry fundamentals (see Chapter 6). These forces must be watched for specific developments, and the investor should also understand the broad direction of events in each of these areas.

Current Signs of Change

Specific signals that alert investors to current events which should be studied in detail are described below.

Weakening Industry Performance
The relationship between the industry's five-year average, the industry's latest median returns on equity (ROEs), and the all-industries figures deserves careful attention. The reasons for a weakening of industry performance in either the long-term average or the latest period should be determined. These reasons may be cyclical, or they may indicate more serious long-term problems.

Price Wars
Persistent price wars are usually indicative of industry overcapacity or a balanced competitive situation which can lead to growing sales but stagnant profitability. However, price wars are not necessarily a long-term problem for a company with decisive competitive advantage, because it can usually match competitors' initiatives, suffering only temporary ill effects. Price wars in the form of factory rebates were common in the U.S. automobile industry throughout the 1980s, when the domestic companies were weak in relation to foreign companies.

Technological Developments

Technological developments may enhance the position of substitute products, reduce barriers to entry, or significantly enhance the cost performance of competitors. Such threats to an industry usually start in a small way, but new technology almost always has the potential for significant further development and new applications, giving it an advantage over mature technologies. The threat, however, is not usually as imminent as the market perceives it to be, so that panic is not usually necessary.

Demands for Government Intervention

Demands for government protection by prominent executives or industry trade associations usually indicate that a domestic industry is developing structural problems. The government intervention demanded may take the form of tariffs or quotas on imports, regulation or re-regulation of the product or the market, or subsidies. Companies in the industry may be at a competitive disadvantage in relation to other domestic companies that are developing substitutes, or they may be threatened by foreign companies that are encroaching upon their markets. These structural problems may threaten the profitability of companies operating within the domestic industry, or may even plunge the industry as a whole into the decline phase.

Even if the government does grant an industry's demands for protection, government actions rarely solve the problem. Take the example of the U.S. automobile industry. The government created a problem for the domestic industry in 1975 when it imposed average fuel consumption limits on the cars produced by a given manufacturer. To meet the fleet average, U.S. manufacturers were forced to produce a relatively large proportion of small cars. They lost money on these cars because of their manufacturing inefficiency as compared to that of Japanese companies.

Appealing for help, the industry was successful in convincing the government to impose quotas on imports of Japanese cars, effective in 1984. Ironically, the quotas not only did little to improve the situation but ultimately backfired. Because of the quotas, the Japanese companies accelerated their move to establish North American assembly operations. Furthermore, since the quotas were based on numbers rather than value, the Japanese focused on the luxury car market, thus increasing their competitiveness in the area in which the domestic manufacturers had been profitable.

For the long-term investor, the lesson to be learned from this example is that government intervention rarely solves an industry's problems. Instead, by temporarily postponing adverse effects, it reduces managers' sense of urgency and encourages them to postpone the strategic actions that would more effectively insulate their companies against the perceived threat. Whenever an industry's spokespersons demand government protection, investors should reconsider the wisdom of continuing to hold a position in that industry.

Long-Term Developments

While the specific signals cited above are indicative of current problems on a national level, there are also longer-term, global developments which should be kept in mind as background indicators of potential changes in an industry. The points listed below are not intended to be predictive, but only to illustrate current trends and potential discontinuities.[1]

Degradation of the Environment   Increasing population pressures and industrial growth in emerging nations will accelerate global environmental degradation. It is estimated that countries do not become concerned about the environmental effects of economic development until per capita gross domestic product (GDP) reaches $8,000. The GDPs of China and the main Southeast Asian countries are nowhere near this level. The resource base for economic growth is likely to be weakened worldwide, and military tensions over the control of resources will escalate, as a consequence. Developed nations will have to spend more to counter the threat of environmental degradation in their own countries.

Political Instability and Military Action   Miniwars between and within states divert resources from economic development and slow the growth of the global economy. Such wars have become almost commonplace in recent times. Given the range of ethnic, tribal, racial, and religious animosities that prevails throughout the world, they are likely to persist if not intensify. It is not only small and comparatively undeveloped nations which face this likelihood; indeed, in both Russia and China the risk of internal instability is high.

International Terrorism   As a consequence of the same conditions that are making miniwars almost inevitable, the international terrorism that has captured headlines and frightened both the governments and the citizens of politically stable as well as unstable countries will also continue and escalate.

Proliferation of nuclear capability implies that terrorists might eventually be equipped with portable, "suitcase"-size nuclear weapons. If this came to pass, national levels of internal security measures would sharply increase. Individuals' freedom to travel internationally would inevitably be inhibited, and economic activity would become decentralized. Vulnerable city core facilities such as the World Trade Center in New York City, which was attacked though not destroyed by international terrorists in 1993, would no longer be the locations of first choice for financial institutions. Winners from such a scenario would be commercial real estate in secondary centers, domestic tourism, and providers of security equipment and services. Among the many losers would be international airlines and commercial real estate companies in the present major financial centers.

Resurgence of Government Intervention   Threats such as those described above, if combined with a serious stock market crash, would weaken investment on a global scale. Protectionism would consequently be reinvoked as a shield for domestic industries. Curbs on imports would lead to trade wars, which in turn would create serious worldwide recessions. Governments would be forced to resume interventions in the economy, reversing a long period of increasing free market liberalization. The main risk to investment markets would likely arise from excessive global trading in unregulated derivatives.[2]

The dire scenarios presented above is not to be taken as my personal prediction of worldwide disaster. Rather, I have described them only to arouse investors' sensibilities concerning the fragility of world political and economic orders. Investors should be aware of world events as a broad background upon which possible long-term events may significantly affect a wide range of industries. Given the increasing globalization of the economy, few companies would be immune, but each such development would affect different industries in different ways, either favorable or unfavorable.

MONITORING A COMPANY

Five aspects of company development are crucial to a company's continuing viability as a long-term investment. The first two, (1) *sales and earnings progression* and (2) *changes in return on equity (ROE),* are discussed together below, as they are interrelated. The progression of sales and earning should be in line with expectations. Any fluctuations must be evaluated to determine whether they are due to short-term developments rather than indicative of changes in industry structure or loss of competitive advantage. Changes in ROE rank in the industry, either as compared to the long-term industry median or in the latest period, should be assessed. The reasons for any significant decline in the company's standing in the latest period in relation to the long-term industry average should be investigated thoroughly.

Each of the other three critical aspects of company development will be discussed separately. These three aspects are (3) *company strategy*, or the strategic initiatives being pursued by the company; (4) *changes in management*; and (5) *management priorities*. The company's strategic initiatives should have a strong likelihood of being productive and enhancing long-term performance. The probable effect of changes in management on the direction of the company should be positive, and management priorities should not be such as to inhibit the long-term potential of the company.

Sales and Earnings Progression, and Changes in ROE Rank

The investor's primary interest in an investment is its earnings record and its performance relative to competitors. The reasons for any significant deviation from an established trend should be determined, whether they are the result of developments that affect the structure of the industry as a whole or the competitive position of the company. Though an ROE for the latest 12 months that falls below the company's five-year average may be due solely to short-term developments, the reasons for it should be determined. If the company decline is greater than the decline in the industry median, the deviation is to be considered significant and should be thoroughly investigated.

Temporary setbacks in earnings, which do not affect the long-term potential of a company, can be caused by cyclical factors. In evaluating short-term developments, investors should try to ignore short-term market sentiment, which often makes an adverse judgment because earnings fall short of immediate expectations.

The forces that cause change were discussed in Chapter 6, along with their implications. Some industries are particularly sensitive to economic causes. In addition, write-offs or charges may be incurred in disposing of certain operations that were not generating adequate returns; in restructuring the organization by downsizing, for instance; and/or in meeting new statutory requirements, such as pension funding.

Some management actions, however, though they are outwardly similar to these harmless or beneficial ones, may actually be drastic signs of management bloat or errors in judgment. These signs are best evaluated in the context of assessment of management, which is discussed below.

Certain developments can indicate a deterioration of industry fundamentals and/or a weakening of a company's competitive position and earnings potential in the long term. One such development is a *weakening of product or market leadership.* Product or market leadership is a common basis for strong competitive advantage (see Chapter 5). Its weakening is often one of the first signals of serious long-term problems. This was true of both GM and IBM. GM held a 45.8 percent share of the North American automobile market in 1980. This was steadily eroded to 37 percent in 1987. Its competitors had stopped their traditional copying of GM, a fact convincingly demonstrated by Ford's introduction of the drastically designed Taurus in 1985. IBM lost its attempt at leadership of the PC market, the primary area of growth in the computer industry. Not only was its initial entry, the PC Jr., a disappointment, but subsequent models have been unable to claim the market leadership that might be expected from a company that had so long dominated its industry.

Another signal that alerts the investor to a possible industry deterioration or company weakness is *continuing labor problems which cause strikes or other operating disruptions.* In addition to the temporary disruption of sales, such conflicts distract management and create difficulties in obtaining labor cooperation in other areas of the business. They can also require management to attempt to improve its bargaining power with a major supplier—labor—to offset weaknesses in the other determinants of industry structure. Furthermore, morale throughout the company can be seriously damaged by managerial hypocrisy in which the organization is urged to tighten its belt but the CEO and executive receive large bonuses (as did GM executives) or the fleet of executive jets is expanded.

Some symptoms of long-term problems are highly visible; others are not. Fortunately, the business press has become quite vigilant about management problems and is often quick to point them out. Investors should be concerned when the company, in its annual report or other statements, fails to comment on known problems, or dismisses them as not significant. Of course, any problem must be evaluated in the context of the company's ability to cope with it. In general, a company that is in a strong competitive position or that is operating in an attractive industry has scope for acting effectively to handle problems.

Changes in Strategy

Before making an investment decision, an investor should first understand the thrust of the candidate company's strategy (see Chapter 5 if you need a review), as well as whether the strategy is likely to enhance the company's competitive advantage (see Chapter 5) and whether the company is capable of adapting to change (see Chapter 6).

Even then, the investor's work is not finished. No company strategy is, or should be, carved in stone. It is necessary to assess on a continuing basis what the company is actually doing. With respect to many aspects of strategy, it is difficult or impossible for an outsider to find out what is really going on inside the company. How vigorously and how effectively, for example, is the company pursuing an action such as cost reduction? Company statements about such matters tend to be reassuring but not necessarily candid.

One aspect of strategy cannot be hidden—and this one aspect fully reveals the thrust of the strategy. This aspect is, of course, the nature of the company's acquisitions and divestitures.

Acquisitions

Acquisitions, which are virtually an everyday event in corporate news, are one of the most common vehicles used to carry out a corporate strategy. Acquisitions can be accomplished quickly, and they can provide an immediate contribution to corporate earnings. This is in contrast to the process of developing a new business internally, which can be done only slowly and which inevitably penalizes short-term earnings. Further, few large companies have the entrepreneurial skills needed to promote a new venture. An acquisition can also overcome barriers to entry and minimize the further fragmentation of a crowded industry.

Acquisitions can be either productive or unproductive. The acquisitions that a company makes provide a good indication of its management's thinking. The long-term investor should therefore pay close attention to a company's acquisitions, to determine whether and to what extent they will contribute to future earnings.

Productive Acquisitions The logic of an acquisition can be judged by its productiveness, or its contribution to the competitive strength of the parent company and the closeness of its relationship to the parent's core business. Actions which can contribute to competitive strength include the purchase of a supplier or a major customer to improve bargaining power; the acquisition of the maker of a substitute which poses a current or potential threat; and the acquisition of a competitor to fill out the product line, to rationalize the industry, to expand geographically to provide room for additional growth, or to enhance economies of scale (see Chapter 5).

By embarking on biotechnology research during the 1980s, Merck gained representation in a substitute industry. The company's 1993 purchase of one of its major distributors helped to restore some of the bargaining power with buyers which had been eroded in recent years. Both of these actions contributed to Merck's competitive strength.

Wal-Mart's purchase of Woolworth's Woolco operations in Canada is another example of a productive acquisition. Wal-Mart achieved quick entry into a new market as well as access to good locations without further fragmenting a crowded industry.

The need for relatedness is important, as it can help to keep the acquisition within the scope of management expertise. However, relatedness alone does not guarantee success; nor is relatedness always easy to assess. In the late 1970s, Coca-Cola bought three vintners. The reasoning of management was that wine, like Coca-Cola, was a beverage. Furthermore, wine markets were showing rapid market growth, and it was believed that Coca-Cola's soft-drink marketing expertise would be easily transferable to wine. However, wine turned out to be a vastly different business from soft drinks. After making a number of mistakes, Coca-Cola sold its wine business in 1983 for the same price it had originally paid for the three vintners.

General Electric's acquisition of Kidder Peabody & Co. in 1986 seemed initially to be a good fit with GE Capital Services Inc. in that it broadened the company's range of financial services. However, GE Capital deals primarily with hard assets, which have tangible value that can be assessed, while Kidder is primarily a trading operation. Thus, there was little synergy between the two. GE's failure to understand the business was a factor in Kidder Peabody's $350 million pretax loss in 1993 due to trading irregularities.[3]

Even acquisitions that can be considered strategically productive must be evaluated in the context of the price paid. If the premium over the current market price is very high, a significant portion of the future benefits will have been discounted.

Unproductive Acquisitions The long-term investor should be wary about acquisitions made for the purpose of diversification, one of the most common objectives of such moves. On the surface, broadening the revenue base of a company through diversification may appear to be a logical move which would help to insulate the company from cyclical fluctuations. In fact, a diversification strategy is often an indication of internal problems as well as a poor record of results.

The pursuit of diversification indicates that management has lost faith in the ability of the existing business to produce the expected results. Managers dissipate the company's resources to make the acquisition and then turn their attention to trying to manage it. Thus they neglect the company's core business and create a self-fulfilling prophecy: the core business may falter.

Acquisitions made for the purpose of diversification often fail to live up to expectations. For one thing, the acquisition is usually made at a substantial premium over its market price, with the recent premium being about 36 percent. If we assume that the current market price represents reasonable value, it follows that management must extract higher earnings from the acquisition to justify the cost. Such an improvement in performance is especially difficult to achieve because the acquiring management has no experience in the new industry. The problem is often compounded by the departure of the acquired management after the transaction.

A second reason for the failure of acquisitions to satisfy managers' expectations is that they usually involve heavy debt for the parent company. Servicing this debt obviously diverts financial resources from other needs of the business.

In recent years, there has been a move toward making acquisitions for stock. This method has the unfortunate effect of exposing shareholders to dilution from the issue of additional shares to the extent of the premium paid for the company.

Announcements of acquisitions for the purpose of diversification are often accompanied by elaborate justifications based on the potential of the acquired business and the way that it will "fit." In most cases these fits are illusions. Investors should be particularly wary about pursuit of diversification by resource companies. The specialized management expertise of these companies is rarely applicable to other businesses. Studies have shown that 36 to 50 percent of acquisitions are later divested, often with heavy write-offs. The management effort that went into trying to make the acquisitions work undoubtedly took its toll on the existing businesses.[4]

In 1974, for instance, Inco acquired a battery maker, ESB Inc., partially on the grounds that the emerging battery technology would make this company a captive customer for nickel. At best, ESB would have been a minor user of nickel. Inco's probable real reason for the purchase was the hope that the higher price/earnings (P/E) ratios of energy stocks would rub off on its own stock. The company ended up writing off more than $250 million on the deal.

Acquisitions are inherently difficult to absorb, and the problem can be compounded if heavy debt limits the ability of the company to make productive investments in the existing businesses. It was shown in Chapter 7 that RJR Nabisco had difficulty in responding to Philip Morris's strategic initiatives to counter the inroads of generic cigarettes into the premium brand markets because of its heavy debt load. This debt was incurred to finance an acquisition, a change of ownership by way of a leveraged buyout (LBO).

In general, long-term investors should consider making a change whenever a company in which they hold shares pursues diversification. The overall thrust of the strategies of the best performers in recent years has been toward specialization. These successful companies stick to what they do best and broaden their capabilities through strategic alliances. An argument can be made that this strategy creates reliance on a relatively narrow base and therefore increases the investment risk. This argument is offset by the fact that such a strategy also provides the basis for decisive competitive advantage, which is much more valuable than diversification in sustaining superior performance in a volatile world.

Investors must, however, remain alert to potential changes that might affect the performance of even the most successful company. Neither decisive competitive advantage nor a long-term record of superior performance is a guarantee of future success. Eventual change is the only thing that can be guaranteed, in investing as in other aspects of life.

Divestitures

Divestitures can usually be considered favorable developments, except when they are desperation measures to raise cash. The most common reason given is that the company is returning to its core business. This usually means that it is undoing an attempt at diversification which has not worked out. However, divestitures can also be made to dispose of only the parts of a larger acquisition that do not fit well with the company's core business.

Divestitures usually have the direct, practical effect of allowing management to focus attention on improving the company's basic business. They also often indicate that managers have given thought to the future of the company and are taking decisive action.

It is possible, however, for a divestiture to be an unfavorable development, in a given situation. The implications of each divestiture must be worked out by the analyst.

Changes in Management

Management pronouncements, particularly those of a public nature, usually give the impression that decisions made within a company have been deliberated thoughtfully and are based on a logical foundation. All too often, outsiders, such as traders, take these pronouncements at face value. In truth, however, decisions are made by human beings, not all of whom are invariably thoughtful, insightful, and rational. Every management decision is subject to the human biases and preferences of the individuals involved.

A change in management may, or may not, bring into play a set of priorities that is new to the company. The existing management style may be perpetuated under the guidance of a new, but similarly oriented, set of managers. On the other hand, if managers who have a drastically different idea of the future of the company assume power, they will institute totally new management policies.

The astute investor can evaluate the implications of a change in management by determining the nature of the succession.

Favorable Changes in Management

Under some circumstances, changes in management should not usually be a cause for concern. For example, suppose a company which is a strong performer in a stable industry appoints the heir apparent to the CEO position. In such cases, the new CEO usually understands both the capabilities of the organization and the basis for its success, having played a part in its favorable performance to date. As a result, there is not likely to be a drastic change in the success formula. The succession of David Glass in 1988 to the CEO position at Wal-Mart, following Sam Walton, was of this character.

Another type of favorable management succession occurs when a company with a satisfactory though uninspiring performance record appoints an insider, though not the expected successor, to the CEO position. For most boards of directors, bypassing the normal line of succession is a fairly drastic step. Such an appointment signals the board's recognition that some changes are necessary. On the basis of the new CEO's strong past performance, the board is satisfied that this person can bring the necessary changes to fruition. Jack Welch of GE was such an appointee in 1981, following long-time CEO, Reginald Jones. Welch was an improbable choice because of his relative youth (he was only 45) and because he was considered too rough around the edges for GE's culture. In his favor were the technical background provided by his PhD in chemical engineering and his appreciation of the rise of global competition.[5]

Another circumstance in which a change in management is usually favorable occurs when a company with a weak performance record appoints an outsider as CEO. The outsider, particularly if he or she has a proven record of performance in other organizations, is not inhibited by having taken part in past decisions and is therefore free to take any action necessary. As a result, such outside appointments are almost always necessary in turnaround situations. The stock market tends to react favorably to such changes in management, particularly if the outsider has a strong track record. The long-term investor, however, should wait to see the direction of the new CEO's actions before making a commitment.

Unfavorable Changes in Management

Companies with poor or deteriorating performance records are not usually good candidates for long-term investment. The prospects for a favorable turnaround are diminished when a company with weak or deteriorating performance appoints the former CEO's nominee as CEO. This new CEO, having been involved in the company's decisions to date, has a vested interest in the actions which have resulted in the deterioration of the company's performance. CEOs of this sort are likely to work hard to prove that past decisions have been right, rather than embarking on alternative courses of action. Similar pressures to continue past policies can occur when the former CEO remains a member of the board of directors. In 1977, for example, Harold Geneen of ITT intervened in the attempt of his successor (Lyman C. Hamilton Jr.) to slim down the ITT empire and had him fired. The divestitures were eventually started in 1979 under a new CEO, Rand V. Araskog, after Geneen's departure from the board, but the conditions were much less favorable due to the delay.

Changes in management are an issue only when the company's long-term performance problems are primarily caused by weaknesses in its competitive position. As Warren Buffett has pointed out, even the best management cannot be expected to accomplish much in the face of weak industry fundamentals. There are exceptions, however. Herb Kelleher's accomplishments at Southwest Airlines constitute one such exception. Kelleher was practicing law in San Antonio, Texas, when he was approached by an investor who saw an opportunity for a new airline in the region. The new airline commenced operation in 1971, broke into the black in two years, and has remained profitable ever since. Kelleher is credited with recognizing the existence of a profitable market niche, as discussed in Chapter 5, and with having the freewheeling, entrepreneurial style necessary to exploit it.

Evaluating Changes in Management

The process of evaluating the implications of management changes is obviously not a precise science. These changes have to be evaluated on a case-by-case basis. An indication of how they may be interpreted can be obtained by looking at developments in three companies, Eastman Kodak, Polaroid, and Merck. The decisions made under the circumstances described for these companies can be used as guidelines to the implications of changes and how they may be interpreted.

Eastman Kodak   Despite its status as a household name, Eastman Kodak would not seem to qualify as a long-term investment candidate under the criteria outlined in this book. Its performance has been mediocre, with an average ROE of 14.3 percent in the decade of the 1980s and only 10.2 percent in the most recent five years. This is below the all-industry median of 11.5 percent, and particularly poor for a business based on sophisticated proprietary technology. Not surprisingly, the company's stock price grew at an average annual rate of only 3.5 percent over a decade.

The photography and toys industry is basically attractive, with high barriers to entry, strong brand preferences on the part of buyers, and high bargaining power over suppliers. Eastman Kodak's competitive strength is based on its strong technology, high brand awareness, and strong distribution capability. The company's strengths have not, however, been mobilized to realize the potential inherent in its industry situation.

The roots of the company's problems go back to the 1970s, when its executives apparently became concerned about the future of silver halide photography. Kodak was the global leader in this technology, which was the foundation upon which the company's success was based. The company strategy came to be driven by concern over the risk of substitution, mainly by electronic imaging. Attempts to copy Polaroid products failed. The result was heavy losses, including damages for patent infringement. An attempted entry into reprographics was beaten back by Xerox, despite Kodak's superior technology. Several publishing ventures faltered because Kodak managers were not equipped to deal with the entrepreneurial aspects of the publishing world. Another mistaken attempt at diversification was the purchase of Sterling Drug in 1988 for $5.5 billion—a purchase that might have been ill-advised under any circumstances, because Sterling's five-year average ROE performance was below the pharmaceuticals industry median.

Caught up in these various attempts to diversify, Kodak managers neglected the company's core business, the silver halide photography upon which its success had been built. The unfortunate consequence was that Fuji caught up.

During the period in which the company was thrashing about, from the 1970s through late 1993, Kodak was led by three successive CEOs. All three were insiders who had technical backgrounds and were steeped in the Kodak culture, and each was picked by his predecessor. The third was Kay Whitmore, who was appointed CEO in 1989. After he was ousted in 1993, *Forbes* commented, "[Kay Whitmore's] whole career prepared him to run a Kodak which no longer existed."[6]

Because of this three-pronged combination of mistakes—unproductive attempts to diversify, departure from the company's core business, and continuation of internal management succession despite failures to improve performance—Kodak in this period was clearly not a suitable candidate for long-term investment. Beginning in 1994, however, there were obvious signals that the company's potential in this regard should be reevaluated.

First, the industry fundamentals remained favorable. The threat of substitution from electronic photography, which dominated Kodak's strategy for so long, was developing more slowly than expected. Electronic imaging was now expected to complement rather than to replace conventional photography. The number of pictures taken was growing at a rate of 4 percent per year.

Second, Kodak had regained its competitive edge in film technology and was now estimated to hold 55 percent of the world film market.

Third, in late 1993, the board had appointed George Fisher as Kodak's first outside CEO. Fisher, the former CEO of Motorola, had a strong performance record. He proceeded to sell off Sterling Drugs and to cut costs, refocusing the company on its core business.

Kodak's earlier problems lay in its failure to exploit its competitive strengths. The company's story illustrates a counterproductive diversification strategy. Since the industry fundamentals remain strong, the company's change in management and return to its core business may make it a good prospect for long-term investment.

Polaroid In the discussion of the sustainability of competitive advantage in Chapter 5, Polaroid's ability to establish itself in electronic imaging was called into question. Because of the aging of the company's instant photography technology, this excursion into a substitute technology was deemed necessary. An experienced executive was needed to develop and run the electronic photography business. In late 1993, the company recruited Larry Gerhardt, CEO of Test Systems Strategies Inc., who seemed suitable for the position. In an astonishing and damaging move, however, this recruit left the company after only one week.[7] Though his exact reason for leaving is unknown, it is possible to speculate. One plausible explanation is that he found the company's electronic imaging technology weak, and assessed it as being unable to contribute significantly to CEO I. MacAllister Booth's publicly announced pledge to lift pretax operating profits from 8 to 12 percent of sales. If this speculation is correct, the newly hired Gerhardt may not have wanted to be associated with a losing cause.

This incident accentuates the questionability of a key element of Polaroid's long-term potential. The company is thus not a suitable candidate for long-term investment.

Merck Though the implications of a change in management in either a successful or a troubled company may be clear, as described above, they can be quite difficult to assess in more ambiguous instances. Merck, for instance, in mid-1994, after an 18-month search, hired Raymond V. Gilmartin to succeed Dr. P. Roy Vagelos, who was soon to retire as CEO.[8] This appointment was a departure from the company's past practice of drawing senior managers from its product development ranks. The company needed someone who was capable of merging the diverse cultures of Merck and its recent acquisition, Medco Containment Services. In the course of searching for a new CEO, the committee responsible for conducting the search had rejected all the existing senior executives of Merck, and three of these executives had left the company.

Gilmartin had been CEO of Becton Dickenson & Co., a much smaller company which manufactured medical equipment and had no experience in development of pharmaceuticals—traditionally the key to success in the pharmaceuticals industry. Counteracting Gilmartin's lack of specific experience with pharmaceuticals was his reputation as a team builder and a strategic thinker. He also had an excellent record with Becton Dickenson.

Thus, in hiring Gilmartin, Merck's board of directors traded specific industry experience for the ability to take an objective view of the future and to make the company's diversification into Medco's business a successful one. The board's action was also an implicit acknowledgment that changes were taking place in the pharmaceuticals industry (see Chapter 6) and that new management approaches were needed. For this reason, the management change can be viewed as a favorable development despite the fact that it is contrary to Merck's traditional practice in choosing CEOs.

Management Priorities

Ideally, long-term investors should be entitled to make certain assumptions about the management priorities of companies in which they hold shares. First, the management team should be dedicated to the pursuit of consistent, long-term growth in the company's earnings. The effort to fulfill this goal should be made through the effective and balanced operation of the business. Second, shareholders should be able to assume that the company is being managed for their benefit.

Unfortunately, neither of these desirable conditions can be assumed. Often, the long-term investor's interest is sacrificed to the needs of the market player. Management action in such instances favors short-term share prices but is detrimental to the company's long-term potential.[9] In companies that have powerful managements and passive boards of directors, executives may work to advance their own agendas—and these agendas may be quite contrary to the interests of shareholders.

Such deviations from the best interests of long-term investors are signaled by the following developments:

- Signs that the company is being managed for short-term share prices
- Action to preserve management independence (that is, to avoid takeover)
- The development of illusions of grandeur
- The development or existence of a personality cult

While no one of these developments alone is totally adverse to the interests of shareholders, the long-term investor should be alert to each of them as a possible danger signal, and should search for explanations.

Managing for Share Price

The market value of North American stocks is heavily dependent on expected short-term earnings. Thus, it is not surprising that the managements of many companies give high priority to producing the consistent earnings growth that maximizes short-term share prices. This approach to management leads to distortions of earnings. (You may want to refer back to Chapter 2 to review both the historical background of management for share price and the resulting earnings distortions.)

Management's preoccupation with short-term earnings can be detrimental to a company's development of its long-term potential. While the outsider can rarely know what is going on inside the company, certain actions and situations signal caution to the long-term investor. These include the reduction of R&D expenditures; the publication of ambitious, rigid performance goals; announcements of drastic downsizing; and disagreements with auditors.

Reductions in R&D Expenditures   One key factor in the long-term success of many companies is the quality of its product and process technology, which enables a company to keep the cost and the marketability of its products competitive. In this environment, R&D spending should rarely be reduced, and any such reduction requires explanation. The current level of R&D spending in comparison to the previous year's level is published annually by *Business Week*'s "R&D Score Card" in a June issue. If a current or potential investment shows a decline in spending coincident with only a marginal increase in earnings, the investor should seek an explanation.

Ambitious Performance Goals   Though setting performance goals is a valid and useful aspect of business planning, the objectives for growth in sales and earnings which managers announce are often both overly ambitious and overly specific. When they make such announcements, the managers are obviously attempting to impress investors by showing that they are tough and dedicated. In truth, there is rarely much substance behind the inflated objectives. Actual performance will be strongly influenced by factors that are largely beyond management control.

Once they have staked their reputations and their egos on achievement of certain results, the executives are hampered in their efforts to undertake sound long-term programs. Instead, they must sacrifice the long term in order to achieve more immediate objectives—the only way they are able to give shareholders an indication that their efforts are having some sort of effect.

Drastic Downsizing   Perhaps one of the most common corporate announcements of the past few years has been the intention of reducing costs by slashing the fat out of the company's labor force. Usually a certain percentage is the goal, often 15 to 20 percent worldwide. When they hear such an announcement, shareholders should raise these questions: "If there's so much fat in the company, why was it allowed to accumulate in the first place? Why hasn't it been cut out before?"

Undoubtedly, the efficiency of most companies could be increased by using new management approaches. There are also circumstances, such as the loss of a major contract, in which fixed-target cutbacks could be appropriate. However, in many other situations, drastic downsizing may not be in the long-term best interests of the company and its shareholders. This is true for several reasons, including the likelihood that the cutbacks will include R&D personnel, since research is often viewed as offering no immediate contribution to the company's profitability. Even outside the R&D department, the company effort as a whole may suffer. The staff members who remain are expected to assume the additional load of doing the work of the "laid-off" personnel. Thus they become overloaded and find themselves in the position of having to neglect their own previously assigned functions. Burnout and poor morale are the unfortunate results.

No conclusive studies have yet been published on the effectiveness of drastic downsizing for the sake of cutting costs. Some early work, however, suggests that its benefits are at best short-term, in that any performance gains soon disappear.[10]

Though the stock market generally appears to like cutbacks in personnel, the long-term investor should not interpret cutback announcements as predictors of long-term improvement in performance. It is probably best to defer a decision to invest in a company that has announced a drastic downsizing long enough to see whether its performance will confirm that the action was sound. An announcement of downsizing of a company in which an investor holds stock may be indicative of problems that are not yet reflected in the company's earnings. Close monitoring should be undertaken.

Disagreements with Auditors Change of auditors, an action which is generally taken at an annual meeting, is a relatively rare occurrence. Usually it takes place as a result of management's dissatisfaction with the auditor's performance.

Even though most people believe that "figures don't lie," accounting is not a precise science. There is room for legitimate differences of opinion on accounting standards. The most frequent cause of disputes between management and auditors, in fact, is the accounting standards by which earnings are calculated. Management, because of its quest for earnings growth, tends to prefer relatively liberal practices and may even advocate changes in standards. The auditor may disagree, on the grounds that calculating the reported profit on a different basis would make it inconsistent with previous years' reporting.

Either a change in auditors or a dispute about accounting standards in a company in which a long-term investor holds a position raises a question which the investor ought to consider carefully. The question is: "Is this company's immediate earnings performance so important and so fragile that management must resort to changes in accounting practices to achieve it?" A "yes" answer may indicate that the investment is no longer useful to the shareholder.

Excessive Debt or Dividend Payout   A high level of debt strains the company's ability to service it and tends to lead to a short-term focus. Management's actions become driven by the need to generate cash to service the debt. In other words, decisions are based on accounting needs rather than on operating considerations. Emphasis on generating the needed cash can result in cuts in R&D, advertising, maintenance, supervision, levels of inventory (and therefore customer service), capital expenditures, and so forth. All of these cuts can be expected to have adverse effects on future results.

In a less common situation, a company may pay excessive dividends to help sustain its share price. This action saps funds that ought to be available for other purposes. In an extreme version of this situation, a company may borrow to pay dividends, as Avon did in the early 1980s, when it continued its customary $2 per share payout despite a negative cash flow. By thus increasing its debt from $3 million to $1.1 billion in eight years, the company was, in effect, liquidating itself. Pulling back from this self-destructive action, Avon halved its dividends in 1988 and saved itself from liquidation. The company has since enjoyed a strong recovery, and has gone on to achieve the leading average ROE performance in its industry in the past five years.

Either an excessive debt load or a very high proportion of earnings paid out in dividends serves as a definite caution signal for the long-term investor. It casts serious doubt on the ability of the company to sustain the level of internal spending necessary to improve future performance.

Preservation of Management Independence
Not only companies with mediocre performance records but also companies with strong fundamentals may someday face the threat of takeover. It is the managements of companies that have long histories of mediocre performance, however, who are likely to have severe reactions to these threats. Among the forms these reactions may take are the following:

- Managers sometimes propose *poison pills*, changes in bylaws which will make it more expensive or more difficult for the bidder to get representation on the board of directors.

- They may make the company less attractive to the bidder by dissipating its cash resources. For instance, they may pay out a large one-time dividend to shareholders, or they may make a major panic acquisition.
- They may succumb to greenmail—that is, they may buy back the bidder's initial position at a high price.
- They may demand high severance penalties for themselves—so-called golden parachutes. If big enough, these penalties may deter raiders. In any event, they will provide security to managers, whether or not they deserve it.

The usual justification for these takeover defenses is the contention that the takeover bid does not reflect the "real" value of the company. This raises the question of what the real value of the company is, if not the price that a buyer is willing to pay. (American management has shown itself to be a believer in free markets for everything but stock prices.)

The problem here is that successful defenses against takeover entrench the existing management, which is often mediocre. After all, the bidder may see potential in the company which is not reflected in its share price—potential that could be developed by a vigorous new management team. Worse still, the company may borrow heavily to finance such defenses, particularly to pay a big dividend. In 1986, Owens-Corning Fiberglas Corporation, trying to escape a takeover by Wickes Cos., executed a leveraged recapitalization, taking on $1.6 billion in additional debt to pay a $52 per share one-time dividend. The company was then forced to emphasize cash flow rather than long-term expansion. Its five-year average ROE since that time has been negative.

My suggestion for long-term investors is to consider accepting the best offer they receive, in order to get rid of any stock they hold in a company whose management mounts a vigorous antitakeover defense. A possible exception would be when a strong combination of competitive advantage and industry attractiveness offsets the problems implied by management's reaction.

Incidentally, there is also a question whether a company that already has antitakeover devices, such as a poison pill, in place should have been considered a candidate for long-term investment in the first place. If the fundamentals are sound, the answer is yes. The investor, as always, looks to operating performance as the basis for returns. If performance has been sound, the guarantee of independence has probably not lulled management into complacency.

A related question is whether an issue of shares by a company that has undergone a LBO should be considered as an investment. Considerable caution is indicated for two reasons. First, the company is probably heavily in debt as the result of the buyout, though buyout debt serves no productive purpose as far as operations and earnings are concerned. Second, usually one shareholder, the LBO specialist, remains in control. This shareholder's interests are short-term, with the priority of harvesting the investment. Ensuing business actions taken may therefore not be in the best interests of the long-term investor. In 1994, for instance, investors in RJR Nabisco expressed concerns about the move by Kohlberg Kravis Roberts and RJR Nabisco Holding Corp. to take over Borden, Inc., which was viewed by many as a way for KKR to exit from RJR Nabisco.[11] The concern was not only the dilution of existing shareholders' equity involved but also fear that KKR would force RJR Nabisco to buy some of Borden's brands at a premium price, to the benefit of the holding company controlled by KKR.

Illusions of Grandeur

The most common manifestation of illusions of grandeur is the building of expensive, elaborate, and opulent head office buildings by relatively young companies. This has been dubbed "the Versailles syndrome."[12] The justification is usually that such buildings provide a productive working environment for employees. Not surprisingly, they are most commonly favored by high-tech companies, which build campuslike complexes.

The investor should view these grandiose buildings as a signal of problems for a number of reasons. First, they are expensive and not a good use of money, as real estate can be leased relatively cheaply. Second, planning and construction draw heavily on management time, to the detriment of operations. Third and most damaging, they send a message to the employees, telling them, "We've got it made." This message tends to reduce the sense of urgency which employees of most dynamic companies have. Fourth, the cost of the facilities, as shown on the balance sheet, probably overstates their market value. Such facilities tend to be designed for a specific type of business, and successful competitors are not usually interested in them.

Borland International, under its founder and chairman Philippe Kahn, provides an example. In 1992 this software developer tied up almost one-half its net worth in building a $100 million, luxurious, campuslike headquarters facility. Though the amphitheater of this facility seats 2,500, the company was down to 1,100 employees at the end of 1992, because business conditions had forced the firing of 350 employees late in that year. Its

ROE, both in the most recent year (1994) and in the average for the past five years, has been a deficit.

Even in large, well-established companies, elaborate headquarters and extensive executive perks should be of concern to the investor. Even though these frills may account for a relatively small part of total costs, they may indicate a lack of concern about costs and an attitude that places management's interests ahead of shareholders's interests.

Take the case of RJR Nabisco under Ross Johnson prior to the 1989 LBO by Kohlberg Kravis Roberts. This company maintained one of the most elaborate set of perks in the United States, including an opulent head office building, a large fleet of corporate jets, and condominiums in major cities and resorts. In proposing the LBO in 1988, Johnson's group bid $75 per share despite the indications in KKR internal documents that the company was worth $80 to $111 per share. Johnson lost the subsequent bidding war to Kohlberg Kravis Roberts at $108 per share. However, Johnson strongly resisted any bid above $75 per share. The level of debt required to support a higher bid would have required cost cutting by the company. This would have threatened the lavish lifestyle of the senior management group, which Johnson insisted must be preserved. Thus, the question was whether the company was being run for the benefit of management or the shareholders.[13]

Personality Cults

While strong overall management is essential to any company, a dominant CEO combined with a tame board of directors presents a danger signal. Strong CEOs soon surround themselves with like-minded people. There are no internal checks and balances, and the CEO reigns supreme. There is not even a critical evaluation of the strategy being pursued. The company strategy becomes highly personalized, and is influenced by the biases and even whims of the CEO.

The seemingly rational investment world is not immune to hero worship. The CEO of a company that has a strong record of earnings and share price growth will often develop a following among securities analysts. When this happens, analysts' conclusions are based not on the logic of corporate actions but on the track record of the CEO, as if he or she were infallible. Flaws in corporate strategy are overlooked, or seemingly logical explanations of action are invented, even though no real logic exists.

During the 1960s and the early 1970s, Harold Geneen led ITT through a period of consistent earnings growth by continuously making acquisitions. He made a total of more than 350 acquisitions. The companies were acquired because they were available, not because they fit. Though there were an objective (growth of earnings) and a means (making continued acquisitions), there was no real strategy to connect the two. Under tight head office control, the acquisitions were pressured to contribute to short-term earnings. Many analysts became fans of Geneen despite the fatal flaws in his actions. The acquisition process with its mounting debt could not go on indefinitely, particularly because the performance of the acquisitions started to falter. In 1986, ITT's core telecommunications business virtually collapsed and had to be sold. The need for cash to continue acquisitions had denied the core business the R&D funds necessary to keep up to date technologically. There were two basic flaws in the ITT situation: first, that the action was driven by a dogma, not by long-term logic, and second, that the high priest who could do no wrong, rather than the action which he took, became the focus of attention.

Another personality cult developed in Canada and the United States in the 1980s. Robert Campeau developed a following among analysts because of a record of strong growth by the Campeau Corporation in the commercial real estate industry. In 1986, Campeau embarked on an almost totally leveraged acquisition of, first, Allied Stores and, soon after, Federated Department Stores. A number of analysts imagined reasons for the deals and attributed to Campeau the shrewdness of finding hidden real-estate values in these companies. In fact, the driving force behind the deals was nothing more than Campeau's considerable ego and blind ambition. Some analysts continued to recommend the stock down through its ultimate collapse into bankruptcy. Perhaps even more surprising was the fierce competition by a number of major U.S. brokerage houses to participate in the disaster.[14]

The presence of a strong leader who is closely identified with a company does not in itself constitute a personality cult. The issue is how leadership is exercised. Both Geneen and Campeau were authoritarian and dogmatic leaders. In contrast, though Jack Welch is closely identified with General Electric and is a strong leader, he delegates responsibility for strategy throughout the organization. While some of GE's setbacks in 1994 tarnished Welch's reputation, they have not invalidated his basic approach.

Sound management is an essential ingredient in the success of a company, but any management must be continuously evaluated on the basis of what it is doing, not solely on the basis of its past record. If a corporate development can be justified only on the basis of faith in management, it may be time for the long-term investor to sell.

POINTS TO REMEMBER

The key points in this chapter are as follows:

1. Long-term investments must be monitored for possible changes that may increase or decrease risks. These changes may be the result of a change in either industry fundamentals or the company's competitive strength. As they monitor companies in which they already hold shares, the investors should also remain alert to changes in other companies which may make them good investment prospects.

2. The basic monitoring process consists of following developments in five areas: the progression of sales and earnings, changes in ROE, strategic initiatives undertaken by the company, changes in management, and management priorities.

3. A key aspect of the monitoring of sales and earnings and the performance of the company relative to competitors is assuring that earnings setbacks or shortfalls reflect temporary developments rather than fundamental changes in the industry or the company's competitive position.

4. Signals that problems are developing in the industry or in a company include continuing price wars, loss of product or market leadership, persistent labor problems, and demands by industry spokespersons or company managers for government intervention.

5. The failure of a company's management to acknowledge or discuss problems should be regarded as an adverse development.

6. A good indicator of the basic thrust of the strategic initiatives being undertaken by a company is provided by the nature of its acquisitions. Acquisitions that enhance competitive strength or improve the structure of the industry should be considered favorable. In contrast, acquisitions made for the purpose of diversification should be regarded with suspicion, as they indicate a loss of faith in the potential of the existing business and may take the company into businesses in which the company's managers have no expertise.

7. Changes in management involving orderly internal succession should not be of concern in companies in which performance has been consistently strong. However, if the company's performance has been weak or deteriorating, a management change by

internal succession should be a signal for caution.

8. If a company's performance has been weak despite strong industry fundamentals, the appointment of a new outside CEO with a strong performance record suggests the need for reevaluation of the company's suitability as a long-term investment.

9. Management priorities that may be detrimental to the long-term potential of a company include management for the share price with its short-term prospective, antitakeover defenses which preserve management independence, illusions of grandeur as demonstrated by lavish spending on nonproductive assets, and the existence of a personality cult in which the CEO rather than management action is the basis of faith in the company's future.

10. The long-term investor should be wary of companies that are being managed for share price. Action that gives priority to immediate results is often detrimental to long-term potential. The signals of such a short-term focus include reductions in R&D expenditures, ambitious fixed performance targets, plans for drastic but unspecified downsizing, disputes with auditors, and the assumption of excessive debt.

NOTES

1. The long-term changes discussed here are derived in part from John Rossant with John Pearson, "Landmines on the Road to Utopia," pp. 136–40, and Sharon Moshavi, "So Many People, So Little Time," p. 142, both in *Business Week*, 1994 Special Edition, "21st Century Capitalism," December 1994.

2. Carol J. Loomis, "The Risk That Won't Go Away," *Fortune*, March 7, 1994, pp. 40–57.

3. Tim Smart, "Wall Street's Bitter Lesson for GE," *Business Week*, August 22, 1994, p. 60.

4. Steven E. Prokesch and William J. Powell Jr., "Do Mergers Really Work?" *Business Week*, June 3, 1985, pp. 88–93; and Terence P. Pare, "The New Merger Boom," *Fortune*, November 28, 1994, pp. 95–106.

5. Robert Slater, *The New GE: How Jack Welch Revived an American Institution* (Burr Ridge, IL: Business One Irwin, 1992).

6. Subrata N. Chakravarty and Amy Feldman, "The Road Not Taken," *Forbes*, August 30, 1993, pp. 40–41.

7. Gary McWilliams, "Larry, We Hardly Knew Ye," *Business Week*, December 27, 1993, p. 40.

8. Joseph Weber, John Byrne, Mike McNamee, and Gary McWilliams, "Merck Finally Gets Its Man," *Business Week*, June 27, 1994, pp. 22–25.

9. John J. Curran, "Companies that Rob the Future," *Fortune*, July 4, 1988, pp. 84–89.

10 John A. Byrne, "There Is an Upside to Downsizing," *Business Week*, May 9, 1994, p. 69.

11. Laura Zinn with Greg Burns, "The RJR-Borden Deal: Is the Investor the Odd Man Out?" *Business Week*, October 10, 1994, pp. 110–11; and Eric S. Hardy, "Be Careful of Those Retreads," *Forbes*, December 5, 1994, pp. 256–57.

12. This term and the example are derived from Julie Pitta, "The Versailles Syndrome," *Forbes*, July 19, 1993, p. 201.

13. Brian Burroughs and John Helyar, *Barbarians at the Gates: The Fall of RJR Nabisco* (New York: Harper and Row, 1990).

14. John Rothchild, *Going for Broke* (New York: Simon & Schuster, 1991).

PART

V

COMPREHENSIVE
INDUSTRY STUDIES

Certain industries become popular favorites with investors, and some remain popular for many years, or even decades. Chapters 9 through 12 present detailed examinations of several industries which have had a wide investor following. The industries have been chosen for this detailed study because their different characteristics illustrate numerous issues concerning investment decisions. Chapter 9 deals with the automobile and the automotive parts industry as an example of a mature manufacturing business of the type which is commonly called a smokestack industry. Chapter 10 covers the computer industry, a high-tech business in which intellectual rather than physical assets are necessary to success. Chapter 11 is devoted to the forest products industry as an example of a producer of commodity raw materials. Chapter 12 examines the banking industry as an example of a business in which the output is not a good but a service.

Though some of the companies discussed in these chapters have been touched on earlier in the book, the more detailed study of their respective industries provides the opportunity to also examine in more detail how changes in the industry have evolved and their effect on the competitive position of some of the major players.

In each chapter, industry characteristics and developments are presented first, followed by analysis of the strategies and performance records of major companies. Finally, I draw conclusions about the status of the companies as long-term investment candidates.

9

THE AUTOMOBILE INDUSTRY AND THE AUTOMOTIVE PARTS INDUSTRY

Taken together, the automobile industry and the automotive parts industry provide an example of a mature manufacturing business which has long been a favorite of investors. After examining the structure of each of these industries, the changes which are affecting the structure, and the strategies pursued by the major companies, we will also examine the market performance of these companies' stocks. Finally the monitoring signals discussed in Chapter 8 will be used to show the effects of investment decisions during the decade 1984–94.

AUTOMOBILE INDUSTRY

The primary force driving economic development in the first half of the twentieth century was the internal combustion engine, the basis of the automobile. While automobile production became a major industry in itself, it also made possible the efficient distribution of other products which could be made in highly efficient centralized factories. The development of the tractor enabled a large improvement in the productivity of farmers, thereby making available the supply of labor necessary for the growth of manufacturing.

During the first half of the century, the automobile industry pro-gressed through the emerging and growth phases to maturity, in a typical phase progression (as described in Chapter 4). By the late 1950s, the large number of small producers typical of the emerging and early growth phas-es had been reduced to a relatively small number of large manufacturers. Some of these might have dropped out earlier if they had not been sus-tained by armament production during World War II. From this war-relat-ed work they gained the financial strength necessary to continue operation and to participate in a strong market created by deferred demand, which existed until the early 1950s. From the late 1950s to the late 1970s, the automobile industry was attractive to surviving major North American automobile producers, as a result of the structure of the industry.

INDUSTRY STRUCTURE

Traditional Industry Fundamentals

The traditional characteristics of the automobile industry are described below.

Substitutes

There were no substitutes. The vast majority of members of the North American public were apparently fully convinced of the efficacy and desir-ability of the private car as their major means of transportation. With improved roads, the popularity of the car resulted in the decline of train trav-el. To economize, railways reduced service, hastening their own decline.

Barriers to Entry

Barriers to entry were prohibitive. A great deal of capital would have been needed for initial product development, and also to build and equip the physical plant required for manufacture of a line of automobiles. A rela-tively large market share would have been necessary to achieve economies of scale, and this would have entailed establishment of an extensive deal-ership structure. Nevertheless, at least three companies did attempt to enter the industry. Kaiser-Frazer Corporation made an attempt in 1949–58, and Tucker Corporation tried in 1946–48. These were followed by Bricklin Vehicle Corporation in 1974. Not surprisingly, all these attempts failed.

Bargaining Power

Automobile manufacturers' bargaining power with buyers was high. Brand loyalties were well established, and the producers wielded a great deal of promotional power. It was the producers themselves, in fact, who had created and promoted the concept of the car as a status symbol rather than merely a means of transportation. Furthermore, the manufacturers were well entrenched as the arbiters of style and taste in automobiles.

Producers' bargaining power with suppliers was also relatively strong. A high degree of backward integration into the manufacture of components gave the companies an edge in their dealings with suppliers of materials and components.

In addition, though the unions were powerful, they had been successfully bought off by the manufacturers, who had continually made concessions on virtually every aspect of the unions' demands. The labor contracts between unions and manufacturers were almost identical throughout the industry. Thus labor costs were stable and did not affect the competitive positions of the companies, as they could be readily passed on to consumers.

Industry Life Cycle

The automobile industry has been in the mature phase since the mid-1950s. Its well-defined long-term growth trend was highly cyclical, and was based on economic factors and the replacement cycle. As is typical of a mature phase, the rationalization of the industry progressed in a relatively orderly way through the 1960s and 1970s. The smaller companies merged, were acquired, or dropped out. In the process, a large number of long-established brand names such as Packard, Hudson, Nash, and Studebaker disappeared. There were only four domestic automobile manufacturers left in 1980. This rationalization of the domestic industry was completed with the acquisition of American Motors Corp. by Chrysler in 1987. (The term *completed* is used here because there is little if any competitive advantage to be gained by any further mergers among the surviving Big Three.)

Fixed Costs

Due to product development and tooling costs, mechanized manufacture, and the supplementary unemployment benefits that had been granted as union concessions, fixed costs were high.

Effects of Changes in Industry Fundamentals

The industry as a whole had long been a profitable one, despite its cyclicality. By 1980, however, it had become apparent that the industry fundamenatals were changing drastically, in several respects.[1]

Inroads by Japanese Manufacturers

Many changes had been brought about by Japanese automobile manufacturers' actions. First, the Japanese manufacturers had overcome barriers to entry into the North American car market by achieving economies of scale while operating in their own protected domestic market. All the while, they had also been gradually and patiently adapting and improving their products, to make them more appealing to their target, the large North American market.

Second, consumer tastes had changed. The market had become increasingly price-sensitive due to both the increase in fuel prices as the result of the oil price increases of 1973 and 1979 and the increase in the price of cars due to the high rate of inflation during the 1970s. Instead of looking at their cars as status symbols, buyers had begun to view them more as utilitarian transportation. The lower-priced and more fuel-efficient Japanese cars, which were concurrently developing a reputation for quality, were well positioned to take advantage of these developments. While the American producers introduced their initial lines of front-wheel-drive economy cars in 1979 and 1980, their lack of experience in this area resulted in products of relatively poor design and quality. These developments significantly weakened the American producers' bargaining power with their traditional captive market.

Third, Japanese manufacturers enjoyed highly productive plants as the result of both the nature of their labor force and their organizational practices. Their well-educated and highly dedicated labor gave them both high productivity and high quality. They had pioneered disaggregation in the industry combined with such innovative practices as just-in-time delivery of components. Combined with a favorable exchange rate, these factors gave them a significant cost advantage over North American producers.

Fourth, superior product development practices enabled Japanese manufacturers to drastically shorten the lead time needed to bring a car from concept to showroom. The Japanese lead time was 36 months, which was 12 months less than the North American capability. This enabled the Japanese to retain and improve customer preference for their cars by keeping up to date on both stylistic and technological innovations. This product development process involved the use of teams in which all the necessary technical and other functions were represented. Close liaison and joint responsibility enabled the Japanese teams to make quickly and effectively the multitude of decisions and trade-offs involved in the development of a complex product. This *multifunctional team approach* was subsequently adopted by the American industry as well.

Political Developments

North American automobile companies were harmed also by politically inspired developments. In 1975 the U.S. government imposed a fuel consumption limit which had to be met by 1985 by each manufacturer on the basis of average fuel consumption over all the cars it made in a given year. As a result, U.S. auto manufacturers were forced to produce relatively high proportions of subcompact and compact cars, on which they lost money. In producing cars of these sizes, they were at a disadvantage in relation to Japanese producers, which already had the design and manufacturing capabilities for small cars in place. The Japanese auto makers also had the efficiency to produce these cars profitably.

The U.S. automobile industry successfully lobbied the government, with the result that quotas were imposed on Japanese imports in 1981. The seeming success of this move was short-lived, and ultimately it backfired. Japanese manufacturers responded by accelerating the transfer of their assembly operations to North America. Thus not only did they successfully avoid the intended ill effects of the quotas upon their ability to sell in North America, but also they were insulated to a significant extent from unfavorable currency fluctuations. The lasting effect of the quotas was that, by the mid-1980s, Japanese producers had established themselves more securely and more permanently in the North American market.

What happened next was even worse for North American car manufacturers, which up to this point had been able to maintain their profitability in the market for luxury cars. Being limited in the numbers of cars that they could export, the Japanese turned their focus from numbers to value. By developing new lines of luxury cars, starting with the Acura in 1985, they quickly took market share away from U.S. manufacturers in this area as well. Japanese auto makers had already established a reputation for providing quality cars, and the new luxury cars they marketed in North America were an almost immediate success.

Even as late as 1994, American automobile manufacturers had not yet fully recovered from Japanese inroads into their domestic markets. Mounting a gallant effort, they had dramatically improved their products, notably the Cadillac and the Lincoln. The new generation of luxury car buyers, however, had grown up yearning for foreign luxury cars, and not even seductive updating could influence many of them to switch to American luxury cars. Sales of both Cadillacs and Lincolns were disappointing. Ironically, the quotas for which the industry had lobbied had the net result of forcing North American manufacturers to sell more of the small cars on which they lost money, while preventing them from selling enough profitable luxury cars to make up the difference.

Protected Market Segments

The developments described above would have left domestic automobile manufacturers in dire straits indeed, had they not been able to exploit two protected market segments: (1) light trucks and other so-called utility vehicles, and (2) minivans. These two market segments have their roots in somewhat different circumstances, though both have been affected by demographic factors.

Light Trucks and Utility Vehicles Light trucks and utility vehicles became attractive to American producers during the 1970s because they were subject to comparatively lenient fuel economy standards. Furthermore, they had been largely ignored by the Japanese, who were discouraged by a 25 percent import tariff. By the mid-1980s, demographic factors caused a rise in the market for these vehicles. As baby boomers found themselves increasingly tied down by family responsibilities (a phenomenon which is sometimes called "cocooning"), they began to seek ways to escape, if only through fantasy. Driving light trucks contributed to their images of themselves as rugged individualists who were ready for adventure. In actuality, it is doubtful whether most of the many four-wheel-drive vehicles that have been sold will ever see any terrain more rugged than an unpaved parking lot. However, the American manufacturers, who had already been making these vehicles for some years, were in a position to take advantage of the surge in demand.

Minivans The minivan, in contrast, was a totally new product developed in response to the family-oriented needs of the same period. Chrysler pioneered the product, introducing it in 1983. It was built on an automobile chassis and drove like a car. Both GM and Ford were slow to respond. When they did finally respond, several years later, they produced vehicles built on light truck chassis, which did not have the Chrysler's easy handling characteristics. This response extended the duration of Chrysler's advantage. The Japanese manufacturers did not even begin to move into the minivan market until quite late in the 1980s.

Leasing

In the early 1990s, in response to tax changes which eliminated the deductibility of interest on car loans, the industry turned heavily to leasing.

The leases appealed to customers because they reduced monthly payments. What was ignored by the 75 percent of buyers who had previously relied on financing when they purchased cars was the sizable price increases that were camouflaged by the leasing arrangements.[2] For manufacturers, one advantage of the limited-term leases was a decrease in the necessity for price discounts in the form of factory rebates. A further potential benefit for producers was that leasing was thought of as a possible way to restore some of the brand loyalty that had flagged during the changes of the previous decade or more. However, the question of the effect of leasing on future new car sales remained unanswered as of late 1994.

Leasing was a highly successful tactic. It was used in 25 percent of car transactions in 1994, for instance. However, it also restored price competitiveness to the Japanese, who had been under severe pressure because the appreciation of the yen drove up their costs for products which had to be priced in U.S. dollars. Since Japanese cars have higher resale value than American cars, Japanese producers were able to set lease rates at a competitive level. Thus, the practice of leasing handed back to the Japanese producers some of the profit margins which had been eroded by the rise of the yen.

American Companies' Responses to Changes

The substantial structural changes in the American automobile industry in the 1980s and the early 1990s found domestic companies largely unprepared to respond effectively. A part of their problem was the long lead times required to develop a new automobile. Inertia created by the combination of management attitudes and the intransigence of the powerful unions was another major factor. In fairness to unions, the companies continued to engage in self-destructive practices, such as giving executives large bonuses, even while they were demanding concessions from the unions—all this without altering their traditional adversarial relationship.

Disaggregation is an aspect of auto manufacturers' response to change that has been rather profound. Unfortunately, while it creates some positive benefits for existing companies, it also creates further problems. In disaggregation, responsibility for design and development of critical components is often contracted to outside suppliers.[3] This retreat from the vertical integration that had been traditional in the industry creates enormous benefits in cost reduction, flexibility, and access to new technologies, as well as a reduction in the amount of working capital required.

The downside to disaggregation is that it significantly reduces the barriers to entry into the industry. A new entrant can readily contract out the manufacture of its parts, and does not have to suffer as the existing companies do from being stuck with aging plants and restrictive union contracts. Already disaggregation has enabled several foreign manufacturers—Honda, Toyota, BMW AG, and Daimler-Benz AG—to establish assembly plants in the United States.

In effect, it has taken more than a decade for the domestic companies to recognize and adjust to the new realities, and even now their adjustment not only remains incomplete but also is creating further changes which will have to be coped with in turn.

Prospects of Future Changes

Besides the changes already mentioned, some of which the companies themselves are causing or exacerbating, some additional changes may be expected and will likely have to be dealt with. First, strong pressure by governments to reduce air pollution, along with mandated standards, can be expected to continue primarily at the state level. Auto makers will have to continue the efforts they have already begun to improve pollution abatement equipment, and they will also have to continue their ongoing efforts to improve car engines so as to reduce fuel usage.

Second, though ample global reserves have contributed to a feeling of complacency about oil prices, these prices are in truth likely to rise, as oil consumption continues to increase. The lessons of the past with regard to product development time and volatile political influences appear to have been discounted, but both automobile manufacturers and investors should be aware that a sudden sharp rise in oil prices is possible. Should such a rise occur, a company that had strong representation in the economy car segment of the market, and that also possessed the capacity for quickly diverting additional manufacturing capability to this segment, would be in a highly advantageous position.

In addition, the industry will face further evolutionary changes in product preferences, as demographic factors continue to change. There is a question as to whether light trucks and utility vehicles, for which the manufacturers are adding capacity, will continue to be popular as the population ages. The next cyclical downturn, however, may be less severe for domestic automobile producers, as they have become more competitive with the Japanese in terms of quality, costs, and product mix. The Japanese manufacturers, in fact, are likely to have to share the pain.

COMPANY PERFORMANCE

The performance of the key domestic players in the automobile industry—General Motors, Ford, and Chrysler—is shown in Exhibit 9–1.

Key Performance Statistics for the Major Manufacturers in the
Automobile Industry, 1990–94

Company	Return on Equity, %		Return on Capital, %	
	5-Year Average	Latest 12 Months	Latest 12 Months	Profit Margin, %
Chrysler	11.2	53.3	26.5	6.7
GM	9.8	163.5	20.8	3.5
Ford	5.1	33.1	9.8	3.6
Industry median: 1994	4.4	11.3	6.7	1.6

Overall, Chrysler has outperformed the industry, with Ford slightly above the median. The strong return on equity (ROE) performance of GM in the latest 12 months is in part attributable to the company's being highly leveraged, with debt at 77 percent of capital as compared to 44 percent for Chrysler. Chrysler significantly outperformed GM in return on total capital. (This points out one of the weaknesses of analyses that rely on ROE alone as a measure of performance.) The five-year average statistics reflect the down part of the industry cycle, in which the industry underperformed the all-industries median five-year average ROE of 11.5 percent by a considerable margin. During the strong part of the economic cycle, up to 1988, the median five-year average ROE for the automobile industry was 23.5 percent, well above the all-industries median of 13.9 percent.

In reacting to changes in the industry, as discussed above, General Motors, Ford, and Chrysler have each responded in different ways. Let's look at the events reflected in their respective performances.

General Motors[4] GM started the decade of the 1980s as the dominant company in the industry, with a 46 percent market share. While it remains the largest producer in 1994, its market share has dropped to about 35 percent and it is no longer considered a leader in any category. The company has been slow to respond to change. Even when it has responded, its actions have not had the expected results. Here are some specifics.

• On a positive note, GM had already introduced its front-wheel-drive compact models by 1980. However, its full-sized cars were relatively new and were vulnerable to the oil price increase of 1979.

- The company's first major attempt to revamp its larger products and to use front-wheel drive also involved rationalization of manufacture in an attempt to reduce costs by increasing the commonalty of components between brands. The result was a loss of differentiation between brands. (Ford took advantage of this mistake by poking fun at GM's look-alike cars.) Cadillac was particularly hard-hit by the loss of its traditional high quality.

- The company's designers lacked feel for changes in market tastes. GM's first aerodynamic designs, produced in response to the success of the Ford Taurus, were outdated by the time they were introduced. The designers overreacted in the design of their first minivan with a chassis based on a traditional automobile chassis. Introduced in 1989, this minivan had too futuristic a look and did not sell well.

- GM was the slowest of the major domestic auto producers to adopt disaggregation by increasing its reliance on outside suppliers. This move introduced a particular problem because GM was the most vertically integrated of the Big Three. The sale of the company's component operations did not pick up steam until the 1990s. Many of these operations were parts of larger plants, and the unions were able to hold the company hostage by shutting down key component operations. Such shutdowns quickly halted production at the assembly plants, because of the just-in-time inventory practices which the company had picked up from the Japanese. For example, a nine-day walkout by only 240 workers at its Lordstown, Ohio, tool and die shop in 1992, in protest of a plan to close down the operation, cost an estimated $70 million in pretax profit because it shut down production at assembly plants.

- Organizational turmoil, starting with the reorganization of 1984, both created problems and hampered attempted reforms. Attempted decentralization added new layers of management, and internal communication suffered seriously. Attempts to reform the company were impeded. In this confusion, CEO Robert Stemple was forced out in 1992, in favor of Jack Smith.

In 1980, GM was almost universally considered the king of the global automotive hill and was expected to continue to dominate the industry. It was the lowest-cost domestic producer, had the financial resources to continue to develop and produce a full line of cars and trucks, and had a well-established and loyal customer base. In contrast, Ford's financial position would allow it to develop only a limited number of new models and Chrysler was seeking a government bailout to avoid bankruptcy.

GM's disappointing performance since 1980 is indicative of how much the market has changed and the inadequacy of its strategic responses. In order to maintain its overall level of sales, it must try to appeal to the broadest possible market. Therefore it fragments its efforts into a multitude of overlapping models. It has usually failed to read the market correctly, and even when its readings have been correct, its organization has lacked the ability to respond to changes quickly. Despite its size, which theoretically should provide it with economies of scale, GM has had the economic characteristics of a group of smaller companies.

In sum, GM's problems are both structural and managerial. Structurally, the task of undoing the high degree of vertical integration in the face of union resistance is daunting. Most of the company's remaining component manufacturing operations are physically integrated with other operations, which means they cannot be readily separated and sold. Managerially, the company has been inbred and has lacked decisive leadership, resorting to an adaptive strategy (as discussed in Chapter 2). Only in 1994 did GM executive indicate that they were looking outside the company for marketing management.

Ford Ford was the only U.S. car maker to gain market share in the decade of the 1980s. It did this by being both lucky and smart.

- Starting the 1980s with two popular compact models, the Escort and the Lynx, Ford was able to take advantage of the demand for economy cars that was caused by the large oil price increase of 1979. Though these models were not profitable, they did help to pay the rent.
- In the middle of the 1980s, the company made major investments to increase its truck capacity and upgrade the product. Thus it was able to take advantage of the boom in the truck market.
- The Taurus, a major gamble in design by a multifunctional team, was introduced in 1985. It proved an enormous success and contributed to Ford's outearning GM in 1987 and 1988.
- With capital fully committed elsewhere, Ford was not able to downsize the Lincoln in 1979 and early in the 1980s. In a stroke of good fortune, however, the Lincoln began to sell well as oil prices declined.
- The autocratic and finance-oriented Ford family management ended in 1980. After this, the company was directed by highly competent automotive professionals. Lacking GM's resources, it was unable to try to be all things to all people and so had to pick

its niches carefully. It chose well, and was rewarded for its wisdom in this regard.

By the end of the 1980s, Ford was running out of steam. Its product mix, including the compact cars, had low margins, and it lacked the capacity to increase its output of profitable trucks.[5] It had to spend heavily to develop new engines and transmissions because it had delayed such spending in the 1980s. It did not follow up on the use of multifunctional teams which had been so successful with the Taurus, and its new product offerings were warmed-up versions of old products. Not until 1993 and 1994 was a new line of Ford products unveiled.

Ford's current strategy is to pursue growth by globalizing the company. This would involve merging the various regional auto operations (American, European, South American, and Asian) into one unit, to eliminate duplication of product development costs and allow use of fewer global suppliers. The basic global designs would be customized for the various national markets. While this strategy has been successfully used in other industries and is sound in theory, it will be difficult to implement.[6] Infighting within the organization will have to be overcome, and there is also a risk of producing vehicles that please no one, due to the necessary compromises. Ford's pursuit of a massive global organization also has the disadvantage of being contrary to current organizational preferences for smaller, more flexible units. The company's first product development effort under this strategy was slow (it took six years to develop the product) and expensive (the cost was $6 billion). While there is obviously a learning curve in such a process, these initial results show how far Ford has still to go.

Chrysler[7]   If Ford was limited in its scope of action by a lack of resources, Chrysler had no options whatsoever. Rescued from bankruptcy by government loan guarantees in 1980, it was kept alive by the K-car. Introduced in that same year, the K-car benefited from the sharp oil price increase of 1979. The subsequent events can be summarized as follows:

- Chrysler's Caravan minivan was introduced in 1983 and was an outstanding success. It was the brainchild of Lee Iacocca, who had brought the idea over from Ford (with Ford's permission) when he joined Chrysler in 1979. Ford did not think the idea had merit, but Iacocca's involvement with the Ford Mustang had taught him how profitable specialty niche cars can be.
- In 1985, Chrysler used its newfound profitability to diversify. It bought several defense-related companies, including Gulfstream

Aerospace Inc. for $637 million and Electrospace Systems Inc., a defense contractor, for $367 million. It also purchased four rental car companies. Chrysler was not alone in its diversification effort. GM had spent $10 billion for Hughes Aircraft Company and Electronic Data Systems Corporation, and Ford had invested $5 billion in a savings bank, a finance company, and a leasing operation. The difference was that the outside investments starved Chrysler's auto business for funds. Further, these acquisitions diverted management attention from the company's core business. Gulfstream was sold in 1990.

- Perhaps due to the diversion of managers' attention from the automobile business, the cars introduced in the middle and late 1980s were flops. They had a high, squared-off appearance, and archaic styling touches like vinyl roofs and chrome wheel covers completed their out-of-date look. (This look was attributed to Iacocca's influence.) During the second half of the decade, the company was kept alive only by its minivan and its trucks.

- In 1987, being denied further nonautomobile acquisitions by its board, Chrysler bought American Motors for $718 million. Thus it acquired the Jeep line of utility vehicles for a booming market, as well as AMC's state-of-the-science Canadian assembly plant.

By 1994, Chrysler had become the most disaggregated of the U.S. auto companies, as it was making 34 percent of its own parts (versus 38 percent for Ford and 47 percent for GM, but compared to only 25 percent for Toyota). Partially due to its disaggregation, Chrysler was the lowest-cost domestic producer; it was also the producer with the most quality problems. However, it was the leader in the new product development process, having adopted the Japanese multifunctional team approach. This approach was supported by a new $1 billion R&D facility.

As of 1994, Chrysler was again a full-line supplier. It was producing compact, midsize, and full-sized cars, as well as trucks, all introduced within the previous two years. A new minivan is due in 1995. All the company's new products have had a good market reception. Chrysler's overall product line strategy is very similar to Toyota's, but Chrysler sells under more nameplates. This differentiation is useful for pricing purposes, as the differences between the products are minimal and not cost-additive.

Of the Big Three, Chrysler announced by far the most focused strategy. The company will concentrate on the North American market. Only minor joint ventures, such as a possible minivan plant in China, will require low investment elsewhere. It will also continue aggressive product development. Further, it plans to build up a cash reserve of $10 billion to sustain investment during the next cyclical industry downturn. Unlike its domestic competitors, the company has both a management and an organizational structure that have demonstrated the ability to deliver the potential inherent in its strategy. This potential for success was a major factor in its subsequent takeover attempt, which will be discussed in Chapter 13.

Thus, in the Big Three North American manufacturers, we see three well-defined strategies: GM's traditional industry perspective, Ford's global plans, and Chrysler's domestic focus. These three strategies characterize the present situation and provide a basis for consideration of the industry's potential from the investor's perspective.

THE INVESTOR'S PERSPECTIVE

Exhibit 9–2 shows the market performance of GM, Ford, and Chrysler stock prices relative to the S&P 500 for the period 1982–1994.

The Market's Judgment

For the reasons indicated above, GM was a disappointment to investors, as its performance fell well short of the market as a whole. Both Ford and Chrysler gave investors a roller-coaster ride over the 12-year period, but only Chrysler would have left a long-term investor who held a position throughout the period well ahead of the broad market.

While the auto stocks are highly cyclical, it should be noted that Chrysler stock started to decline in 1987, the third year after its peak earnings of 1984. It is apparent that investors thought the company was running out of steam. To the long-term investor, the caution signal occurred in 1985, when the company acquired Gulfstream Aerospace and other defense-related companies. This was a clear indication that Iacocca was losing faith in the company's automobile business and had nothing in the pipeline to revive it. Chrysler's new products were warmed-over copies of old designs. Though the sale of Gulfstream in 1990 may have been an act of financial necessity, it may also have indicated that Iacocca was ready to turn his attention back to the automobile business. The revival of Chrysler's stock in 1992 occurred partly in anticipation of a cyclical recovery of the industry, but also reflected enthusiasm for the new LH and Neon product lines.

Comparative Performance of Major Manufacturers in the
Automobile Industry, 1982–94 (Indexed to S&P 500, 1984 = 160)

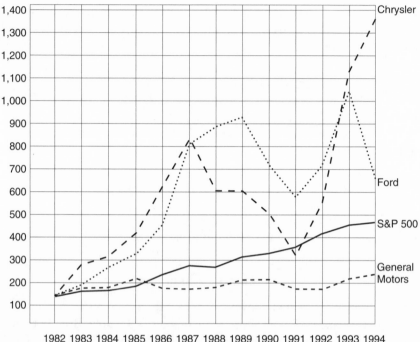

Note: The index for each year is shown at the mean between the high and the low for the period.

Ford stock did not decline until 1990, because of the continued strength of its truck and Taurus lines. The company's recovery in 1992 appears to be largely cyclical, as it had no immediate new product prospects; the Windstar minivan and the new compact lines had yet to be introduced. However, investors' disappointment with Ford's performance showed up in 1994.

There has been a significant improvement in the competitiveness of U.S. industry as a whole. As a result, its vulnerability to the next cyclical downturn will tend to be reduced, and foreign producers are likely to share the U.S. market decline to a much greater extent than they have in the past.

The stock market, however, does not appear to have reached the conclusion that improvements in competitiveness will reduce the vulnerability of

U.S. automobile companies to cyclical downturns. Apprehensions about cyclicality have caused investors to value auto stocks quite conservatively. As of the end of 1994, for example, GM, Ford, and Chrysler had an average price/earnings (P/E) ratio of 5.7, as compared to the S&P 500 P/E ratio of 17.

According to the historical pattern, the P/E ratio for auto companies has been about one-half the market multiple.[8] On this basis, assuming that earnings were reaching a cyclical peak, auto stocks should have been selling at about 8.5 times current earnings. The difference between market perceptions of the strength of the automobile industry and the analysis presented here, in fact, is one of the bases upon which my recommendation that long-term investors consider investment in this industry is predicated.

Industry Structure and Competitive Advantage

These historical stock price developments provide the background necessary for an assessment of the state of the industry and the relative competitive strengths of the Big Three. Listed below are some assumptions concerning the present state of the industry, the basis of competitive advantage, and the nature of the changes expected in the industry. These assumptions will be used in assessing these companies as long-term investment candidates.

1. For North American producers, the automobile industry can be described as moderately attractive, though still highly cyclical. Barriers to entry remain high, and substitutes are nonexistent. The decline of companies' bargaining power with suppliers has been offset by the suppliers' contribution to the funding of product development, and also by cost reductions and the shortening of lead times for new products. High domestic labor costs are no longer a significant disadvantage, as the production process has become increasingly automated. Bargaining power with customers, which was severely eroded by a decade of weak design and indifferent product quality, has to some extent been restored by contemporary design and an improved reputation for quality. In total, the North American auto manufacturers have closed much of the competitive gap with foreign competitors, irrespective of any advantage derived from the fall of the U.S. dollar.

2. Competitive advantage for a company in the automobile industry must be based on the following factors:

   • The ability to produce high-quality products at low cost

- Sensitivity to market tastes and demands
- The ability to rapidly develop and introduce new products

3. The changes that the industry faces can be described as evolutionary in nature. They are likely to be relatively slow and orderly, and highly predictable.

Assessment of Three Automobile Manufacturers

Within the overall automobile industry situation, there are significant differences between the competitive strengths of the Big Three companies. These differences, which should be recognized in any long-term investment decision, are summarized in Exhibit 9–3. The P/E ratios cited in the exhibit are in comparison to the prevailing S&P 500 P/E ratio of 17.3.

Chrysler can be considered as a long-term investment candidate based on its capability: the lowest costs and the most effective market response capability in an industry with improving fundamentals. While investors seem to be leery of the company because of its checkered history, its management appears to have learned from the lessons of the past and will likely stay focused on the car business and on a primarily U.S. manufacturing base. The managers understand the company's core business and appear to be willing to devote to it the continuing investment that it will require. This long-term perspective does not rely heavily on the popularity of current product offerings, even though these products will be important to earnings for several years. Strong earnings will be required in the intermediate term, to allow Chrysler to accumulate the cash necessary to maintain its position during the next downturn in the cycle. As of March 31, 1995, these advantages were available for a stock price of only 4.1 times current earnings.

AUTOMOTIVE PARTS INDUSTRY

In comparison to the oligopolistic automobile industry, the automotive parts industry is much more fragmented. The *Forbes* list contains 32 companies, and many of these have interests in other industries. What these 32 companies have in common, however, is a high degree of reliance on business related to automobiles.

Like the automobile industry, this industry has undergone a substantial change in structure. And like companies in the automobile industry, each of the companies in the automotive parts industry has reacted differently.

E X H I B I T   9–3

Assessment of the Major Manufacturers in the Automobile Industry as Long-Term Investment Candidates (As of March 31, 1995)

General Motors

Market Price, March 31, 1995: 44   P/E Ratio: 7.1   52-Week Range: 60 1/8–36 1/8

Competitive Strength

Moderate. GM's 1994 ROE performance improvement can be attributed to a strong cyclical sales recovery and its highly leveraged position. The company is vulnerable to a cyclical downturn. Though it is very strong in Europe, where it has been turned around, it is far from solving its structural problems in North America, as indicated by loss suffered in operations during the third quarter of 1994. New models introduced are catch-up at best, and GM's brand names have become tarnished during several years when indifferent products were put out. The company's organizational structure has been changed, but management's attitudes have remained the same. GM's future performance is likely to be a repeat of the 1980s, though at a somewhat higher level. In the absence of any definable or sustainable competitive advantage, the investor should maintain an attitude of skepticism in regard to optimistic predictions about the company's future (which have been common in recent years) until such a time as enduring improvement may be demonstrated. Recent P/E ratios and stock prices reflect continuing, justifiable investor skepticism.

Ford

Market Price, March 31, 1995: 26   P/E Ratio: 5.4   52-Week Range: 32 3/4–24 1/2

Competitive Strength

Moderate. Ford has shown good ability to read market tastes and has an up-to-date, balanced product line, but lags behind competitors' product development capability in regard to both speed and cost. The company has been slow to update the Taurus, but the popularity of the line should assure good market reception when new models become available. Ford's global strategy may help to increase its rate of sales growth but carries a high risk that the expected cost reduction benefits may or may not materialize. The company's competitive advantage is sustainable and appears to be adequate to provide solid though not spectacular performance.

Chrysler

Market Price, March 31, 1995: 41 3/4   P/E Ratio: 4.1   52-Week Range: 55 3/8–38 1/4

Competitive Strength

High. This company is the lowest-cost North American producer, with a full, up-to-date product line which is being well received by the market. It has demonstrated an ability to read market preferences, and it has rapid response capability with its product development teams and new facilities. However, it must still resolve product quality problems. Its strategy of focusing on North American operations except for relatively minor joint ventures elsewhere is sound. The company's announced intention of accumulating cash reserves to sustain its investment capability in cyclical downturns is sound strategy. In light of these factors, the company should be able to increase its competitive edge over its North American rivals.

INDUSTRY STRUCTURE

The automotive parts industry grew in parallel with the automobile manufacturers. Until the early 1980s, the industry was inherently unattractive.

Traditional Industry Fundamentals

The traditional characteristics of the automotive parts industry are described below.

Barriers to Entry

Most manufacturing operations in the industry involved relatively standard metalworking or plastics-molding capability. No significant proprietary technology existed for these operations. As a result, barriers to entry were low.

Bargaining Power

In at least two respects, the bargaining power of companies in the industry was disadvantageous. The buyers—the major automobile manufacturers—had high bargaining power. Auto producers were large, cost-conscious customers which either already maintained their own partial internal supply capabilities or possessed a credible likelihood of being able to establish such capabilities.

The unionized labor forces of the parts manufacturers also exerted high bargaining power. Among other things, the unions could always either strike or threaten to strike if they were dissatisfied with wages, benefits, or working conditions. Strikes could significantly inhibit the companies' ability to guarantee a continuing supply of automotive parts to their powerful customers—an ability on which parts suppliers' competitive advantage depended to a high degree, as discussed below.

Only in relation to their suppliers of raw materials, which were standard, undifferentiated commodities, did automotive parts suppliers have any real bargaining power.

Fixed Costs

Because manufacture of automotive parts (even the standard, comparatively simple parts that were widely used in the automobile industry prior to the 1980s) requires specialized facilities, the parts supply companies had a relatively large investment in fixed-cost facilities.

Industry Life Cycle

While parts suppliers were under constant pressure to renew their contracts because of their fixed costs, they were also subject to the same cyclicality that affected their customers. The degree of cyclicality, however, was not uniform throughout the industry. Though suppliers that relied primarily on sales to automobile producers shared their customers' cyclicality, companies that produced parts for the replacement market were to some extent contracyclical. Demand for parts rose as cars aged, and demand often rose sharply when replacement of cars was deferred due to a down cycle in the automobile industry.

Basis for Competitive Advantage

In the automotive parts industry, competitive advantage rested on several interrelated factors: a company must be able to produce a standard part to detailed specifications, it must be able to maintain acceptable quality, and it must offer the lowest possible price. In addition, suppliers to the replacement market also had to have superb distribution capabilities. The parts themselves were treated as virtual commodities, and quick availability was important to the customer.

Effects of Changes in Industry Fundamentals

Changes in the automobile industry, starting in the early 1980s, were described earlier in this chapter. These same changes had significant effects on the structure of the automotive parts industry. Changes in barriers to entry, bargaining power with customers and suppliers, contractual arrangements with customers, and new domestic business had positive effects on the industry. On the other hand, a change in the competitive arena, from domestic to global, had the negative effect of introducing new competition from low-wage countries. All these changes are described below.

The overall effect of the changes was to make the automotive parts industry more attractive as the result of higher barriers to entry and an improvement in its bargaining power with customers. It also altered the basis of competitive advantage. Whereas previously all a company had to do was make a standard product and deliver it on time at a low price, now it was required to have an R&D function. Parts suppliers began to work with auto makers to develop highly specialized and increasingly sophisticated versions of long-used components such as ignitions and brakes, as well as completely new technology such as air bags. The increasing sophistication of both old and new technology will tend to limit future competition in the replacement market.

New Requirements
As automobile producers became more demanding, the companies in the automotive parts industry were required to qualify as continuing suppliers by demonstrating both quality and just-in-time delivery capability. In addition, they were now required to work interactively with auto producers on the R&D aspects of automotive parts. Thus the suppliers became both designers and manufacturers of components. A much broader combination of resources was required, in contrast to the earlier, more limited capabilities needed by suppliers that did simple manufacturing only. The result was that barriers to entry rose sharply.

Differentiation and Specialization of Products
As parts suppliers added R&D to their capabilities, they became able to differentiate their products. Often they were able to develop proprietary technology, which increased their bargaining power with customers. Related to differentiation was specialization in a specific product area, such as seating, which created opportunities for suppliers to greatly increase their efficiency.

Long-Term Contracts
A trend toward the granting of longer-term contracts by auto makers enabled parts suppliers to undertake the investment necessary to reduce costs. However, these new contracts usually also required suppliers to continually reduce their prices, on a year-by-year basis.

Industry Life Cycle
Companies in the industry obtained a large volume of new business when auto manufacturers started to discontinue their internal supply operations, in the early 1980s. Technically, this development constituted an upside breakout in industry evolution (see Chapter 4 for a discussion of upside breakouts).

Industry Expansion
Low-wage competition caused by expansion of the industry to a global scale during the late 1980s had a negative effect on parts suppliers, as mentioned above. This was true even though domestic sourcing rules initially afforded some protection. However, when the North American Free

Trade Agreement (NAFTA) took effect in 1994, Mexico acquired the ability to offer severe wage competition within the definition of North American sourcing.

Prospects of Future Changes

Cars are likely to last longer in the future because of improvements in the standards for their initial manufacture. Higher quality and improved durability, which are provided by the use of corrosion-resistant body panels, for instance, will contribute to the longevity of automobiles. This longevity, in turn, will tend to increase the demand for replacement parts.

In addition, probable changes in the automobile industry, which were described earlier in this chapter, will have reverberation effects on the automotive parts industry.

COMPANY PERFORMANCE

The changes in the fundamentals of the automotive parts industry, which have been described above, can be illustrated by the strategies and developments of four companies. The performance statistics for these companies are shown in Exhibit 9–4. The companies—Cooper Tire and Rubber Co., AlliedSignal Inc., Goodyear Tire and Rubber Company, and Dana Corporation—have been selected because they are representative of segments of the industry that have differing potentials for long-term performance.

EXHIBIT   9–4

Key Performance Statistics for Selected Suppliers in the Automotive Parts Industry, 1990–94

Company	Return on Equity, %		Return on Capital, %	Profit Margin, %
	5-Year Average	Latest 12 Months	Latest 12 Months	
Cooper	22.4	21.3	19.5	8.8
AlliedSignal	15.8	30.5	18.7	5.9
Goodyear	12.9	23.6	18.8	4.5
Dana	9.3	25.6	15.2	3.2
Industry medians:				
1994	9.9	16.6	12.8	4.3
1988	12.5	13.9	NA	3.7

With the exception of Cooper, which has shown consistently sound long-term ROE performance, these companies show dramatic increases in ROE performance in the latest 12 months included in the exhibit. Following are brief summaries of the developments underlying the performance of each of the four companies.

Cooper Tire & Rubber Company   The tire-manufacturing segment of the automotive industry has traditionally been a low-ROE business, and its ROE in fact only occasionally rises above the all-industries median. About one-third of the output of tire manufacturers goes to the cost-conscious auto makers at low margins. The balance goes to the replacement market, which is growing faster because cars are being kept longer. In the past, car owners tended to upgrade their tires when they replaced them, but this tendency has been decreasing in recent years. Car owners are also increasingly price-sensitive, and they exhibit little brand loyalty when it comes to tires.

Within this relatively unattractive industry environment, Cooper has been able to achieve consistently strong performance by consistent adherence to a strategy that exhibits the following characteristics[9]:

- Cooper concentrates on the replacement market. By not selling to auto manufacturers, the company earns a comparatively high margin. This tactic also minimizes cyclicality; in fact, it reverses the cyclicality of the automobile industry, because replacement tire sales drop in years of high new car sales.
- The company sells about one-half its volume under its own name; the other half is sold as private brands to various large distributors, oil companies, and mass merchandise retailers. Thus Cooper obtains economies of scale from an overall high volume, as well as higher margins from its own brand.
- Cooper's own brand is sold by independent retailers, who account for two-thirds of replacement tire sales. The company obtains preference from these dealers by giving them higher margins and by not competing with them by establishing Cooper-owned outlets. (The makers of Goodyear and Bridgestone and Firestone brands do compete with independent retailers and thereby lose preferential status.)
- Cooper is able to provide its dealers with higher margins because of its efficiency. The company has a highly cost-conscious, austere culture. It adds capacity by buying and refurbishing old plants. By copying competitors' successful products, it is able to minimize R&D costs. Performance-based incentives in its pay practices help to enlist the full cooperation of employees.

In short, the Cooper strategy has two basic thrusts. First, the company actively creates its bargaining power with buyers. It selects its own customers by selling only to the replacement market and avoiding the price-sensitive original equipment manufacturer (OEM) market. It reinforces this bargaining power by providing incentives to the independent dealers who, because brand preference is not a factor, are able to influence consumers' purchase decisions.

The second basic thrust of Cooper's strategy is to pursue low costs through internal efficiencies. Cultivation of a cost-conscious company culture is one aspect of this effort, and the other is achievement of economies of scale by producing tires for private labels. The company is able to trade off some of its production cost advantage by offering higher margins to dealers, as part of its incentive program.

As a result of this strategy, Cooper earns a margin of 8.8 percent of sales. It runs at close to full capacity, versus 80 percent for the tire manufacturers as a whole. The company has not taken on a new private brand customer since 1985. This sensible refusal to overexpand is one factor in Cooper's ability to maintain its operations at nearly full capacity. All in all, this is a highly competent company. Its capability is further demonstrated by rapid increases in sales of its nontire products (hoses and seals, for example) to the quality-conscious Japanese auto manufacturers.

Goodyear Tire & Rubber Company Goodyear is the largest rubber manufacturer in the US. It operates in the same industry environment as Cooper but until the latest 12 months had consistently underperformed Cooper. It sells about one-half of its output to the auto industry as original equipment. The other half is sold to the replacement market. Goodyear owns 1,000 auto service stores and also sells through 2,500 independent dealers and, recently, through major discount retailers. It is the most vertically integrated of the rubber companies, as it owns six rubber plantations.

A major factor in the company's recent profit improvement has been its success in identifying specialty market niches for high-margin premium replacement tires. To differentiate these products, it has focused on an element of performance that is important to buyers—traction. Specifically, Goodyear has developed several specialized lines, as follows[10]:

- The Aquatred line not only claims good wet weather performance but looks the part. This discernable differentiation gives the line an advantage with the buyer, who is otherwise usually unable to evaluate the merits of various tread designs.

- The company has developed lines of high-performance tires for sports cars, which must be bought in sets of four because the tire for each wheel differs slightly from the other three tires. This somewhat esoteric development appeals to technology-minded customers in Goodyear's specialized market niche.

- The company's tires for four-wheel-drive vehicles have a sporty appearance, and the treads come in different patterns. These tires were specially designed to sell to the adventurous baby boomers, described earlier in this chapter, who purchase light trucks and utility vehicles. Goodyear dominates this market niche, which grew from 10 percent of the market in 1987 to 23 percent in 1994.

These new lines, introduced in 1992 and 1993, account for 14 percent of the manufacturer's unit volume and 20 percent of its gross profits. However, Goodyear's high proportion of low-margin original equipment tires reduces its overall profit margin to 4.5 percent, slightly more than half of Cooper's. Goodyear's sharp improvement in ROE in the latest 12 months reported in Exhibit 9–4 results from a combination of new product contributions and other recent measures, including selling off nonessential businesses, cutting costs, and reducing debt.

Goodyear's improvement in performance can be attributed to its success in differentiating its products and in a one-time cost-reduction effort. However, imitators have diluted much of the company's advantage, and the company has alienated its own dealers by selling to discount merchandizers. For these reasons, the sustainability of Goodyear's current competitive advantage is in doubt and the company is vulnerable to the cyclical downturn in the OEM market.

Analysis of Goodyear's recent strategy, which has been described briefly here, reveals that it is characterized by a number of shortsighted actions. Thus the question of motivation arises. Since the present CEO Stanley Gault was scheduled for retirement at the end of 1994, it is possible that these actions may have been motivated by a desire to dress up the company's performance for the purpose of further enhancing his record.

AlliedSignal Inc.   About 37 percent of AlliedSignal's sales are in automobile components (braking systems and components, air bags, spark plugs, turbochargers, and filters), 41 percent in aerospace equipment (auxiliary power plants, environmental control systems, wheels, brakes, and turbo fan/prop engines), and 22 percent in engineered materials. The company has high technological capability which it applies in its automotive business to produce technologically advanced products. Further, there is high replacement demand for virtually all its automotive products.

AlliedSignal has achieved a strong improvement in ROE in the latest 12 months shown in Exhibit 9–4. While this improvement reflects in part a cyclical improvement in OEM demand, as well as a sharp upswing in the demand for air bags and for more sophisticated, higher-value braking systems, it is mainly the result of aggressive cost cutting by management. The company's strategic thrust is based on use of its technological resources to produce high-value components, thereby enhancing its bargaining power with both OEM and replacement market customers. This strategic thrust provides the basis for future earnings improvement, but this potential remains to be realized.

Dana Corporation   Essentially a metalworking business, Dana manufactures commodity parts which are used primarily by OEMs. Incidentally, the concept of "manufactured commodities" is not exclusive to the automotive parts industry. It also applies to a wide range of products, including metal cans as well as glass and plastic containers. These commodities are manufactured to meet an industry standard, and they do not enhance the value of the end product in which they are used. The manufacturers which purchase these necessary but usually unglamorous products choose their sources on the basis of cost.

Dana's products include axles, frames, transmissions, clutches, and engine parts. Because there are no proprietary differences in these products, economies of scale are important to Dana's success. A recent expansion of operations to Mexico was part of an effort to achieve cost leadership by reducing labor costs. The company has also expanded to Germany to be closer to its European Customers.

Dana's improvement in ROE in the latest 12 months shown in Exhibit 9–4 may be attributed to its increased sales to the recovering automobile industry. Because of the company's dependence on economies of scale, its earnings are highly vulnerable to the cyclicality of the industry.

THE INVESTOR'S PERSPECTIVE

Exhibit 9–5 shows the market performance of Cooper, AlliedSignal, Goodyear, and Dana relative to the S&P 500 for the period 1984–94.

EXHIBIT 9–5

Comparative Performance of Selected Suppliers in the Automotive Parts
Industry, 1984–94 (Indexed to S&P 500, 1984=160)

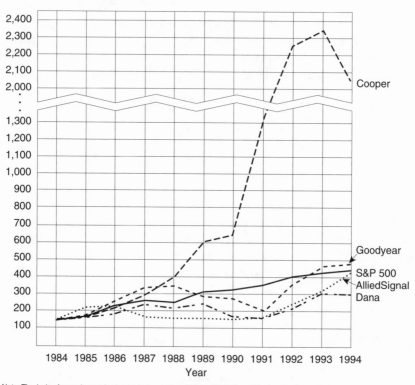

Year

Note: The index for each year is shown at the mean between the high and the low for the period.

The Market's Judgment

Cooper was the strongest market performer during this period, reflecting
its competitive strength in the tire segment of the industry, which has
stayed relatively stable. The other three companies have outperformed the
S&P 500 since 1990 to varying degrees, as might be expected for cyclical stocks. Goodyear's recent improvement reflects both its cyclicality
and its new product introductions. AlliedSignal and Dana moved roughly in parallel until 1994. Both of these companies underperformed the
broad market, reflecting the relatively unattractive conditions in their segments of the automotive parts industry during the period. The improvements in their stock prices in the past few years appear to reflect cyclical
factors, rather than recognition of an improvement in industry fundamen-

tals. Dana moved down slightly in 1994, which was likely due to cyclical factors, but AlliedSignal continued to rise. It is not possible to tell whether the stock market has recognized differences between these two companies, as AlliedSignal has other interests.

Industry Structure and Competitive Advantage

My assessment of these four companies as long-term investment candidates will be based on certain assumptions about the industry situation and the basis for competitive advantage within it. These assumptions are described below.

The automotive parts industry, which had traditionally been rather unattractive to its participants, has become more appealing in recent years. Barriers to entry have increased, partly as the result of an increase in long-term contractual commitments with auto makers. Another factor is that the suppliers have acquired new responsibilities for R&D, which has increased their bargaining power with their customers. In addition, there is room for further growth in product development, because the disaggregation movement among automobile companies is expected to continue.

To achieve competitive advantage, a company in the automotive parts industry must have the ability to design products to meet buyers' specifications, as well as the ability to develop new technology so as to improve product performance. In addition, it must be able to meet quality standards and precise delivery specifications. Besides all this, replacement markets must exist, to offset the inherent cyclicality of OEM demand.

Assessment of Four Automotive Parts Suppliers

Exhibit 9–6 provides brief assessments of Cooper, AlliedSignal, Goodyear, and Dana as long-term investment candidates. The P/E ratios cited in the exhibit are in comparison to the prevailing S&P 500 ratio of 17.3. My conclusions, on the basis of these assessments, are as follows.

Of the four companies considered here, Cooper may be considered as a current candidate for long-term investment and AlliedSignal as a potential candidate. Cooper's competitive advantage is sustainable because of its low costs and its well-established distribution channels. In addition, the company is not exposed to the extremes of the industry's cyclicality.

AlliedSignal has the capability to enhance its products' value by the use of technology, which should be in part provided by its engineered materials business. Recent improvements in performance have largely

E X H I B I T   9–6

Assessment of Selected Automotive Parts Suppliers as Long-Term
Investment Candidates (As of March 31, 1995)

Cooper

Market Price, March 31, 1995: 28 1/2   P/E Ratio: 18.5   52-Week Range: 29 5/8–21 5/8

Competitive Strength

   High. The company is a low-cost producer with strong distribution capability concentrated in the less cyclical part of the market. Its management understands its basis
of profitability. Cooper's competitive advantage should be sustainable, as it is rooted in
both the structure and the culture of the company. Room for growth is provided by
slow growth in the number of cars on the road and in the mileage driven. The P/E ratio
does not make it unduly expensive considering the company's potential.

Goodyear

Market Price, March 31, 1995: 36 3/4   P/E Ratio: 9.8   52-Week Range: 44 1/2–36 3/4

Competitive Strength

   High, but sustainability is in doubt. The company's return to its core business and
reduction of costs and debt should yield long-term improvement in ROE, but
Goodyear's segment of the industry remains inherently unattractive. In addition, the
company is still heavily reliant on low-margin, cyclical, OEM business. Backward integration is providing short-term benefits by lowering the cost of rubber in the current
shortage. The company's sustainability of advantage from product design initiatives is
in doubt, as the designs can be imitated. The company will have to run hard just to
hold its position. Goodyear has antagonized its independent dealers by selling to discounters, a shortsighted decision which provides immediate sales volume at the risk of
long-term damage.* The P/E ratio appears to recognize this situation.

AlliedSignal

Market Price, March 31, 1995: 39 1/4   P/E Ratio: 14.6   52-Week Range: 39 7/8–30 3/8

Competitive Strength

   High. The company has the technological capability to enhance product performance and develop proprietary products. There is sufficient replacement demand for
the product line to reduce the effects of the automobile industry's cyclicality. The
company's advantage should be sustainable, with a continuing R&D effort. The company's diverse sales base and its position in replacement market make this company
less cyclical than OEM suppliers.

Dana

Market Price, March 31, 1995: 25 1/2   P/E Ratio: 11.0   52-Week Range: 30 5/8–19 5/8

Competitive Strength

   Marginal. Dana's profitability is heavily dependent on achievement of low costs. Margins will be under continuous pressure from price reductions in contracts. The product
line is primarily intended for OEMs, a situation which will expose it to customer cyclicality.

---

*Seth Luove, "The Last Bastion," Forbes, February 14, 1994, pp. 56-58.

been the result of effective cost cutting by a very aggressive management. The company has yet to demonstrate an ability to take advantage of the potential inherent in the industry situation. Therefore, some caution is necessary and the company is categorized as a potential long-term investment.

While Goodyear's performance improvement has been impressive, the sustainability of the improvement is in doubt because the company's product differentiation initiatives are vulnerable to imitation. The apparent strategy of increasing sales of a less cyclical product, replacement tires, is leading to increased reliance on highly price-sensitive discount retailers, as well as antagonizing Goodyear's established dealers.

While Dana's earnings performance may well improve in line with more attractive industry fundamentals, it is not considered a long-term investment candidate. Its products resemble commodities, in that there are few opportunities to improve bargaining power with customers by differentiating them. In view of the continued demands by its powerful customers for lower prices, the company will have to run hard on cost reduction to merely stand still.

POINTS TO REMEMBER

Automobile Industry

The automobile industry has been examined in this chapter as a mature, manufacturing-based business. A typical mature industry, it is slow-growing and cyclical. It has evolved into an oligopoly, with three companies making up the North American manufacturing operations. Developments in both technology and markets are evolutionary.

However, the industry has not been immune to change. The seemingly insurmountable barriers to entry have been overcome by a combination of the resurgence of the Japanese economy and a major discontinuity in oil prices. These developments in turn have forced changes in product lines and in the way production is organized. The three major companies have reacted in different ways, with the result that, in little more than a decade, the top- and bottom-performing companies have changed places.

The changes described in this chapter have had two overall effects, as follows:

1. The industry has become more attractive to the North American producers, as they are now capable of being competitive in their own back yard.

2. Whereas, before the early 1980s, the basis of competitive advantage was economies of scale provided by vertically integrated production, it has now become sensitivity to market needs and the ability to quickly respond to them. The disaggregation of operations has come to play an important role in competitiveness.

The assessment of long-term investment candidates in the automobile industry must be based on recognition of the new basis of competitive advantage. A company's ability to respond to changes depends primarily on the quality of its management, but also to some degree on luck. This situation, again, is typical of a mature industry.

Automotive Parts Industry

The changes in the automobile industry which were described in this chapter and summarized above have had substantial repercussions upon the automotive parts industry. Barriers to entry have risen sharply. Thus the industry has become more attractive to its participants, due to a closer association between parts suppliers and their primary customer base, the auto makers. Parts suppliers have come to play an expanded role in the production of automotive parts. They are now frequently called upon to assist in R&D, whereas formerly all they did was manufacture standard parts to industry specifications.

The expansion of the role of parts suppliers has resulted in a substantial increase in the size of the parts industry's market. Though a company's competitive advantage once was based solely upon its ability to produce automotive parts at low cost, now it also encompasses the ability to successfully undertake product development. In many instances, the R&D departments of today's parts suppliers have been able to develop or acquire proprietary technology, thus further enhancing the company's competitive advantage.

The assessment of long-term investment candidates in the automotive parts industry is difficult. Industry developments are still relatively new, and the capabilities of many companies have not yet been demonstrated. However, two companies have been identified which may have strong and sustainable competitive advantage on the basis of either low costs or technological leadership, combined with the ability to reduce cyclicality by taking advantage of the replacement market. One of these is categorized as a potential long-term investment because, while its strategic thrust is sound, it has not yet demonstrated its full potential.

NOTES

1. Sources of information on the industry and on developments within specific companies include: Alex Taylor III, "US Cars Come Back," *Fortune*, November 16, 1992, pp. 52–85; and Alex Taylor III, "The New Golden Age of Autos," *Fortune*, April 4, 1994, pp. 49–66.

2. David Woodruff, Larry Armstrong, John Templeman, Julia Flynn, Christopher Farrell, and Jon Berry, "Leasing Fever: Why the Car Business Will Never Be the Same," *Business Week*, February 7, 1994, pp. 92–96.

3. Alex Taylor III, "The Auto Industry Meets the New Economy," *Fortune*, September 5, 1994, pp. 52–60.

4. Background information on GM is based in part on the following sources: Maryann Keller, *Rude Awakening: The Rise, Fall, and Struggle for Recovery of General Motors* (New York: Macmillan, 1989); William J. Hampton and James Norman, "General Motors: What Went Wrong," *Business Week*, March 16, 1987, pp. 102–110; Alex Taylor III, "Can GM Remodel Itself?" *Fortune*, January 13, 1992, pp. 26–34; and Jerry Flint, "A Brand Is Like a Friend," *Forbes*, November 4, 1988, pp. 267–270.

5. Kathleen Kerwin and James B. Treece, "There's Trouble Under Ford's Hood," *Business Week*, November 29, 1993, pp. 66–67.

6. James B. Treece with Kathleen Kerwin, Heidi Dawley, "Ford: Alex Trotman's Daring Global Strategy," *Business Week*, April 3, 1995, pp. 94–104.

7. Background information on Chrysler based in part on the following sources: David Woodruff and Karen Lowry Miller, "Chrysler's Neon: Is This the Small Car Detroit Couldn't Build?" *Business Week*, May 3, 1993, pp. Alex Taylor III, "Will Success Spoil Chrysler?" *Fortune*, January 10, 1994, pp. 82–92; Alex Taylor III, "Iacocca's Minivan," *Fortune*, May 30, 1994, pp. 56–66; and Jerry Flint, "Old Stay at Home," *Forbes*, November 7, 1994, pp. 62–67.

8. R. S. Salomon Jr., "Time for a New Car," *Forbes*, March 14, 1994, p. 144.

9. Alex Taylor III, "Cooper Tire and Rubber: Now Hear This, Jack Welch," *Fortune*, April 6, 1992, pp. 94-95.

10. Myron Magnet, "Goodyear Rubber: The Marvels of High Margins," *Fortune*, May 2, 1994, pp. 73–74.

10

THE COMPUTER INDUSTRY

$\mathbf{T}$he key resources of the computer industry are intellectual in nature, being vested in the knowledge of its participants, both managers and employees. The computer industry thus presents a striking contrast to the automobile industry, which numbers among its key resources material objects such as plants and machinery (see Chapter 9).

Another way in which the computer industry differs from the mature automobile industry is that it is now in the transition phase and is only beginning to verge on maturity. This technology-based industry took 40 years to go through its emerging and growth phases.

In an industry in the mature phase, established companies jockey for market share. Emerging and growth situations, on the other hand, are much more complex and volatile. In these phases too, participants compete for market share, but many other things are also happening. The market is broadening, technology is evolving rapidly, and an influx of new entrants presents challenges. As the transition phase begins to emerge, the competitive ground shifts again. Priorities such as distribution capability, cost reduction, and price competition take on new importance.

The volatility inherent in the transition phase means that companies operating in a transition phase industry are unlikely candidates for long-term investment (see Chapter 4). Only after the industry enters its maturity phase is it common for a clear picture to emerge, showing which companies will be the long-term winners.

This analysis of the computer industry will illustrate the difficulties inherent in making investment decisions while an industry is still in the unpredictable transition phase. The present structure of the computer industry will be examined, the courses of action pursued by the companies in the industry will be reviewed, and the consequences of these actions will be followed up. An attempt will be made to identify potential candidates for long-term investment.

The computer industry has three sectors, in a technological sense: major systems (including mainframes, minicomputers, and microcomputers), peripherals and equipment, and software. The main focus in this chapter will be on companies that build or package major systems, for two reasons: this is the area in which changes in the computer industry have had the strongest effect, and this is also the area in which the market's errors in judgment may have been the greatest.

INDUSTRY STRUCTURE

The electronic computer has had an effect on the second half of the twentieth century as profound as the automobile's effect on the first half. A little over 30 years ago, the computer was a scientific curiosity, the stuff of science fiction. Now it is a ubiquitous tool in everyday life, an intrinsic part of commerce and society. While these once unimaginable changes were taking place, a different sort of evolution has also been occurring: the once highly attractive computer industry has become relatively unattractive.

Traditional Industry Fundamentals

The attractiveness of the industry, which was high from the early 1960s through the early 1980s, was based on several factors.

Barriers to Entry

The primary product of the major systems sector of the computer industry was technologically sophisticated mainframes, which were designed for and exclusively used by large companies. A high level of support services was required to develop and maintain these systems. Once a customer adopted a supplier's system, the cost and effort of switching was high. Thus barriers to entry were high.

Substitutes

When mainframe computers first hit the market, their ability to process data was considered an almost awe-inspiring phenomenon. No substitute could even approach their performance.

Bargaining Power

The industry enjoyed an advantageous position between its suppliers and its buyers, in terms of bargaining power. The major companies were highly integrated, producing their own components, writing the necessary software, and distributing and servicing the product through their own organizations. Thus neither suppliers nor customers had bargaining power. In terms of bargaining power with buyers, the domination of the overall computer industry by two companies—IBM in mainframes and Digital Equipment Corporation (DEC) in minicomputers—created an equally advantageous situation. Further, both IBM and DEC had proprietary systems. Customers had little choice in either service and maintenance or updates and improvements.

Market Growth

The rapid computerization of virtually all industrial and commercial data processing functions provided plenty of room for growth. IBM in fact frequently had long lead times for delivery. While costs and prices declined rapidly, as is typical of a growth industry, the companies in the industry were able to achieve high profit margins. As of 1981, the computer industry's five-year average median return on equity of 19.0 percent was in the upper quartile of the all-industries performance, well above the all-industries median of 15.5 percent.[1]

Effects of Changes in Industry Fundamentals[2]

The highly favorable conditions described above started to come to an end in the early 1980s, as the result of technological advances which reduced the barriers to entry. The major technological development was a rapid increase in the power of microprocessors which made the microcomputer possible and enabled it to challenge the mainframe inexpensively and in an increasing range of functions. As long as the industry consisted primarily of complex and expensive mainframes, the barriers to entry were high, as discussed earlier. However, the barriers dropped sharply with the introduction of the relatively simple and inexpensive microcomputer in 1976 and with the subsequent reaction of IBM. IBM obviously underestimated the growth potential of the microcomputer market and was a late entrant. The IBM PC was introduced in 1981 after a crash program of development. In seeming panic and because of a desire to reduce the lead time necessary to enter the market, the company abandoned its established practice of integration. Instead, it assembled its PCs from externally sourced components. In a further effort to reduce the lead time, it avoided the slow but critical process of developing its own software by disclosing its machine's internal architecture, in order to encourage other companies to develop the software necessary to broaden the uses of its machine. Since the electronic technology was no longer secret, and the Intel Corp. microchip and Microsoft software which IBM chose to use were available to anybody, the industry was quick to produce clones. The term *IBM compatible* became the industry standard, creating instant respectability for a wide range of imitators. By 1987, more than 300 firms had duplicated the IBM PC and captured 48 percent of the market.

With hardware becoming an increasingly cheap commodity, customer interest focused on the user-friendly software that allowed executives and professionals to work directly with computers, freeing them from reliance on computer specialists as intermediaries. Since software was available off the shelf from various developers, the barriers to entry into the industry fell sharply.

The early 1980s saw the beginning of the disaggregation of the industry into three distinct sectors, as follows:

- Major systems producers or packagers, who designed and marketed the products but often contracted out the assembly of the hardware
- Suppliers who provided software, semiconductor chips, and microprocessors; peripheral equipment such as printers; and services such as systems integration
- Distributors who sold the products

These sectors had very different results in the ensuing years.

The Current Situation[3]

As of late 1994, the situation in the computer industry can be summarized as described below.

Market Growth

The rapid growth of the computer industry through the 1980s and into the 1990s was provided by microcomputer sales. With their increasing power and with the advent of technology to link machines, microcomputers have taken over many of the functions of minicomputers and even of mainframes. The miniaturization of hardware has made the computer portable and provided another source of growth. The market for computers has continued to grow rapidly, but the major source of growth has shifted to microcomputers for the home market, which accounted for about 40 percent of shipments in 1994. The consumer market is traditionally more price-sensitive than the business market. Sales of mainframes continue to be stagnant.

Competition
Major economies of scale are possible in manufacture and high volume is necessary to efficient distribution, which means that market share is becoming important. A relatively large number of players remain, and barriers to exit are high because of the specialized nature of the companies and the industry. Fierce competition results in rapidly declining prices and price wars.

Bargaining Power
Unlike the purchaser of a mainframe, who acquires an integrated system, the microcomputer buyer is interested in three separate factors in making a purchase decision: the performance of the hardware, the capabilities and friendliness of the software, and the quality of service. Since differences between manufacturers in the performance of the hardware have become minor, efforts to establish bargaining power with buyers are moving toward a focus on software and service factors. The majority of purchase decisions are made by unsophisticated individuals rather than by corporate computer specialists.

Barriers to Entry
Economies of scale and the need for increased access to distribution through retailers have become necessary, and brand awareness and preference has emerged. Thus barriers to entry are rising.

Technology
As of late 1994, computer technology has to some extent reached a plateau, at least for the moment. This has occurred because improvements in speed, capability, and capacity are mainly incremental. Unlike the situation in the earlier period, the magnitude of the improvements no longer justifies the replacement of relatively new existing machines by the home and business machines that dominate the mass market. The technological

frontier has moved in two directions: first, in business and professional usage, toward linking computers and data sources, and second, in the area of consumer electronics, toward broadening the functions of computers by assigning to computers roles similar to those played by TV sets and CD players. Despite the high barriers, this increasing intrusion of the microcomputer into the entertainment field of consumer electronics may be creating the risk of entry into the computer industry by consumer electronics companies. These companies in turn are feeling threatened about their ability to maintain positions in their own industries.

Rationalization

With rising barriers to entry and severe competition, the rationalization of the industry is progressing. Survival is contingent on possession of well-defined competitive advantage. The top 10 computer companies captured 70 percent of the market in 1994, as compared to 52 percent in 1991.

In Conclusion

The computer industry as a whole is showing many of the conventional signs of transition from growth to maturity: price wars; falling profit margins; battles for market share necessary to take advantage of economies of scale; and the inevitable, rapid rationalization of the industry. However, the falloff of sales that typically occurs in the transition phase of a durable goods industry has not occurred. Even though the computer is a durable product, demand has been sustained by a rapid improvement in product performance combined with falling prices. Further, the market is more receptive to computers because the education system has produced a generation of computer-literate customers who regard possession of a computer as a necessity, overcoming the cultural resistance to home computers which was discussed in Chapter 6. There are likely to be enough new products and enough new markets to avoid a slump in industry sales. (Refer back to Chapter 4 if you need to refresh your memory on the characteristics of the transition phase of an industry's life cycle.)

The computer manufacturers have become packagers, and their function is primarily to assemble externally sourced components and market the machines. The abilities to introduce new products and to achieve low costs are the key factors to success.

For the reasons stated earlier, the industry environment for the packagers is hostile. In 1994, the five-year average median return on equity for the major systems manufacturers was 5.6 percent, as compared to 13.7

percent for the peripherals and equipment producers and 16.2 percent for the software developers. The shift of power to the suppliers is shown by the fact that the earnings of the two main suppliers, Microsoft with its software and Intel with its microprocessor chips, together totaled $3.7 billion in 1994, as compared to a total of $4.0 billion for 25 major systems manufacturers. These two companies are exploiting the bargaining provided by their unique, proprietary products. The biggest single factor in any possible improvement in the industry fundamentals would be the emergence of credible competition for these two companies.

COMPANY PERFORMANCE

The computer industry includes many companies, not only the five that have been selected for scrutiny here. Because of the way the industry has evolved, the companies within it employ different strategies. Dell, for example, which was discussed in Chapter 5, exploited the emerging power of distribution, as hardware became a commodity. Sun Microsystems Inc. has been highly successful in network systems, taking advantage of the decentralization of information within corporations.

The five companies that I have chosen for analysis in this chapter are IBM, Digital Equipment, Apple Computer Inc., Compaq Computer Corporation, and Hewlett-Packard Company. The performance and strategies of these companies will serve to illustrate major developments in the industry. Key performance statistics for the five companies are shown in Exhibit 10–1.

The historical developments described in the following brief commentaries are the forerunners of the current positions held by these five companies.

IBM[4] IBM, founded in 1924, initially produced weight scales. The company's product line evolved from these scales to punch-card tabulating equipment to typewriters and eventually to electronic computers. IBM rode to industry dominance on the strength of its immensely popular System/360 line of mainframes. Introduced in the mid-1960s, these mainframes offered superior performance and were almost totally proprietary. They were helped by the fact that the computer specialists being recruited by industry were largely former IBM employees, who naturally favored the systems that they understood. IBM continues to be the leading mainframe producer in the industry.

E X H I B I T   10–1

Key Performance Statistics for Selected Companies in the
Computer Industry, 1990–94

Company	Return on Equity, %		Return on Capital, %	
	5-Year Average	Latest 12 Months	Latest 12 Months	Profit Margin, %
Compaq	18.7	27.7	27.5	7.9
Apple	16.7	15.0	11.9	3.4
Hewlett-Packard	15.1	18.2	17.6	6.4
IBM	Def.	11.4	7.9	3.4
Digital Equipment	Def.	Def.	Def.	Def.
Industry median:				
1994	5.6	9.9	8.5	3.4
1983	15.1	8.9	13.6	NA

Note: Def. = deficit. NA = not available.

As discussed earlier, IBM's difficulties started in 1981 when the
company abandoned vertical integration to speed up its entry into the
microcomputer market. This sharply reduced the barriers to entry into the
segment of the industry which not only would grow the fastest but would
eventually displace a significant portion of the mainframe business. The
PC did, however, make a major contribution to IBM earnings for several
years until the company's position in PCs was eroded by the emergence
of cheaper clones. Compaq, the market leader in microcomputers in 1994,
got its start producing IBM PC clones in 1982.

In 1987, IBM attempted to displace the clones by replacing its original PCs with the PS/2 line, which used a proprietary format. By then,
IBM's share of U.S. microcomputer sales had slipped to 30 percent, and
customers balked at making the necessary adjustments to their systems.
Further, within a year, four clones of the PS/2 line had appeared on the
market. IBM has never caught up in the microcomputer segment.

It is interesting to speculate about what would have happened if
IBM had begun to develop its microcomputer earlier and had developed
a proprietary system. The company's power and reputation would likely
have allowed it to dominate the market. The large number of small, fragmented rivals would have been forced to try to cooperate in agreeing on
another standard. At best, the advent of competition would have been

delayed for some time and IBM would have been able to establish a strong base.

In 1991, John Akers, who was then the newly appointed CEO of IBM, broke up the company into 13 business units. His goals were to make the company more responsive and to dissolve the well-known and long-standing IBM culture, which had been a major cause of the company's problems. Between 1993 and mid-1994, IBM's share of the PC market in the United States declined from about 18 percent to under 10 percent. The company dropped to third place in the home market, and its strength was still concentrated in business applications. By 1994, questions were arising about whether Aker's seemingly bold approach was still too cautious. He was replaced by Louis Gerstner in 1993.

In November 1994, IBM and Apple announced a joint effort to develop a new hardware platform. The platform is to be used by both companies and is expected to be available in 1996. This effort may yield some economies of scale, but it does nothing to create compatibility in software, a much more important competitive factor.

The lessons from Microsoft's profitability have not been lost on IBM. It has spent heavily on the development and promotion of its competing OS/2 Warp operating system in an attempt to break Microsoft's virtual monopoly position. However, it faces the formidable challenge of overcoming Microsoft's installed base of more than 100 million largely satisfied users who appear to be willing to wait for Microsoft's forthcoming upgrades.

Digital Equipment [5] DEC's history parallels IBM's in many respects. Founded in 1957, it focused on minicomputers for small businesses and for scientific and technical applications, just as IBM focused on mainframes. DEC was particularly successful through the 1980s with its VAX line. This success may have created a culture of complacency. In any event, the company failed to recognize the importance of the emerging microcomputers and workstations. It entered the microcomputer field in 1981, the year after IBM entered it. While DEC retains a loyal following in minicomputers, and particularly in scientific and technical applications, it has lagged in the fastest-growing aspect of the computer industry, the microcomputer market. In the early 1990s, it embarked on a major R&D program to update its product line; at that time it also replaced its founding CEO. The company's recovery will likely be slow.

Apple [6] Apple was the pioneer of the microcomputer industry, introducing the first model in 1976. After a number of intermediate models, the first

Macintosh was introduced in 1984. Apple has always been noted for its user friendliness, a characteristic that has allowed it to gain a dominant 28 percent share of the worldwide educational market and a strong 14 percent share of the global home market (all 1993 figures). While its superior graphics capabilities make it popular in fields such as advertising, desktop publishing, and art, its share of the overall world business market is under 6 percent. As the result of IBM's influence, the business market has adopted the IBM-compatible standard. Apple's overall worldwide shipments were less than 10 percent of the industry's total in 1993.

However, Apple occupies a somewhat isolated position in respect to other computer companies, in that it still uses its own proprietary software rather than Microsoft software, which is based on Intel's microprocessing chip and has become the industry standard. Apple's attempts to license its system to other companies had not been very successful as of late 1994. Its relatively small market share discourages software developers from writing programs for it. Though in other respects it matches competitors in costs and efficiency, Apple must therefore spend heavily to develop its own software. It is unable to take full advantage of the products of other developers, which are usually keyed to the much larger IBM-compatible market. Though software has been developed to bridge the systems, Apple remains an orphan. Its November 1994 decision to join forces with IBM in developing common hardware does nothing to resolve the software issue.

A parallel between Apple's current position in the microcomputer market and Sony's position in the video market in the 1970s is too striking to be ignored. Sony introduced its Betamax videocassette recorder (VCR) in late 1975. The following year the Betamax was challenged by the VCR systems that were introduced by a number of other companies. Among all these contenders, it was Japan Victor Company (JVC) that eventually won out, with its Video Home System (VHS) system. Though the Betamax was technically superior, the VHS offered a longer playing time and thus successfully ousted Betamax, even though the Betamax had been the first entrant.

Compaq[7]   This company was founded in 1982 by a group of Texas Instrument Inc. engineers, who made the first of the IBM clones. It therefore started in the small end of the market and has stayed there, specializing in microcomputers. It has been very quick to recognize the changes in the industry and to respond by rapidly introducing new products, including portable models; by cutting costs and prices; and by marketing its products aggressively. In this respect, it has recently moved into the mass market through retailers such as Wal-Mart. This strategy has moved it into the top position in the PC market in the United

States and is giving it the economies of scale necessary for survival. It has expanded into China, to find room for growth.

Compaq has developed close relationships with Intel and Microsoft, which have helped the company to expand its capability into areas such as servers that anchor office networks.

Hewlett-Packard This company has had a remarkable performance record, moving up from No. 7 to No. 2 among U.S. computer makers in one decade. It has done this by putting out a relatively broad but still focused product line. Hewlett-Packard makes midrange systems that have the capability to serve as data repositories in office networks, so that they can replace minicomputers. It also makes PCs for the corporate market, as well as electronic devices, particularly printers. Further, it has built a substantial business in medical electronic devices. The company's policy of continuing to improve its line, even when this means cannibalizing established products, has kept it in the forefront of many markets.[8] Because of this policy, and because Hewlett-Packard is not burdened with old technology, it has been able to take market share from both IBM and DEC.

In Conclusion

These brief summaries of the histories of key players in the computer industry explain their respective ROE performances. IBM and DEC have faltered because of the strategic inertia that kept them doing what had been successful in the past. Apple and Compaq have had highly focused strategies, concentrating on the fastest-growing segment of the market. Hewlett-Packard has to some extent bridged the minicomputer and microcomputer segments of the market and exploited proprietary technology.

THE INVESTOR'S PERSPECTIVE

Three bases will be used in assessing the five companies described above as candidates for long-term investment: The structure of the industry, the companies' competitive strengths, and each company's past market performance.

The Market's Judgment

Exhibit 10–2 shows the market performance of the stock of IBM, DEC, Apple, Compaq, and Hewlett-Packard relative to the S&P 500 for the period 1984–94. Given the turmoil prevailent in the computer industry during this period, the weak market performance of four of these compa-

E X H I B I T   10–2

Comparative Performance of Selected Companies in the Computer
Industry, 1984–94 (Indexed to S&P 500, 1984=160)

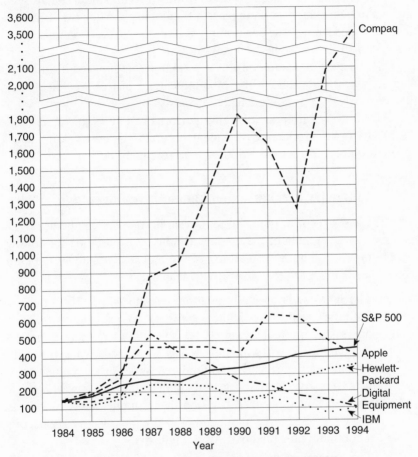

Note: The index for each year is shown at the mean between the high and the low for the period.

nies should not be a surprise. Only Compaq significantly outperformed
the broad market. Both IBM and DEC, the traditional leaders in the industry, significantly underperformed it.

Since IBM in particular had been a buy-and-hold favorite of investors
for a long time, the question is when the policy of holding IBM stocks
should have been reconsidered (the monitoring of investments was discussed in Chapter 8). By the mid-1980s, IBM's long-term dominance of the
industry should have been seen as cause for caution. The company's fum-

bling efforts in the PC field and the emergence of smaller, more nimble competitors should have been a signal to the astute analyst that IBM was losing control of developments in its industry, that its dominance had been breached, and that its better days were behind it. While these signals seem obvious in hindsight, they were more difficult to spot while the IBM mystique remained strong. The business press continued to carry optimistic articles and analyses about the company's future.

IBM's story tends to confirm my opinion that long-dominant companies, in particular, should be monitored for signs of weakness—and that any such signs should be taken seriously.

Hewlett-Packard was a lagging performer until 1990. At this time the results of its product development program started to show, and it began to outperform the S&P 500 by a narrow margin.

Industry Structure and Competitive Advantage

The assessment of potential long-term investment candidates in the major systems segment of the computer industry is based on the following assumptions about the condition of the industry and about the companies' needs in regard to competitive advantage.

1. The industry is basically unattractive and will likely remain so until the transition to maturity has been completed and the packagers gain more bargaining power with their main suppliers. Bargaining power with buyers has weakened as hardware has become a price-sensitive commodity. Superior proprietary products have given certain suppliers high bargaining power. Thus the packagers are squeezed between their suppliers and an increasingly price-sensitive market. As a result, price wars have become a continuing characteristic of the industry.

2. The nature of the changes confronting the industry may be described as rapid but evolutionary and relatively predictable.

3. Competitive advantage must be based on low costs (which are in part dependent on economies of scale derived from significant market share), and on the ability to bring out a continuing line of new products and to provide a high level of service to the customer. Some firms may still find room to concentrate on high-margin niches based on their specialized customer bases.

4. The industry will likely become polarized around several software-hardware combinations. Eventually the major players will

opt for one or another system, and the industry ultimately will be rationalized, with perhaps four major players remaining.

Assessment of Five Computer Companies

The status of five selected computer companies as long-term investment candidates is assessed in Exhibit 10–3. References to P/E ratios are based on comparison to the prevailing S&P 500 P/E ratio of 17.3.

Many investors are eager to have some representation in the computer industry, if only because it is the third largest industry in the world, after automobiles and oil. However, the long-term investor should take certain industrywide factors into account before making a decision to invest in any computer company.

It is undeniable that the industry as a whole is not at present a good candidate for long-term investment. As of early 1995, the industry is unattractive and appears likely to remain so for some time. In fact, its fundamentals may deteriorate still further. The industry is also in a newly disaggregated state, in which it is almost impossible for any company to be all things to all people.

In the face of these weak industry fundamentals, the investor should look for sustainable competitive advantage in specific market segments. In this context, both Compaq and Hewlett-Packard appear to have sufficient competitive strength to be considered as long-term investment candidates—though investors must be prepared to be patient and must recognize the possibility of some setbacks.

Additional Opportunities for Investment

The analysis in this chapter has focused on the major systems component of the computer industry. There may also be opportunities among the suppliers in the industry. Both Microsoft and Intel, which were mentioned in the chapter, have had dramatic growth records. Both have used their bargaining power to advantage in raising their own profitability. However, the same caution which was urged above in relation to other long-dominant companies should be applied here.

Specifically, though Microsoft's domination of the software segment of the industry is not currently threatened, it will likely be somewhat eroded. The company's position appears to be relatively secure for the next three to four years, but it will have to develop new markets to stay competitive. A recent agreement with the U.S. Department of Justice to

E X H I B I T   10–3

Assessment of Selected Computer Manufacturers as Long-Term Investment Candidates (As of March 31, 1995)

IBM

Market Price, March 31, 1995: 85 1/8   P/E Ratio: 16.4 52-Week   Range: 85 1/8–51 3/8

Competitive Strength

IBM has very strong competitive advantage in mainframes, which is unfortunately a weakening market in which prices and margins are falling. IBM has not yet demonstrated capability in PCs against nimble competitors, as indicated by recent loss of market share. The company's name recognition and brand preference have been tarnished but are still formidable. A new alliance with Apple covers hardware only and does nothing to challenge the strong position of the Microsoft-Intel combination. IBM's rewriting of OS/2 to allow it to introduce its new line of desktop computers based on the PowerPC RISC microprocessor is more than a year behind schedule. Restructuring may be too little to restore competitiveness in an increasingly cost-sensitive business and in any event places IBM in much lower-margin businesses than in the past, with little prospect of regaining its former highly profitable monolithic glory. Therefore the company's ability to regain competitive advantage in a vastly changed industry remains in sufficient doubt to disqualify it as a long-term investment candidate. IBM's P/E ratio is likely highly optimistic but indicates that the mystique is still alive.

Digital Equipment

Market Price, March 31, 1995: 37 1/7   P/E Ratio: Def.   52-Week Range: 38 7/8–18 1/8

Competitive Strength

While some vestige of DEC's once-strong competitive advantage (vested in a strong following in traditional scientific and technical markets) remains, this company's overall competitive strength is at best marginal. DEC's future depends on the success of its current R&D effort against strong competition. It is likely to survive for the intermediate term but as a smaller company, and it will likely be an acquisition candidate as industry rationalization progresses.

Apple

Market Price, March 31, 1995: 35 1/4   P/E Ratio: 9.0   52-Week Range: 48 1/8–24 5/8

Competitive Strength

Apple has strong competitive strength in educational and home markets, where its user friendliness gives it a competitive advantage. However, this advantage has been eroding in recent years because of the aggressiveness of Microsoft. The alliance with IBM does not solve Apple's software problem. The company has been losing market share in PCs and is falling behind in independent software development. It will have to regain market share to avoid being marginalized. Its best hope lies in offshore markets where Windows is not yet dominant. This major challenge makes the company's P/E ratio optimistic. Apple has been rumored to be an aquisition candidate, a strong possibility as it would provide one of the Japanese consumer electronics giants with entry into an industry that is making inroads into its U.S. markets.

Exhibit 10–3, *Concluded*

Compaq

Market Price, March 31, 1995: 34 3/8   P/E Ratio: 10.6   52-Week Range: 44 3/8–29 1/2

Competitive Strength

   Compaq's very strong competitive strength is based on a combination of product development capability; low operating costs due to outsourcing, effective scheduling, and logistics; and aggressive marketing which has created strong brand recognition. The company has achieved the economies of scale necessary to survive price wars, but has suffered some sacrifice of profit margins. Its competitive advantage is sustainable if management remains aggressive. Compaq's P/E ratio appears to be influenced by short-term pressures and may underestimate the company's long-term potential.

Hewlett-Packard

Market Price, March 31, 1995: 120 3/8   P/E Ratio: 17.1   52-Week-Range: 125–71 7/8

Competitive Strength

   Hewlett-Packard has strong competitive strength, due to a combination of an up-to-date product line with some diversity, strong distribution, and excellent name recognition. It has a leadership position in printers, with potential for further improvement. Its reputation will help it in the field of server technology, which is expected to be a major area of growth. Its market share in PCs is improving, but it will likely have to focus on products for the less price-sensitive business market. It will need to avoid the severe price competition of the home market, as its No. 7 standing in this market may make cost competitiveness difficult to achieve. Its P/E ratio does not appear to overly discount its long-term prospects.

Note: Def. = Deficit.

change some of its competitive practices did not create significant limitations for Microsoft. The company is lagging in introducing the Windows upgrade, and its Windows NT server system is not making much headway against its competitors, Unix International and Novell Inc. However, the competitors' efforts are also lagging, so Microsoft's delay has not been critical up to this point.

   Microsoft's management, under the guidance of its founder, Bill Gates, is visionary. However, as the company heads into the unmapped information superhighway, where its traditional dominance is not assured, anything could happen.[9] In addition, as always when a cult following develops for a CEO, Microsoft's heavy dependence on Bill Gates should make investors uneasy.

   Investment in Intel likewise may be an interesting possibility but should be approached with caution. Intel faces a challenge by clones of its products as well as by IBM's PowerPC RISC microprocessor, an IBM-

Motorola venture which is also backed by Apple. However, Intel's aggressive R&D program is pushing out new products and reducing prices rapidly, at a rate of about 30 percent per year.[10] As a result, it remains well-positioned to take advantage of the price-sensitive home computer market.

While the leadership position of neither Microsoft nor Intel is seriously challenged at present, the competition these companies face may affect their pricing and profitability. Because of this possibility, along with the vulnerability that accompanies industry dominance, caution is suggested.

As of March 31, 1995, Microsoft and Intel had P/E ratios of 34 and 16, respectively, reflecting the stock market's opinions of the sustainability of these companies' respective competitive advantages and earnings growth expectations. These opinions are probably relatively accurate. Microsoft has a very large customer base; its customers are generally satisfied and would find a switch to a competitor significantly inconvenient. Further, the market also expects a significant surge in earnings from the eventual Windows upgrades. While Intel is dominant in its industry sector, it must continue to run hard on product improvements and cost reduction to retain its advantage. Unlike Microsoft, it is vulnerable to some extent to a technological breakthrough by competitors; with few barriers to switching, its loss of market share could be rapid.

POINTS TO REMEMBER

In this chapter the computer industry has been examined as an example of a knowledge-based industry in the process of making the transition from the growth phase to the maturity phase. During this transition, the following developments have been taking place:

1. This originally attractive industry has become unattractive. The barriers to entry, which were high until the late 1970s, became low in the mid-1980s and now are rapidly increasing. Market growth has been slowing, while price sensitivity has been increasing. There have been large increases in the power of suppliers and distributors. These changes in the industry, while they are occurring rapidly, are evolutionary in nature and fairly predictable.

2. The computer industry has disaggregated into three main segments: the suppliers of software and microprocessors, the packagers who develop and market the products, and the distributors.

3. The rationalization of the industry is being driven by software. For now, there are three main software systems: Microsoft, IBM, and Apple. The packager segment of the industry will also rationalize, because economies of scale will be necessary to survival.

4. Integration no longer provides competitive advantage. The investor must look for opportunities in the supplier segment and/or the packaging segment. The key factors in establishing competitive advantage in the packaging component of the industry will be achievement of the size necessary to realize low costs through economies of scale and other measures, the ability to develop new products quickly, and the establishment of name recognition and brand preference.

Long-term investment in companies in an industry which is in a state of transition is inherently risky. Even relatively sound companies in such an industry experience a long period of low profitability because of the competitive pressures characteristic of the phase. In view of the changes in the structure of the computer industry, investment candidates must be evaluated in the context of their competitive advantage in the industry segment in which they are operating and must therefore have very high competitive strength in the functions that are important to success.

NOTES

1. Kathleen K. Wiegner, "Computers," *Forbes*, January 4, 1982, pp. 144–47.

2. Analysis of the changes in industry fundamentals is derived in part from: Stuart Gannes, "Tremors from the Computer Quake," *Fortune*, August 1, 1988, pp. 42–60; Andrew Kupfer, "Who's Winning the PC Price Wars?" *Fortune*, September 21, 1992, pp. 80–82; Stratford Sherman, "The New Computer Revolution," *Fortune*, June 14, 1993, pp. 56–80; John W. Verity, "Deconstructing the Computer Industry," *Business Week*, November 23, 1992, pp. 91–100; Catherine Arnst with Lois Therrien, "PC Land's Little Guys Get Slaughtered," *Business Week*, February 15, 1993, pp. 105–06.

3. Analysis of the current situation is derived in part from: David Kilpatrick, "How PCs Will Take Over Your Home," *Fortune*, February 21, 1994, pp. 100–04; David Kilpatrick, "What's Driving the New PC Shakeout," *Fortune*, September 19, 1994, pp. 109–22.

4. Background on IBM is based in part on: Paul Carrol, *Big Blues: The Unmaking of IBM* (New York: Crown Press, 1993); Charles H. Ferguson and Charles R. Morris, *Computer Wars: How the West Can Win in a Post-IBM World* (New York: Times Books, 1993); Susan Gelford, "Here Come the First Wave of PS/2 Clones," *Business Week*, May 9, 1988, p. 138C; Geoff Lewis with Thane Peterson and Jo

Ellen Davis, "If the PS/2 Is a Winner, Why Is IBM So Frustrated?" *Business Week*, April 11, 1988, pp. 82–83; David Kilpatrick, "Breaking Up IBM," *Fortune*, July 27, 1992, pp. 44–58; Judith H. Dobrzynski, "Rethinking IBM," *Business Week*, October 4, 1993, pp. 86–97; David Kilpatrick, "Gerstner's New Vision for IBM," *Fortune*, November 15, 1993, pp. 109–26; Stratford Sherman, "Is He Too Cautious to Save IBM?" *Fortune*, October 3, 1994, pp. 78–90; Amy Cortese, "IBM Rides into Microsoft Country," *Business Week*, June 6, 1994, pp. 111–12.

5. Background on and current developments at DEC are based in part on: Stratford P. Sherman, "Digital's Daring Comeback Plan," *Fortune*, January 14, 1991; Gary McWilliams, "DEC's Comeback Is Still a Work in Progress," *Business Week*, January 18, 1993, pp. 75–76; Gary McWilliams, "Desperate Hours at DEC," *Business Week*, May 9, 1994, pp. 26–28.

6. Background on and current developments at Apple are based in part on: Brenton R. Schlender, "Yet Another Strategy for Apple," *Fortune*, October 22, 1990, pp. 81–87; Alan Deutschman, "Odd Man Out," *Fortune*, July 26, 1993, pp. 42–56; Kathy Rebello, Ira Sager, and Richard Brandt, "Spindler's Apple," *Business Week*, October 3, 1994, pp. 87–96.

7. Background on and current developments at Compaq are based in part on: Jo Ellen Davis and Jeoff Lewis, "Who's Afraid of IBM," *Business Week*, June 29, 1987, pp. 68–74; Catherine Arnst and Stephanie Anderson Forest with Kathy Rebello and Jonathon Levine, "Compaq: How It Made Its Impressive Move Out of the Doldrums," *Business Week*, November 2, 1993, pp. 146–51; Stephanie Losee, "How Compaq Keeps the Magic Going," *Fortune*, February 21, 1994, pp. 90–92; Peter Harrows, "Compaq Stretches for the Crown," *Business Week*, July 11, 1994, pp. 140–42.

8. Alan Deutschman, "How H-P Continues to Grow and Grow," *Fortune*, May 2, 1994, pp. 90–100.

9. Richard Brandt with Amy Cortese, "Bill Gates's Vision," *Business Week*, June 27, 1994, pp. 57–62.

10. David Kirkpatrick, "Intel Goes for Broke," *Fortune*, May 16, 1994, pp. 62–68.

11

THE FOREST PRODUCTS INDUSTRY

Since the early 1980s, the action of the stock market has been in high-technology industries. In this so-called post-industrial age, knowledge has been said to replace the traditional industrial inputs. Rather than labor, capital, and natural resources, it is now knowledge that drives economic growth, according to the many books and articles that have been written on this topic. The emphasis on technology has attracted investors' attention and diverted their interest away from industries based on natural resources.

In this climate, the forest products industry is generally regarded as mundane. An investor would have been hard-pressed to find articles on companies in this industry in the major business magazines during the past several years.[1] Another reason for investors' apathy about forest products has been that commodity prices have generally declined or remained low, with the result that commodity producers have become either low-profit or losing operations. Many investors have assumed that the long-term depressed condition of the industry would be perpetual. (This assumption is in keeping with findings about psychological influences on investing that were discussed in Chapter 7.)

In fact, however, while resource industries have become a smaller part of the economy as a whole, they are nevertheless important. The need for metals, paper, and other basic materials remains strong. The basic problem facing the natural resource industries has been an oversupply of products. As in the case of all undifferentiated products, this condition translates directly into low prices. Further, since the market for commodities is global, North American producers have been directly affected by supplies coming onstream in other countries. In some of these countries, the motivation for production may be more political than economic. In addition, exchange rates may have tremendous influence on effective prices.

Few industries have experienced the degree of change that has faced the forest products industry over the past decade. The traditional economics of the industry have been altered by political, economic, and technological factors. The effects of these factors are only now beginning to show, but they must be recognized in investment decisions.

The forest products industry is used in this chapter as an example of how long-term investment opportunities in a natural resource-based industry can be evaluated. Producers of both lumber and paper will be included, along with, in some cases, makers of products directly derived from lumber or paper through vertical integration. Within the overall classification "forest products," there are four segments with differing characteristics. As a result, evaluating a company solely on the basis of the broad characteristics of the industry can be misleading. However, the investor must understand the structure of the industry in order to have a context in which to consider its segments.

INDUSTRY STRUCTURE

The history of the exploitation of forests started with early humans cutting firewood for fuel. Forests played a major role in the economic development of North America from the establishment of the first colonies to the late nineteenth century. Abundant forests provided the primary materials for building construction, shipbuilding, and fuel. During this time "lumber barons," along with "railway barons," built many of the great American family fortunes. Since the late nineteenth century, other industries such as manufacturing have taken up the role of economic leadership. The forest products industry has gradually diminished in importance to the economy as a whole, although it remains the mainstay of the economies in remote regions of the United States and Canada. There have been periodic major booms in the industry. Around the Great Lakes in the late 1800s, for instance, vast quantities of lumber were required to rebuild Chicago after the great fire of 1871. In the 1950s, the suburbanization of the country caused a similar boom.

The common denominator in this industry is its dependency on the harvesting of trees. The four sectors of the industry are as follows:

1. The *lumber* sector processes wood into building materials.
2. The *heavy papers* sector processes wood into paper, primarily for packaging purposes.
3. The *white papers* sector produces papers for various printing purposes, including books and periodicals, and for tissues and other personal-use papers.
4. The *newsprint and groundwood specialty papers* sector produces paper for newspapers, directories, and other such publications.

The various paper producers use highly specialized production processes and cannot readily switch to other products.

Traditional Industry Fundamentals

The traditional characteristics of the forest products industry are described below.

Barriers to Entry

The industry is capital-intensive, and long lead times are required for building or expanding plants. Since prices are volatile and beyond the control of the producer, there is always uncertainty about whether the prices that will be in effect by the time the new facilities come onstream will justify the expansion. The overall lead time for constructing or even expanding a plant can be up to five years, or even longer when environmental approvals are taken into account. Thus barriers to entry are, in general, forbiddingly high. However, there has been significant subsidization of entry by certain foreign governments, which have granted cheap timber-cutting rights, tax concessions, and comparatively lenient pollution regulations.

Bargaining Power

Bargaining power with buyers is low, because the products are undifferentiated commodities which are graded in accordance with industry specifications. In virtually every use, paper is a major cost of production for buyers, and thus they are highly price-sensitive.

On the other hand, for the paper sectors of the industry, the bargaining power of the principal suppliers—the suppliers of wood—has been relatively high. Wood is obtained through a combination of sources: private tree plantations, cutting rights on government land, and a company's own lands. Backward integration into the ownership of woodlands is indicative of a company's need to limit the bargaining power of its suppliers.

Substitutes
The risk of substitution is generally low, but it does vary from product to product. Since no generalizations are possible, the substitutions for specific products will be discussed later in the chapter.

Barriers to Exit
Papermaking machinery is specialized and cannot be converted for use in producing other products. The companies are often vertically integrated, so that the various parts of the business are interdependent. Further, the environmental costs of closing include cleaning up lagoons, spills, and other areas. These costs can be very high. Thus barriers to exit are high.

Industry Life Cycle
Though the forest products industry is mature, demand is cyclical, due in large part to variations in the economic cycle. For lumber, the main variable is housing starts. For packaging products and newsprint, demand tends to fluctuate with overall economic activity, as measured by the GDP.

Fixed Costs
The processes involved in operating in this industry are capital-intensive and highly automated. The mills cannot be run economically at part capacity, nor can they be readily shut down and restarted according to need. The main factors in determining costs are fiber (whether wood or recycled paper), energy, and economies of scale based on machine size. The combination of cyclical demand with the high fixed costs caused by these factors has resulted in major fluctuations in industry earnings.

In total, this has been a highly unattractive industry, which accounts in part for investors' apathy toward it. The latest median five-year average ROE is only 6.4 percent, as compared to the all-industries median return of 11.4 percent. This mediocre performance can be accounted for in part by the cyclical low point of the industry, which occurred in 1990. However, the industry's problems have been aggravated by its longstanding practice of starting to add capacity at the peak of the cycle, when such decisions seem to be justified by current prices. Because of the long lead times needed to construct mills and the size necessary to achieve economies of scale, large additions to industry capacity then come onstream in the down portion of the cycle, aggravating the oversupply situation. Despite these adverse factors, the United States is the world's lowest-cost producer of forest products, primarily due to the accessibility of low-cost, high-quality raw materials.

Effects of Changes in Industry Fundamentals

The traditional characteristics of the industry have been affected by political and ecological changes, as well as by technological advances.

Recycling

Politically mandated recycling of paper has created a new major source of fiber. In the case of newsprint, recycled paper has displaced raw wood by as much as one-half of mill requirements. Municipal regulations imposed in the late 1980s specifying recycled-materials content were motivated primarily by the need to reduce landfill volume. An additional requirement of 20 percent recycled content for U.S. government paper purchases went into effect in 1994. Large capital spending requirements have also been imposed on the industry by recycling requirements that result in low rates of return for the companies that have to lay out the money. Industry expenditures for adaptation to use of recycled paper have been estimated to total $1 billion as of the mid-1990s. There is a further penalty for companies in the industry, in that use of recycled fiber reduces the efficiency of machines by 10 to 15 percent.

Despite these seeming disadvantages, the industry has not strenuously opposed recycling legislation. Indeed, laws about recycling have been viewed as affording some protection for domestic companies, because they have the effect of restricting import of foreign-made papers that do not meet industry specifications. Further, they imposed cost penalties on competing Canadian mills which are far from the major population centers where the recycled paper is generated.

Wildlife Protection

In support of movements to protect the habitats of endangered species, the U.S. government reduced timber-cutting allowances in the Northwest by 60 percent starting in 1994.

Air and Water Pollution Legislation

More stringent water and air pollution standards were also imposed on the industry by the U.S. government, again major capital expenditures were necessary just to stay in business.

Technological Advances

There were significant advances in technology in some segments of the industry, as well as advances in the technologies of substitute industries. These have been specific to the various sectors of the industry and will be discussed later in the chapter.

Changing Global Economics

There has been a significant improvement in the prospects for a prolonged period of growth of demand from the global manufacturing sector due to the liberation of the economies of formerly communist nations, and from economic growth primarily in the Far East. As discussed in Chapter 6, this can be regarded as a discontinuity in the evolution of the world economy.

STRUCTURE IN INDUSTRY SEGMENTS

The effects of the favorable developments described above have not yet been reflected in the industry's performance statistics; indeed, the effects have been disguised by cyclical woes. The relative recency of some of the events is another reason the effects have not yet shown up. The need for heavy investment to accommodate recycling and pollution needs without any corresponding contribution to productivity or efficiency has been a factor in the industry's low return on equity (ROE). The various segments of the industry have been affected in different ways, and the present condition of the industry can be best assessed by examining each segment separately.

Lumber

The lumber segment of the forest products industry is primarily a supplier of construction materials. The nature of the segment has changed considerably. Traditionally it consisted of suppliers of logs and sawn lumber. It now has manufacturing operations as well, which produce not only plywood but also such materials as oriented structural boards, a comparatively new product. The evolution of lumber into a two-tiered business has come about because of politically influenced developments in the forest products industry as a whole (which were described above), and also because of technological developments in construction materials. The lumber business differs from the forest products industry as a whole in the following ways:

Bargaining Power

Lumber companies' bargaining power with suppliers has weakened. They are heavily reliant on the supply of logs, and the power of log suppliers has increased sharply. As mentioned above, the U.S. government has reduced allowable cuts in the Northwest. In this area, which is the main U.S. timber source, cuts were reduced from 3 billion board feet to 1.2 billion board feet, commencing in 1994.[2] The logs must be cut from mature trees, and the added growing time increases the cost of inventory and becomes a part of the cost structure. Since the domestic industry must now compete with exporters for the supply of logs, material prices are likely to rise.

Substitutes

Substitutes for sawn lumber are emerging rapidly in the form of oriented structural boards. These boards are made from lower-grade wood, and a much greater portion of the tree is used. To manufacture structural boards, a company must have access to new technologies as well as to channels of distribution. While the products are more expensive than plain wood, their strength makes them competitive on a systems basis. In an effort to create what is known as "draw-through" demand, some producers have even begun to advertise to consumers, making claims for such benefits as "squeak-proof floors." This sort of advertising, however, appears to be rather futile. Usually it is the builder who chooses the materials to be used. The choice is based on cost. Since a feature such as flooring is not sufficient to influence the marketability of a house, advertising to consumers is not likely to be effective.

Success in the manufacturing portion of the lumber business depends on access to the necessary technological and distribution capabilities. Prices for sawn lumber will continue to increase, and the availability of mature logs will be a key determinant of success. The exception is likely to be low-grade structural products such as studs; plantations will probably offset a loss of pulpwood markets (discussed below) by letting their trees grow to sawable size. Use of wood-based, engineered structural products (which are made by gluing together fiber from comparatively plentiful tree species) as substitutes for sawn lumber is expected to grow rapidly. While some companies are integrated forward into ownership of retail lumber dealers, the lumber segment of the industry remains highly fragmented. Any benefits lumber companies may receive from improving their bargaining power with buyers will therefore be rather limited.

Heavy Papers

The term *heavy papers* is used here to mean papers used for packaging. These include kraft papers used to make bags for various purposes, corrugated paper boxes, and paperboard for use in light containers such as cartons for cereals and other consumer products. The structure of the heavy papers business differs from that of the forest products industry as a whole in the following ways:

Barriers to Entry

Barriers to entry are high. The capital-intensive nature of the heavy papers business, combined with a prolonged period of low prices, has made the industry unattractive. There has been relatively little increase in industry capacity since the mid-1980s, and significant new capacity will not be coming onstream until 1995–96. Heavy paper manufacturing is like all capital-intensive businesses in that a high rate of capacity utilization is required for profitability. Increasing capacity is difficult because lead times are long and because wood and energy supplies must be assured and environmental conditions met. Though a number of min-imills using recycled materials have been constructed, they have not provided a significant increase in total capacity.

Bargaining Power

Companies that manufacture heavy papers have considerable bargaining power over suppliers. Unlike lumber manufacturers, which require mature trees, these companies use smaller-sized pulpwood trees, many of which are grown on tree farms in the southern part of the United States and reach harvestable size relatively quickly. In addition, these companies can use wood chips (the waste material from sawmills) and recycled papers as basic materials. The recycling infrastructure of heavy paper manufacturers, however, is not as well developed as that of newsprint manufacturers, and thus their ability to use recycled material is still limited.

Substitutes

There are currently no substitutes for the corrugated containers and paperboard boxes into which heavy papers are made, nor do these products face any significant substitution threat. The substitution of plastic for paper grocery bags, however, is resulting in the conversion of kraft paper bag machines to linerboard production. This substitution may still have some way to go.

Cyclicality

Demand for heavy paper products is cyclical, as it is dependent on buyers' manufacturing activity. This cyclicality, however, is dampened by the fact that the relatively steady food and beverage industry is a major user. Prices can be highly volatile; for instance, the price of the linerboard used to make corrugated cartons rose by 32 percent between October 1993 and October 1994. The long-term demand trend is favorable, as it is related to global manufacturing activity. Virtually every manufactured product is packaged or shipped in paper boxes.

Most packaging paper manufacturers are integrated forward into conversion operations, particularly corrugated box manufacture. This is the only segment of the forest products industry in which forward integration is economically feasible. Forward integration improves the companies' bargaining power with buyers. After integrating, rather than dealing with a relatively large number of large converters, they have a large number of small customers for boxes and bags. Further, they also acquire the opportunity to differentiate their products by adding quality and service.

Traditionally, the main economic benefit of vertical integration for these manufacturers was that, even if the conversion was only a break-even operation, it helped to keep mill capacity utilization high, one of the keys to profitability in the industry. Recently, however, new technology in the conversion segment has created at least two opportunities for improving the profitability of operations. First, because of new technology, companies have been able to increase the capacity and productivity of existing plants at relatively low capital cost. This is resulting in some rationalization of the industry. Companies with multiple plants can combine the volume of several plants into one, thereby dramatically improving their profitability.

New processes involving the preprinting of linerboard have significantly improved the graphics capability of the corrugated papers industry, bringing it up to consumer product display standards. Thus these papers are becoming the primary packaging for a wide range of products, displacing paperboard folding cartons in this function. The strength of corrugated packaging also makes it possible to eliminate use of a secondary shipping container, resulting in major systems savings. As a result, paperboard growth is flat while corrugated shipments have been growing at 4 percent per annum, well ahead of what could have been expected from economic recovery alone.

A very sharp (30 percent) rise in the price of linerboard began in October 1993 and continued throughout 1994. While this rise is in part a cyclical development, it also likely indicates the first stage of a significant improvement in the attractiveness of this segment of the industry. The combination of improved long-term prospects for global manufacturing with the increased role of linerboard in packaging provides a basis for more rapid market growth. Given the supply constraints, this growth is likely to place a higher floor under the cyclical price declines. Technological developments have significantly changed the role of the converted parts of the integrated companies. No longer do they simply serve as marketing operations: now they profitably add value to the product and provide a higher rate of market growth.

Not all the companies in the industry are recognizing the potential benefits of conversion and making the necessary investments. In fact, many of the companies are having trouble in transcending their traditional view of the role of their downstream operations.

White Papers

The white papers segment of the forest products industry includes a wide variety of products, ranging from highly specialized, low-volume filter, cigarette, and bond writing papers to high-volume commodity papers, such as those used in printing and computer applications. Some of these products are coated or otherwise processed. The characteristics of the various companies in the industry can therefore be quite different.

Barriers to Entry

Traditionally, barriers to entry into the white papers business have been high. In general, they remain high, but there has been some conversion of old, small machines that are no longer competitive in the making of commodity products for use in making specialty papers. Because of this conversion, there is a risk of overcrowding in the specialty markets.

Bargaining Power

Though companies that produce low-volume specialized papers can have quite high bargaining power with buyers, producers of high-volume commodity-grade papers have much less leverage with their customers.

Substitutes

In the 1980s it was thought by many people that an electronic revolution in office products would create the so-called paperless office. A more realistic view of the possibilities of electronic products, including computers, prevails in the 1990s, and this perceived threat to the white papers business has faded. For example, computer printout formats are very often great wasters of paper.

The profitability of companies in the white papers segment of the forest products industry varies widely. Depending on the product, a company may fit anywhere in a range from attractive to unattractive. The rate of market growth likewise varies widely, depending on the end use of the individual products. Following the pattern of the industry as a whole, this segment added heavily to capacity in the late 1980s, a move that added to its distress in the 1990–91 recession.

Newsprint and Groundwood Specialty Papers

Newsprint and groundwood specialty papers are used in newspapers and directories. With variations in the nature of the wood pulp used and with additional processing, these papers can also be used in higher-value products such as magazine stock. The basic long-term growth of demand for newsprint in the United States and other developed economies averages only about 1 percent per annum; it also fluctuates cyclically with the economy. In developing countries, the basic growth is about 2 1/2 percent per annum. Within this overall market situation, the characteristics of the industry are as follows:

Barriers to Entry

Barriers to entry are relatively high but not prohibitive. There is no shortage of the wood pulp used by this segment of the industry, and in any event, advances in recycling technology have freed mills from heavy dependence on wood supplies. As a result, new mills are being built in a number of countries to serve local markets. However, the barriers to entry for new wood-based operations are especially high, due to capital and energy intensity in the face of uncertain markets. Probably the highest barrier to entry is a lack of capital due to the weak profit performance of the industry. Recent entrants have been minimills using recycled fiber, but sharp increases in the price of old newspapers have made the economics of these operations marginal, thus discouraging the building of additional new plants. There were significant increases in capacity in this segment of the industry in the 1989–92 period.

Bargaining Power

Companies that make newsprint and groundwood papers obtain their raw materials in almost equal parts from recycled newspapers and from pulp.

U.S. government-mandated recycling programs have resulted in a short-age of material, driving up the price of old newspapers to above that of fiber from trees. The infrastructure for the collection of old newspapers has not kept up with the demand created by their mandated use. Further, continued recycling results in the breakdown of the fiber so that a portion of input tonnage is wasted. Since most pulpwood is obtained from tree farms, the decrease in use of pulp has improved these paper makers' bargaining power with suppliers, stabilizing pulpwood costs.

The customers for this segment of the industry are a relatively small number of large publishers, which gives them high bargaining power. A number of mills are owned jointly with publishers, in a form of backward integration. In the most recent recession, the cyclical decline in demand resulted in price declines as high as 50 percent. Debt-laden mills were forced to compete for the available business of the publishers.

Substitutes
A substitution threat arising from the advent of electronic media and communication processes has not yet run its course, but the erosion of newsprint's market share is reasonably reflected in the slow rate of growth of demand. While there are fewer newspapers, increases in advertising and particularly in inserts have offset the decline in numbers. This segment of the industry is probably most vulnerable to substitution in directories applications, because electronic directories can be continuously updated.

Fixed Costs
Fixed costs among newsprint and groundwood specialties companies are high, making earnings sensitive to capacity utilization. Until the 1990-91 recession, prices tended to be relatively stable during economic declines. The mills usually reduced their operating rates, suggesting the existence of an informal cartel. This pattern changed during the most recent recession. Prices fell sharply as mills maintained their operating rates. It is likely that their motivation was an attempt to generate cash in order to meet debt service requirements.

Barriers to Exit
Barriers to exit are high. Contributory factors are specialized manufacturing facilities, debt servicing requirements, and the typically single-product nature of the companies.

This segment of the forest products industry is inherently unattractive, though it is likely to show short-term cyclical improvement. In this segment as in the white papers segment, the problems of the early 1990s were aggravated by new capacity coming onstream. By 1994, however, this capacity had been absorbed. In addition, many of the one-time costs of adapting to recycling and environmental protection requirements had been met and the debt that had been incurred was being worked down.

In Conclusion

This brief review of the characteristics of the four sectors of the forest products industry has shown that the industry is not monolithic. Investment decisions must take into consideration the characteristics of the segment of the industry in which investment candidates operate. The key factors are, first, the long-term balance between supply and demand which determines prices and capacity utilization and, second, the costs entailed by the company under consideration. A company's costs depend to a significant extent on its supply situation.

COMPANY PERFORMANCE

Exhibit 11–1 shows the performance of selected companies in the forest products industry. These companies are P.H. Glatfelter Company, a manufacturer of white papers; Louisiana-Pacific Corporation, which produces

E X H I B I T   11–1

Key Performance Statistics for Selected Companies in the
Forest Products Industry, 1990–94

Company	Return on Equity, %		Return on Capital, %	
	5-Year Average	Latest 12 Months	Latest 12 Months	Profit Margin, %
P.H. Glatfelter	13.4	2.4	1.8	2.4
Louisiana-Pacific	12.3	18.9	13.3	11.3
International Paper	6.3	5.9	4.2	2.6
Chesapeake	4.8	8.3	6.5	3.4
Bowater	Def.	Def.	Def.	Def.
Industry median:				
1994	6.4	6.8	5.4	2.6
1988	11.8	21.8	NA	7.9

Note: Def. = deficit. NA = not available.

lumber and other building supplies; International Paper Company, which makes diverse paper products; Chesapeake Corporation, a maker of integrated corrugated packaging; and Bowater Inc., a newsprint manufacturer.

The cyclicality of the industry can be seen by comparing the five-year average rates of return and the respective latest-12-months figures for 1988 and 1994. The inherent unattractiveness of the forest products industry is shown by the fact the five-year average ROE of the best performer is only slightly above the all-industries median.

Following are brief commentaries on the circumstances of and developments in these five companies, which have led to their past performance on the stock market.

P.H. Glatfelter For this leading producer of uncoated book publishing papers, 78 percent of sales is provided by the company's 34 percent share of the uncoated paper market. The balance of P.H. Glatfelter's sales are in tobacco papers and other specialty papers. The company's relatively low profit margins reflect the increasingly competitive nature of the specialty paper markets. Its ROE for the latest 12 months shown in Exhibit 11–1 is down in part because of a decline in sales due to the loss of a major cigarette customer.

Louisiana-Pacific Louisiana-Pacific, which focuses on production of building materials, including panels, lumber, windows, and doors, is one of the largest lumber producers in the world. Its engineered structural products account for 41 percent of sales. Its 1.6 million acres of timberland provide about 15 percent of its log requirements. The company's sales are heavily dependent on housing starts, which are heavily cyclical in response to the overall economic cycle and which turned favorable in 1994. This development explains the company's improvement in ROE in the latest 12 months shown in Exhibit 11–1. Another 30 percent of sales are made to the less cyclical remodeling and construction markets.

International Paper International Paper is the largest and most diversified forest products company in the United States and one of the largest in the world. Its products include paper, paperboard, packaging, pulp, lumber, panels, laminated products, chemicals, and minerals. Directly and through partnerships, it controls a total of 6.1 million acres of timberland in the United States. The company's current emphasis is on containerboard, for which it is adding mill capacity and recycling capability, as well as modernizing its converting plants. International Paper has demonstrated both its courage and its long-term priority by starting construction of a major new linerboard mill during the cyclical low, which will come onstream in 1995 to take advantage of the current market strength and higher prices.

Chesapeake This integrated operation holds 350,000 acres of tree farm, a packaging (linerboard) mill, and 11 converting plants that manufacture corrugated cartons and serve Eastern Seaboard markets. Chesapeake also manufactures and sells commercial and industrial tissues and treated wood. The company has pursued a strategy of maximizing value added through its conversion operations and by treating lumber. To this end, it has spent heavily to upgrade its conversion operations to state-of-the-science capability. It is well positioned to take advantage of the new markets for corrugated containers.

Bowater This company is the largest producer of newsprint and other coated and uncoated commodity papers in the United States. It converts some of its commodity papers into stock, continuous business forms. Bowater has five mills, with major publishers holding a minority interest in two of them. Its mills are supplied by a total of 4 million acres of forestland.

THE INVESTOR'S PERSPECTIVE

The first step in assessing the five companies under consideration in this chapter as long-term investment candidates is to examine the companies' past market performance, the structure of the forest products industry, and the basis of each company's competitive advantage.

The Market's Judgment

Exhibit 11–2 shows the stock market performance of the five companies in relation to the overall market during the decade 1984–94. An interesting characteristic of the performance of these companies is the extent to which, as a generalization, their stocks matched the S&P 500 up to 1988. Louisiana-Pacific has outperformed the market since 1992 because of a recovery in the cyclical housing market. Chesapeake was among the first to fall below the overall market but recovered slightly in 1994. This company is highly dependent on industrial production which started to recover after 1992, although box prices did not start to rise until 1994. Bowater significantly underperformed the market during the period under consideration, as a result of its focus on commodity products.

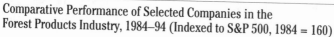

EXHIBIT 11-2

Comparative Performance of Selected Companies in the
Forest Products Industry, 1984–94 (Indexed to S&P 500, 1984 = 160)

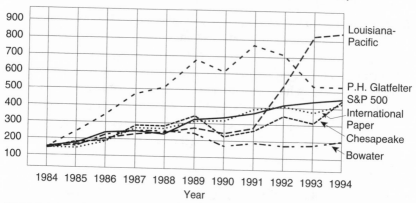

Note: The index for each year is shown at the mean between the high and the low for the period.

P.H. Glatfelter was the only papermaker that outperformed the market during these years. Because of its position in a specialty niche, it has continued to outperform the market. However, its stock prices began to fall in 1992; this fall has been taking place because even the specialty niches have been squeezed in recent years by companies looking to escape the price sensitivity of the market for commodity-type papers.

Industry Structure and Competitive Advantage

Certain assumptions about the condition of the forest products industry and the five companies' bases of competitive advantage underlie my assessment of the companies as long-term investment candidates. These assumptions are as follows:

1. The industry will remain inherently unattractive except for cyclical periods of better performance. Most of its products are price-sensitive commodity papers, and there are no significant supply constraints. However, the long-term balance of supply and demand may be more favorable in some segments of the industry.

2. A company's competitive advantage relies heavily on two factors: (a) low costs due to a combination of access to cheap inputs and economies of scale and (b) concentration on an industry segment

in which the long-term supply-demand relationship is comparatively favorable and in which there are opportunities to add value, and hence enhance profit, through forward integration, so as to increase bargaining power with buyers.

3. Change in the industry as a whole will be slow and evolutionary. The main stabilizing factors are as follows: (a) the companies are heavily invested in their mills, plantations, and so forth; (b) the industry's technologies are mature; and (c) most markets in this industry can be expected to grow slowly. To a significant extent, the mandated recycling and environmental protection investments and costs (which together can be classified as a discontinuity) of the 1980s have been absorbed and are reflected in the current industry situation. The developments only now starting to show their effect are the growth of global manufacturing and certain technological advances in the packaging industry.

While there is no doubt that the markets for paper will remain highly cyclical, there are indications that the companies in the industry are currently less inclined to exacerbate their future woes. Repetition of the past mistake made by many companies—adding capacity during an upturn, only to have it come onstream just in time for the next downturn—seems unlikely. The recession of 1990–91 had severe repercussions for the forest products industry, and left many companies on the verge of bankruptcy. This lesson is well remembered in the industry. Companies are tending to give priority to repairing their balance sheets and paying down their debt, rather than adding capacity. If this priority continues to prevail, price declines are likely to be less severe in the next economic downturn than they have been in the past.

Two potential political developments may also help the industry. First, the U.S. Congress is considering restoring some of the cutting rights on public lands that had been taken away by past legislation. Second, constraints may be placed on the imposition of stricter environmental standards on mills.[3]

Notwithstanding these developments, the forest products industry can be expected to remain relatively unattractive as a whole. The one segment that has better prospects will be discussed below.

Assessment of Five Forest Products Companies

The basic criteria used throughout this book for identifying a long-term investment candidate are that the company must have competitive strength and/or the industry must either be attractive or have the potential to become attractive in the long run. Exhibit 11–3 provides brief assessments of five companies as candidates for long-term investment.

E X H I B I T   11–3

Assessment of Selected Companies in the Forest Products Industry as Long-Term Investment Candidates (As of March 31, 1995)

P.H. Glatfelter

**Market Price, March 31, 1995: 18 3/8   P/E Ratio: Deficit
52-Week Range: 18 3/8–14 5/8**

Competitive Strength

High but weakening. The company has an established position in high-margin specialty markets, which are less cyclical than the industry as a whole. The relative attractiveness of its industry niches is at risk of erosion as the industry converts small, marginal machines from commodity to specialty products. The company's relatively high share of the uncoated publishing paper market makes it a natural target for new entrants, and price pressure is likely to increase as a result. The stock price has been held up by the dividend, which substantially exceeds earnings.

Louisiana-Pacific

**Market Pric, March 31, 1995: 27 5/8   P/E Ratio: 8.8
52-Week Range: 36 1/8–24 3/4**

Competitive Strength

Marginal. Almost one-half of sales are provided by panel products, which are price-sensitive manufactured commodities and difficult to differentiate. Thus the company has heavy investment and high fixed costs in products in which the industry is adding capacity and which must be sold in a highly cyclical housing market. An internal wood supply of 15 percent of requirements is not sufficient to provide advantage in the sawn lumber segment. The market will continue to be highly cyclical; this appears to be recognized in the company's modest P/E ratio. Even so, the market's view may be overly optimistic in the long term.

International Paper

**Market Price, March 31, 1995: 75   P/E Ratio: 21.7
52-Week Range: 80 1/2–60 5/8**

Competitive Strength

High. The company will be able to take advantage of the expected prolonged strength in the packaging segment of industry, though this strength will be diluted to some extent by cyclical weakness in other product groups. Major new linerboard capacity is coming on line at a good time, and the decision to build this new mill is an indication of the long-term view held by management. International Paper's stock has shown an ability to hold up through cycles. However, the company's P/E ratio discounts some of these strong fundamentals.

Exhibit 11–3, *Concluded*

Chesapeake

Market Price, March 31, 1995: 32   P/E Ratio: 20.3
52-Week Range: 35 7/8-22 5/8

Competitive Strength

   High. Chesapeake holds a strong position in the most attractive segment of industry. The rapidly increasing price of linerboard will sharply increase the company mill's profitability. A significant portion of its higher prices are likely to be sustainable in the long term, because the global shortage of linerboard is likely to be prolonged as manufacturing activity grows but long lead times constrain supply increases. This company has been aggressive in upgrading its converting plants to take advantage of cost reduction and market-broadening opportunities. Traditionally, producers of linerboard have engaged in converting operations with the objective of keeping their mills busy. Chesapeake has invested in the technology to enable its converting plants to produce higher-value products to take advantage of the profit contribution opportunity from this activity. Chesapeake's high P/E ratio anticipates the effect of increases in linerboard prices in the past year.

Bowater

Market Price, March 31, 1995: 35 3/8 P/E Ratio: Deficit
52-Week Range: 37 5/8–20 3/4

Competitive Strength

   Marginal, though the company is trapped in the least attractive segment of the industry. While Bowater is likely to exhibit considerable short-term improvement in performance, it will be weighed down by the weak fundamentals of newsprint and groundwood specialties sector of the industry in the long term.

   In the forest products industry, there are two sources of competitive advantage: first, a company's ability to operate at low costs, and second, its ability to add value to its products either through differentiation or through forward integration. Prospective improvements in industry attractiveness have meaning for the long-term investor only if they are based on long-term trends rather than on cyclicality alone.

   Though the forest products industry as a whole is inherently unattractive, its structure may be improving, for two reasons. First, most of the companies in the industry are holding back on adding capacity, a voluntary constraint that may help to alleviate the severity of the next cyclical downturn. Second, the threat of increased strictness in environmental regulations has receded for the moment. In addition, the fundamentals are somewhat different in certain segments of the industry.

The segment that manufactures heavy packaging papers such as liner-board is an exception to the relatively weak condition of the overall industry fundamentals. A shortage of capacity in this area has been created by a steady increase in demand due to global manufacturing growth, combined with an increasing share of the consumer products packaging market. The shortage of capacity is likely to last for an extended period because of the long lead times involved in building new plants. The major companies in this segment also have an opportunity to integrate forward into the conversion of commodity papers into finished products, thus adding value to their products and consistency to the volume of demand. The two candidates for long-term investment that are suggested below are both in this segment.

Despite the positive factors cited above, the basic unattractiveness of the overall industry limits the appeal of many forest products companies to long-term investors. Only when segment-specific variations in fundamentals are considered along with the competitive positions of specific companies do two possible candidates for long-term investment emerge. These are International Paper and Chesapeake. Of all the candidates for long-term investment that are discussed in this book, these two are most heavily dependent on their ability to take advantage of changes that are taking place in their industry but that have not yet shown up in their operating results. Thus caution is advisable.

International Paper's inherent strength is revealed by its 11-year trading record. As shown in Exhibit 11–2, the company's stock prices have remained close to the S&P 500 price throughout this period. A combination of the possible improvement in overall industry structure with this company's strength in the packaging segment is likely to enable it to outperform the industry and the market as a whole in the long term.

Chesapeake has been discussed in this chapter as a relatively specialized company. Its long-term performance potential is provided both by an improvement in the packaging segment of the industry and by the company's investment strategy, which will allow it to take advantage of opportunities to add value to its products. Chesapeake is a likely candidate only for the long-term investor who is also somewhat aggressive.

The assessment that the fundamentals of the linerboard and packaging sector of the industry are improving for the integrated producers raises the question of why the industry's largest producer, Stone Container Corp., is not being considered as a long-term investment candidate. This company has high debt, which was incurred in its rapid growth through acquisitions, together with relatively old converting plants. For the time being, the cash required to service and pay down debt precludes investment in upgrading its plants. While Stone should do well as the result of price increases in paper alone, its converting activities will continue to be confined to the manufacture of low-margin commodity-type boxes. This makes it highly vulnerable to the economic cycle.

POINTS TO REMEMBER

The forest products industry is far from a monolithic entity. Rather, it consists of four well-defined sectors: lumber and building materials, heavy packaging papers, white papers, and newsprint and groundwood specialty papers. The three paper segments have different fundamentals, which are determined by the end uses of their products. Papermaking machinery is specialized in nature. Conversion to production of different kinds of paper is difficult but has sometimes been done successfully.

The traditional lack of attractiveness of this industry is caused by its very nature, in that its products are commodities and thus low costs are the primary basis of profitability. Adding to this disadvantageous fundamental nature is the high degree of cyclicality of demand in virtually all segments of the industry. Cyclicality is a particular problem for the paper producers, which have high fixed costs and cannot easily adjust to fluctuations in demand. In the past, periods of prosperity have inevitably been followed by years of marginal profitability or even losses. The problems caused by cyclicality have been aggravated by the propensity of companies in the industry to add capacity at the wrong time.

As of early 1995, most segments of the industry were showing cyclical improvement. The only suggestion of a basic long-term improvement in overall industry fundamentals was the limitations on additions to capacity that were being initiated by the companies in the industry. The heavy papers segment of the industry was characterized by stronger fundamentals.

NOTES

1. Because of the lack of significant amounts of news coverage, the discussion of current developments in the industry is based in part on interviews with executives in the different segments of the industry and in part on my own background in the industry. The following published sources have also been useful: Mathew K. Berber, "Paper and Forest Products," from Donaldson, Lufkin & Genrette, *To the Millennium: A Roadmap to Investing in the 1990s*, pp. 127–31; Resource Information Systems, Inc., *Pulp and Paper Review*, October 1994.

2. Robert La Franco, "Forest Products and Packaging," *Forbes*, January 2, 1995, pp. 156–57.

3. Alex Taylor III, "Why an Industry that Is up a Tree Is on a Roll," *Fortune*, April 17, 1995, pp. 134–42.

12

THE BANKING INDUSTRY

In the past, a *bank's* function was to hold money and pay it out, to lend and borrow money, and to exchange it for other currencies. In earlier times, banks even issued currency. Banks nowadays have expanded into a broad range of additional functions, to such an extent that the distinction between banks and other financial institutions has become blurred.

A bank, however, is still a service institution, and service industries obviously differ from goods-producing industries, in which products change hands. Chapters 9, 10, and 11, on the automobile, computer, and forest products industries, respectively, dealt with businesses in which physical objects are the reason for the interactions between companies, their suppliers, and their customers.

Service industries can involve physical activities. In retailing industries, for example, the physical movement of goods is what is required. In the airlines industry, it is people who must be moved in order for the business of a company to be transacted.

Banking is an exception. The "product" is an exchange of "value" between parties, and the exchange involves little or no physical activity. This is one reason for taking a closer look at the banking industry. Another reason is the industry's traditional status as a favorite of long-term investors. This status has been based on the reputation of banking as a conservatively managed business that often offered opportunities for high yields.

Banking's reputation for conservatism was severely shaken during the late 1970s and the 1980s, when the industry embarked upon a quest for growth and higher profit margins. In pursuit of these goals, banks loaned heavily to less developed countries (LDCs) and to commercial real estate developers. Many of these loans had to be written down or restructured, and industry earnings were severely affected. By the late 1980s, the industry had lost much of its reputation as a good investment.

The banking industry has changed in other ways as well. Since the mid-1980s, it has been in a state of "creeping" deregulation. Constraints upon the services that banks can provide are being lifted, and regulations restricting a bank's geographic areas of operation are being loosened. The pace of deregulation may even be accelerating. In addition, the industry is in the process of adapting to new technology that is changing the way it delivers services to customers. Consequently, the banking industry must be evaluated in the context of a range of new functions, risks, and the new competitive environment which these changes are creating.

INDUSTRY STRUCTURE

Traditionally, the banking industry has had the following three tiers:

- *Money center banks,* which provide a comprehensive range of services and operate on a global level
- *Regional banks,* which also provide a wide range of services but are mainly confined to a domestic geographic region
- *Local banks,* which operate in a specific community

Money center banks and major regional banks have certain industry fundamentals in common but differ in important respects from local banks. These similarities and differences will be described below.

Another way to classify banks is by the range of services that they provide, as follows:

- *Commercial banks* primarily take deposits and make loans. They also provide a comprehensive range of other services to a broad market.
- *Investment banks* underwrite bonds and stocks, sell securities, and use their own capital in various trading activities to make a profit.

Banks obtain revenue from a number of activities, including the following:

- *Wholesaling and retailing money.* Banks operate as both wholesalers and retailers of money. They borrow from many sources, including depositors, and they lend to industrial, commercial, government, and individual customers.
- *Providing services.* Banks charge fees for a wide variety of services, including maintaining and servicing checking accounts, credit card accounts, and trust services; syndicating loans and leases; and providing advice.
- *Engaging in trading activities.* Banks underwrite stock and bond issues, make investments, and perform risk management activities such as issuing derivative securities. In certain instances, they carry inventories of financial instruments.

Traditional Industry Fundamentals

The multinational money center segment of the industry, which was consistently unattractive during the decade 1985–94, remains unattractive as of early 1995. The median returns on equity (ROEs) of companies in this industry for the five-year periods ending in 1988 and 1994 were 5.9 percent and 10.2 percent, respectively. Losses on LDCs and commercial real estate loans were a major cause of these mediocre ROEs.

The performance of the regional banking industry was somewhat better, with median ROEs of 11.8 percent and 14.0 percent for the five-year periods ending in 1988 and 1994, respectively. The performance of this industry segment improved from below the all-industries median to slightly above it during this period.

The industry fundamentals that are shared by money center banks and major regional banks can be summarized as follows:

Barriers to Entry

The nature of the banking activities has an effect on barriers to entry. Other financial institutions have entered the fields of industrial and commercial lending and credit card services, as relatively low-risk extensions of their traditional businesses. Barriers to entry into other types of banking activities are high. Capital requirements for full-service retail banking are high. Regulatory conditions must be met. Only if a bank is able to establish and maintain a favorable reputation will it be able to build the large, strong, and consistent customer base it needs. An extensive branch network is required, in order to attract a high level of deposits and provide a market for consumer and business lending.

Bargaining Power

Banks' bargaining power with large customers is relatively high due to the long-established business relationships that are characteristic of the industry. However, bargaining power with the large number of small customers who make up the consumer market is low. Banking services for these customers have become commodities, and the key factors in establishing customer preference have become location and convenience. One of the the traditional mainstays of relationships with customers, friendly personal service, has declined in importance now that small customers' main contacts with banks take place increasingly through impersonal automated teller machines (ATMs).

Banks have two major suppliers of money: large lenders and depositors. Large banks with strong financial positions and good credit ratings have relatively high bargaining power with the large lenders, from whom they can obtain funds on relatively favorable terms and conditions. Their bargaining power with depositors is based almost entirely on the interest rates they are able to offer. Since most deposits are protected by federal deposit insurance, depositors do not have to be concerned about the financial health of the institution to which they entrust their funds. (Incidentally, this circumstance shows that governmental regulation has a distorting effect—no matter how justified it may be in a larger context—in that it places financially weak companies on an equal competitive basis with stronger ones.)

Substitutes

While there are no direct substitutes for banking services, many of the services that banks provide, including financing, credit cards, and investment services, are also provided by a large number of substitute providers. There include finance companies, factors, stockbrokers, and merchant banks.

Industry Life Cycle

Banking can be regarded as a mature industry. Internal rivalry is intense. The rate of market growth varies from product to product, and according to the geographic area of operation. Industrial, commercial, and consumer lending have slow underlying growth trends but are also cyclical. The demand for banking services in general is growing slowly but has some cyclical components, including credit card use.

Some products, such as trade in derivative securities, are still in the growth phase, as are markets for banking services in general, in developing countries.

Fixed Costs

Banking is a high-fixed-cost business. The organization and its entire infrastructure must be available and ready to provide services regardless of the level of customer activity. Many banking functions, in addition, require high levels of skill. Operating costs, excluding interest payments, consume about 60 percent of the total revenue dollar. Cyclicality of earnings is a result, because of declining lending opportunities and rising loan defaults in periods of economic weakness. (Another cause of cyclicality is the spread between the cost of borrowing and the lending rate, depending on the difference between short- and long-term rates.)

The automation of transactions with retail customers by way of automated teller machines (ATMs) has increased the fixed-cost component of the business. An ATM system, once installed, can handle an increasing number of units and transactions at very low additional cost. Therefore it has very high economies of scale.

Barriers to Exit

Withdrawing from the industry by selling out is relatively easy. The banking industry, in fact, is rapidly rationalizing through its high rate of acquisitions, in a scenario typical of a mature industry. Acquisition is particularly attractive under two circumstances: when the branch structures of banks overlap, so that the additional business can be handled by one office, and when the acquisition will broaden the acquiring bank's geographic market and/or broaden the range of services which it can provide.

Governmental Regulations

The U.S. banking industry is heavily regulated both by the federal government and by individual states. Federal regulators set and monitor reserve requirements, and various state laws limit interstate banking activities. The Glass-Steagall Act, which was enacted by the U.S. Congress in 1935, separated investment banking and stock brokerage from commercial banking. The original intention of this act was to curb the speculative excesses of banks which take deposits, and what it offered in exchange was federal deposit insurance. This was necessary to restore public confidence in the industry which had been severely shaken by the bank failures of the early 1930s.

The various provisions of the Glass-Steagall Act, including interest rate ceilings, have been dismantled on a piecemeal basis. Reinterpretation of the act, beginning in the mid-1980s, has enabled banks to enter such fields as underwriting and futures trading, albeit on a limited basis. Glass-Steagall still maintains a substantial wall between commercial and investment banking, but a significant overlap now exists between investment banks and brokerage houses that engage in underwriting and trading activities.

Commercial banking must be regarded as an unattractive segment of the industry. This conclusion is based on the following structural elements, which are specific to this segment of the industry.

Commercial Lending

The volume of commercial and business lending, the traditional bread-and-butter business of commercial banking, has been flat for about a decade. Commercial banks have become more selective about credit risks, both because of their loan loss experiences in the 1980s and the early 1990s and because of increased regulatory surveillance. A cyclical downturn in loan demand due to economic developments has only made things worse. Corporations have become much more efficient in their management of working capital, lowering their traditional need for operating loans. Thus, one of the main activities of the commercial banks has been migrating toward the securities industry. There has been a diverse range of new entrants into commercial lending, including finance companies and even stockbrokers, such as Merrill Lynch.[1] Since there are no regulatory constraints on such activity, these companies regard the extension of operating loans to selected clients not only as an opportunity for growth but as a way of reinforcing relationships with important customers.

Substitutes

The level of deposits, the source of "cheap" money upon which banks have long depended, has been falling. Other investment instruments, such as mutual funds and treasury bills, are readily available to an increasingly sophisticated consumer market. The share of financial assets held by depository institutions has fallen from two-thirds of the U.S. total in the mid-1940s to one-third today.

Foreign Competition

Foreign banks, particularly European banks, have entered the U.S. market in increasing numbers, using the business provided by U.S. subsidiaries of their national companies as a base.

Domestic Competition

Fee-for-services revenue in the banking industry tends to be consistent and to entail only low risks, while not requiring an increase in a bank's capital base. Thus new entrants have been attracted to this area, creating a highly competitive atmosphere. Price cutting has developed.[2]

The industry structure of commercial banking is further complicated by its adaptation to provision of services via technological innovations. These services include basic banking through ATMs and consumer loan arrangements that may be ordered on the telephone. ATMs already account for about 75 percent of cash-dispensing transactions.[3] Technological developments have allowed banks to significantly extend the range of customer services they offer, and to do it at a low cost per transaction and without expanding their expensive branch networks. A proliferation of ATMs has resulted. It is almost inevitable that the eventual result will be an overbuilt and underutilized ATM network, which will lead to dilution of the advantages of efficiency.

Consideration of the overall situation of commercial banks leads to the conclusion that there are built-in constraints upon these banks' room for growth in domestic markets, due to the slow growth and increasing competition in their traditional core businesses.

Earnings Performance

Banks, like companies in all other industries, experience significant differences in earnings performance. The variables upon which earnings depend in banking may be described as follows:

- The *spread* or *margin* between the interest rates at which a bank borrows and the interest rates at which it can lend. The spread in turn is a function of the nature of the suppliers of funds upon which the bank relies and the direction of interest rate movement.
- The bank's *opportunities to lend and provide services.* For any given bank, these opportunities are determined by the geographic area in which it operates, the product mix it provides, and the lending risks it is willing to take.

• The *quality of judgments* made by the bank's officers in lending and trading operations. These judgments determine the level of loan losses incurred and the positions held by the bank's own accounts in currencies, bonds, and other securities.

• The *size and cost of the organization and infrastructure* necessary to accommodate customers' needs and to define the size of the market the bank can serve.

Basis of Competitive Advantage

Competitive advantage in the banking industry can be pursued in two ways, which are determined by the industry's characteristics. First, a bank may obtain competitive advantage by achieving low costs through economies of scale and by providing a wide range of services, the costs of which can be shared by the organization and its infrastructure. Differentiation is based on reputation, a high level of customer service, and convenience. This usually requires that the geographic area of operation be relatively concentrated so as to minimize the need to duplicate support facilities.

Second, a bank may choose to focus its activities in a limited range of services in which it develops a high level of skill and expertise and a reputation for superior performance. Since the range of services is limited, high market share with its economies of scale must be obtained together with large geographic markets, often global.

Strategic Responses

The strategic responses of the commercial banks to industry developments have had three basic thrusts: a broadening of the geographic area of operation, the rationalization of the structure and services offered, and the improvement of internal efficiency by "reengineering" operations.

The broadening of the geographic areas of operation has been a result of the relaxation of interstate banking restraints at both the federal and the state levels. This has led to the creation of large "super-regional" banks through mergers and acquisitions. A total of 1,422 bank mergers took place between 1986 and late 1994. This provided the new units to achieve significant economies of scale, particularly in the retail sector, as it spread the high fixed costs of the business over a larger customer base.[4]

Inherent in the economic logic of these mergers was the rationalization of operations to reduce duplication and overlaps. The action of First

Union Corp. provides an example of the impact of rationalization. Over the 10-year period 1985–94, this company purchased 31 banks in Florida, acquiring a total of 900 branches. By closing 442 of the branches, it boosted deposits per branch by 60 percent and doubled loans per branch, thus achieving a fivefold increase in net income.

Rationalization is also occurring in the range of services being offered. After a rush to get into all the areas of services which the relaxation of regulations made possible, many banks are withdrawing from crowded areas such as mortgage banking and corporate trust services.

Because of the need to reduce costs while improving the quality of service, banks have undertaken a fundamental rethinking and redesign of their business processes. This reengineering process has already yielded dramatic results for some banks. Fleet Financial Inc. has simplified its organization by cutting layers of management, simplifying record keeping, and centralizing services on the branch level.[5] The generally accepted target in the industry is to improve the overhead efficiency ratio (noninterest expenses divided by total revenues) to below 60 percent.

Investment banks have also sought growth. Their efforts have been concentrated in two areas: development of foreign markets and aggressive entry into fast-growing activities such as derivatives trading.

Prospects of Future Changes

As of early 1995, the question of whether to repeal or significantly amend the Glass-Steagall Act was under consideration by congressional committees. This political development, if it occurs, will have a significant effect on the future of the banking industry. Constraints on the activities of commercial banks will be eliminated or substantially reduced. These banks will then be able to offer a much broader range of products, possibly including insurance, mutual funds, and derivatives trading. Investment banks likewise will have broader possibilities, as their access to commercial banking activities will be less restricted or unrestricted. The implications for investors will be examined below.

In Conclusion

The banking industry in the United States has become unattractive. Barriers to entry have fallen and will likely continue to fall, as the lines are blurring between the various components of the financial services industry: banks, thrift institutions, brokers, and lease and finance companies. Bank services have become commoditized, and as a result the industry has lost bargaining power with its customers. Some of the industry's major suppliers, its depositors, have gained bargaining power as a result of having available other forms of short-term, liquid investment opportunities. Further, the domestic market is expected to remain relatively flat, intensifying competition for market share. The banking industry is overbuilt, a situation which is typical of an industry that has grown in a relatively protected, regulated environment.

Decisions about investment in the banking industry can no longer be based on expected earnings in the industry as a whole. The level of economic activity and cyclical developments in interest rate spreads are no longer reliably predictive of expected earnings in this industry. Earnings now depend more on the competitive advantage of the individual companies. Though a sharp improvement in industry and company ROEs occurred in 1993–94, it is not likely to be sustainable. In part, the improvement reflects a favorable spread between low short-term and high long-term interest rates. Other factors are the general economic recovery, which has led to a higher demand for loans, and a slowdown in the write-off of bad loans. These developments are tending to mask the structural deterioration of the banks' core business.

COMPANY PERFORMANCE

The banks selected for review here represent different types of banking operations and different geographic areas of operation. Bankers Trust New York Corporation, State Street Boston Corporation, and J.P. Morgan & Company, Inc., can be considered investment banks, in that they offer a limited range of services to specific markets. BankAmerica Corporation, Fleet Financial Group, and Citicorp are primarily commercial banks, providing a broader range of services to either domestic or foreign markets, or both.

Differences in the scopes of operations of these companies, together with developments in the banking industry, have led to differences in performance, as shown in Exhibit 12–1. The overall improvement in the performance of the banks in the latest 12 months shown in the exhibit, as indicated by an increase in the median ROE, must be interpreted cautiously. A similar increase was shown in 1988, but performance in the subsequent five years was dismal. Cyclical economic reasons and the need to write off the lending excesses of the previous years were the causes of this poor performance.

E X H I B I T   12–1

Key Performance Statistics for Selected Companies in the Banking
Industry, 1990–94

Company	Return on Equity, %		Return on Capital, %	Profit Margin, %
	5-Year Average	Latest 12 Months	Latest 12 Months	
Bankers Trust NY	22.0	17.4	9.1	10.5
State Street Boston	19.1	18.0	16.9	11.4
J.P. Morgan	18.7	14.4	10.3	12.0
BankAmerica	15.2	13.0	8.3	13.0
Fleet Financial	9.4	15.9	11.1	13.2
Citicorp	5.8	24.8	13.3	9.1
Medians:*				
1994	12.1	16.0	12.0	13.2
1988	8.8	14.7	NA	6.5

*Medians are an average of the multinational and regional bank classifications.
Note: NA = not available.

Brief reviews of the nature of operations in each of the six companies selected for analysis in this chapter follow. The more specialized
investment banks, State Street Boston, Bankers Trust NY, and J.P.
Morgan, which have been among the best long-term performers, will be
described first, followed by the commercial banks.

State Street Boston This is the most specialized of the companies
reviewed in this chapter. It obtains 60 percent of its revenue by providing financial services to mutual funds, pension funds, banks, and individual trust customers. These services, which include the custody and
clearance of securities, shareholder accounting, transaction processing,
and investment management, are performed by 13 domestic and 16 over-
seas offices. State Street Boston does engage in lending, mainly commercial. However, its lending activities are usually on a short-term, col-
lateralized basis.

In early 1995, the company will complete the acquisition of
Investors Fiduciary Trust Co., reinforcing its position in the financial services business. State Street Boston has been aggressive in technologically strengthening the accounting and information exchange capability
upon which its core business is heavily dependent.

Bankers Trust NY This company provides commercial banking services to industrial, commercial, financial institution, and government clients, and to high-net-worth individuals. Its investment portfolio is about two-thirds domestic and one-third foreign. It has traditionally been a strong performer as the result of its concentration on an elite market. Recently, it has entered into the trading of equity derivatives and sovereign bonds, as well as into fee-based activities such as securities underwriting and loan and lease syndication.

Though the company has gained a leading position in derivatives trading, it is being sued by a number of clients (including Procter & Gamble) who have incurred heavy losses and claim that they were not advised of the nature of the risks that they were incurring.[6] These lawsuits do not threaten the survival of the company, but they do damage its reputation and may limit its growth in an important area of new business.

J.P. Morgan Like Bankers Trust, J.P. Morgan operates in an "elite" market, providing financial services to corporations, government clients, financial institutions, and individuals with a net worth in excess of $5 million. Its products include financial advice and the execution of transactions, underwriting, trading, and investment services as well as trust, agency, and operating services. Its portfolio is one-third domestic and two-thirds foreign.

J.P. Morgan has been a leader in giving priority to investment banking and global activities. Constrained by regulation at home, it originally developed underwriting and capital market expertise in Europe. Now able to use this expertise at home, it holds ninth place among U.S. bond and stock underwriters.[7] Again like Bankers Trust, J.P. Morgan has also been aggressive in its entry into derivatives trading.[8] About three-quarters of its current revenue is provided by trading, underwriting, and investment management activities, and only one-quarter by interest income on loans. This product mix, with its emphasis on high-growth activities, has provided the company with a strong ROE performance but has tended to make its earnings unpredictable.

BankAmerica[9] Offering a diverse range of financial products to corporations and government agencies, BankAmerica operates in 18 states through subsidiary companies. It also operates in a total of 42 states in the consumer financing business through its 1992 acquisition of Security Pacific Corp. Its portfolio is about 50 percent consumer loans and 8 percent foreign commercial and industrial loans. In recent years it took heavy losses on its commercial real estate portfolio, by selling most of it at 35 to 70 percent of face value.

In 1994, the company acquired the Chicago-based Continental Bank Corp. The large corporate account base of this acquisition broadened BankAmerica's mainly western state geographic base. BankAmerica's recent acquisitions have been made at high prices. When the costs of combining operations are added in, these acquisitions may weigh down the company's ROE for some time.

Fleet Financial Fleet Financial is a combination of Norstar Bankcorp Inc. and the original Fleet plus the Bank of New England, which was acquired in 1991. This company operates through 800 branch offices in Maine, Massachusetts, New Hampshire, Rhode Island, Connecticut, and New York. Its areas are mortgage banking, asset-based lending, leasing, consumer finance, and investment management.

Fleet Financial represents a new breed of aggressive banks that are pursuing regional dominance through acquisition. It has embarked on a cost-cutting program with the objective of improving its efficiency ratio (noninterest expenses divided by revenues) from 67 percent of revenues in 1993 to less than the generally accepted industry standard of 60 percent.

Citicorp[10] Citicorp, the largest commercial bank in the United States, also has the most diverse product mix, making it a "full-service" bank. It is involved in commercial banking and trust activities, mortgage banking, consumer finance, investment brokerage, credit card services, equipment leasing, and factoring. It also issues travelers' checks and various payment instruments.

While Citicorp's domestic operations are concentrated in New York State (it has 218 branches), the company is also well represented in Europe, with 303 branches in Germany alone. It has the largest number of foreign banking licenses of any U.S. bank. Its portfolio is about 60 percent consumer (of which 57 percent is domestic and 43 percent foreign) and 40 percent commercial (41 percent domestic, 59 percent foreign). It is therefore the most diverse, geographically and in product mix, of the U.S. banks.

Citicorp is moving cautiously into investment banking activities, offering services only to its existing clients and gradually building up its capability. However, the size of its customer base still puts it into thirteenth place in U.S. stock and bond underwriting. Citicorp has strong representation in emerging nations but has been implicated in various financial scandals in India and elsewhere. Its historic ROE has been seriously affected by losses on real estate, LBOs, and LDC loans.

While the company has embarked on a drastic cost-cutting effort, it is not yet clear whether all its loan problems have been worked out. The scope of its operations, both with regard to geography and product mix, makes Citicorp an inherently high-cost operation.

In Conclusion

The basic strategic thrusts of the companies described above are fairly clear.

State Street Boston is pursuing a specialized market segment. Strengthening its position in client financial services, which are fee-based and less cyclical than lending, provides the company with an opportunity to exert some bargaining power over less price-sensitive customers. The company is enhancing the skills necessary to serve this market and is also making an acquisition which will improve its economies of scale.

By emphasizing investment banking and derivatives trading, both Bankers Trust and J.P. Morgan are concentrating on market segments with high growth and high profit margins. These banks get economies of scale by concentrating on large customers, both corporate and individual. Their rationalization is that most transactions take approximately the same amounts of time and effort, and that large transactions therefore are more profitable. However, derivatives trading is a relatively new product which will soon mature, making it a more competitive business. Bankers Trust and J.P. Morgan may be affected by the large-scale entry of commercial banks into investment banking. Price wars may ensue as the various banks battle for market share, which is considered to be very important by the industry.

BankAmerica and Fleet Financial are pursuing stronger positions in commercial lending and retail banking by making acquisitions. The broader geographic coverage that these banks are creating with their enlarged branch structures has a number of advantages, as follows:

- Money, in the form of deposits, which is gathered over a wide area can then be loaned out where the best opportunities exist.
- Branch networks can be used to sell a wide range of services at relatively low incremental cost. By providing convenient access to customers, the banks gain bargaining power.
- A large and geographically dispersed branch structure can be efficiently managed by using standardized procedures, centralized electronic communications, and a data processing network.

Canadian banks, which provide national coverage, have demonstrated the opportunities for major economies of scale as well as improved efficiency that are afforded by such a branch structure. This approach may offset the lower margins that are developing in the United States because of the price war in services. In addition, BankAmerica has shown that the pursuit of size is also necessary to success in global operations.

Citicorp is pursuing both product and geographic diversity, in an attempt to be all things to all people. It is also placing heavy emphasis on development of its foreign business. A relatively low five-year average ROE reflects the serious loan losses suffered by the company in the 1980s, whereas an improved ROE in the latest 12 months shown in Exhibit 12–1 reflects its strong foreign business and improved internal efficiency.

THE INVESTOR'S PERSPECTIVE

First the past market performance of the six banks described above will be reviewed. Next the current industry structure will be assessed. Finally the competitive advantage of each company will be described, and likely candidates for long-term investment will be selected.

The Market's Judgment

Exhibit 12–2 shows the stock market performance of our six selected banks for the period 1984–94. In general, the six banks have followed the S&P 500, but only two of them, State Street Boston and J.P. Morgan, both relatively focused operations, have consistently outperformed the market. These results are not surprising in light of the difficulties which the industry has faced.

Industry Structure and Competitive Advantage

A significant unknown factor that affects any assessment of the banking industry at present is the fate of the Glass-Steagall Act. The implications of changes to the act on the status of banks as investment candidates can be shown in part by the arguments for and against its abolition.

Most companies operating in the industry are vociferous in their advocacy of repeal of the act. Their arguments contend that broadening the business base of banks would lower risks to taxpayers by lowering

EXHIBIT 12-2

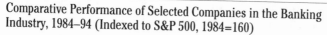

Comparative Performance of Selected Companies in the Banking
Industry, 1984–94 (Indexed to S&P 500, 1984=160)

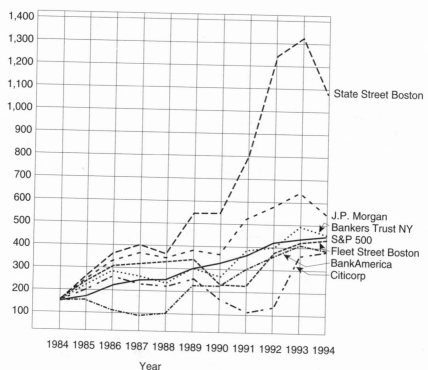

Year

Note: The index for each year is shown at the mean between the high and the low for the period.

deposit insurance claims. If the act were abolished, they argue, banks
would be allowed to pursue growth in a variety of areas such as consumer
finance, mutual funds, and insurance products, rather than by engaging in
the looser loan practices that lead inevitably to losses. (This, be it noted,
is a rather curious argument, as it suggests that banks need to be given an
incentive for avoiding bad management practices.)

Many parties have specific interests that would be served by abolition of the act. Investment banks, for instance, would presumably become
eligible for low-cost loans from the Federal Reserve in times of liquidity
crunches. Insurance companies see the banks as offering an efficient distribution system for their products—a system that would replace their
own costly networks of insurance agents.[11]

Arguments against repeal of the act assert that if commercial banks were allowed to engage in investment banking activity, their risks would be compounded. They would be exposed to trading losses of the type that brought down Barings PLC and placed Lehman Brothers Inc. and Kidder, Peabody & Co. in such dire straits that their respective parent companies had to bail them out.[12]

There is general agreement that trading leads to an increased likelihood of high risks, much as lending does. The proponents of repeal of the act acknowledge the validity of this point. They propose to require segregation of the bank's capital and its securities units, to prevent trading losses from spreading to the banking system.

The enthusiasm of the banking industry in the 1990s about the possibility of less restrictive competition is reminiscent of the airlines industry's eager advocacy of deregulation in the late 1970s. All banks see the opportunities, but few if any of them realize the destructive potential of an intensification of competition within the industry. Bank services have already become commoditized, and the removal of barriers to entry would intensify competition in virtually every activity. High fixed costs would require banks to pursue their shares of a slowly growing market even more avidly. As in the case of the airlines industry, deregulation would likely accelerate rationalization and force a significant restructuring of the industry, making it less attractive for a considerable time. The superior performers in the long term will be the companies that can either establish strong competitive advantage in a broad market or exploit specialized niches. (This is not an argument against competition; I am only pointing out that, while competition is healthy for the economy as a whole, intense competition does not usually create an attractive environment for the long-term investor. This applies particularly to the type of competition which ensues from a discontinuity such as deregulation).

Assessment of Five Banking Companies

In view of the current and potential industry situation, a bank's competitive advantage must be primarily derived from whatever bargaining power it can establish with buyers and from economies of scale. Bargaining power can be based on the superior capability and skills necessary to provide specialized services and/or on possession of the branch structure necessary to conveniently serve a large market. Economies of scale can be achieved through marketing as well as by establishing standardized procedures for effectively controlling a large, geographically dispersed branch structure. Sustaining competitive advantage means holding a position in a market niche and/or making it difficult for competitors to imitate a successful infrastructure. In light of the competitive situation and the relatively slow growth of demand, room for growth requires that a company be able to increase its share of the domestic market and/or to take advantage of global opportunities.

Assessments of the selected companies are summarized in Exhibit 12–3.

Overall, the banking industry must be classified as unattractive. Its future is subject to continuing uncertainty because of possible deregulation and also because of the confusion arising from the adoption of new technology. Long-term investment candidates in such a situation must be able to compensate for questionable industry circumstances with a high degree of competitive advantage. In the banking industry, competitive advantage must be based primarily on bargaining power with buyers, superior capability, and/or operating cost advantages. Also necessary will be room for growth in an industry in which domestic growth will likely be slow and competition for market share fierce.

The basic difficulty in selecting long-term investments in the banking industry is that it is in a state of transition. The traditional lines between the various types of financial institutions are becoming blurred. Many banks will continue to diversify into a wide range of other services, such as insurance, which they will not always understand. As a result, selection of companies for investment must be based on their possession of a well-defined and focused strategy that can give them competitive advantage. On this basis, I consider two companies to be the most likely candidates for long-term investment. These companies are State Street Boston and J.P. Morgan.

State Street Boston is focused on a specialized range of services. The company is strengthening its ability to serve these areas and has room to grow in both domestic and global markets.

J.P. Morgan, which serves an elite market, has demonstrated its capability in investment banking. It has the financial strength and global reach necessary to play this game. While its earnings have tended to be unpredictable, the stock market appears to recognize the inherent strength of this company, so that the stock price has not been volatile. While the company has a staid image, it does a relatively small number of things very well. Bankers Trust is a somewhat similar company, but J.P. Morgan is preferred on the basis of its strength in investment banking, its lower

Assessment of Selected Companies in the Banking Industry as Long-Term Investment Candidates (As of March 31, 1995)

State Street Boston

Market Price, March 31, 1995: 31 7/8   P/E Ratio: 12.0
52-Week Range: 43 1/8-27 5/8

Competitive Strength

Strong. This company is pursuing a focused strategy by concentrating on a well-defined market segment in which it is reinforcing its position with an acquisition and improving its capability. It is experiencing overall growth in securities transactions both domestically and in global markets, where it is well represented. Because of the nature of its business, State Street Boston usually has continuing relationships with customers. The nature of its markets and services make its revenue and earnings less cyclical than that of banks that are dependent on loan business; it is also less vulnerable to changes in the industry. While price cutting due to other banks' entry into the fee-based services business may hurt it in the short term, its strength in this activity should allow it to expand its position.

Bankers Trust NY

Market Price, March 31, 1995: 52 1/8   P/E Ratio: 7.3
52-Week Range: 74-49 3/4

Competitive Strength

Marginal to strong based on established position in an elite market. The company's reputation, however, has been tarnished by what may have been an overly aggressive pursuit of derivatives trading business. Its room for growth may be diminished by the maturing of the derivatives business and the entry of commercial banks into the underwriting business. As a long-term investment candidate, Bankers Trust NY suffers in relation to the main candidate in this segment of the industry, J.P. Morgan. Bankers Trust NY's P/E ratio may reflect market concern over litigation, but even a worst-case outcome does not threaten the viability of the company.

J.P. Morgan

Market Price, March 31, 1995: 61   P/E Ratio: 10.1
52-Week Range: 67 1/8-55 1/8

Competitive Strength

Strong, on the basis of an established position in the elite market. J.P. Morgan has skills and experience in the high-growth investment banking sector, as well as a strong financial position (an AAA rating), along with less reliance on derivatives and trading than Bankers Trust. Concentration on a relatively small number of large customers enables J.P. Morgan to have an efficiency ratio of 58.6 percent.* A strong global position provides it with room for growth. Its P/E ratio does not appear to unduly discount either the company's potential or the industry's cyclicality.

Exhibit 11–3, *Concluded*

BankAmerica

Market Price, March 31, 1995: 48 1/4   P/E Ratio: 9.0
52-Week Range: 50 1/4-38 3/8

Competitive Strength

Strong. BankAmerica has traditionally been a relatively strong ROE performer and is moving toward becoming a national bank with an extensive retail branch network. The high cost of necessary acquisitions may weigh on its ROE in the intermediate term. Its future profitability will depend heavily on how effectively it can integrate the various parts into an effective whole to take advantage of the full potential of its position. Room for growth is provided by an increase in domestic market share. The company has sufficient global presence to expand in that area. Its extensive branch network would be expensive to imitate, providing significant sustainability. However, it will have to weather the confusion in the industry in the intermediate term.

Fleet Financial

Market Price, March 31, 1995: 32 3/8   P/E Ratio: 8.6
52-Week Range: 41 3/8-29 7/8

Competitive Strength

Marginal but with potential for improvement. While the overall strategic initiative of the rationalization of the industry is a move in the right direction, this company has not yet demonstrated the ability to integrate its parts into an effective whole. It remains dependent on the economy of its region and will likely be highly cyclical. Fleet Financial's basic strategy may make it a winner in the long term, but investors would do better to wait until the company demonstrates the ability to implement its potential effectively.

Citicorp

Market Price, March 31, 1995: 42 5/8   P/E Ratio: 6.0
52-Week Range: 47 3/4-36 1/4

Competitive Strength

Marginal to strong. Citicorp's diverse product and geographic base has proved difficult to manage, making this company a chronic underachiever. Some of its problems are being cleared up, but the durability of its turnaround remains to be proved. Its domestic business, particularly in services, will remain intensely competitive. Its strength in global markets provides room for growth, and the company has shown impressive growth in Europe.[†] Operations in LDCs have been shown to create control problems. The company's P/E ratio indicates that the market remains wary because of its past problems.

*J.P. Morgan's efficiency ratio was taken from Matthew Schifrin, "Chase Manhattan's Unsung Turnaround," Forbes, October 25, 1993, pp. 141–146.

[†]Information on Citibank's global situation was taken from Richard C. Morais, "Citi uber Alles," Forbes, January 17, 1994, p. 150.

dependence on derivatives trading, its greater financial strength, and its stronger global position.

Two other companies, BankAmerica and Citicorp, present somewhat higher risk but are also worth consideration by the more aggressive investor. BankAmerica is developing the geographic spread and branch structure to be effective in full-service banking, with potential economies of scale. It is likely to find room for growth by increasing its share of the domestic market, while maintaining its global representation. Its future, however, will be heavily dependent upon its ability to take advantage of its size and geographic coverage.

The investor who is interested in Citicorp must make several assumptions: that the company will be able to maintain its domestic position, that it will be able to exploit its strength in foreign markets, and that it will be able to stay out of trouble. The investor must also feel confident that the company has overcome its past operating problems.

There are other prospects for investment in the banking industry. *Forbes* lists 53 regional banks. The investor who is interested in this industry should choose some of these regional banks for evaluation. As always, both the industry situation and the company's competitive advantage should be considered.

POINTS TO REMEMBER

The mature banking industry, which has long been the core of the financial services business, has become somewhat unattractive. Banking services have become commodities, and creeping deregulation has enabled other financial services to encroach on the banks' traditional areas of operation. Furthermore, the industry is in an overbuilt condition which is creating severe internal competition. The future may bring significant further deregulation, possibly including repeal of the Glass-Steagall Act. The transition to use of highly cost-effective technology is creating further turmoil, as well as a risk of market saturation.

In the context of this unsettled and unattractive industry situation, a candidate for long-term investment must have well-defined competitive advantage. For a bank, the primary basis of competitive advantage must be an ability to establish bargaining power with customers. Such bargaining power may be achieved either by demonstrating superior capabilities in specific, limited markets, or by providing customers with convenient access to bank services in a broad market. If a bank wants to serve a broad market, it must have the infrastructure to take advantage of economies of scale.

To sustain its competitive advantage, a bank must have room for growth, either by increasing its share of the domestic market or by taking advantage of global markets; some banks are able to do both.

NOTES

1. Mike McNamee, Geoffrey Smith, John Meehan, and Karen Thurston, "Jumping into the Credit Gaps," *Business Week*, October 19, 1992, pp. 94–95.

2. Kelley Holland, "Banking on Fees," *Business Week*, January 18, 1993, pp. 72–74; and Kelley Holland with Richard A. Melcher, "Twilight of a Banking Bonanza," *Business Week*, October 17, 1994, pp. 218–219.

3. Robert Lennzer and Philippe Mao, "Banking Pops Up in the Strangest Places," *Forbes*, April 10, 1995, pp. 72–76.

4. Kelley Holland with Mike McNamee, "It's a Bank-Eat-Bank World," *Business Week*, January 11, 1993, p. 101; Kelley Holland and David Greising with Amy Barrett, "The Big Banks Set Out to Branch Out in Earnest," *Business Week*, May 2, 1994, p. 120: Mathew Schifrin, "Next Down the Aisle?" *Forbes*, November 22, 1993, pp. 78–80; and Terence P. Pare, "The New Merger Boom," *Fortune*, November 28, 1994, pp. 95–106.

5. Geoffrey Smith, "Fleet's Can-Do Spirit: We Can Do Without," *Business Week*, March 21, 1994, pp. 106–07.

6. Kelley Holland with Gary Schiller, "Did Procter & Gamble Play with Fire?" *Business Week*, April 25, 1994, p. 38; and Kelley Holland with Michael Schroeder, "A Lingering Black Eye at Bankers Trust," *Business Week*, November 14, 1994, p. 42.

7. Richard D. Hylton, "Can Banks Make It on Wall Street?" *Fortune*, October 31, 1994, pp. 199–202.

8. Carol J. Loomis, "The Risk that Won't Go Away," *Fortune*, March 7, 1994, pp. 40–56.

9. The discussion of developments at BankAmerica is based in part on: Russell Mitchell with Richard A. Melcher, "'Dick Rosenberg's Manifest Destiny'," *Business Week*, February 14, 1994, p. 31; and Richard D. Hylton, "Go Where the Money Is," *Fortune*, March 21, 1994, p. 70.

10. The discussion of developments at Citicorp based in part on Carol J. Loomis, "Citicorp's World of Troubles," *Fortune*, January 14, 1991, pp. 90–98; Carol J. Loomis, "The Reed that Citicorp Leans On," *Fortune*, July 12, 1993, pp. 90–93; Pete Engardio and Shekhar Hattangadi, "Citibank's 'Taj Mahal' May Be Crumbling," *Business Week*, October 26, 1992, pp. 76–78; and Mathew Schifrin, "The Wizard of Citi," *Forbes*, March 13, 1995, pp. 44–48.

11. The arguments in favor of repeal are taken in part from Amy Barrett and Dean Foust, "It's Time to Guillotine Glass-Steagall," *Business Week*, March 13, 1995, p. 33.

12. The arguments against repeal are taken in part from Allan Sloan, "Helping Banks Lose Their Bearings," *Newsweek*, March 13, 1995, p. 51.

VI

OVERVIEW AND UPDATE

A set of concepts has been outlined in this book, and a method for conducting strategic analysis has been described and illustrated with copious examples. On the basis of these concepts and this methodology, candidates for long-term investment can be identified and evaluated, and investment decisions can be made. Many examples of actual industry and company situations have been used to illustrate the process of strategic analysis and to demonstrate its relevance. In keeping with the long-term perspective of this book, I have used a statistical database which is updated annually. Data derived from this database have been used to evaluate many companies and to recommend a number of them for consideration as long-term investment candidates.

The monitoring of investments is an essential follow-up to the analytical processes that culminate in the choice of one or more companies for investment—companies that appear to be able to outperform the market in the long term. *Monitoring*, which can be a fascinating exercise in itself, is the process in which the investor "plays detective," so to speak, by checking on whether the assumptions underlying the original investment decisions remain valid. (See Chapter 8 for a detailed description of the process of monitoring.)

The basic analytical concepts of strategic analysis are reviewed, to refresh the reader's memory, in "Strategic Analysis: A Review," the first major section of Chapter 13. The final text section, "Updates," examines recent developments in selected companies and industries—a few of the many that were discussed earlier in the book. These developments occurred after March 31, 1995 (the latest date as of which long-term investment candidates were evaluated earlier in the book), and took place in a wide range of contexts: economic, political, social, and technological. This examination of recent developments provides an example of the monitoring process.

13

OVERVIEW AND UPDATE

STRATEGIC ANALYSIS: A REVIEW

An investor whose technical knowledge of the stock market is limited or nonexistent may initially feel unqualified to perform a process so seemingly mysterious as analyzing a company's strategy. The term *strategic analysis* has an interesting—and intimidating—mystique. The origin of the word *strategic* is the ancient Greek term *strategein,* meaning "maneuver" or "general," which was used in military contexts. In modern times, the uses of the term *strategic* have been extended to a wide range of contexts, ranging from technical designations for basic survival techniques (in the insect world, for instance), to loose descriptions of the sophisticated—or sometimes not so sophisticated—ways in which consumer goods are advertised in the media. In the context of investments, *strategic* seems to hint at some sort of black magic involving esoteric maneuvers or calculations that are forever beyond the ken of the ordinary investor. The term *analysis,* which also originated in ancient Greece—it comes from *analyein,* meaning to break up or loosen—is not much better. Its scientific connotations appear to remove it too from the realm of everyday activity.

My hope is that my readers no longer feel intimidated by strategic analysis. The concepts explained and illustrated in this book reveal that the average investor can readily use strategic analysis in a rational and systematic way to evaluate the implications of industry and company situations.

Far from being a corporate version of black magic, the strategy of a business is a practical combination of industry conditions and corporate capability. Though corporate managers have long understood the concepts of industry structure and competitive advantage, as well as the implications of change, the world of investors has lagged in applying these concepts to securities analysis.

The main hypothesis of strategic analysis is that the long-term earnings potential of a company rests upon two primary factors: first, the nature of the industry, which determines the overall profitability of the companies that are operating in it, and second, the strategy of the company itself, which determines its performance relative to its competitors' performance.

Following, for handy reference, are summaries of the concepts and reasoning that underlie strategic analysis.

Company Performance

The performance of any company being considered as a long-term investment is derived from a combination of two factors: (1) the characteristics of the industry in which it is operating, which determines whether the company has room to make a profit, and (2) the company's own actions, which determine its performance relative to that of competitors.

ROE

The performance of both an industry and a company can be measured by their respective returns on equity (ROEs). ROE has been shown to bear a close relationship to the market value of a stock. High-ROE industries, as shown in stock price indexes, consistently outperform the broad market; the same is true of companies with ROEs that outperform their industries. It follows that the stock of a company with a continuing high ROE will outperform the broad market.

Industry Attractiveness

The would-be investor's first task is to determine why some industries outperform others and why some companies outperform their competi-

tors. The overall profitability, or attractiveness, of an industry is determined by a combination of five variables: (1) the barriers to entry into the
industry, (2) the threat posed by substitutes, (3) the industry's bargaining
power with suppliers, (4) its bargaining power with customers, and (5) the
intensity of internal competition. The fifth variable, the intensity of internal competition, is dependent in turn on the rate of market growth, the
cost structure of the industry, and the barriers to exit.

Competitive Advantage

The performance of a company in its industry, regardless of the industry's
attractiveness, is dependent on the extent to which its strategy can provide
sustainable competitive advantage along with room for growth.
Competitive advantage can be derived from a combination of superior
capability and/or positioning in a comparatively less competitive segment
of the market. A company can find room for growth by concentrating on
growing markets, entering new markets, and/or increasing market share.

Effects of Change

While the investor's analysis of an industry and a company provide an
explanation of its a company's past and current performance, whether this
performance can be expected to continue is a matter of judgment. If the
industry is expected to remain relatively stable, this judgment can be
based primarily on two factors: (1) the company's ability to sustain its
competitive advantage and (2) its room for growth. However, it is often
the case that change is expected. The nature and magnitude of the change
and how it may affect the industry and company must be estimated.
Change may be caused by economic, social, political, and technological
influences. Its potential effects can be determined by judging how it may
change the industry structure and the company's basis of competitive
advantage. The assessment of change involves determining whether it is
occurring as part of a cycle or trend, or whether it should be categorized
as a discontinuity.

The Investment Decision

To make a long-term investment decision, the investor must weigh the
combination of industry and company performance, to determine what
results the combination can be expected to provide. A company's performance potential, as supplied by the extent and sustainability of its competitive advantage, is the more important of these two factors. A conser-

vative investor may base the decision on the expectation of strong long-term performance by the company. A more aggressive investor may decide to rely on the expectation of a favorable change in an industry in which a company with competitive strength can thrive.

Monitoring

The monitoring of an investment requires, at the outset, keeping track of events and developments that can affect the industry. However, it is usually even more important to keep abreast of company developments and to assess how the company's actions and priorities affect its competitive advantage.

The overall approach outlined above can be applied in two ways, as pointed out in Chapter 2. First, it can be used to enhance the fundamentalist and value investment schools of thought. These approaches depend heavily on extrapolations of past results and/or on assumptions about a company's performance potential based on its current financial position. Strategic analysis can add greater depth to these established methods.

The second, and simpler, way to apply the method of strategic analysis is predicated on a recognition that estimates of future earnings are highly uncertain at best. Thus no attempt is made to quantify these expectations; rather, the analyst assumes that a company that is operating in a sound industry and that has strong or decisive and sustainable competitive advantage will outperform its competitors and the market as a whole, in the long term. In this approach, it is also necessary to make judgments about the extent to which the potential of the company is being discounted by the price/earnings (P/E) ratio of the stock. This is the approach that has been used throughout this book in identifying candidates for long-term investment.

THE EXTERNAL ENVIRONMENT: A REVIEW

It would be difficult to overestimate the potential effects of changes in the external environment on the quality of specific investment opportunities and the mood of the stock market as a whole (see Chapter 6). The long-term investor must stay abreast of national and worldwide developments that are likely to have far-reaching effects on the stock market as a whole and on specific investments. In effect, these changes too must be monitored.

The external forces for change that must be monitored are economic, political, social, and technological in nature.

Economic Developments

In mid-1995, economists were locked in debate about the current stage of the economic cycle and whether it would end in a hard or a soft landing. The nature of the debate was confirming the old adage, "If all the economists in the world were laid end to end, they would not reach a conclusion." Though economic cycles occur regularly and should not be of concern to the long-term investor except in timing the purchase of stocks that are clearly cyclical, certain elements of the mid-1995 economic situation should be recognized by the long-term investor.

First, as of mid-1995, the value of both the deutsche mark and the Japanese yen had risen sharply against the U.S. dollar. (This was widely reported by the press as the "collapse" of the U.S. dollar.) While such corrections usually overshoot their mark, there is evidence that the role of the U.S. dollar as a global reserve currency is diminishing because it is overweighed in relation to the United States' share of world economic activity. Further, the persistence of the U.S. balance-of-payments deficit and concerns about the level of U.S. foreign debt suggest that some portion of the 1995 decline in the value of the dollar may be longer-lasting. Such a development would be favorable to exporting industries and to companies that derive a significant portion of their earnings from activity in foreign markets in which earnings in local currencies will have a favorable exchange rate when converted to dollars.

Second, the duration of the economic recovery has come into doubt. Though cycles do recur, it cannot be assumed that they will repeat past patterns, because the underlying reasons for their recurrence may differ (see Chapter 6). The character of markets will continue to change due to demographic changes, but there is also evidence that, because of the weakening of traditional job security, consumer attitudes may be evolving toward a more cautious stance. Thus both the recovery from the recession of the early 1990s and subsequent developments may well present a picture that differs from past patterns.

Political Developments

The election of a Republican majority to the U.S. Congress in November 1994 set in motion a further round of deregulation and a generally more favorable attitude toward business. The likely results include a relaxation of many regulations, less vigorous enforcement, and the devolution of authority toward the state level. Many such measures enjoy bipartisan support and are considered likely to endure. However, both investors and political commentators tend to extrapolate current developments. The forecasts of such gurus must be treated with caution, because political developments rarely evolve in a linear progression. Rather, they tend to swing back and forth, like a pendulum.

Social Developments

Though the primary causes of social change are usually demographic, there is increasing evidence of profound changes in consumer values, due to increasing and widespread distrust of both business and government. Specifically, many of the activities that have traditionally been entrusted to others are now being done by consumers for themselves. They are making their own transportation arrangements, rebuilding their houses with their own tools, running their own businesses, and planning their own finances. It has been estimated that the value of time spent on do-it-yourself activities, if paid to others instead, would amount to 40 percent of the U.S. GDP.[1] The many beneficiaries of this trend include "category-buster" merchandisers, warehouse clubs, do-it-yourself building suppliers, manufacturers of light trucks and utility vehicles, suppliers of computer software, and even discount stockbrokers. Charles Schwab & Co., Inc., for instance, offers software for use in direct entry of stock orders from home computers.

Technological Developments

Both the news media and investor interest have been dominated by developments in computer and communications technology. In particular, the rapid development of such on-line services as the Worldwide Web and the Internet for computer communications has caught the public's imagination. In Chapter 6 it was pointed out that the effects of new technology are almost always overestimated in the short term but underestimated in the long term. On-line computer services are no exception. The situation is chaotic, and the Internet in particular has been often misused, to such an extent that the possibility of its being regulated has been raised. It is already becoming saturated with information, despite its relatively small number of users. This situation is typical of the emerging phase which as was suggested in Chapter 4, should be avoided by the long-term investor.

The cost of electronic technology continues to fall at a rapid rate, with the result that its various markets are being broadened. For example, the proliferation of cellular telephones has changed the basis of interpersonal communications and probably increased the rate of traffic accidents. As technology becomes cheaper, its providers are having to change their strategic priorities. This necessity has been recognized by microcomputer producers such as Dell, which established a special relationship with its customers by focusing on service. Dell's approach is being imitated in other sectors. For example, Computer Associates International Inc. gave away the first 1 million copies of its Smart Money accounting program software, thereby establishing a customer base and the basis for favorable word-of-mouth advertising, along with the expectation that customers will buy upgrades and related programs.[2] This approach is not new. King Gillette gave each U.S. soldier embarking for Europe in 1917 one of his newly developed safety razors, thereby establishing a continuing market for replacement blades.

The lesson for the long-term investor continues to be that the technology area is volatile and requires extreme caution. Profits do not necessarily accrue for the developer of the better mousetrap itself; rather, it is the exterminator who uses the mousetrap to satisfy a customer need which wins out in the long run.

UPDATES

Day-to-day developments in the business world are well covered by the media, and thus easy to follow. Developments of long-term significance must also be monitored and evaluated (see Chapter 8 and Appendix B).

Many industries and many companies have been analyzed in previous chapters of this book. Five sample industries, and selected companies within them, were used to illustrate a range of attractiveness, from the profitable pharmaceuticals industry to the money-losing airlines industry. The sources of competitive advantage for companies in a broad spectrum of industries were also described. These companies were chosen because their different performance records illustrated varieties of competitive advantage. Finally, four industries, and selected companies within them, were subjected to intensive scrutiny.

IMPLICATIONS OF RECENT DEVELOPMENTS

Numerous developments of long-term significance took place in the first half of 1995. Many of the companies and industries that have already been analyzed will be affected by these events.

Five Sample Industries

Recent developments in the pharmaceuticals industry, the tobacco industry, the drug and discount retailing industry, the recreational products manufacturing industry, and the airlines industry have had a variety of differing impacts on companies in these industries.

Pharmaceuticals Industry This already attractive industry has been assisted by recent developments and is likely to receive further boosts from proposals that are still pending. Specifically:

- The threat of health care reforms which might squeeze the industry's profitability has temporarily receded as the result of the election of a Republican-controlled U.S. Congress. However, the question of health care reform continues to smolder as costs continue to inflate, and may well be reignited as a major public issue in the future.

- Introduction of regulatory reforms by the U.S. Food and Drug Administration (FDA) is likely to sharply reduce the time and cost of bringing new pharmaceuticals products to the market.[3] The downside of the new drug approval procedures will be some degree of reduction of barriers to entry into the industry, though only narrow market niches will be thus opened up.

- Proposed tort reform would sharply limit product liability damages for all companies, and particularly for companies in the pharmaceuticals industry.

Meanwhile, the rationalization of the pharmaceuticals industry continues. A number of major takeovers have been completed, and others are obviously being planned. Merck remains a strong long-term investment candidate because of its overall competitive advantage. Pfizer's status as an investment candidate is enhanced by its pursuit of a focused research-based strategy; this company will be a major beneficiary of the streamlined regulatory approval processes.

Tobacco Industry The tobacco industry also may benefit from the new Republican Congress, which is sympathetic to its needs and may forestall proposed regulatory initiatives, such as declaring tobacco a drug. However, the main arena for this industry has moved from the legislature to the courts. The industry has demonstrated its influence with politicians by successfully lobbying the Florida state legislature to repeal an adverse law. This law was the basis for the state's lawsuit against the industry to recover Medicaid costs of treating smokers, and its repeal is still subject to the veto of the governor.

The industry is still threatened by anti-smoking bylaws, which are under municipal jurisdiction. Action such as New York's bylaw against smoking in restaurants continues to flourish. Further, the industry's efforts to enlist new smokers among black youth, once a prime market toward which new brands were directed, is floundering because of a lack of effective role models. Smoking among black youth has declined to one-half its rate among white youth.

Recent events confirm tobacco's status as a declining industry. Tobacco companies continue to face high risks of catastrophic legal damages. The seriousness of this threat is indicated by the withdrawal of many suppliers to the industry, which are seeking to reduce their risk of being implicated in successful damage suits.[4]

Drug and Discount Retailing Industry Though recent developments are not affecting the overall stability of the drug and discount retailing industry, a new trend toward warehouse clubs is gaining momentum, as consumer values change. Sam's Club, a subsidiary of Wal-Mart, is the No. 1 operator in this segment of the industry. It has recently acquired the 91 Pace clubs from Kmart and is still struggling to integrate the new acquisition. Even so, it is a major beneficiary of the trend toward warehouse clubs. Together with Price/Costco Inc., in fact, it controls over 90 percent of the warehouse club market.

Recreational Products Manufacturing Industry The trend toward increased do-it-yourself activities may divert time from recreational activities, and a continuation of the current lower level of consumer confidence could inhibit spending on discretionary purchases. Though these developments remain speculative in mid-1995, their potential for causing deterioration in the attractiveness of this industry should be taken into account by investors. Increasingly, long-term investment decisions must be based on the circumstances and competitive advantage of specific companies in this diverse industry. In this context, Fleetwood may be said to retain its relatively favorable position, because its potential depends more on demographic factors than on consumer values.

Airlines Industry While many of the companies in the domestic airlines industry have returned to profitability as the result of a combination of cost cutting and economic recovery, there has been no change in the fundamental unattractiveness of the industry. Many of the gains from cost cutting continue to be dissipated by fare wars. Barriers to entry remain low.

The woes of the industry are illustrated by the experience of one new entrant, ValuJet Airlines Inc., which is a clone of Southwest that was started up in 1994. Cloning is typical of industries with low barriers to entry, in which successful strategies can be easily imitated. ValuJet flies to 24 cities. It has 29 planes, used DC-9s which it acquired for only $5.2 million each. The combination of used aircraft, ticketless flying, and low wages (achieved by contracting nonpilot employees from a temporary service agency) has enabled the company to set fares at low levels. The low fares have attracted so many customers that ValuJet achieved 75 percent capacity utilization and earned a profit in its second month of operation.

Accompanying this success, however, is the threat of unionization, which has forced the company to pay higher wages. A tightening market for used aircraft has increased prices to the point that ValuJet is having trouble meeting its growth requirements. The relative ease of entry and the effectiveness of this company's strategy virtually guarantee additional competition, keeping the industry unattractive. Even so, investors have seen ValuJet's stock rise from $6.25 at initial issue in 1994 to $27.50 in mid-1995, with a highly optimistic P/E ratio of 26. This company's stock offers to speculators the possibility of significant gains but is hardly of interest to long-term investors.[5]

Another example of the relative ease with which strategic initiatives may be imitated in this industry is offered by United Airlines' new Shuttle service, operating in the heart of Southwest's California market. This service is winning passengers and is a major factor in Southwest's recent profit decline.[6] While United is not likely to earn a profit on this service for some time, its persistence and Southwest's need to match its offers to customers, so as to minimize its own loss of revenue, are indicative of the woes of the industry.

As pointed out in Chapter 5, a necessary strategic move for the major U.S. airlines is the establishment of strategic alliances with foreign airlines, so as to cross-feed traffic and share capacity. One such alliance, between Northwest Airlines Inc. and KLM Royal Dutch Airlines is showing the potential of such a move. The arrangement, triggered by KLM's purchase of a 20 percent stake in Northwest and made possible by an exemption from antitrust action, has resulted in a sharp reduction in costs and an increase in capacity utilization. Both airlines have returned to profitability.[7] This success will likely lead to further rationalization of the industry. Probably only seven or eight international airlines will survive in the long term.

Despite this and other strategic successes, the airlines industry remains one to be avoided by the long-term investor. As *Fortune* magazine commented; "Chaos may just be the nature of the business."[8]

Selected Company Developments

In Chapters 3 to 6, a number of companies were used as examples in the examination of the implications of industry circumstances and the effectiveness of their respective strategies. These companies were evaluated as long-term investment candidates in Chapter 7. The monitoring of investments requires following developments and interpreting their implications to assure that the assumptions underlying the original investment decision remain valid. The principles of monitoring were discussed in Chapter 8.

In order to further illustrate the monitoring process, this section will examine recent developments affecting three companies which were discussed earlier in the book: Boeing, General Mills, and Inco.

Boeing   Boeing was selected in Chapter 7 as a long-term investment candidate because its technological strength and large customer base gave it competitive advantage and because its industry was expected to strengthen due to a combination of market growth and a forthcoming replacement cycle. In early 1995, Boeing won a major 35-plane order from Scandinavian Airlines System (SAS) for its new 737-600, beating out McDonnell Douglas Corp.'s proposed MD-95. However, to do this, it had to slash its price by one-third of the $35 million per plane originally asked.[9]

Strategically, this may have been a good move on two counts. It may have blocked or at least significantly delayed the launch of a major competing product, and it may ultimately be a factor in McDonnell Douglas's withdrawal from the manufacture of civil airliners despite the very high barriers to exit. If the MD-95 does not proceed, Boeing should more than recover its immediate price sacrifice in the long term, through additional orders. This recovery would make a large contribution to profits, as it would overabsorb the fixed development costs. In the short term, profitability on the order will depend on Boeing's ability to significantly reduce its manufacturing costs even beyond announced objectives and programs.

The squeeze on airline profits is therefore being transferred backward to the plane makers, where the basis for success has expanded beyond the traditional aircraft development capability into the ability to manufacture airplanes cheaply without sacrificing quality. Boeing obviously faces weak earnings for several years. Given the market's preoccupation with short-term earnings, this prospect may knock down its stock price somewhat. It may be preferable for the long-term investor to defer an investment decision. However, this company's size and product range still make it a relatively attractive long-term investment prospect.

General Mills The competitive advantage and strong ROE performance of General Mills are derived from the strength of its brands and the effectiveness of its new product development efforts. The company has also expanded into the food service industry. Its Red Lobster and Olive Garden chains now provide about 35 percent of sales revenues.

The company intends to divide the food service and restaurant businesses into separate companies in a share-for-share split, so that each can pursue its respective endeavors aggressively. General Mills will also force the restaurant business, which is to be named Darden Restaurants, Inc., to raise its own capital. For years, the growth of the restaurant business has absorbed one-half of General Mills's capital spending while providing only one-quarter of operating profits.[10] Of the company's two industries, food processing is the more attractive, with a five-year average median ROE of 15.4 percent as compared to 13.8 percent for restaurant chains.

The food-processing operation should benefit substantially from the additional management attention and capital that will be made available to it. While the company's success in introducing new products has lagged in the past few years, such flat spots are not unusual over the long term and it has recovered market share in cereals. This strategic separation significantly enhances the status of General Mills as a long-term investment candidate.

Inco The competitive advantage of this company has been based on its control of vast, scarce ore reserves which make it a relatively low-cost producer. While the situation in the former USSR (see Chapter 6) is depressing nickel prices, the opinion expressed in Chapter 7 was that after this discontinuity ran its course, Inco had the potential to become a good long-term investment prospect. Quite surprisingly, during 1995, a nickel discovery at Voisey Bay in the Labrador region of Newfoundland, which was explored by Diamondfields Resources Ltd., has been found to be a very large, high-grade deposit. This discovery could add significant supplies to the market at a very low cost of production.

While it will be 3 to 5 years before production is available from this new site, the combination of this additional supply with the supply expected to become available from the Russion mines after they are eventually rehabilitated dims the potential for consistantly higher nickel prices. The threat posed by Voisey Bay has not been lost on Inco management, which paid a total of about $475 million for a 30 percent interest in the new discovery and obtained an agreement to market its output. This investment, though it is costly, hedges to a considerable extent the risk to Inco posed by this new entrant to the industry. In the inevitable periods of cyclical oversupply of nickel, Inco will be forced to cut its own production to a greater extent than before, but the effect on its earnings will be offset to some extent by the Voisey Bay contribution. Though the implications for Inco's earnings will not be known until the Voisey Bay profit potential has been determined, knowledgeable industry analysts are predicting very high earnings. If these predictions prove to be accurate, Inco may even come out ahead on these developments, leaving its status as a long-term investment candidate unchanged.[11]

Comprehensive Industry Studies

Four industries were examined comprehensively in Chapters 9 to 12. Some of the automobile, computer, forest products, and banking companies that operate in these industries were evaluated as candidates for long-term investment. The implications of recent industry developments are reviewed below.

Automobile Industry The first half of 1995 saw three major developments in the automobile industry (which was examined in Chapter 9). First, there was a slowdown in auto sales; this is a normal cyclical development, though the timing of such slowdowns is often unpredictable. This slowdown is of concern to traders who follow short-term earnings prospects but should not worry long-term investors.

Second, Kirk Kerkorian announced a takeover bid of $20.5 billion for the 90 percent of Chrysler shares not owned by Chrysler. The bid was a surprise even for Kerkorian, a noted takeover artist. This takeover bid provides an opportunity to show how strategic analysis can be used to make a quick evaluation of such a situation. The arrangement would have involved the use of $5.5 billion of Chrysler's cash reserves plus $3 billion in new equity; it would also have loaded the company with $12 billion in additional debt.[12] The announced bid price of $55 per share was not surprising. Chrysler's competitive advantage in its industry, which was due to the company's low costs, product development capability, and focused strategy, verged on decisive.

However, the bid was a loser from any direction. If it had been successful even to the limited extent of providing the acquiring group with control, it would have crippled the company's competitive advantage by destroying its ability to develop new models. The conservation of cash in order to service debt would have required stretching out designs well beyond their active market life and would have preempted the investment required for new facilities. Obviously, the financial community recognized the situation; the financing to support the bid could not be raised. Had the Chrysler board succumbed to the obvious greenmail attempt and bought back Kerkorian's interest at his bid price, it would have seriously depleted its vital cash reserves. Fortunately, the board also recognized the situation and offered a buyback of only a limited number of shares at the market price prevailing at the time of the arrangement, which would not seriously deplete the company's cash.

Investors should have recognized the hopelessness of the situation and sold, to take advantage of the initial market surge which carried the stock price up to $49. Then they should have bought back when the failure of the bid became obvious and a management response that would not hurt the company in the long term was announced. This tactic would have temporarily transformed the long-term investor into a trader. However, when a situation is as clear as it was in this case, trading is desirable.

What I am calling the third major 1995 development in the auto industry actually began in 1994, when GM's results improved so much that the company returned to profitability. Since then, several optimistic articles have predicted a rosy future for GM.[13] It is certainly true that the company is making considerable progress. Its factories are being overhauled to improve productivity and flexibility, the product development process is being revamped, and quality standards are being improved.

However, GM still has a long way to go. Its product lines need pruning, and a coherent image needs to be developed for each item in its range of overlapping brands. As part of a pruning effort, GM announced in May 1995 that it would terminate production of large rear-wheel-drive cars and would convert the plants that had been manufacturing these cars to the production of trucks. This move, incidentally, will allow Ford room to maintain profitable production of large cars. While the market for these cars is declining, substantial residual demand from the police and taxi markets remains. Ford is the logical survivor in this market, because it did not fragment its output into as many brands as GM produced.

GM has other troubles as well. Its product launch of the 1995 Chevrolet Cavalier and Pontiac Sunbird revealed its continuing difficulties. Assembly problems at its Lordstown, Ohio, plant restricted output to 60 percent of capacity for more than 6 months, creating a shortage of product and damaging the momentum of the product launch advertising program. It tried to do too much in starting the production of a new model with 30 percent less labor while imposing higher quality standards.[14] GM's progress in improving operations remains slow. Its traditional problems remain: militant unions and obstacles to greater disaggregation due to the physical integration of component manufacturing with operations.

GM's competitive advantage is still marginal. It is at best making only slow progress toward improving its position—an improvement which is necessary before it can be considered a long-term investment candidate.

Computer Industry The computer industry in mid-1995 continues to be unattractive to long-term investors. According to the analysis in Chapter 10, it was characterized as being in the late part of the transition stage, moving from the growth stage to the maturity stage of the product life cycle. It was continuing to rationalize and was subject to severe price wars. Market growth remained strong because of the influx of new products and the strength of the home market.

In another change typical of the transition phase, power has shifted to distributors, with the result that the industry is squeezed between suppliers and buyers. Nevertheless, two companies, Compaq and Hewlett-Packard, are still worth consideration by the aggressive investor. Each of these companies enjoys a competitive advantage based on new product development capability and low costs.

The volatility of the industry was demonstrated by Packard Bell Electronics, Inc.'s seizure of the volume lead in home personal computers (PCs) from Compaq in early 1995, which dropped IBM to third place. Packard Bell was able to take the lead by virtue of its low costs, the rapid incorporation of new technology into its products, and the strong relationship that it has developed with dealers.[15]

Compaq's vulnerability in the home and laptop computer markets contrasts with its primary strength in desktop PCs and network servers to the business market. To recover, the company is adopting a new strategy for the lower-end market. It will stress brand name, competitive pricing, and distribution, but will back off from providing the costly leading-edge technological features that, its marketers have decided, are not a primary priority for the home market. It will outsource its low-end products to Taiwanese subcontractors, to obtain low costs and a sufficient supply of product to avoid the shortages that have caused problems in the past.[16] An important aspect of this development is that management is taking aggressive action to head off a problem before it loses further ground in the market, even though the strategy itself is not without risks.

A further complication in the home PC market is the entry of Hewlett-Packard, which expects to be able to take advantage of its brand name to attain its objective of becoming one of the top three in the market. Like Compaq, Hewlett-Packard is breaking with tradition by contracting out some of its subsystems.[17]

These developments are indicative of how competitive the fast-growing home market will continue to be. For companies such as Compaq and Hewlett-Packard, in which the home market is supplementary to business markets, it will continue to be relatively profitable. However, the home PC market can present a serious problem for companies that depend on it as a major source of income.

It also poses continuing problems for IBM, which will drop to fourth place if Hewlett-Packard achieves its goal. One of the key elements of IBM's strategy is an attempt to gain bargaining power over Microsoft, one of its suppliers. Development of the OS/2 operating system was an aspect of this strategy. Despite Microsoft's delays in making its Windows 95 available, IBM's attempt is floundering. Microsoft's hold on the market is proving to be very strong. Customers are apparently willing to wait out the delay. IBM's software sales revenue grew by only 2 percent in the first three-quarters of 1994, as compared to Microsoft's 27 percent.[18] IBM has mounted a sales push on the senior executive level and has already started to discount the OS/2.[19] The optimism expressed by some journalists and investors about IBM's ability to recover an industry leadership position is likely premature.

Forest Products Industry Consistently unattractive in the past (see Chapter 11), the forest products industry showed a strong cyclical recovery through the first half of 1995 in the various paper sectors. Shortages of supply are particularly acute in newsprint, where prices rose 64 percent between mid-1994 and mid-1995, surpassing the previous peak, which was set in 1988. As the industry is showing some constraint in planning capacity increases, there will likely be a floor under the inevitable future price declines, meaning that these declines will be well above the previous lows.

In responding to the price and supply squeeze faced by newspaper publishers, Rupert Murdoch announced that all the newspapers in his News Corp. Ltd. stable would be available in electronic form in several years.[20] At worst, however, electronic newspapers present an extremely long-term threat to the paper industry. Only a major technological and cultural leap on the part of the market will significantly replace the paper product.

One sector of the paper industry that is likely to show consistent long-term strength is heavy papers and packaging, because of the global growth of demand from manufacturing and because of the displacement of paperboard packaging by corrugated boxes in many applications (see Chapter 11). Chesapeake Corporation was listed in Chapter 11 as a long-term investment candidate on the basis of its strength in this sector—in particular, because of its ability to provide value-added products with high profit margins.

The largest U.S. producer in this industry, Stone Container, was disqualified in Chapter 11 because of its very high debt. Further, Stone's management has shown a tendency to use the cash and borrowing power generated in previous cyclical upturns to expand aggressively by making acquisitions at very high prices. In the past, this strategy has made the company vulnerable in the ensuing downturns. Stone probably survived the last downturn only because its debt was too high for the bankers to call. However, there are indications that the company's strategy has changed and that the high levels of cash being generated in the current cycle will be used to repair the balance sheet.[21] If this proves to be the case, Stone's strong position in an industry that is becoming more consistently attractive may eventually be considered as a long-term investment candidate by the aggressive investor.

Banking Industry   The banking industry is unattractive because it is undergoing change from two directions: from the politically based transition to deregulation and from the technologically based way in which it delivers its services (see Chapter 12). Politically, the probabilities are increasing that the Glass-Steagall Act will be significantly reformed by the end of 1996.[22] Technological advances are changing the cost structure of the industry. In such circumstances, a candidate for long-term investment must have either strong-to-decisive competitive advantage (derived from a combination of size and geographic scope of operation) or the ability to provide specialized services to an established customer base.

In addition, banks are being influenced by a phenomenon that may be called shareholder activism, which has also affected other industries. Apparently, present-day shareholders are less likely to accept the traditional belief that company performance is more a function of the economic cycle than of management skill. Certainly, company strategy—which is shaped by management—plays a larger role in an era in which competition is less constrained by regulation than in the past. Managers are being forced into mergers or are undertaking them in order to improve performance.[23] Thus activism appears to be accelerating the rationalization of the industry.

Shareholder activism has also influenced another change in banks' behavior. In the past, banks loosened their lending criteria and made increasingly risky loans in the strong parts of the earnings cycle. The losses on these loans showed up in the economic downturn. In recent years, under pressure to improve performance, banks have been tending to use excess capital to buy back shares, a move that increases shareholder equity and does not create a bad loan risk.[24] However, this tendency may be transient. If the Glass-Steagall Act is repealed, banks will need to conserve their capital so that they will be able to enter other activities, such as dealing in securities and making acquisitions in the insurance and securities industries.

These developments do not change my conclusions in Chapter 12 about the lack of attractiveness of the banking industry nor about qualities of the companies within it. State Street Boston and J.P. Morgan are still the most likely candidates for long-term investment.

THE INVESTOR'S PERSPECTIVE

Recent developments have pointed up the truth of certain generalizations concerning the relationship between companies, the stock market, and investors.

The Stock Market's Judgment

The market tends to punish a company for weak past performance by being skeptical about the durability of its present recovery. The stock of a company that has had problems will tend to sell at a low P/E ratio in relation to the stock of its competitors, even when the company begins to show earnings strength. The stock market records of Chrysler and Citibank are examples (see Chapters 9 and 12).

The astute long-term investor can use strategic analysis to take advantage of this tendency. If analysis of a company shows that it has adopted a sound new strategy which has given it sustainable competitive advantage, its stock may offer good value for the long-term investor. The same is true of a company that shows, upon analysis, that it has resolved the problems that caused weak past performance.

Shareholder Value

Pressure on management to provide high immediate stock prices, or what has sometimes been dubbed *shareholder value*, has long been intense. As shareholder activism comes into play, the intensity of this pressure may continue to increase. Companies whose stock is selling at P/E ratios lower than the industry average are particularly under pressure to achieve higher short-term stock prices. Chrysler and companies in the banking industry have been much affected by these pressures (see Chapters 9 and 12).

Under pressure from shareholders, management may make the mistake of focusing on short-term measures that will be counterproductive in the long term. The long-term investor should make a distinction between counterproductive short-term measures and corrective strategic action that will enhance the company's performance in the long term.

Exaggerated Press Reports

Optimistic press reports and commentaries on a company's recovery should be greeted with skepticism by the long-term investor. Developments in old favorites and high-profile news makers, such as GM and IBM, are particularly likely to be reported in a favorable light. Reporters usually turn to the company press contacts they already know when they need perspective on a story. Executives and publicity departments are eager to provide favorable news on their company, and to back it up with so-called facts.

The long-term investor should avoid any temptation to accept an optimistic report at face value, and instead should conduct an objective investigation and evaluation of the underlying facts.

Total Portfolio Performance

There is no foolproof way to choose long-term investments that will outperform the overall market. Uncertainty prevails. The information available is often vague. Assumptions and judgment calls must be made. The environment changes frequently and sometimes unpredictably. Even an investment that has been made on the systematic, reasoned basis described in this book may prove disappointing.

The performance of the total portfolio is what counts. If the initial analysis is sound and if subsequent developments are conscientiously monitored, significant losses should be rare. The presence of only a few large winners in the total portfolio should offset the losses.

The Independent Investor

The investor should keep in mind that only a limited number of industries and companies have been analyzed in this book. These examples were chosen from the *Forbes* database for their usefulness in illustrating the concepts of strategic analysis, not because they are the only prospects or the best prospects. In fact, they constitute only a small portion of the investment candidates available. Only the major companies are included in the *Forbes* annual survey, which covers over 1,300 companies in more than 70 industry classifications. Besides these major companies, a multitude of possible candidates can be evaluated through statistical analysis. The long-term investor can use the evaluation methods described in this book to make many independent and profitable investment decisions.

POINTS TO REMEMBER

This chapter can be used as a model for the continuous monitoring activity that enables an investor to keep up with developments that affect investments and to interpret the significance of these events. The developments that must be monitored are the ones that have strategic implications for the long term. Events of only day-to-day significance should be ignored. Not only company and industry developments must be monitored, but also political and global events.

In the brief span of the first six months of 1995, it was necessary to consider the effects of many news items upon the limited number of companies and industries that have been evaluated in this book. The environment in which a company operates can change quickly—and when the environment changes, the company must cope with it in a timely fashion.

As the result of discoveries made in monitoring developments, the investor may upgrade some companies as long-term investment candidates and downgrade others. In this chapter, for instance, General Mills was upgraded, Boeing was downgraded slightly, and Inco remained unchanged. I altered my previous evaluations of General Mills and Boeing because of the strategic actions which the companies are undertaking. The nickel mining industry faced a discontinuity which would have had an adverse impact on Inco, but the company's strategic action has hedged the threat.

NOTES

1. Alex Taylor III, "Why Every Red-Blooded Consumer Owns a Truck . . .," *Fortune,* May 29, 1995, pp. 87–100.

2. Neil Gross and Peter Coy with Otis Port, "The Technology Paradox," *Business Week,* March 6, 1995, pp. 76–84.

3. John Carey, "The FDA: No Heroic Measures Required," *Business Week,* April 24, 1995, p. 40.

4. Maria Mallory, "For Reynolds, Where There's Smokeless," *Business Week,* March 27, 1995, p. 39.

5. David Greising, "Growing Pains at ValuJet," *Business Week,* May 15, 1995, pp. 50–52.

6. Susan Chandler with Eric Schine, "Not Bad, for a Dumb Idea," *Business Week,* February 20, 1995, p. 40.

7. Stewart Toy, Susan Chandler, Robert Neff, and Margaret Dawson, "Flying High," *Business Week,* February 27, 1995, pp. 90–91.

8. Timothy K. Smith, "Why Air Travel Doesn't Work," *Fortune,* April 3, 1995, pp. 42–56.

9. Howard Banks, "Moment of Truth," *Forbes,* May 22, 1995, pp. 51–62.

10. Greg Burns, "Has General Mills Had Its Wheaties?" *Business Week,* May 8, 1995, pp. 68-69; and Richard Phalon, "Amicable Divorce," *Forbes,* May 8, 1995, pp. 70–74.

11. Conclusions on Inco are based on discussions with Michael J. H. Brown, managing director and mining analyst, Deutsche Bank Securities Canada Ltd.

12. David Woodruff with Jeffrey M. Laderman, Leah Nathans Spiro, Kathleen Kerwin, and James B. Treece, "Target Chrysler," *Business Week,* April 24, 1995, pp. 34–38.

13. An example is Alex Taylor III, "GM: Some Gain, Much Pain," *Fortune,* May 29, 1995, pp. 78–84.

14. Jerry Flint, "No Pain, No Gain," *Forbes,* April 24, 1995, pp. 116-18.

15. Larry Armstrong, "More Red Meat, Please," *Business Week,* May 22, 1995, pp. 132–34.

16. Peter Burrows, "Where Compaq's Kingdom Is Weak," *Business Week,* May 8, 1995, pp. 98–102.

17. Robert Hoff with Peter Burrows, "Hewlett-Packard Heads for Home," *Business Week,* May 8, 1995, p. 102; David Kirkpatrick, "Hewlett-Packard: The Next PC Power," *Fortune,* May 1, 1995, pp. 20–21.

18. Stratford Sherman, "Big Blue Shows Signs of Life," *Fortune,* February 6, 1995, p. 16.

19. Amy Cortese, "Gerstner Goes Into Warp Drive," *Business Week,* April 24, 1995, p. 6.

20. Reuters News Agency, "Murdoch Begs for Paper," *Globe and Mail,* May 20, 1995, p. B3.

21. Matthew Schifrin, "Back from the Brink and Ready to Roll," *Forbes,* February 13, 1995, pp. 110–14.

22. Kelley Holland, Leah Nathans Spiro, and Phillip Zweig, "Waiting for the Glass-Steagall to Shatter," *Business Week,* March 27, 1995, pp. 166–67.

23. Robert Lenzner with Philippe Mao, "Banking Pops Up in the Strangest Places," *Forbes,* April 10, 1995, pp. 72–76.

24. Kelley Holland, "Attack of the Killer Investors," *Business Week,* April 24, 1995, p. 72.

Performance Statistics for American Industry

Key performance statistics for over 1,300 companies in more than 70 industry classifications are presented in this appendix. *Forbes* magazine compiles these industry classifications in 21 industry groups for purposes of its annually updated survey. The table shown here is reprinted from the January 2, 1995, issue. *Forbes* performance statistics are used in analysis of industry performance throughout this book.

Industry (Number of Companies)	Profitability					Growth						Sales	Net Income	Profit Margin
	Return on Equity			Return on Capital	Debt/ Capital %	Sales			Earnings per Share					
	Rank	5-Year Average %	Latest 12 Mos %	Latest 12 Mos %		Rank	5-year Average %	Latest 12 Mos %	Rank	5-Year Average %	Latest 12 Mos %	Latest 12 Mos $Mil	Latest 12 Mos $Mil	Latest 12 Mos %
Health (74)	1	17.3	17.9	13.4	24.2	1	12.7	8.1	1	9.5	16.5	1,921	72	5.8
Drugs (22)		22.8	20.5	16.2	16.5		12.7	8.1		14.3	14.3	6,274	403	8.3
Health care services (32)		18.6	17.6	11.0	32.1		23.6	13.0		10.8	22.3	1,237	51	4.0
Medical supplies (20)		14.9	14.8	12.5	24.2		9.5	3.1		-5.4	6.0	970	69	6.2
Consumer nondurables (58)	2	16.9	16.1	11.5	26.5	4	8.0	5.2	7	-11.5	3.0	1,136	51	5.0
Personal products (23)		16.9	19.0	14.2	21.6		7.8	5.1		-14.3	7.7	1,224	59	6.4
Apparel and shoes (20)		17.8	16.1	12.0	24.6		10.2	8.5		11.1	8.9	742	45	5.3
Textiles (9)		9.2	11.5	8.4	38.0		3.9	4.0		NM	-26.9	1,060	25	3.6
Photography and toys (6)		14.8	12.0	8.4	32.7		11.7	2.3		NM	-14.9	2,481	137	4.2
Food, drink, and tobacco (69)	3	15.9	14.1	10.6	38.1	7	6.4	4.3	6	-8.7	1.7	1,644	61	3.3
Food processors (47)		15.4	15.1	11.0	38.1		5.5	5.0		-4.7	3.3	1,574	47	3.1
Beverages (12)		17.1	21.1	12.4	39.9		7.9	7.0		NM	12.8	2,138	95	7.4
Tobacco (10)		18.4	2.6	4.1	37.3		6.3	-1.3		NM	-37.8	2,049	101	1.9

Industry														
Financial services (99)	4	14.5	16.0	12.3	33.1	16	3.8	4.4	3	6.8	12.0	1,837	232	13.2
Multinational banks (9)		10.2	16.0	10.2	44.2		-2.4	2.9		NM	7.7	11,599	1,289	11.7
Regional banks (53)		14.0	16.0	13.7	25.5		3.5	5.7		5.4	13.4	1,403	223	14.9
Thrift institutions (14)		6.0	12.1	8.5	12.5		-7.1	-0.2		NM	1.7	724	61	8.5
Brokerage and commodity (10)		22.4	18.4	10.2	57.2		14.1	6.3		29.8	-22.3	3,740	189	8.0
Lease and finance (13)		20.1	20.6	8.3	72.9		9.6	12.4		17.9	23.2	2,827	350	11.7
Insurance (80)	5	14.2	12.1	10.9	19.8	8	6.2	3.9	2	7.7	5.1	1,480	100	6.9
Diversified (12)		13.4	8.1	7.7	16.0		5.5	1.1		1.2	-5.0	2,644	90	5.0
Life and health (30)		14.7	13.5	12.4	23.3		6.8	4.3		10.4	14.3	1,460	145	8.6
Property and casualty (35)		13.7	11.9	10.2	20.0		6.2	6.0		8.3	2.8	1,500	75	6.5
Brokerage (3)		23.9	19.4	18.8	22.3		6.6	0.1		1.7	0.0	1,338	40	6.9
Retailing (119)	6	12.8	11.8	9.3	32.6	2	12.1	8.5	8	-13.5	9.4	1,347	28	1.9
Department stores (11)		11.6	9.5	7.6	42.7		4.0	2.9		0.4	18.1	2,779	101	3.0
Apparel (21)		14.5	11.4	9.5	19.8		12.2	6.9		-16.3	-15.1	1,284	25	2.7
Consumer electronics (10)		13.0	13.5	11.8	10.6		32.2	32.1		-7.7	26.3	2,152	17	1.2
Drug and discount (31)		12.8	12.6	9.7	42.0		7.6	7.1		NM	0.0	1,819	30	1.6
Home improvement (7)		8.6	13.9	8.5	43.5		12.6	13.8		-13.5	21.1	2,713	31	1.5
Home shopping (10)		17.9	21.4	14.5	2.6		11.5	14.9		NM	16.4	1,041	44	3.8
Specialty retailers (29)		9.6	7.2	8.4	29.9		14.5	11.1		-26.6	8.0	906	20	1.9

Industry (Number of Companies)	Profitability					Growth						Sales	Net Income	Profit Margin
	Return on Equity			Return on Capital Latest 12 Mos %	Debt/Capital %	Sales			Earnings per Share			Latest 12 Mos $Mil	Latest 12 Mos $Mil	Latest 12 Mos %
	Rank	5-Year Average %	Latest 12 Mos %			Rank	5-Year Average %	Latest 12 Mos %	Rank	5-Year Average %	Latest 12 Mos %			
Aerospace and defense (37)	7	12.7	11.3	10.2	37.3	21	-3.0	-0.8	11	-20.8	10.3	1,493	51	3.4
Entertainment and information (47)	8	12.2	14.8	13.2	28.0	9	5.3	7.0	15	NM	15.2	1,680	88	6.8
Broadcasting and cable (10)		Def	3.7	9.3	59.0		8.1	10.7		NM	-11.1	1,936	79	5.5
Movies (4)		16.5	9.8	8.9	45.6		11.7	3.6		NM	-26.8	4,077	22	2.6
Publishing (27)		12.2	15.4	13.3	25.4		3.4	5.0		-15.7	30.8	1,559	149	7.7
Advertising (6)		16.3	15.7	15.7	32.1		10.3	7.5		NM	1.0	1,747	21	2.8
Food distributors (52)	9	12.1	8.6	8.1	41.5	12	4.5	3.2	5	-4.1	10.7	1,313	24	1.2
Supermarkets and convenience (32)		11.9	8.4	7.8	50.9		3.5	0.9		-11.8	7.1	1,699	24	1.2
Food wholesalers (7)		10.1	8.7	7.7	32.0		4.1	5.1		-10.9	3.1	2,810	17	0.8
Restaurant chains (13)		13.8	14.7	12.5	20.1		5.8	5.2		11.6	18.7	1,053	59	5.3
Chemicals (57)	10	12.1	15.5	11.3	29.3	19	3.4	6.1	13	-29.6	14.8	1,381	54	5.5
Diversified (14)		8.0	15.5	12.6	31.6		0.2	3.5		-24.3	24.1	4,273	242	5.9
Specialized (43)		13.1	15.5	11.2	26.6		5.9	7.5		-35.1	14.8	1,049	52	4.9

	#													
Business services and supplies (69)	11	11.9	14.0	11.2	30.2	6	6.8	9.9	9	−15.5	15.8	984	47	3.3
Business services (25)		13.1	14.6	14.1	26.5		8.8	13.0		−13.9	20.4	1,217	53	2.8
Business supplies (28)		11.3	12.8	11.1	28.8		5.8	6.7		−8.7	15.8	783	43	3.7
Industrial services (9)		8.6	15.1*	10.2	38.3		9.5	4.9		NM	14.5	1,113	55	3.3
Environmental and waste (7)		4.8	0.2	0.4	48.3		9.4	9.8		NM	−93.5	796	0	0.1
Electric utilities (77)	12	11.5	11.7	6.2	37.3	18	3.5	3.3	4	−4.0	−0.8	1,769	147	9.8
Northeast (23)		11.1	10.4	6.0	37.3		5.3	4.6		−2.9	−3.5	1,926	166	9.4
North central (25)		11.8	11.9	6.5	37.3		2.6	2.6		−6.0	−0.8	1,605	93	9.7
Southeast (10)		12.9	12.4	6.9	35.5		3.1	3.5		1.8	−1.0	2,793	266	11.9
South central (7)		10.5	9.6	5.3	38.6		4.6	3.9		−4.0	−10.5	3,672	283	8.4
Western (12)		9.7	11.2	6.0	37.4		3.7	3.1		NM	7.0	1,483	131	9.2
Capital goods (66)	13	10.8	13.0	10.2	29.8	11	5.2	8.4	15	NM	17.6	1,138	43	4.3
Electrical equipment (15)		13.9	12.7	9.6	36.2		3.8	5.3		−27.6	9.9	1,128	58	4.4
Heavy equipment (15)		8.5	16.2	11.3	41.5		4.9	15.4		−26.0	95.6	1,746	74	4.6
Other industrial equipment (36)		11.4	12.5	10.0	25.5		6.5	8.7		NM	17.3	1,055	35	3.8
Travel (24)	14	10.7	8.3	6.5	53.8	5	7.6	7.8	15	NM	18.8	1,473	87	3.0
Airlines (11)		def	1.0	4.1	70.4		9.8	7.9		NM	66.7	7,118	7	0.7
Hotels and gaming (13)		13.4	10.9	8.1	46.5		7.0	7.7		−4.5	16.4	1,223	95	7.7

| | Profitability | | | | | Growth | | | | | | | Sales | Net Income | Profit Margin |
| | Return on Equity | | | Return on Capital Latest 12 Mos % | Debt/Capital % | Sales | | | Earnings per Share | | | | Latest 12 Mos $Mil | Latest 12 Mos $Mil | Latest 12 Mos % |
Industry (Number of Companies)	Rank	5-Year Average %	Latest 12 Mos %			Rank	5-year average %	Latest 12 Mos %	Rank	5-Year Average %	Latest 12 Mos %				
Computers and communications (101)	15	10.2	13.7	10.7	19.6	3	12.0	15.2	15	NM	31.1		1,629	101	5.5
Major systems (25)		5.6	9.9	8.5	10.6		6.1	13.1		NM	36.6		2,108	83	3.4
Peripherals and equipment (41)		13.7	18.2	15.3	17.6		15.3	24.2		7.8	51.6		1,387	79	5.5
Software (11)		16.2	6.6	7.0	1.2		17.7	7.9		NM	9.7		641	28	5.9
Telecommunications (24)		9.6	11.5	8.6	33.5		8.2	8.8		-7.9	5.9		6,582	189	7.6
Transport (30)	16	10.1	12.8	8.2	36.2	10	5.3	9.4	10	-15.5	27.6		1,843	65	3.1
Railroads (11)		8.4	19.9	8.6	34.8		0.6	5.8		NM	30.5		3,657	206	7.9
Trucking and shipping (14)		10.9	7.0	6.7	36.7		5.7	11.2		-16.2	5.7		1,082	26	1.5
Air freight (5)		10.1	12.7	10.2	44.3		8.0	15.9		-8.8	40.2		1,777	43	2.7
Energy (87)	17	9.1	8.9	6.6	39.6	13	4.5	1.1	12	-23.4	0.9		1,581	55	2.8
International oils (7)		10.6	9.1	7.3	18.3		4.5	0.0		-12.7	-9.4		54,924	1,585	3.2
Other energy (37)		5.1	5.6	5.2	43.0		2.4	-1.4		NM	-44.3		1,557	30	1.9

Industry														
Oilfield services (7)		6.0	7.9	6.6	23.6		7.2	2.0		NM	150.0	2,505	45	5.2
Gas producers and pipeliners (11)		10.6	10.3	6.5	43.1		4.3	−0.3		10.5	−7.2	1,869	88	2.7
Gas distributors (14)		10.9	11.7	7.5	41.6		4.7	3.9		0.1	6.6	1,174	49	5.3
Integrated gas (11)		9.6	9.6	6.1	38.6		5.0	0.0		−2.0	14.0	1,398	70	5.0
Consumer durables (80)	18	8.4	15.2	11.6	31.7	14	3.9	11.3	15	NM	30.4	1,769	54	3.4
Automobiles and trucks (10)		4.9	11.3	6.7	44.4		2.3	13.1		NM	58.4	54,434	241	1.6
Automotive parts (32)		9.9	16.6	12.8	27.6		3.7	12.0		−20.5	30.6	1,417	59	4.3
Appliances (13)		4.1	10.0	6.6	38.1		4.4	6.0		NM	35.9	5,181	102	2.2
Home furnishings (16)		10.1	14.0	9.6	29.2		4.9	8.3		−6.6	14.7	1,238	38	3.5
Recreation equipment (9)		7.7	15.2	12.8	24.0		5.3	17.7		NM	13.1	713	34	3.4
Forest products and packaging (37)	19	7.1	5.6	4.7	41.6	15	3.8	5.2	15	NM	13.2	1,426	32	2.6
Paper and lumber (20)		6.4	6.8	5.4	42.6		2.4	4.6		−33.0	16.1	1,959	42	2.6
Packaging (17)		9.2	4.6	4.5	41.3		5.0	6.0		NM	12.5	1,194	29	2.9
Construction (46)	20	5.9	8.4	6.2	39.1	17	3.7	10.4	14	−31.8	24.1	748	18	2.5
Commercial builders (12)		7.0	2.3	4.7	29.9		5.8	2.3		NM	−34.8	1,054	4	0.5
Residential builders (13)		10.5	11.7	8.3	43.4		7.7	26.4		NM	52.1	766	31	3.4
Cement and gypsum (7)		4.6	7.2	6.0	30.8		−2.9	9.7		−32.3	D−P	1,186	34	4.2
Other materials (14)		2.9	4.9	7.9	42.9		−2.7	7.0		−26.8	26.2	645	11	1.9

Industry (Number of Companies)	Profitability					Growth						Sales Latest 12 Mos $Mil	Net Income Latest 12 Mos $Mil	Net Profit Margin Latest 12 Mos %
	Return on Equity			Return on Capital Latest 12 Mos %	Debt/Capital %	Sales			Earnings per Share					
	Rank	5-Year Average %	Latest 12 Mos %			Rank	5-year average %	Latest 12 Mos %	Rank	5-Year Average %	Latest 12 Mos %			
Metals (44)	21	4.6	6.7	7.3	34.0	20	−2.4	7.8	15	NM	27.4	1,300	19	1.9
Steel (27)		4.6	10.7	9.2	35.2		−2.6	11.6		NM	65.1	897	17	2.2
Nonferrous metals (17)		4.3	2.6	4.6	32.0		−1.8	6.0		NM	−16.3	2,232	23	1.8
All-industries median		11.4	12.6	9.4	32.8		5.5	6.3		−18.8	11.8	1,449	60	4.3

Notes: D–P = deficit to profit. Def. = deficit. NM = not meaningful.

Source: *Forbes*, January 2, 1995, pp. 268–269. Reprinted by permission of *Forbes* Magazine © Forbes, Inc. 1995.

Sources of Information

In the field of investment, information on companies and industries is the raw material that can be welded into productive long-term investment decisions, using the analytical tools presented in this book. The quality of any investment decision is highly dependent on the quality of the inputs. Investors need accurate information for the following three purposes:

1. To screen the overall list of potential investment possibilities and identify suitable candidates for more detailed evaluation.

2. To analyze the companies and their industries in sufficient detail to make investment decisions.

3. To monitor both the resulting investments and the overall business environment so as to become aware of (a) developments that may require reevaluation of existing investments and (b) changes that may create new opportunities.

Sources of the information needed to fulfill each of these three purposes are listed below. Much of the information is available in both print and electronic form.

SCREENING FOR OPPORTUNITIES

Business Periodicals

The databases needed to screen for long-term investment opportunities are conveniently available from several business periodicals. *Forbes* is the best primary source of screening information on industries and companies. The other sources listed below supply supplementary information.

Forbes The following surveys are published annually by *Forbes* magazine.

- *Annual Report on American Industry.* Covering approximately 1,300 companies, this report is available in early January. As indicated in Chapter 2, this is the primary database used in this book. It is the most useful database for the purpose of rating industry and company performance, as it provides the required current data in a convenient form and compares them to long-term performance data. Commentary on each industry group covers changes in the industry and often includes a review of the performance of a leading player.

- *The Forbes 500.* Published in April, this report ranks the largest U.S. companies by sales, profits, assets, market value, jobs, and productivity. This is a good source of secondary data, particularly with regard to short-term developments.

In addition, *Forbes* periodically publishes surveys on smaller, "growth" companies. These surveys provide statistical performance data and commentaries on outstanding performers.

Fortune Some annual publications of *Fortune* are listed below.

- *The Fortune 500: The Largest U.S. Industrial Corporations.* Usually published in April, the Fortune 500 ranks 500 companies by sales, profits, assets, shareholders' equity, and market value. It also ranks the companies in 27 industry groups.
- *The Fortune Service 500.* Available in May, this publication covers the largest companies in diversified services, commercial banking, finance, savings, life insurance, retailing, transportation, and utilities. It lists the same information for these companies that the Fortune 500 gives for its listings.

Business Week Listed below are some annual publications of *Business Week.*

- *The Business Week 1000.* Available in March, this report ranks 1,000 corporations by market value. It provides data on sales, profitability (including margins, return on invested capital, and return on common equity), share prices, dividends, and shares outstanding (including the proportion of institutional holdings). In rankings of companies by market valuation, it includes companies that are not usually listed in the other surveys. Its usefulness for the long-term investor is limited, in that current results are compared only to the previous year's results.
- *Hot Growth Companies.* Published periodically, this survey provides current results, three-year averages for increases in sales, profits, return on capital, stock prices, P/E ratios, and market valuations. The 100 companies listed in the survey are derived from Standard and Poor's Compustat database, which lists computerized financial data on 9,000 publicly traded companies.
- *Industry Outlook: 19—.* Published in January, this report provides commentaries on the economic outlook and on developments in selected industries. This information is very useful for monitoring

industry developments. Also included are comments on some of the leading companies.

All of the foregoing are included as a part of a regular subscription.

Investment Newsletters

Available by subscription, investment newsletters can also be useful sources of leads. These publications are of varying quality. They cater primarily to the market player and usually offer a large number of suggestions. The result is enough of them pay off to allow the newsletter to list an impressive string of good picks. *Hulbert's Financial Digest* publishes evaluations of various newsletters based on their past performance.[1]

ANALYZING INDUSTRY AND COMPANY DATA

After identifying a possible investment candidate from the screening information listed above, the investor must undertake a more detailed analysis of the company and its industry. Sources of the information needed for this detailed analysis are listed below, in progressive order from the general to the more detailed.

- *Moody's, Standard and Poor's, and Value Line.* These institutions publish company surveys and update them regularly (usually quarterly). Available on library reference shelves, these surveys provide data on virtually every aspect of a company, including its products, markets, operations, earnings, financial position, 10-year earnings history, and stock price history. These concise reports are particularly convenient for use in researching a number of companies. While each of these surveys contains the same basic data, there are differences in the scope of the information provided. It is usually worthwhile to look at all of them.
- *Corporate annual reports.* Each company's annual report provides current and historical (usually 10-year) earnings and financial data, as well as other information on operations which the management wants investors to know.
- *Regulatory filings.* Each company's 10K statement, which is filed annually with the Securities and Exchange Commission (SEC), provides a detailed outline of all aspects of the company's current operations.

- *Stockbroker's analyses.* These publications usually contain useful information, but investors should be wary of stockbrokers' recommendations. It is always best to form your own conclusions after studying all available information.

MONITORING

Conscientious investors monitor economic and business developments so as to keep up with changes. New developments may make it necessary to reconsider an investment position. The process of monitoring entails continual reading. Thus a general knowledge base is built up, which becomes useful in recognizing potential opportunities and evaluating other opportunities. (The kinds of changes the investor should watch for are discussed in Chapter 8, along with their implications.)

Business Periodicals

Though the monitoring of the business environment and corporate news may initially appear formidable, it need not become an overwhelming task. In fact, the quality of business journalism has improved so much in recent years that regular reading of only three periodicals—*Forbes, Fortune,* and *Business Week*—is enough to constitute comprehensive monitoring. The same three publications were cited above as sources of screening data, and a brief review of each is given below.

Interesting day-to-day developments in corporations and in the economy are covered in the business sections of daily newspapers and in *The Wall Street Journal.* It is a good idea to scan this coverage for news on companies in which a position is held, but most such news items should be recognized as not necessarily having long-term significance.

For most investors, the first problem involved in monitoring is that more information is available than they have time to follow. Selective reading is the answer. *Forbes* with its investment focus, *Fortune* with its insights into socioeconomic developments and its articles on specific companies, and *Business Week* with its general coverage should be considered mandatory. The extent of the information available from these three periodicals is indicated by the fact that almost all the end-of-chapter notes in this book refer to articles in these three periodicals.

The investor's second problem in monitoring is to distinguish significant long-term developments from the mass of day-to-day news. To make this distinction, the investor should adopt a critical stance when reading business periodicals. Looking for answers to the following two questions is helpful: "Why did the company take this action?" and "What does this change mean?" The investor should also look for certain types of developments and should analyze their implications when they occur (refer back to Chapter 8).

It is important to keep in mind that articles in business magazines are not infallible. They may even include interpretations provided by the company that is the subject of the article. The author of an article may have become overly enthusiastic about the subject, particularly if it makes a good story and deals with a high-profile company. During the 1980s, for instance, IBM was the subject of many optimistic articles which were apparently based more on the company's record as a winner than on its obvious current weaknesses.[2] As a safeguard, investors should try to check critical facts in more than one source and should be particularly skeptical about any opinion that goes against factual evidence.

Following are brief comments on the periodicals recommended for regular reading.

Forbes This biweekly magazine takes the investor's perspective. The well-written articles on companies are short and to the point. They often interpret the meaning of events, and they include criticisms of management. Feature articles on economic or other developments, while often rather technical, can be valuable. Six regular columnists write on investment issues from various perspectives and include recommendations that may be worth further evaluation. The magazine's editorial policy suffers from a case of extreme right-wing tunnel vision, but this bias does not affect the news articles.

Fortune The main constituency of this biweekly magazine is senior business executives. *Fortune* is not primarily a newsmagazine. Rather, it covers certain topics in considerable depth. These topics include managing (contemporary management practices) and corporate performance (developments in selected companies), as well as regular features and forecasts on the economy. *Fortune* offers particularly strong coverage of social developments, such as changing demographics and values. Its articles are exceptionally well-written and include generally sound interpretations of the meanings of events.

Business Week Like *Fortune*, this weekly magazine, which covers current events, is written for business executives. Its well-written articles have a news focus and usually include relatively little interpretation. Its feature articles tend to concentrate on management and organizational issues. The excellent book reviews are so good at giving readers the gist of the latest business books that it is often not actually necessary to read the books.

NOTES

1. Mark Hulbert is a regular columnist in *Forbes* and the editor of *The Financial Digest,* which is published monthly by the Hulbert Financial Digest, Alexandria, Virginia.

2. Business journalists have had particular difficulty in believing that IBM's problems were anything but temporary, even though signs of its strategic weaknesses were starting to become apparent. Following are examples of such articles: Stephen Kindell and Gary Slutaker, "While Wall Street and the Media Shout Computer Slump, IBM Quietly Prepares for Another Decade of 15% Annual Growth: Think Again," *Forbes,* November 4, 1985, pp. 38-40; Marilyn A. Harris, "IBM: More Worlds to Conquer," *Business Week,* February 18, 1985, pp. 83-98. Joel Dreyfuss, "Reinventing IBM," *Fortune,* August 14, 1989, pp. 31-39; Catherine Arnst with Bart Ziegler, "A Freewheeling Youngster Called IBM," *Business Week,* May 3, 1993, pp. 134-138.

INDEX